30

Ken Akamatsu

TRANSLATED AND ADAPTED BY
Alethea Nibley and Athena Nibley

LETTERING AND RETOUCH BY
North Market Street Graphics

KODANSHA COMICS

Negima! volume 30 is a work of fiction. Names, characters, places, and incidents are the products of the author's imagination or are used fictitiously. Any resemblance to actual events, locales, or persons, living or dead, is entirely coincidental.

A Kodansha Comics Trade Paperback Original.

Published in the United States by Kodansha Comics, an imprint of Kodansha USA Publishing, LLC., New York.

Publication rights for this English edition arranged through Kodansha Ltd., Tokyo.

First published in Japan in 2010 by Kodansha Ltd., Tokyo, as *Maho sensei Negima!*, volume 30.

ISBN 978-1-935-42957-9

Printed in the United States of America.

www.kodanshacomics.com

9 8 7 6 5 4 3 2 1

Translator/Adapter: Alethea Nibley and Athena Nibley
Lettering: North Market Street Graphics

Honorifics Explained

Throughout the Kodansha Comics books, you will find Japanese honorifics left intact in the translations. For those not familiar with how the Japanese use honorifics and, more important, how they differ from American honorifics, we present this brief overview.

Politeness has always been a critical facet of Japanese culture. Ever since the feudal era, when Japan was a highly stratified society, use of honorifics—which can be defined as polite speech that indicates relationship or status—has played an essential role in the Japanese language. When addressing someone in Japanese, an honorific usually takes the form of a suffix attached to one's name (example: "Asuna-san"), is used as a title at the end of one's name, or appears in place of the name itself (example: "Negi-sensei," or simply "Sensei!").

Honorifics can be expressions of respect or endearment. In the context of manga and anime, honorifics give insight into the nature of the relationship between characters. Many English translations leave out these important honorifics and therefore distort the feel of the original Japanese. Because Japanese honorifics contain nuances that English honorifics lack, it is our policy at Kodansha Comics not to translate them. Here, instead, is a guide to some of the honorifics you may encounter in Kodansha Comics.

-san: This is the most common honorific and is equivalent to Mr., Miss, Ms., or Mrs. It is the all-purpose honorific and can be used in any situation where politeness is required.

-sama: This is one level higher than "-san" and is used to confer great respect.

-dono: This comes from the word "tono," which means "lord." It is an even higher level than "-sama" and confers utmost respect.

-kun: This suffix is used at the end of boys' names to express familiarity or endearment. It is also sometimes used by men

among friends, or when addressing someone younger or of a lower station.

chan: This is used to express endearment, mostly toward girls. It is also used for little boys, pets, and even among lovers. It gives a sense of childish cuteness.

Bōzu: This is an informal way to refer to a boy, similar to the English terms "kid" and "squirt."

Sempai/Senpai: This title suggests that the addressee is one's senior in a group or organization. It is most often used in a school setting, where underclassmen refer to their upperclassmen as "sempai." It can also be used in the workplace, such as when a newer employee addresses an employee who has seniority in the company.

Kohai: This is the opposite of "sempai" and is used toward underclassmen in school or newcomers in the workplace. It connotes that the addressee is of a lower station.

Sensei: Literally meaning "one who has come before," this title is used for teachers, doctors, or masters of any profession or art.

Anesan (or nesan): A generic term for a girl, usually older, that means "sister."

Ojōsama: A way of referring to the daughter or sister of someone with high political or social status.

-[blank]: This is usually forgotten in these lists, but it is perhaps the most significant difference between Japanese and English. The lack of honorific means that the speaker has permission to address the person in a very intimate way. Usually, only family, spouses, or very close friends have this kind of permission. Known as *yobisute*, it can be gratifying when someone who has earned the intimacy starts to call one by one's name without an honorific. But when that intimacy hasn't been earned, it can be very insulting.

A Word from the Author

Negima! volume 30 ended up kind of reeeeally dark.(><) I'm sorry.

But, but, this is Negi's true essence! It's the true past of his parents, Nagi & Arika!

It's hard on the hero (our main character), too.

And it's Negi's 31 students, as well as Nagi's war buddies, who save him from the hardship. I think that's the kind of story Negima! is.

The counter attack begins in the next volume!!

Ken Akamatsu's home page address
http://www.ailove.net/

NEGIMA!
MAGISTER NEGI MAGI

30

Ken Akamatsu

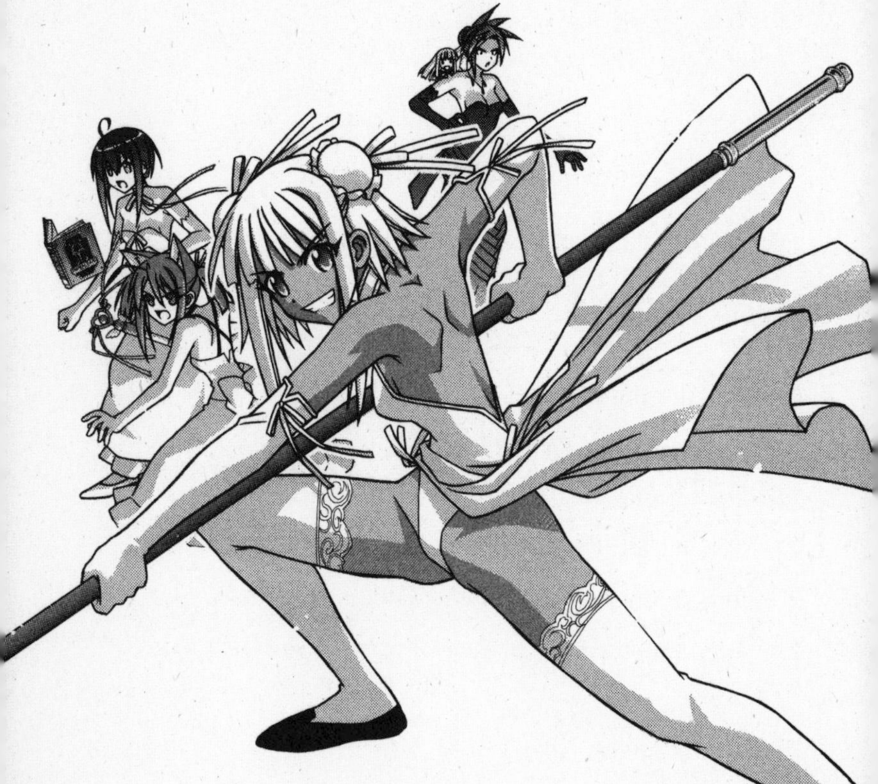

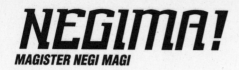

CONTENTS

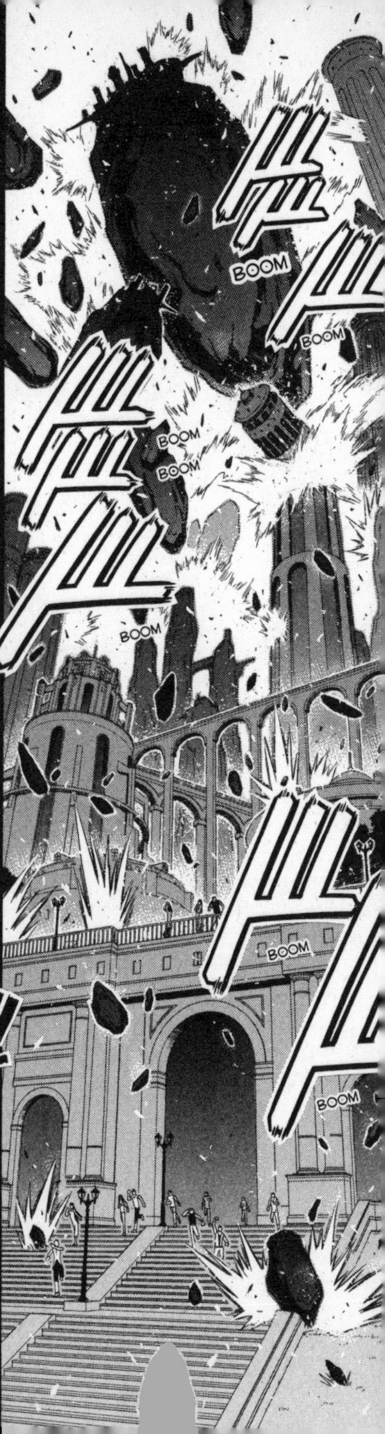
BOOM
BOOM
BOOM
BOOM
BOOM
BOOM
BOOM

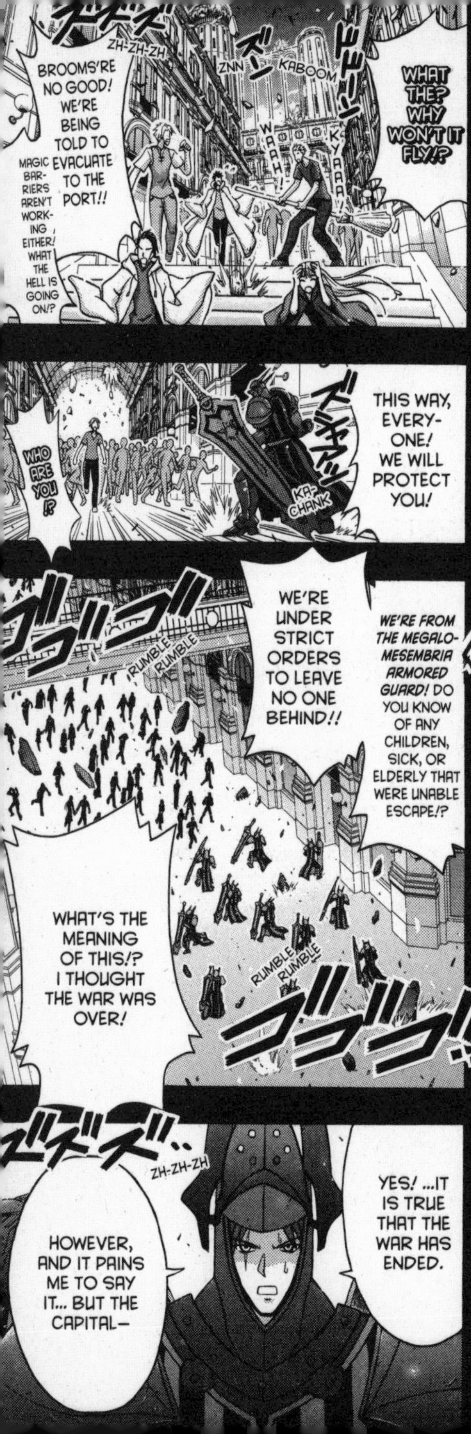
WHAT THE? WHY WON'T IT FLY!?
KYAAAA!
KABOOM
ZNN
WAAH!
ZH-ZH-ZH
BROOMS'RE NO GOOD! WE'RE BEING TOLD TO EVACUATE TO THE PORT!!
MAGIC BARRIERS AREN'T WORKING EITHER! WHAT THE HELL IS GOING ON!?
THIS WAY, EVERYONE! WE WILL PROTECT YOU!
KA-CHANK
WHO ARE YOU!?
WE'RE FROM THE MEGALOMESEMBRIA ARMORED GUARD! DO YOU KNOW OF ANY CHILDREN, SICK, OR ELDERLY THAT WERE UNABLE ESCAPE!?
WE'RE UNDER STRICT ORDERS TO LEAVE NO ONE BEHIND!!
RUMBLE RUMBLE
WHAT'S THE MEANING OF THIS!? I THOUGHT THE WAR WAS OVER!
RUMBLE RUMBLE
YES! ...IT IS TRUE THAT THE WAR HAS ENDED.
ZH-ZH-ZH
HOWEVER, AND IT PAINS ME TO SAY IT... BUT THE CAPITAL—

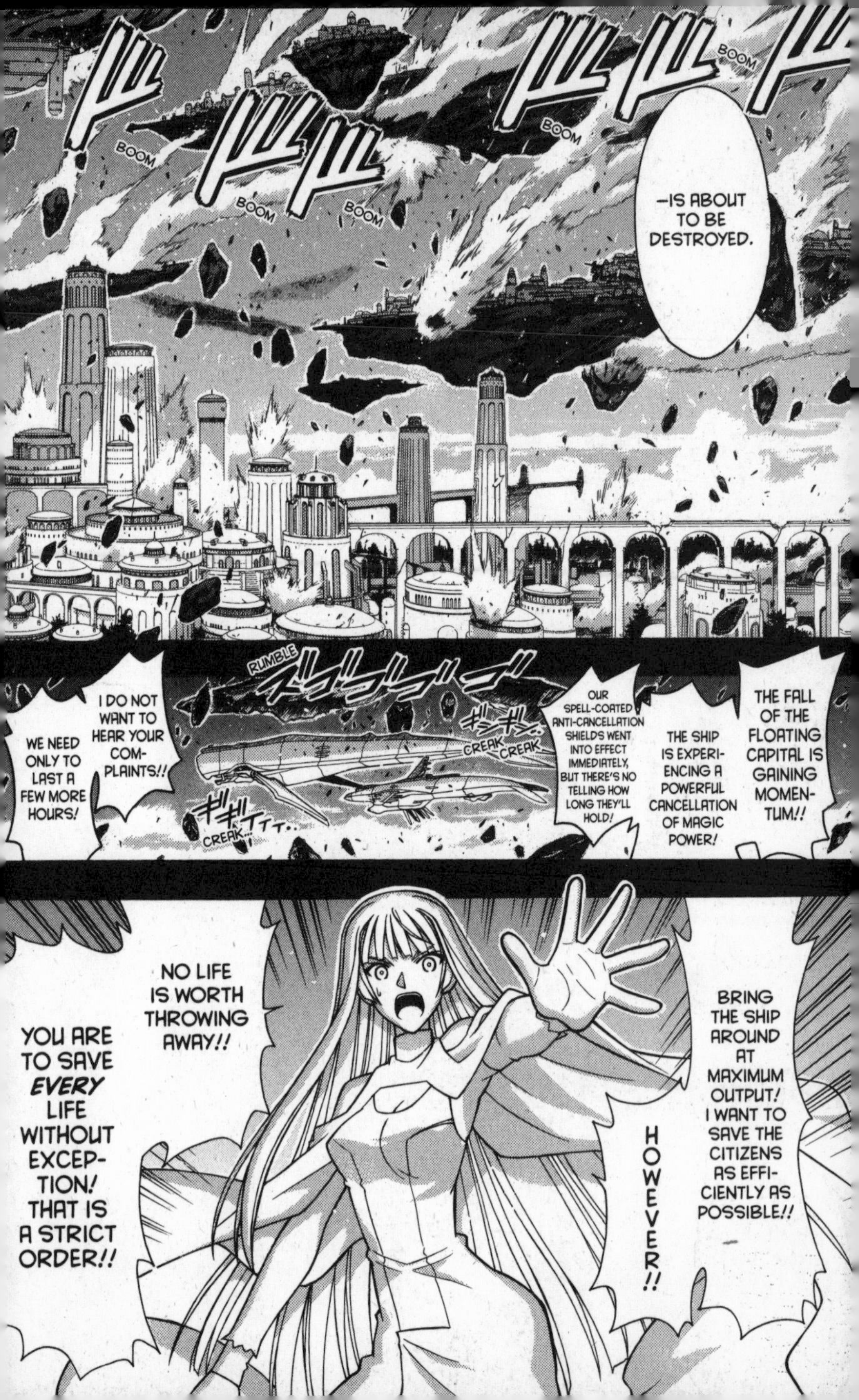
BOOM
BOOM
BOOM
BOOM
BOOM
—IS ABOUT TO BE DESTROYED.
THE FALL OF THE FLOATING CAPITAL IS GAINING MOMENTUM!!
THE SHIP IS EXPERIENCING A POWERFUL CANCELLATION OF MAGIC POWER!
OUR SPELL-COATED ANTI-CANCELLATION SHIELDS WENT INTO EFFECT IMMEDIATELY, BUT THERE'S NO TELLING HOW LONG THEY'LL HOLD!
CREAK CREAK
RUMBLE
I DO NOT WANT TO HEAR YOUR COMPLAINTS!!
WE NEED ONLY TO LAST A FEW MORE HOURS!
CREAK...
BRING THE SHIP AROUND AT MAXIMUM OUTPUT! I WANT TO SAVE THE CITIZENS AS EFFICIENTLY AS POSSIBLE!!
HOWEVER!!
NO LIFE IS WORTH THROWING AWAY!!
YOU ARE TO SAVE ***EVERY*** LIFE WITHOUT EXCEPTION! THAT IS A STRICT ORDER!!

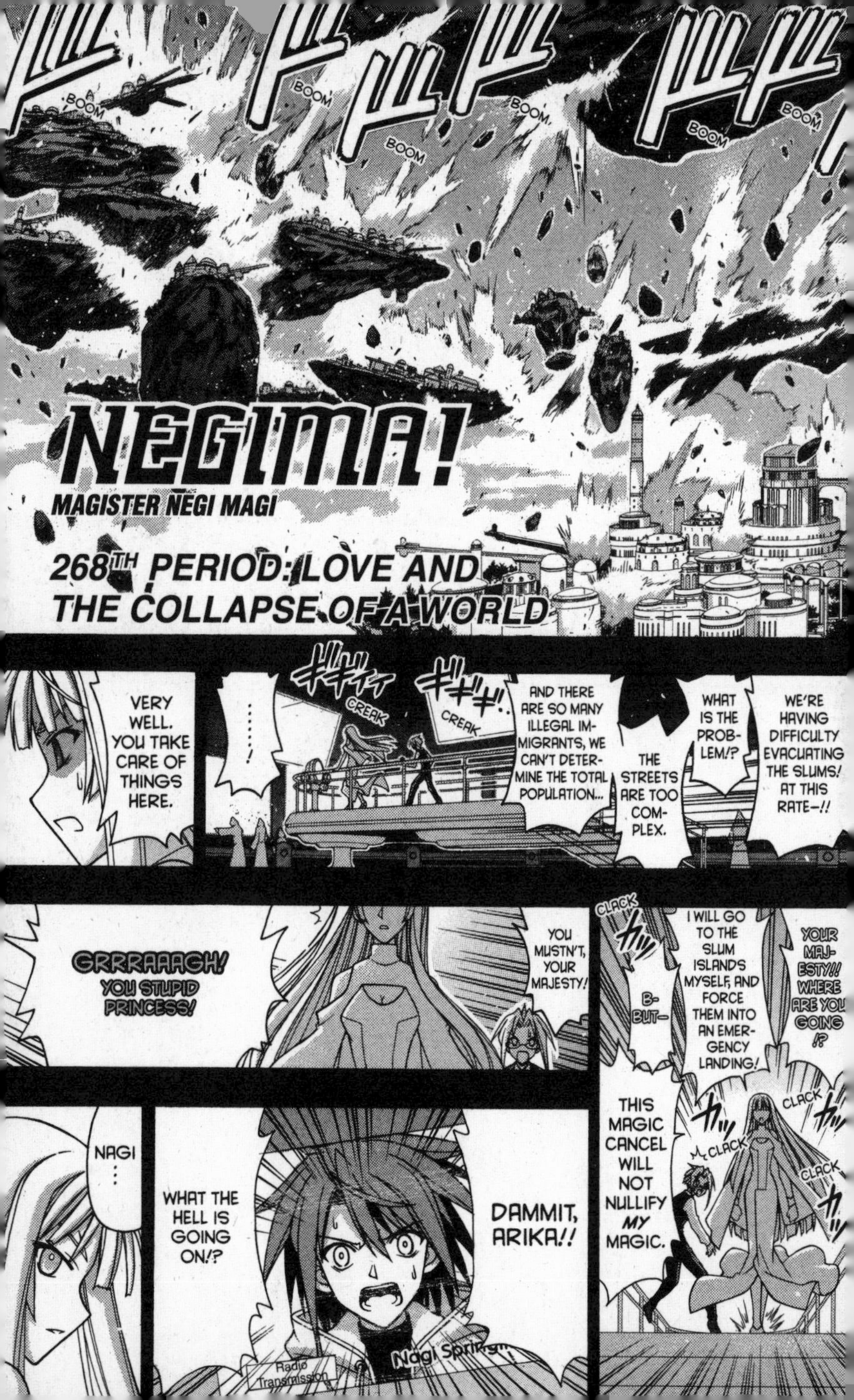
BOOM
BOOM
BOOM
BOOM
BOOM
BOOM
NEGIMA!
MAGISTER NEGI MAGI
268TH PERIOD: LOVE AND THE COLLAPSE OF A WORLD
WE'RE HAVING DIFFICULTY EVACUATING THE SLUMS! AT THIS RATE—!!
WHAT IS THE PROBLEM!?
THE STREETS ARE TOO COMPLEX.
AND THERE ARE SO MANY ILLEGAL IMMIGRANTS, WE CAN'T DETERMINE THE TOTAL POPULATION...
CREAK
CREAK
......!
VERY WELL. YOU TAKE CARE OF THINGS HERE.
YOUR MAJESTY!! WHERE ARE YOU GOING!?
CLACK
I WILL GO TO THE SLUM ISLANDS MYSELF, AND FORCE THEM INTO AN EMERGENCY LANDING!
B-BUT—
CLACK
CLACK
CLACK
THIS MAGIC CANCEL WILL NOT NULLIFY MY MAGIC.
YOU MUSTN'T, YOUR MAJESTY!
GRRRAAAGH! YOU STUPID PRINCESS!
DAMMIT, ARIKA!!
WHAT THE HELL IS GOING ON!?
Nagi Spring
Radio Transmission
NAGI...

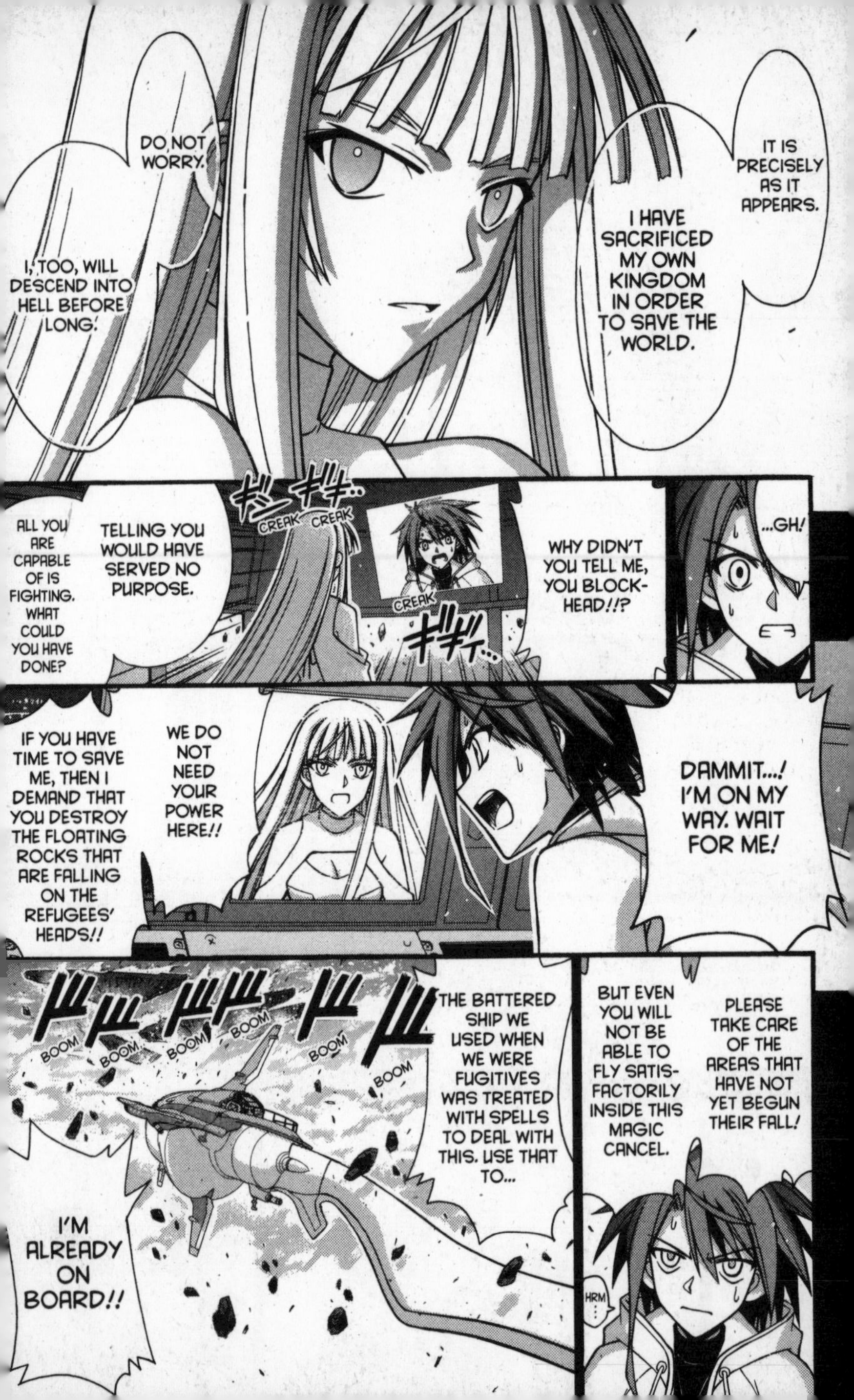
IT IS PRECISELY AS IT APPEARS.
I HAVE SACRIFICED MY OWN KINGDOM IN ORDER TO SAVE THE WORLD.
DO NOT WORRY.
I, TOO, WILL DESCEND INTO HELL BEFORE LONG.
...GH!
WHY DIDN'T YOU TELL ME, YOU BLOCK-HEAD!!?
CREAK CREAK
CREAK
TELLING YOU WOULD HAVE SERVED NO PURPOSE.
ALL YOU ARE CAPABLE OF IS FIGHTING. WHAT COULD YOU HAVE DONE?
DAMMIT...! I'M ON MY WAY. WAIT FOR ME!
WE DO NOT NEED YOUR POWER HERE!!
IF YOU HAVE TIME TO SAVE ME, THEN I DEMAND THAT YOU DESTROY THE FLOATING ROCKS THAT ARE FALLING ON THE REFUGEES' HEADS!!
PLEASE TAKE CARE OF THE AREAS THAT HAVE NOT YET BEGUN THEIR FALL!
BUT EVEN YOU WILL NOT BE ABLE TO FLY SATIS-FACTORILY INSIDE THIS MAGIC CANCEL.
HRM...
THE BATTERED SHIP WE USED WHEN WE WERE FUGITIVES WAS TREATED WITH SPELLS TO DEAL WITH THIS. USE THAT TO...
BOOM BOOM BOOM BOOM BOOM BOOM
I'M ALREADY ON BOARD!!

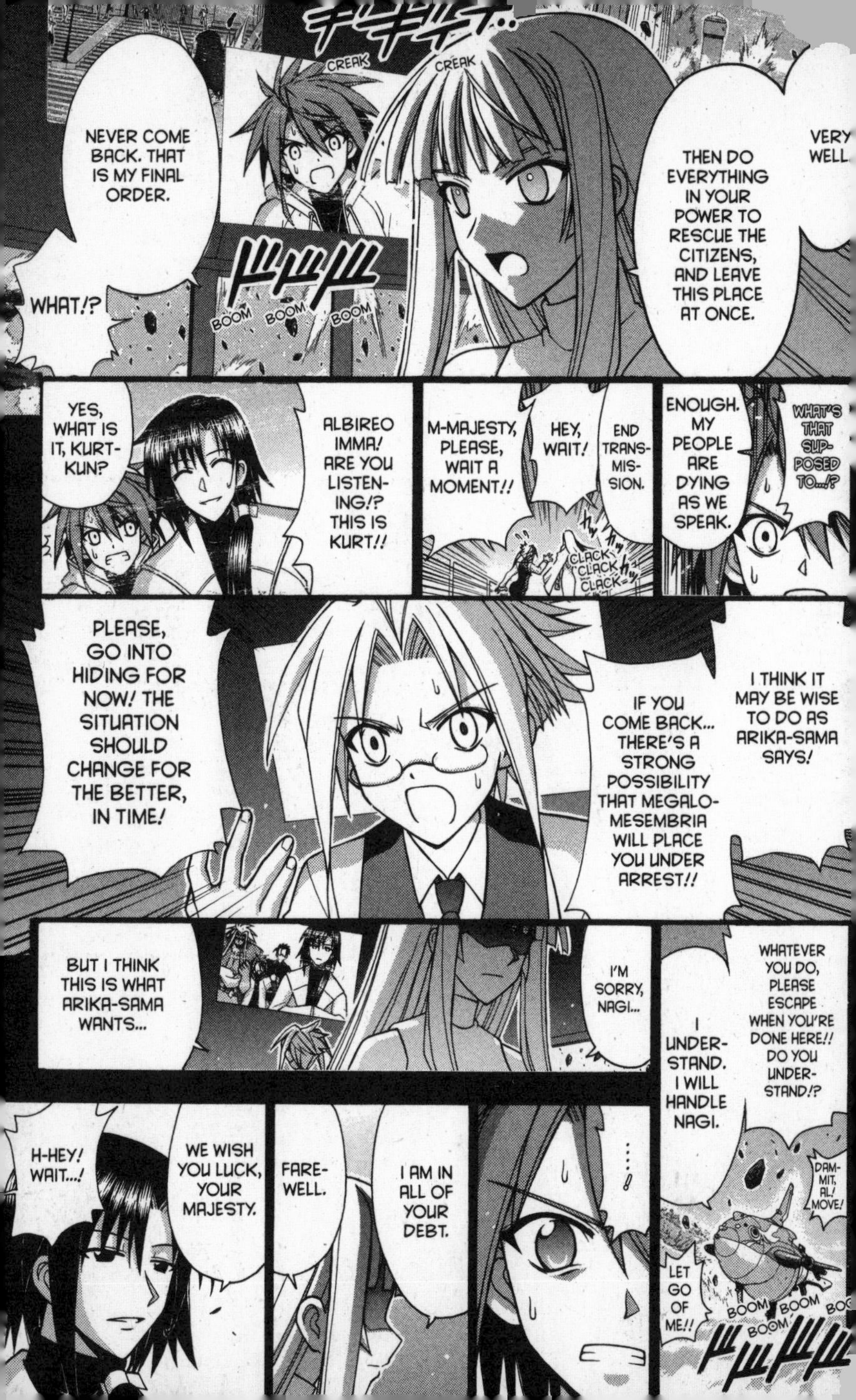

VERY WELL.
THEN DO EVERYTHING IN YOUR POWER TO RESCUE THE CITIZENS, AND LEAVE THIS PLACE AT ONCE.
CREAK
CREAK
NEVER COME BACK. THAT IS MY FINAL ORDER.
BOOM BOOM BOOM
WHAT!?
WHAT'S THAT SUPPOSED TO...!?
ENOUGH. MY PEOPLE ARE DYING AS WE SPEAK.
END TRANSMISSION.
HEY, WAIT!
M-MAJESTY, PLEASE, WAIT A MOMENT!!
CLACK CLACK CLACK
ALBIREO IMMA! ARE YOU LISTENING!? THIS IS KURT!!
YES, WHAT IS IT, KURT-KUN?
I THINK IT MAY BE WISE TO DO AS ARIKA-SAMA SAYS!
IF YOU COME BACK... THERE'S A STRONG POSSIBILITY THAT MEGALOMESEMBRIA WILL PLACE YOU UNDER ARREST!!
PLEASE, GO INTO HIDING FOR NOW! THE SITUATION SHOULD CHANGE FOR THE BETTER, IN TIME!
WHATEVER YOU DO, PLEASE ESCAPE WHEN YOU'RE DONE HERE!! DO YOU UNDERSTAND!?
I UNDERSTAND. I WILL HANDLE NAGI.
I'M SORRY, NAGI...
BUT I THINK THIS IS WHAT ARIKA-SAMA WANTS...
DAMMIT, AL! MOVE!
LET GO OF ME!!
BOOM BOOM BOOM BOO
....!
I AM IN ALL OF YOUR DEBT.
FAREWELL.
WE WISH YOU LUCK, YOUR MAJESTY.
H-HEY! WAIT...!

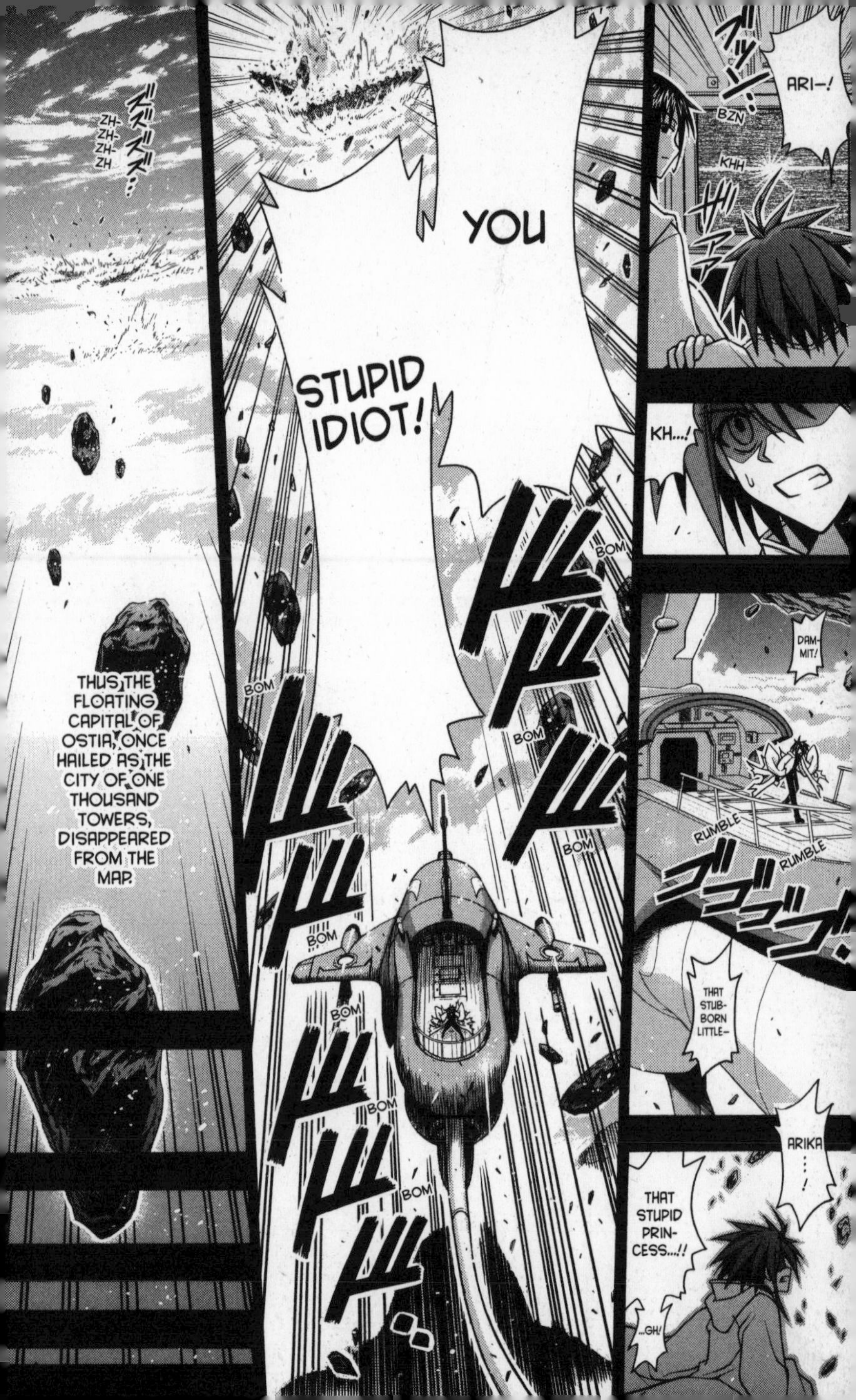
ARI-!
BZN
KHH
KH...!
DAM-MIT!
RUMBLE
RUMBLE
THAT STUB-BORN LITTLE-
ARIKA...!
THAT STUPID PRIN-CESS...!!
...GH!
YOU
STUPID IDIOT!
BOM
ZH-ZH-ZH-ZH
THUS THE FLOATING CAPITAL OF OSTIA, ONCE HAILED AS THE CITY OF ONE THOUSAND TOWERS, DISAPPEARED FROM THE MAP.

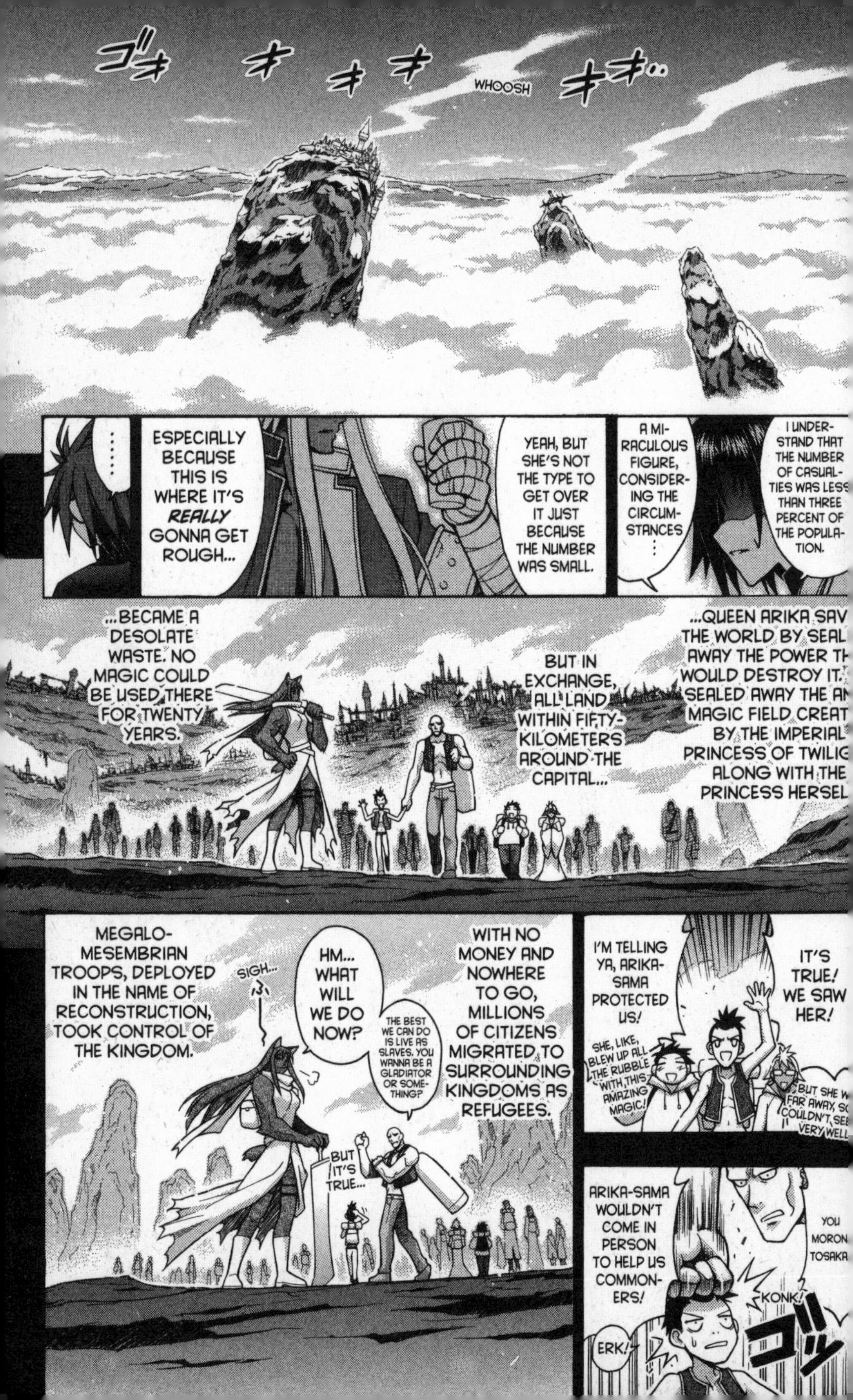
ゴオオオオオオ‥
WHOOSH
I UNDERSTAND THAT THE NUMBER OF CASUALTIES WAS LESS THAN THREE PERCENT OF THE POPULATION.
A MIRACULOUS FIGURE, CONSIDERING THE CIRCUMSTANCES...
YEAH, BUT SHE'S NOT THE TYPE TO GET OVER IT JUST BECAUSE THE NUMBER WAS SMALL.
ESPECIALLY BECAUSE THIS IS WHERE IT'S *REALLY* GONNA GET ROUGH...
......
...QUEEN ARIKA SAV THE WORLD BY SEAL AWAY THE POWER TH WOULD DESTROY IT. SEALED AWAY THE AN MAGIC FIELD CREAT BY THE IMPERIAL PRINCESS OF TWILIG ALONG WITH THE PRINCESS HERSEL
BUT IN EXCHANGE, ALL LAND WITHIN FIFTY-KILOMETERS AROUND THE CAPITAL...
...BECAME A DESOLATE WASTE. NO MAGIC COULD BE USED THERE FOR TWENTY YEARS.
IT'S TRUE! WE SAW HER!
I'M TELLING YA, ARIKA-SAMA PROTECTED US!
SHE, LIKE, BLEW UP ALL THE RUBBLE WITH THIS AMAZING MAGIC!
BUT SHE W FAR AWAY, SO COULDN'T SEE VERY WELL
WITH NO MONEY AND NOWHERE TO GO, MILLIONS OF CITIZENS MIGRATED TO SURROUNDING KINGDOMS AS REFUGEES.
HM... WHAT WILL WE DO NOW?
THE BEST WE CAN DO IS LIVE AS SLAVES. YOU WANNA BE A GLADIATOR OR SOMETHING?
SIGH... ふー
MEGALO-MESEMBRIAN TROOPS, DEPLOYED IN THE NAME OF RECONSTRUCTION, TOOK CONTROL OF THE KINGDOM.
BUT IT'S TRUE...
YOU MORON TOSAKA
ARIKA-SAMA WOULDN'T COME IN PERSON TO HELP US COMMONERS!
KONK! ゴッ
ERK!

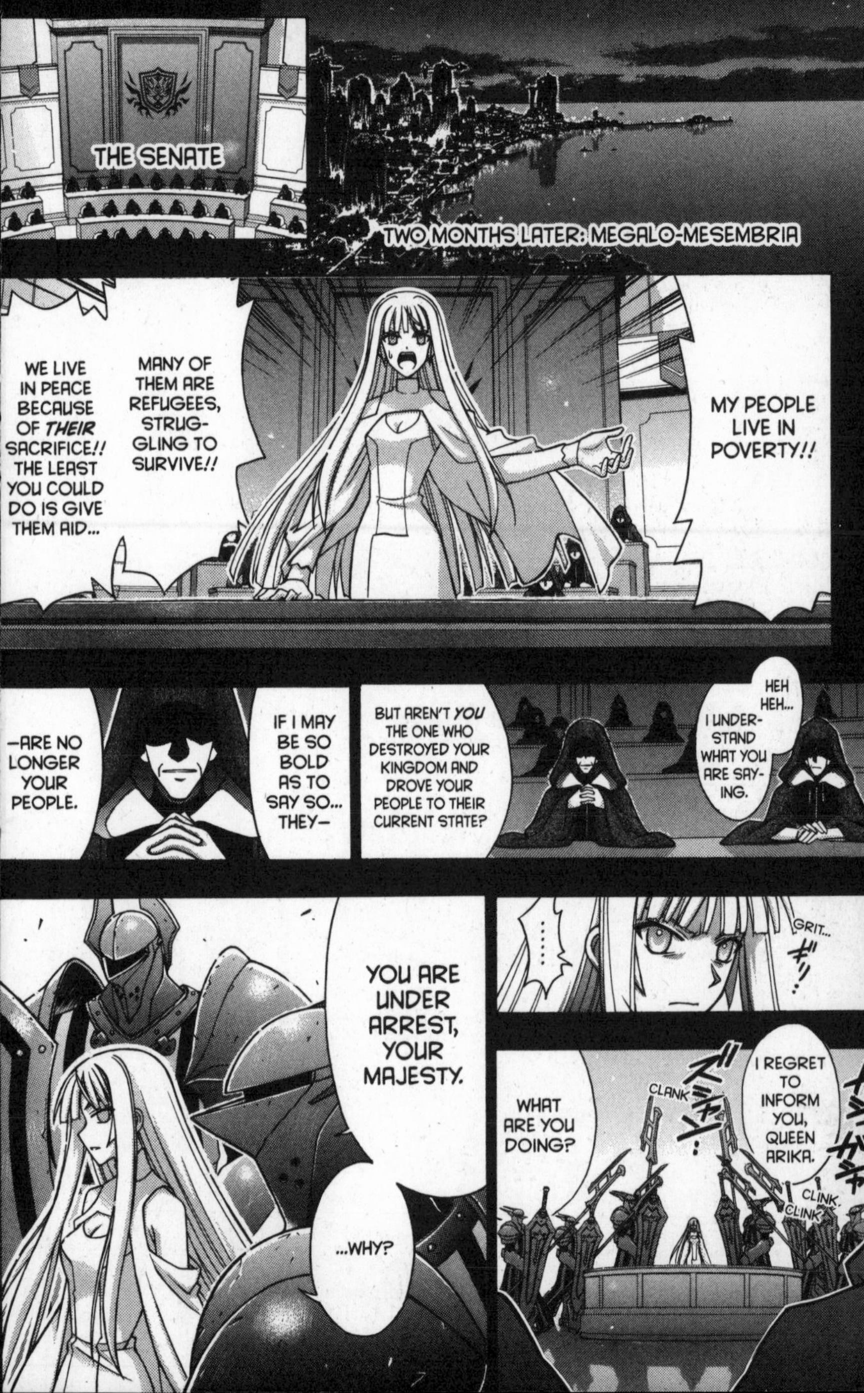
TWO MONTHS LATER: MEGALO-MESEMBRIA
THE SENATE
MY PEOPLE LIVE IN POVERTY!!
MANY OF THEM ARE REFUGEES, STRUGGLING TO SURVIVE!!
WE LIVE IN PEACE BECAUSE OF *THEIR* SACRIFICE!! THE LEAST YOU COULD DO IS GIVE THEM AID...
HEH HEH... I UNDERSTAND WHAT YOU ARE SAYING.
BUT AREN'T *YOU* THE ONE WHO DESTROYED YOUR KINGDOM AND DROVE YOUR PEOPLE TO THEIR CURRENT STATE?
IF I MAY BE SO BOLD AS TO SAY SO... THEY—
—ARE NO LONGER YOUR PEOPLE.
......
GRIT...
I REGRET TO INFORM YOU, QUEEN ARIKA.
CLINK
CLINK
CLANK
WHAT ARE YOU DOING?
YOU ARE UNDER ARREST, YOUR MAJESTY.
...WHY?

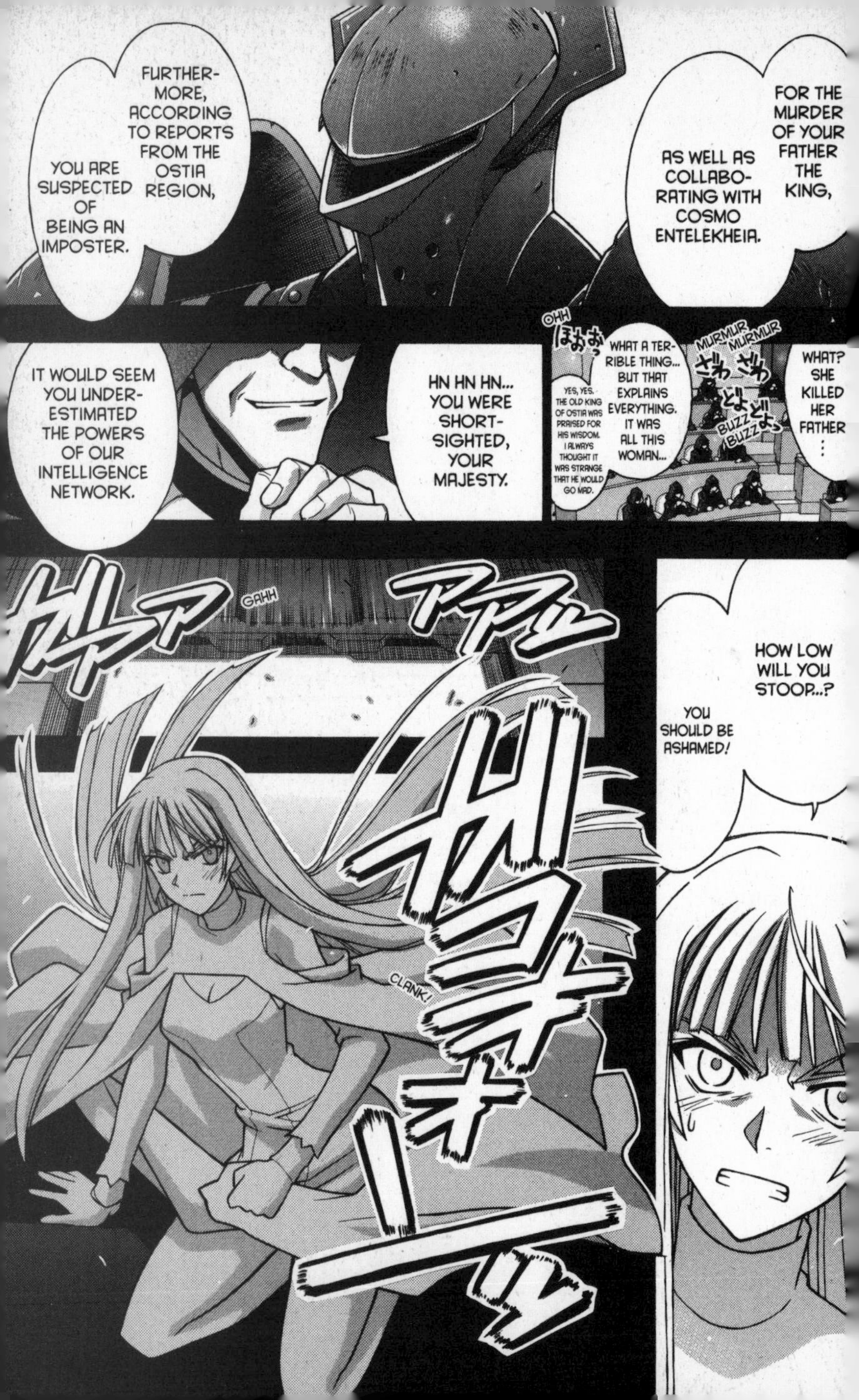
FOR THE MURDER OF YOUR FATHER THE KING,
AS WELL AS COLLABO-RATING WITH COSMO ENTELEKHEIA.
FURTHER-MORE, ACCORDING TO REPORTS FROM THE OSTIA REGION,
YOU ARE SUSPECTED OF BEING AN IMPOSTER.
WHAT? SHE KILLED HER FATHER...
MURMUR MURMUR
ざわ ざわ
どよどよ
BUZZ BUZZ
WHAT A TER-RIBLE THING... BUT THAT EXPLAINS EVERYTHING. IT WAS ALL THIS WOMAN...
YES, YES. THE OLD KING OF OSTIA WAS PRAISED FOR HIS WISDOM. I ALWAYS THOUGHT IT WAS STRANGE THAT HE WOULD GO MAD.
OHH
HN HN HN... YOU WERE SHORT-SIGHTED, YOUR MAJESTY.
IT WOULD SEEM YOU UNDER-ESTIMATED THE POWERS OF OUR INTELLIGENCE NETWORK.
HOW LOW WILL YOU STOOP...?
YOU SHOULD BE ASHAMED!
GAHH
CLANK!

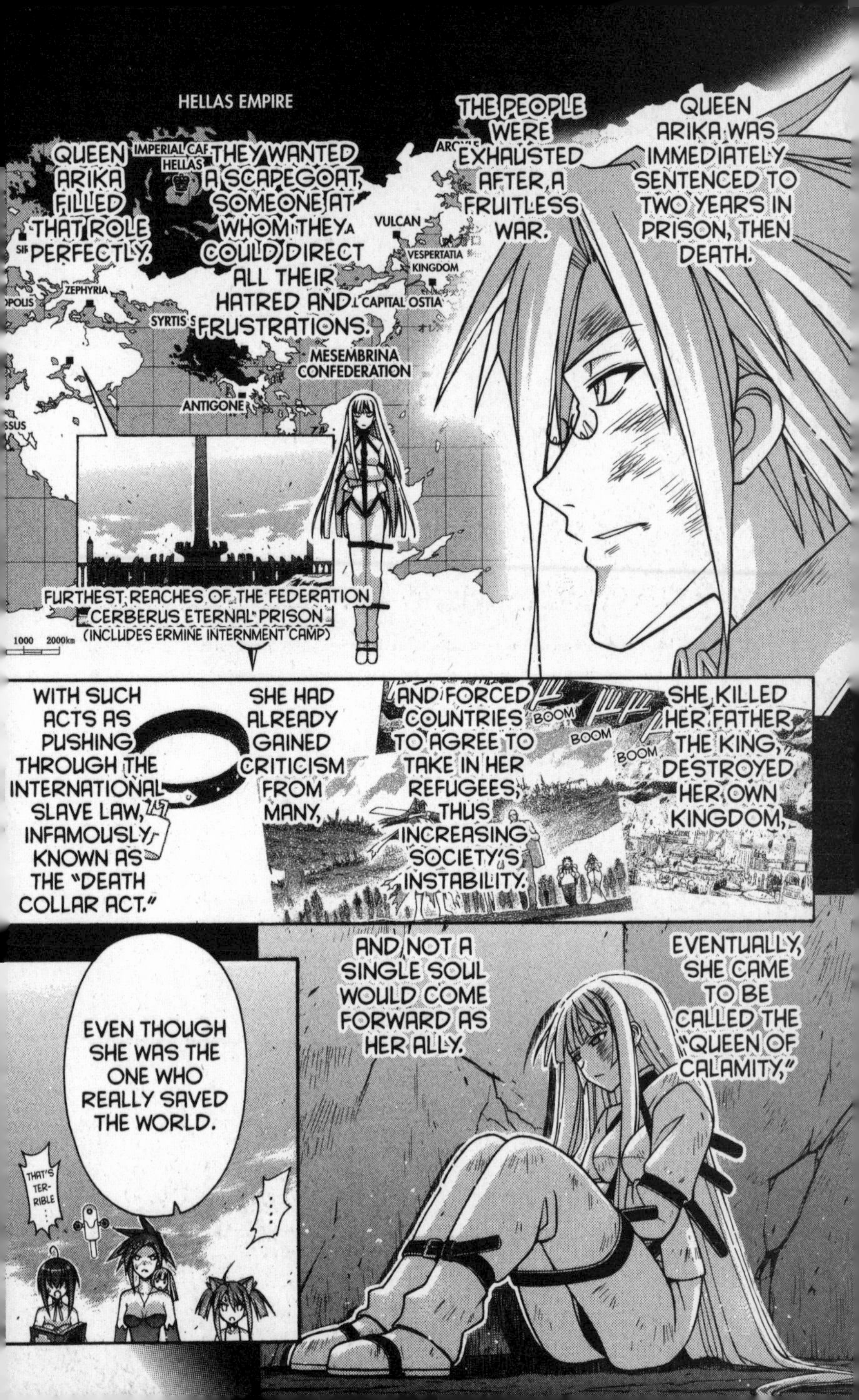

QUEEN ARIKA WAS IMMEDIATELY SENTENCED TO TWO YEARS IN PRISON, THEN DEATH.
THE PEOPLE WERE EXHAUSTED AFTER A FRUITLESS WAR.
THEY WANTED A SCAPEGOAT, SOMEONE AT WHOM THEY COULD DIRECT ALL THEIR HATRED AND FRUSTRATIONS.
QUEEN ARIKA FILLED THAT ROLE PERFECTLY.
HELLAS EMPIRE
HELLAS
VULCAN
VESPERTATIA KINGDOM
CAPITAL OSTIA
ZEPHYRIA
SYRTIS
MESEMBRINA CONFEDERATION
ANTIGONE
FURTHEST REACHES OF THE FEDERATION
CERBERUS ETERNAL PRISON
(INCLUDES ERMINE INTERNMENT CAMP)
1000 2000km
SHE KILLED HER FATHER THE KING, DESTROYED HER OWN KINGDOM,
BOOM
BOOM
BOOM
AND FORCED COUNTRIES TO AGREE TO TAKE IN HER REFUGEES, THUS INCREASING SOCIETY'S INSTABILITY.
SHE HAD ALREADY GAINED CRITICISM FROM MANY,
WITH SUCH ACTS AS PUSHING THROUGH THE INTERNATIONAL SLAVE LAW, INFAMOUSLY KNOWN AS THE "DEATH COLLAR ACT."
EVENTUALLY, SHE CAME TO BE CALLED THE "QUEEN OF CALAMITY,"
AND NOT A SINGLE SOUL WOULD COME FORWARD AS HER ALLY.
EVEN THOUGH SHE WAS THE ONE WHO REALLY SAVED THE WORLD.
....
THAT'S TERRIBLE...

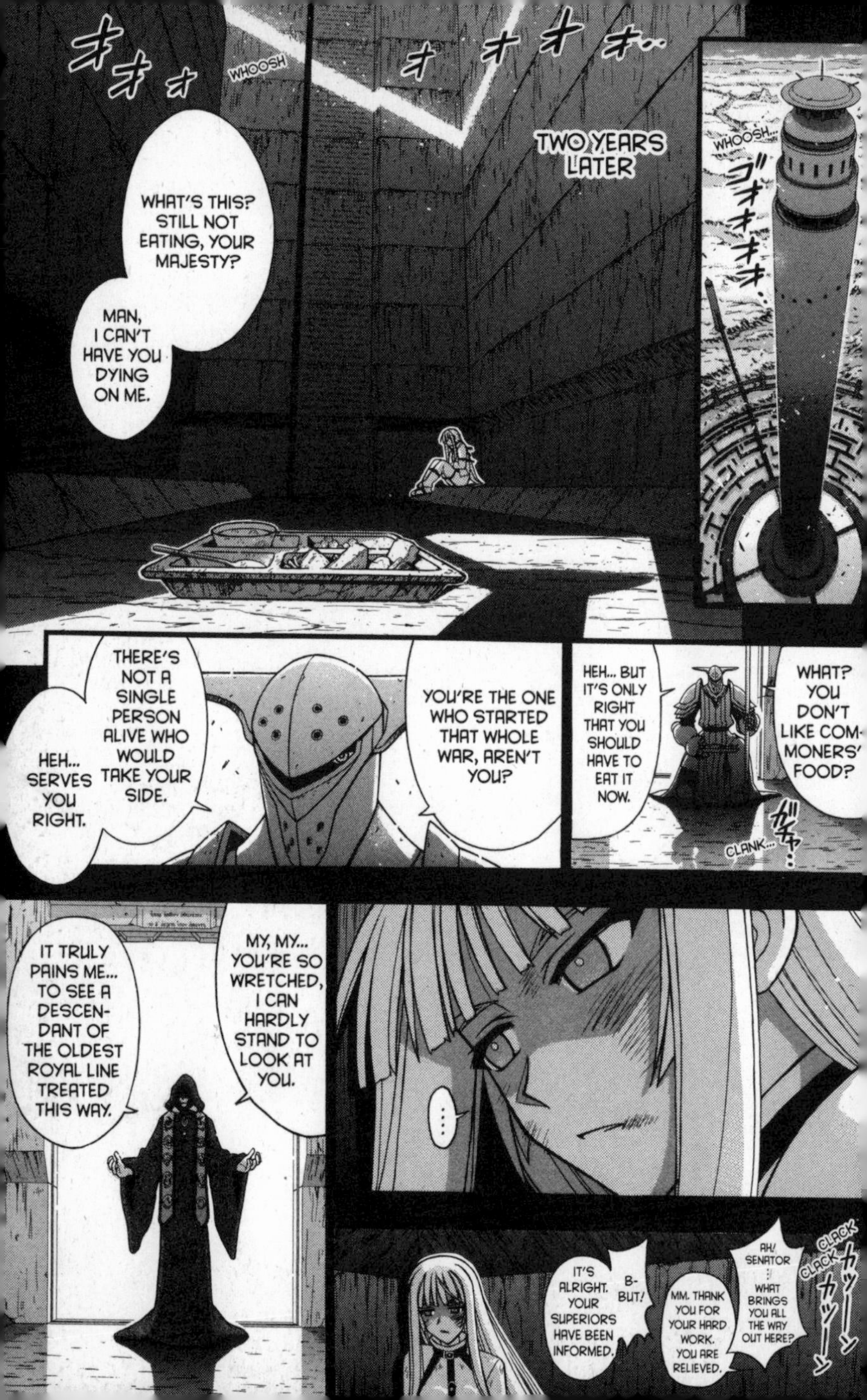
WHOOSH...
ゴォォォォ…
TWO YEARS LATER
オォォォォ…
WHOOSH
オォォ
WHAT'S THIS? STILL NOT EATING, YOUR MAJESTY?
MAN, I CAN'T HAVE YOU DYING ON ME.
WHAT? YOU DON'T LIKE COMMONERS' FOOD?
HEH... BUT IT'S ONLY RIGHT THAT YOU SHOULD HAVE TO EAT IT NOW.
CLANK...
ガチャ…
YOU'RE THE ONE WHO STARTED THAT WHOLE WAR, AREN'T YOU?
THERE'S NOT A SINGLE PERSON ALIVE WHO WOULD TAKE YOUR SIDE.
HEH... SERVES YOU RIGHT.
...
CLACK
CLACK
カツーン
カツーン
AH! SENATOR... WHAT BRINGS YOU ALL THE WAY OUT HERE?
MM. THANK YOU FOR YOUR HARD WORK. YOU ARE RELIEVED.
B-BUT!
IT'S ALRIGHT. YOUR SUPERIORS HAVE BEEN INFORMED.
MY, MY... YOU'RE SO WRETCHED, I CAN HARDLY STAND TO LOOK AT YOU.
IT TRULY PAINS ME... TO SEE A DESCENDANT OF THE OLDEST ROYAL LINE TREATED THIS WAY.

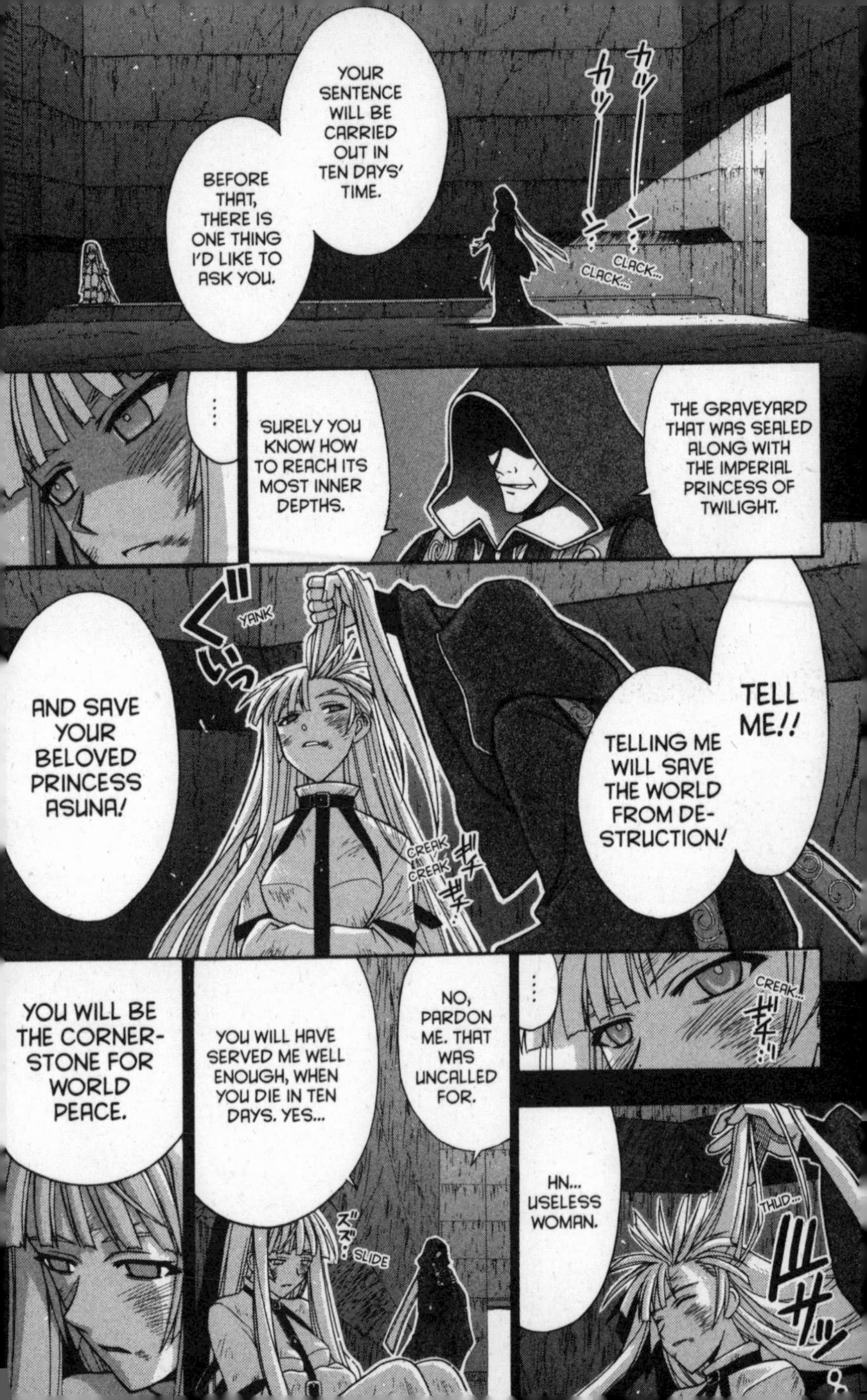
CLACK...
CLACK...
YOUR SENTENCE WILL BE CARRIED OUT IN TEN DAYS' TIME.
BEFORE THAT, THERE IS ONE THING I'D LIKE TO ASK YOU.
THE GRAVEYARD THAT WAS SEALED ALONG WITH THE IMPERIAL PRINCESS OF TWILIGHT.
SURELY YOU KNOW HOW TO REACH ITS MOST INNER DEPTHS.
...
TELL ME!!
TELLING ME WILL SAVE THE WORLD FROM DE-STRUCTION!
YANK
AND SAVE YOUR BELOVED PRINCESS ASUNA!
CREAK CREAK
CREAK...
...
THUD...
HN... USELESS WOMAN.
NO, PARDON ME. THAT WAS UNCALLED FOR.
YOU WILL HAVE SERVED ME WELL ENOUGH, WHEN YOU DIE IN TEN DAYS. YES...
SLIDE
YOU WILL BE THE CORNER-STONE FOR WORLD PEACE.

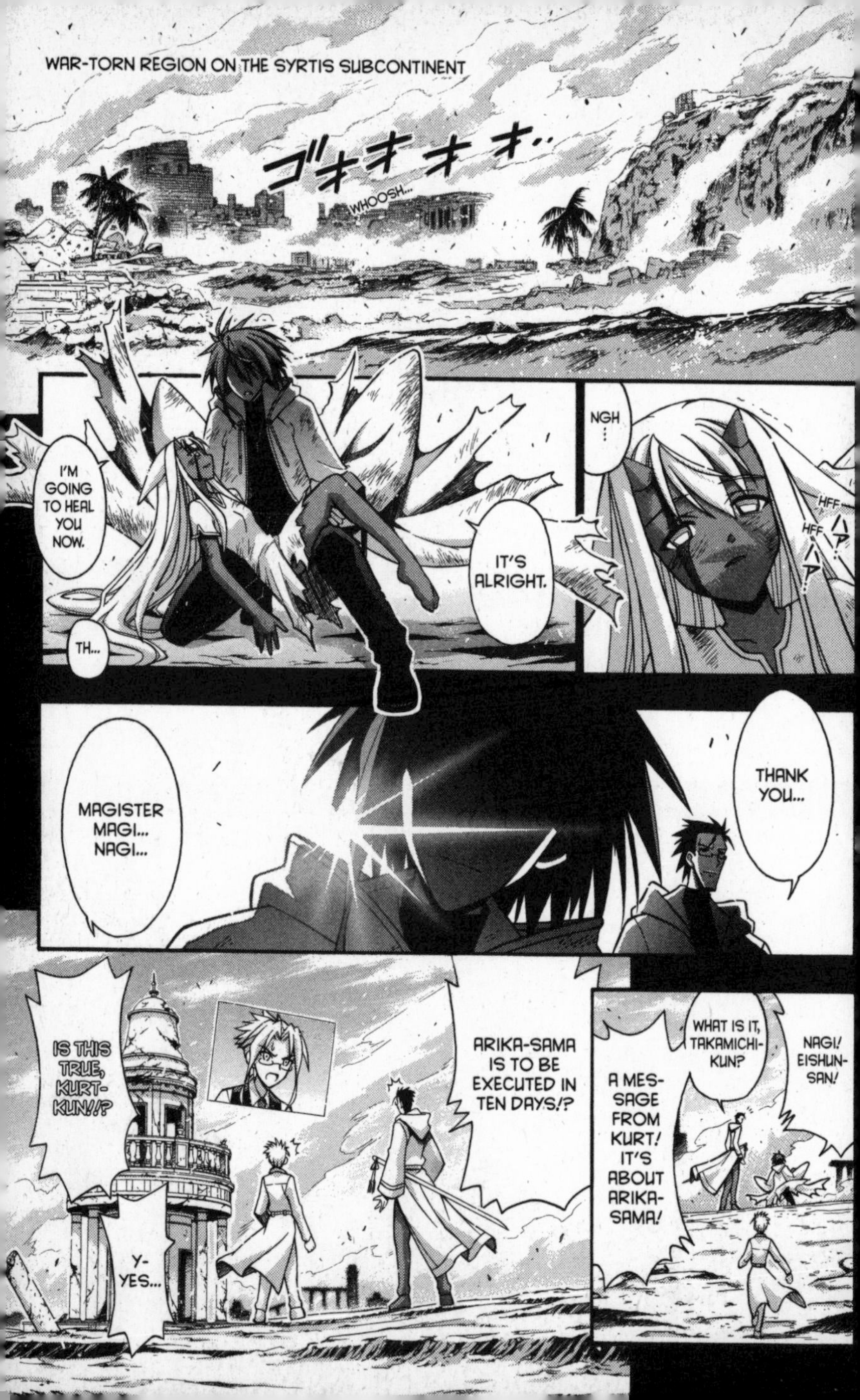
WAR-TORN REGION ON THE SYRTIS SUBCONTINENT
ゴオオオオ..
WHOOSH...
NGH...
HFF HFF
ハァ ハァ
IT'S ALRIGHT.
I'M GOING TO HEAL YOU NOW.
TH...
THANK YOU...
MAGISTER MAGI... NAGI...
NAGI! EISHUN-SAN!
WHAT IS IT, TAKAMICHI-KUN?
A MES-SAGE FROM KURT! IT'S ABOUT ARIKA-SAMA!
ARIKA-SAMA IS TO BE EXECUTED IN TEN DAYS!?
IS THIS TRUE, KURT-KUN!!?
Y-YES...

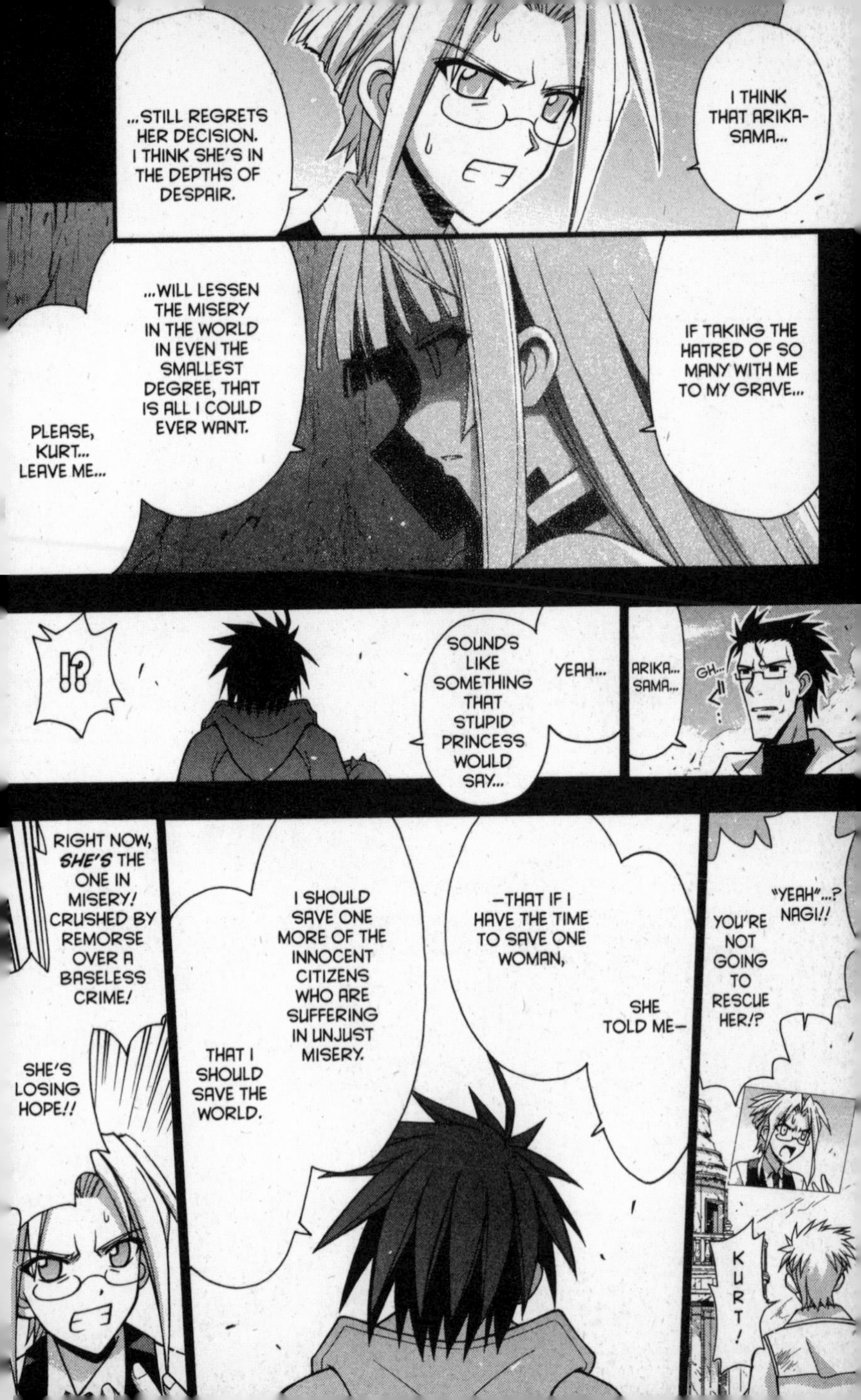
I THINK THAT ARIKA-SAMA...
...STILL REGRETS HER DECISION. I THINK SHE'S IN THE DEPTHS OF DESPAIR.
IF TAKING THE HATRED OF SO MANY WITH ME TO MY GRAVE...
...WILL LESSEN THE MISERY IN THE WORLD IN EVEN THE SMALLEST DEGREE, THAT IS ALL I COULD EVER WANT.
PLEASE, KURT... LEAVE ME...
ARIKA... SAMA...
GH...
YEAH...
SOUNDS LIKE SOMETHING THAT STUPID PRINCESS WOULD SAY...
!?
"YEAH"...? NAGI!!
YOU'RE NOT GOING TO RESCUE HER!?
KURT!
SHE TOLD ME—
—THAT IF I HAVE THE TIME TO SAVE ONE WOMAN,
I SHOULD SAVE ONE MORE OF THE INNOCENT CITIZENS WHO ARE SUFFERING IN UNJUST MISERY.
THAT I SHOULD SAVE THE WORLD.
RIGHT NOW, ***SHE'S*** THE ONE IN MISERY! CRUSHED BY REMORSE OVER A BASELESS CRIME!
SHE'S LOSING HOPE!!

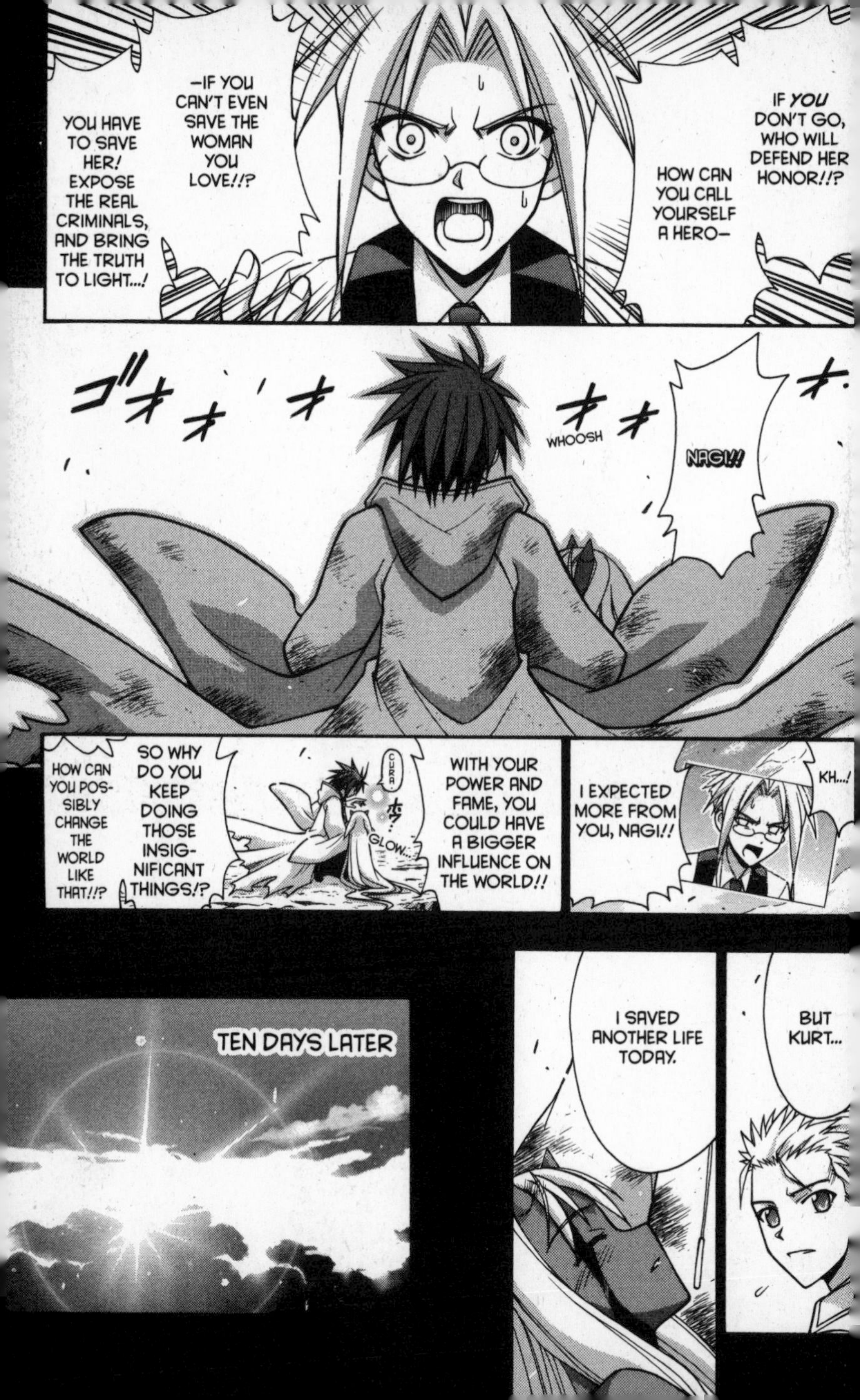
IF YOU DON'T GO, WHO WILL DEFEND HER HONOR!!?
HOW CAN YOU CALL YOURSELF A HERO—
—IF YOU CAN'T EVEN SAVE THE WOMAN YOU LOVE!!?
YOU HAVE TO SAVE HER! EXPOSE THE REAL CRIMINALS, AND BRING THE TRUTH TO LIGHT...!
NAGI!!
ゴオォォォォォ
WHOOSH
KH...!
I EXPECTED MORE FROM YOU, NAGI!!
WITH YOUR POWER AND FAME, YOU COULD HAVE A BIGGER INFLUENCE ON THE WORLD!!
CURA
GLOW
SO WHY DO YOU KEEP DOING THOSE INSIG-NIFICANT THINGS!?
HOW CAN YOU POS-SIBLY CHANGE THE WORLD LIKE THAT!!?
BUT KURT...
I SAVED ANOTHER LIFE TODAY.
TEN DAYS LATER

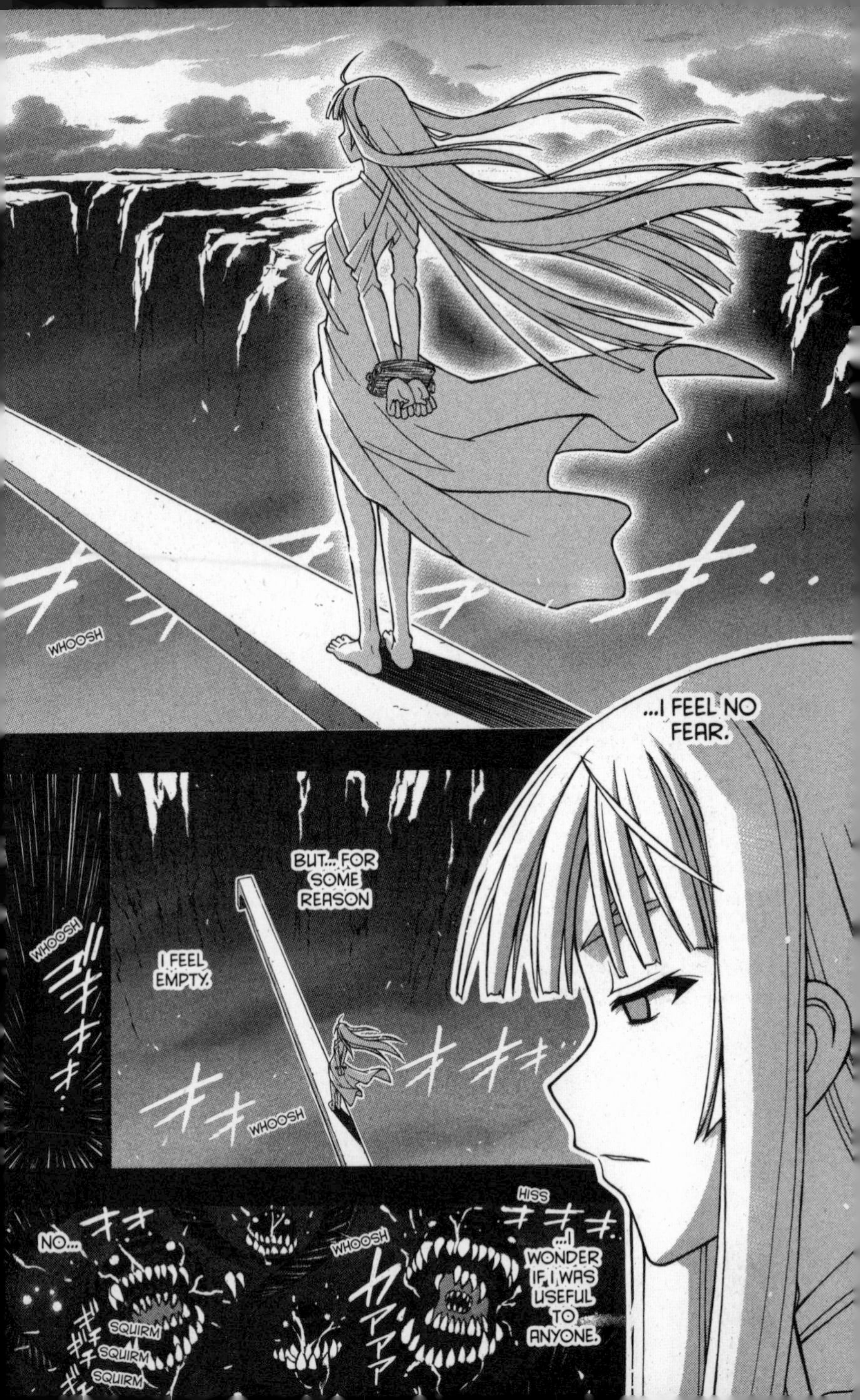
WHOOSH
...I FEEL NO FEAR.
BUT... FOR SOME REASON
I FEEL EMPTY.
WHOOSH
WHOOSH
HISS
...I WONDER IF I WAS USEFUL TO ANYONE.
WHOOSH
NO...
SQUIRM
SQUIRM
SQUIRM

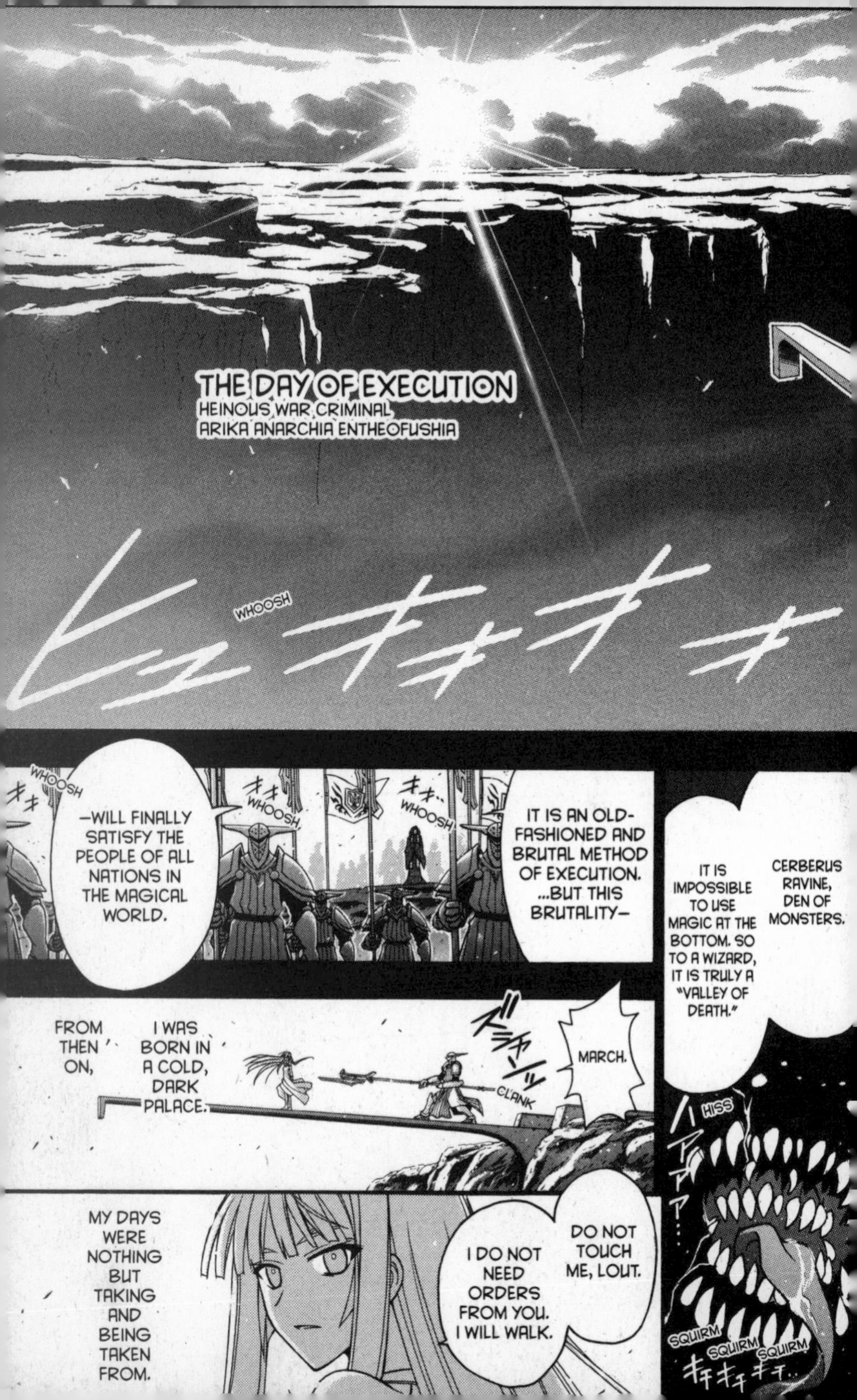
THE DAY OF EXECUTION
HEINOUS WAR CRIMINAL
ARIKA ANARCHIA ENTHEOFUSHIA
WHOOSH
CERBERUS RAVINE, DEN OF MONSTERS.
IT IS IMPOSSIBLE TO USE MAGIC AT THE BOTTOM. SO TO A WIZARD, IT IS TRULY A "VALLEY OF DEATH."
HISS
SQUIRM SQUIRM SQUIRM
IT IS AN OLD-FASHIONED AND BRUTAL METHOD OF EXECUTION. ...BUT THIS BRUTALITY—
WHOOSH
WHOOSH
—WILL FINALLY SATISFY THE PEOPLE OF ALL NATIONS IN THE MAGICAL WORLD.
WHOOSH
MARCH.
CLANK
I WAS BORN IN A COLD, DARK PALACE.
FROM THEN ON,
DO NOT TOUCH ME, LOUT.
I DO NOT NEED ORDERS FROM YOU. I WILL WALK.
MY DAYS WERE NOTHING BUT TAKING AND BEING TAKEN FROM.

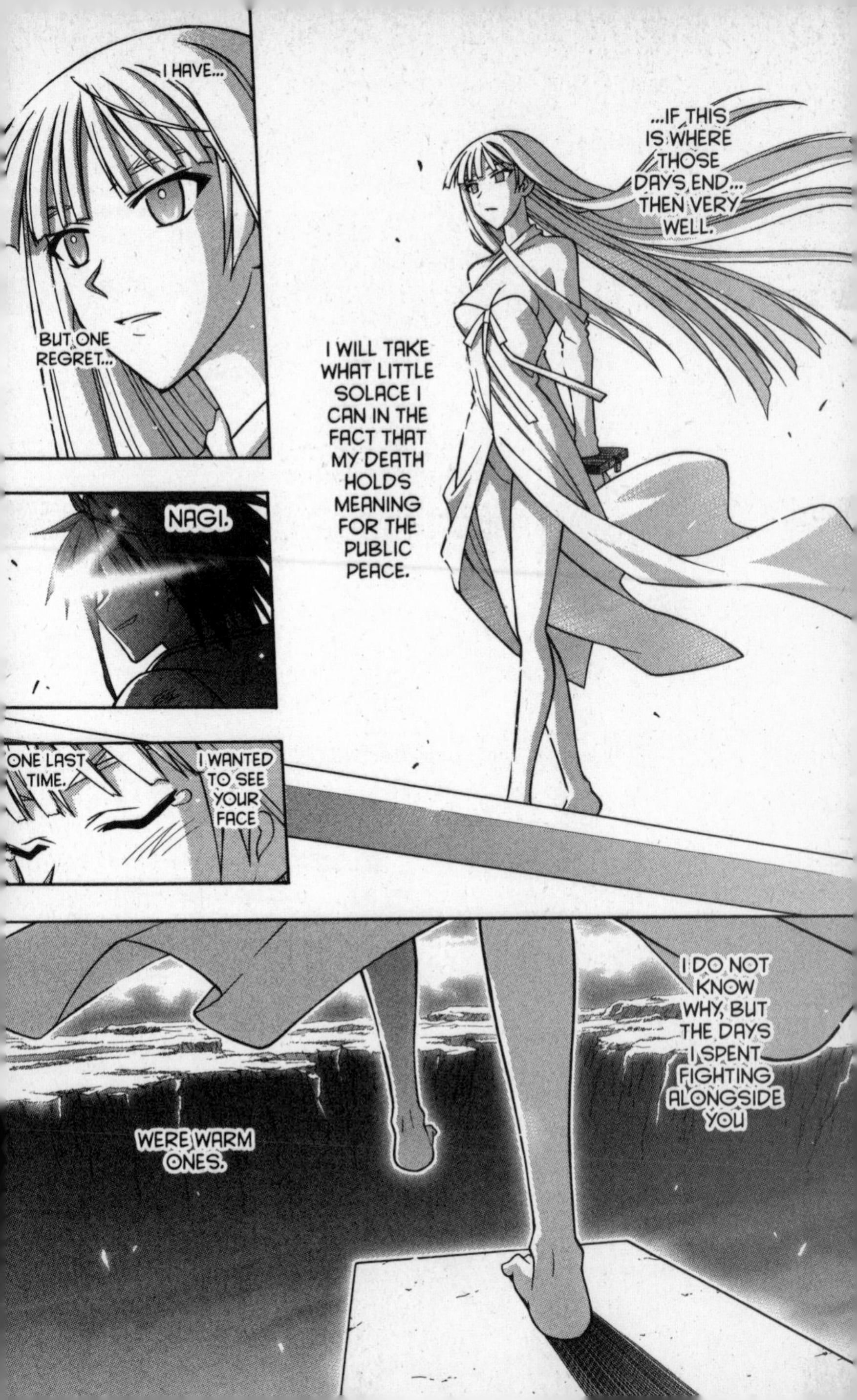
...IF THIS IS WHERE THOSE DAYS END... THEN VERY WELL.
I WILL TAKE WHAT LITTLE SOLACE I CAN IN THE FACT THAT MY DEATH HOLDS MEANING FOR THE PUBLIC PEACE.
I HAVE...
BUT ONE REGRET...
NAGI.
I WANTED TO SEE YOUR FACE
ONE LAST TIME.
I DO NOT KNOW WHY, BUT THE DAYS I SPENT FIGHTING ALONGSIDE YOU
WERE WARM ONES.

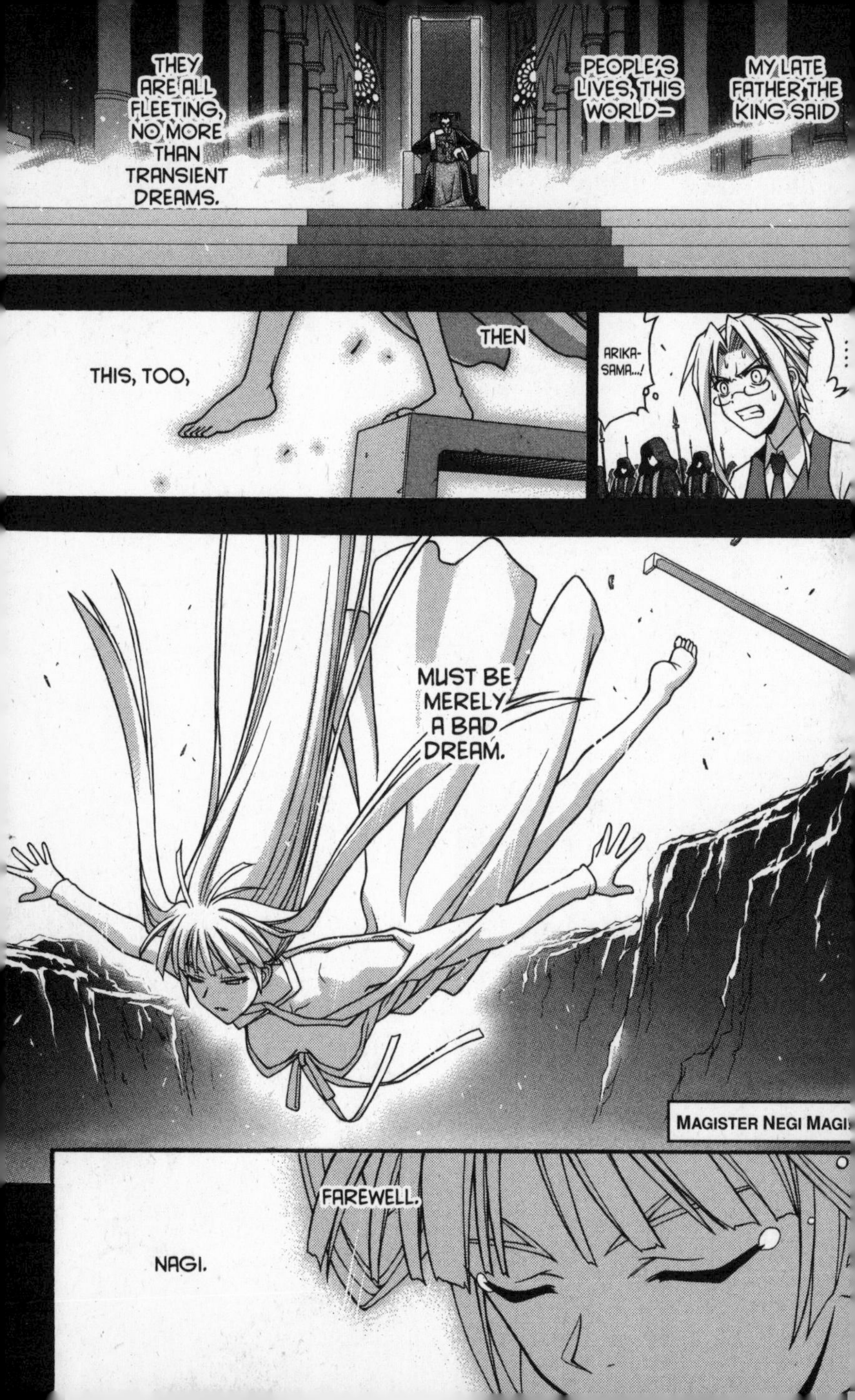
MY LATE FATHER THE KING SAID
PEOPLE'S LIVES, THIS WORLD—
THEY ARE ALL FLEETING, NO MORE THAN TRANSIENT DREAMS.
ARIKA-SAMA...!
THEN
THIS, TOO,
MUST BE MERELY A BAD DREAM.
MAGISTER NEGI MAGI
FAREWELL.
NAGI.

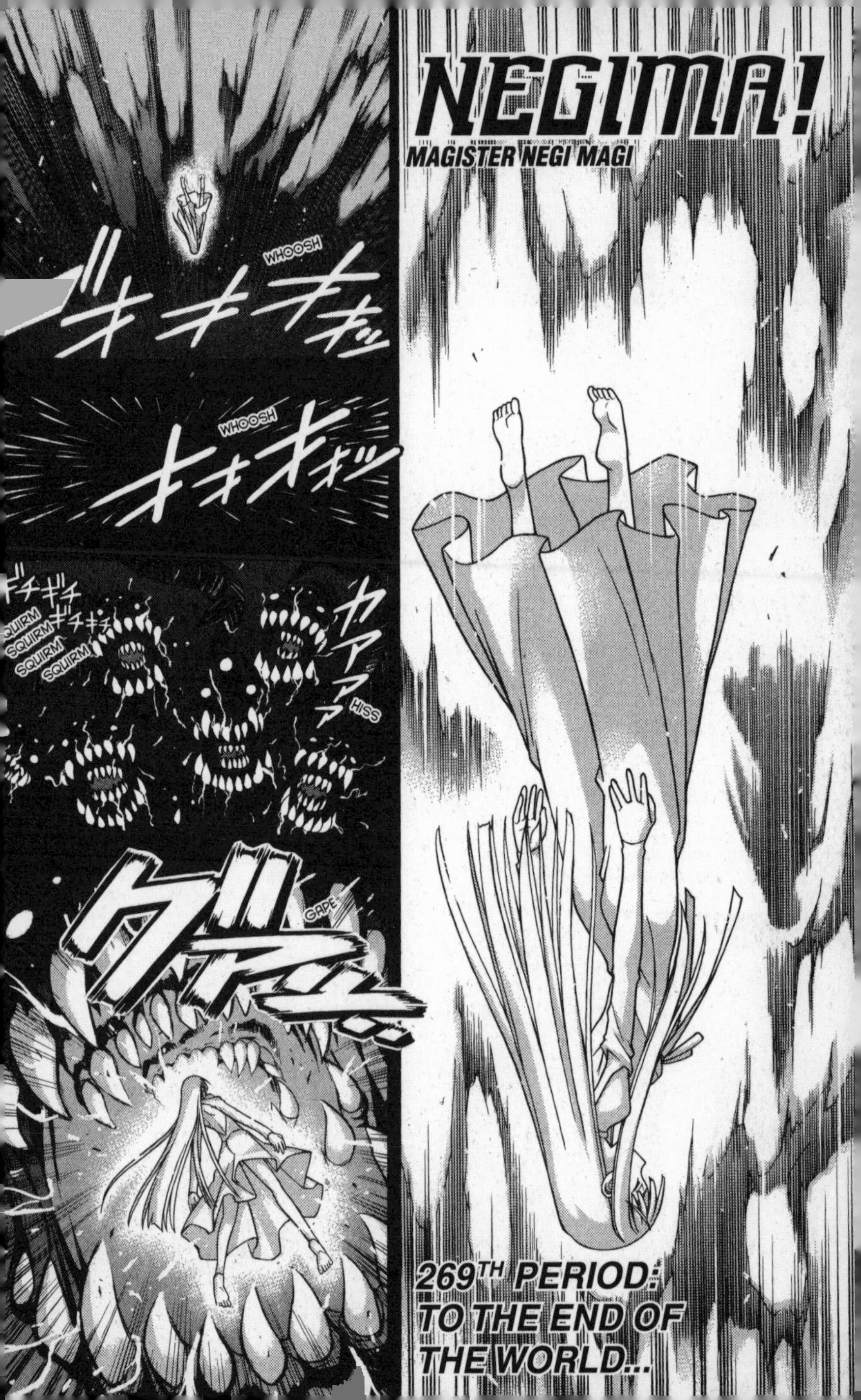
NEGIMA!
MAGISTER NEGI MAGI
269TH PERIOD:
TO THE END OF THE WORLD...
WHOOSH
WHOOSH
SQUIRM SQUIRM SQUIRM SQUIRM
HISS
GAPE

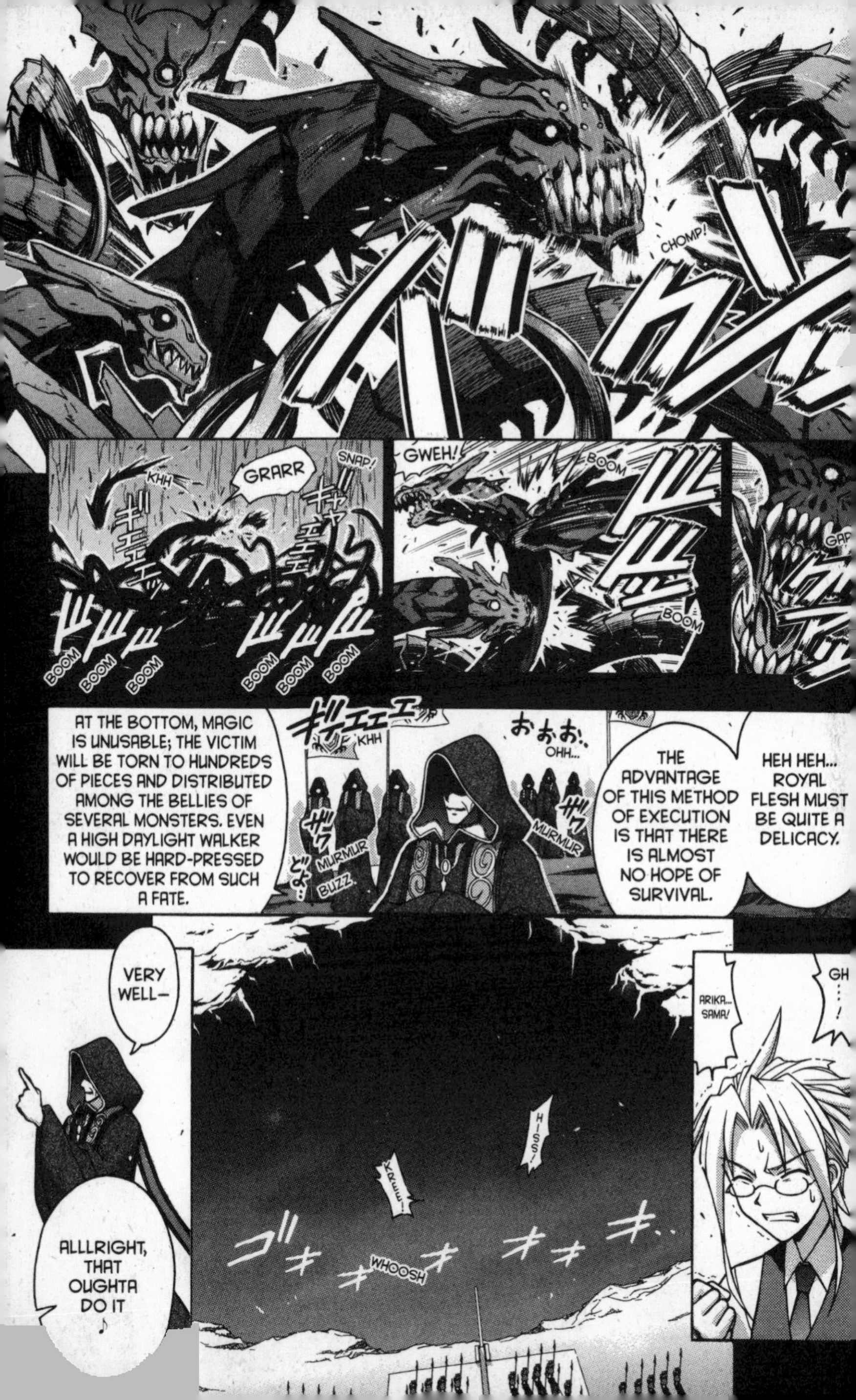

CHOMP!
GAP
GWEH!
BOOM
BOOM
SNAP!
GRARR
KHH
BOOM BOOM BOOM
BOOM BOOM BOOM
HEH HEH... ROYAL FLESH MUST BE QUITE A DELICACY.
THE ADVANTAGE OF THIS METHOD OF EXECUTION IS THAT THERE IS ALMOST NO HOPE OF SURVIVAL.
おおお! OHH...
KHH
MURMUR
MURMUR
BUZZ
AT THE BOTTOM, MAGIC IS UNUSABLE; THE VICTIM WILL BE TORN TO HUNDREDS OF PIECES AND DISTRIBUTED AMONG THE BELLIES OF SEVERAL MONSTERS. EVEN A HIGH DAYLIGHT WALKER WOULD BE HARD-PRESSED TO RECOVER FROM SUCH A FATE.
GH...!
ARIKA... SAMA!
HISS!
KREE!
WHOOSH
VERY WELL—
ALLLRIGHT, THAT OUGHTA DO IT ♪

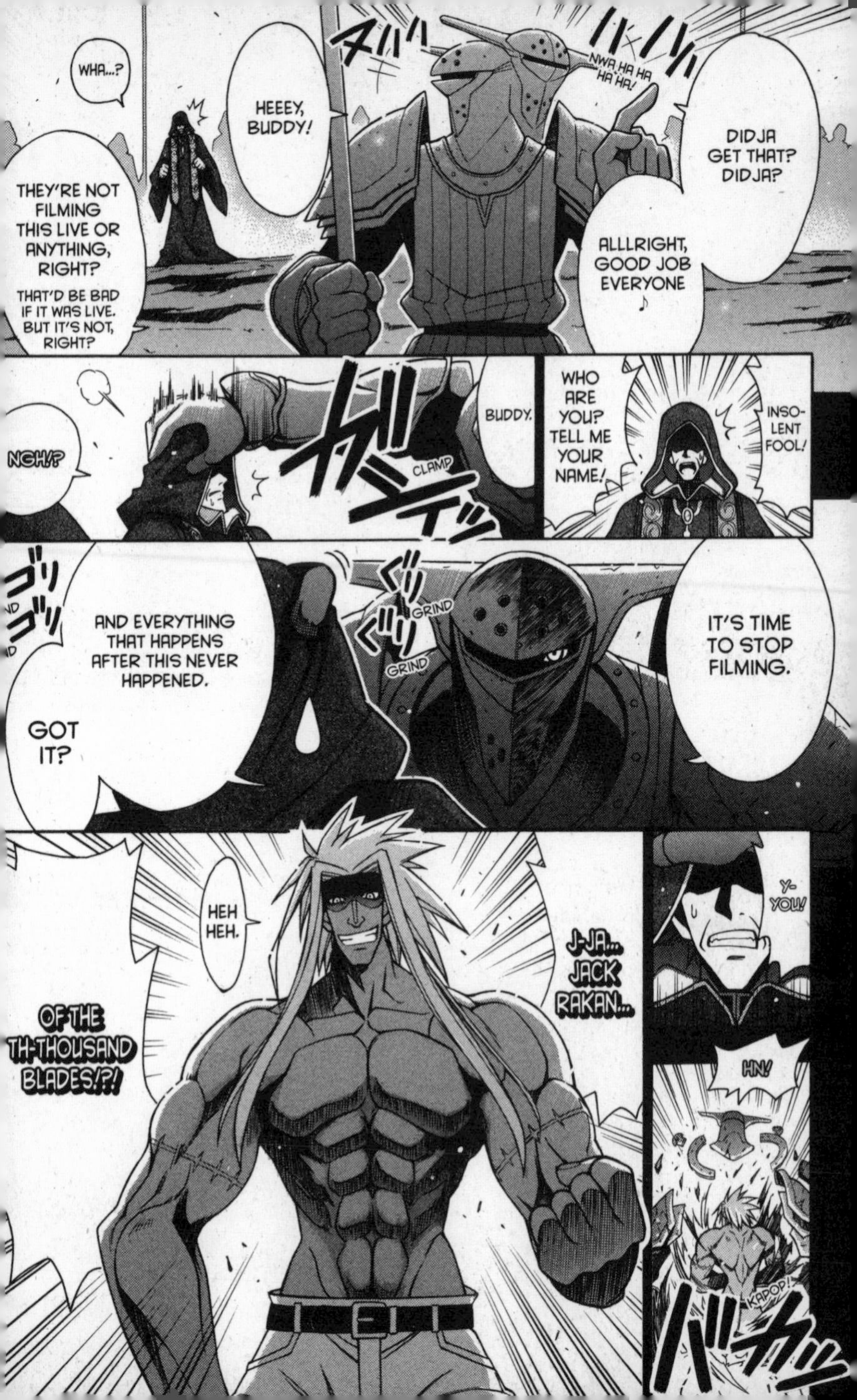

DIDJA GET THAT? DIDJA?
NWA HA HA HA HA!
ALLLRIGHT, GOOD JOB EVERYONE ♪
HEEEY, BUDDY!
WHA...?
THEY'RE NOT FILMING THIS LIVE OR ANYTHING, RIGHT?
THAT'D BE BAD IF IT WAS LIVE. BUT IT'S NOT, RIGHT?
INSO-LENT FOOL!
WHO ARE YOU? TELL ME YOUR NAME!
BUDDY.
CLAMP
NGH!?
IT'S TIME TO STOP FILMING.
GRIND
GRIND
AND EVERYTHING THAT HAPPENS AFTER THIS NEVER HAPPENED.
GOT IT?
Y-YOU!
HN!
KAPOP!
J-JA... JACK RAKAN...
HEH HEH.
OF THE TH-THOUSAND BLADES!?!

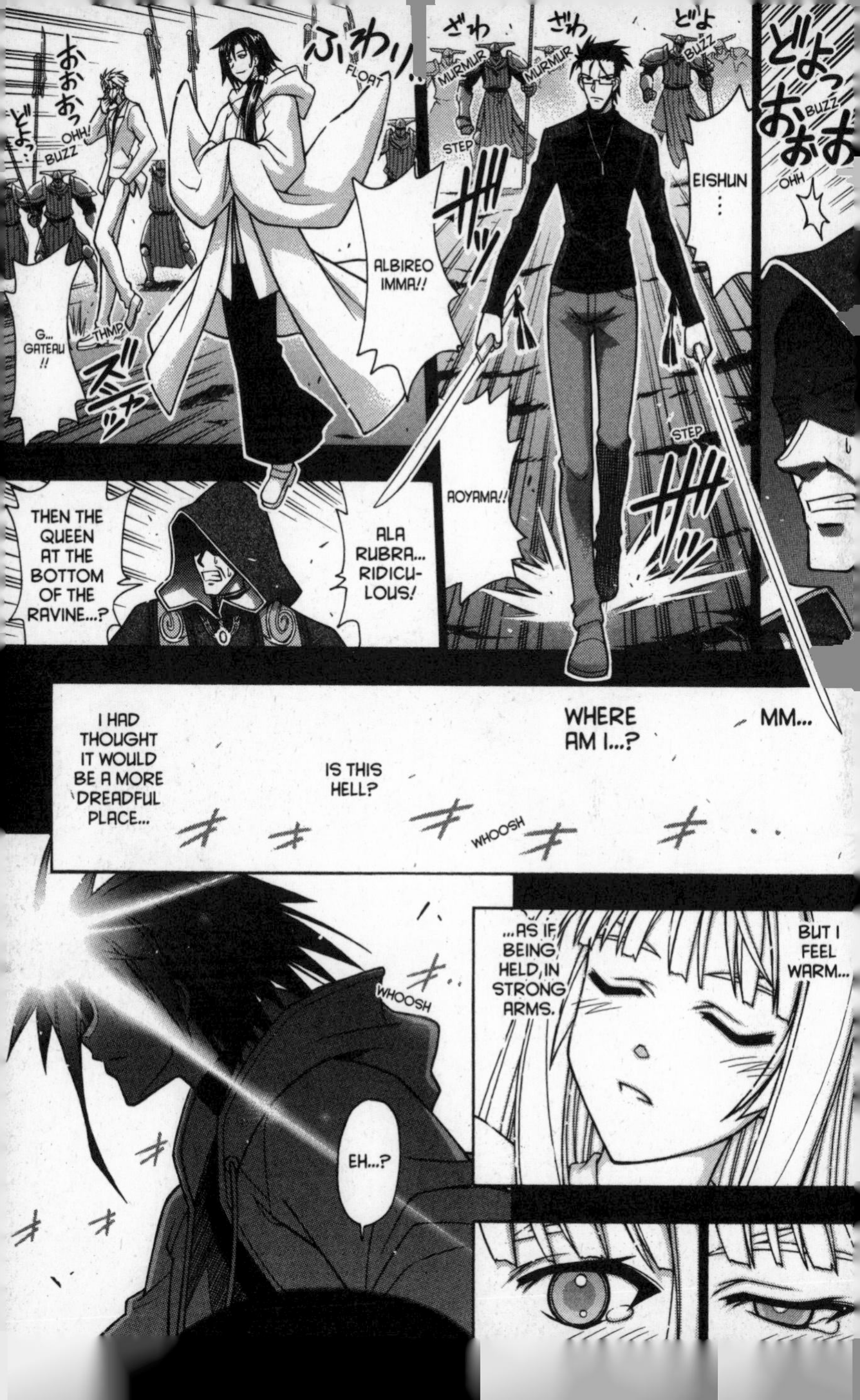
どよっ
BUZZ
おおお
OHH
ざわ ざわ
MURMUR MURMUR
どよ
BUZZ
STEP
EISHUN...
AOYAMA!!
STEP
ふわり
FLOAT
ALBIREO IMMA!!
おおおっ
OHH!
どよっ
BUZZ
G... GATEAU!!
THMP
ALA RUBRA... RIDICULOUS!
THEN THE QUEEN AT THE BOTTOM OF THE RAVINE...?
MM...
WHERE AM I...?
IS THIS HELL?
I HAD THOUGHT IT WOULD BE A MORE DREADFUL PLACE...
WHOOSH
BUT I FEEL WARM...
...AS IF BEING HELD IN STRONG ARMS.
WHOOSH
EH...?

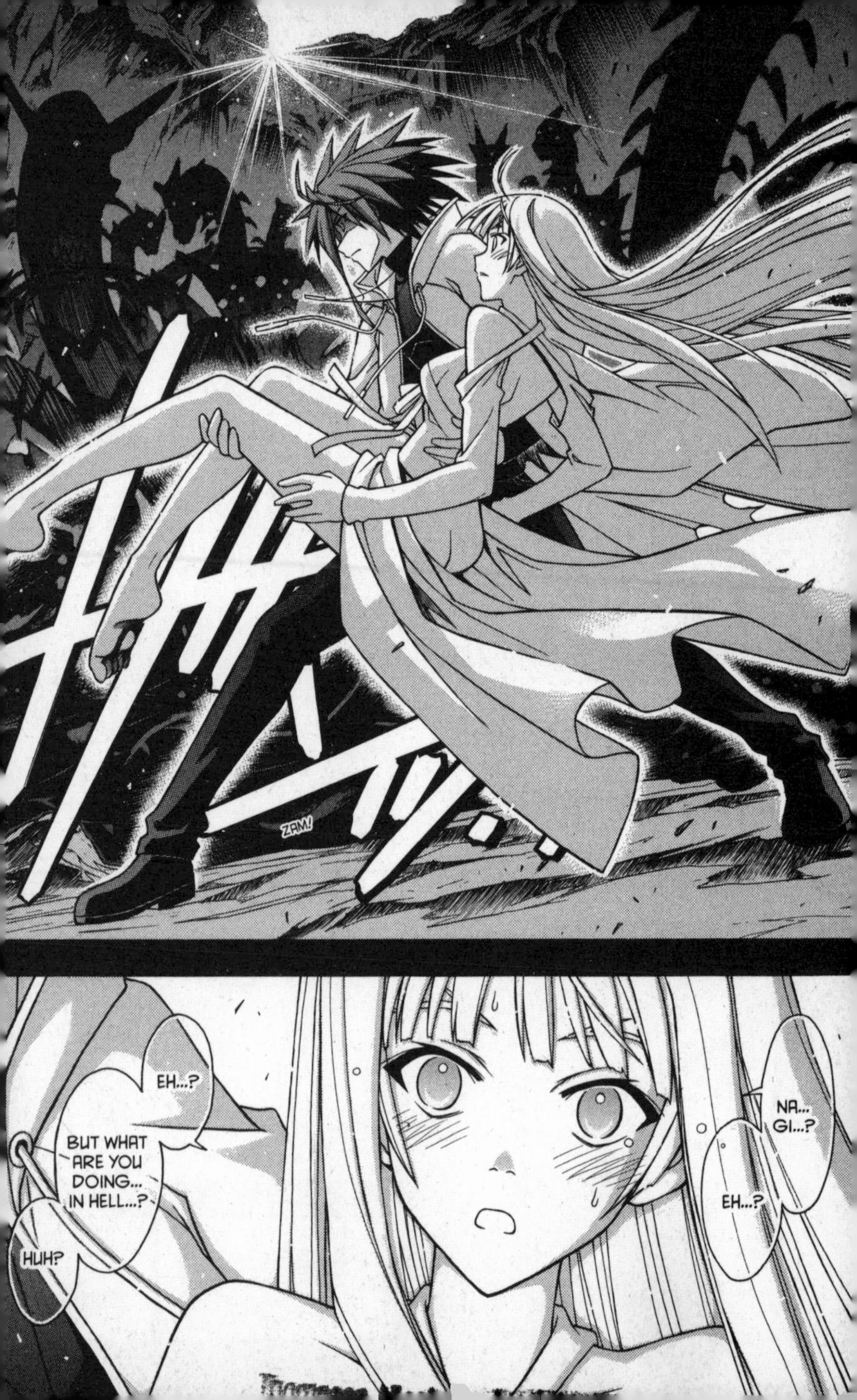
ZAM!
NA... GI...?
EH...?
EH...?
BUT WHAT ARE YOU DOING... IN HELL...?
HUH?

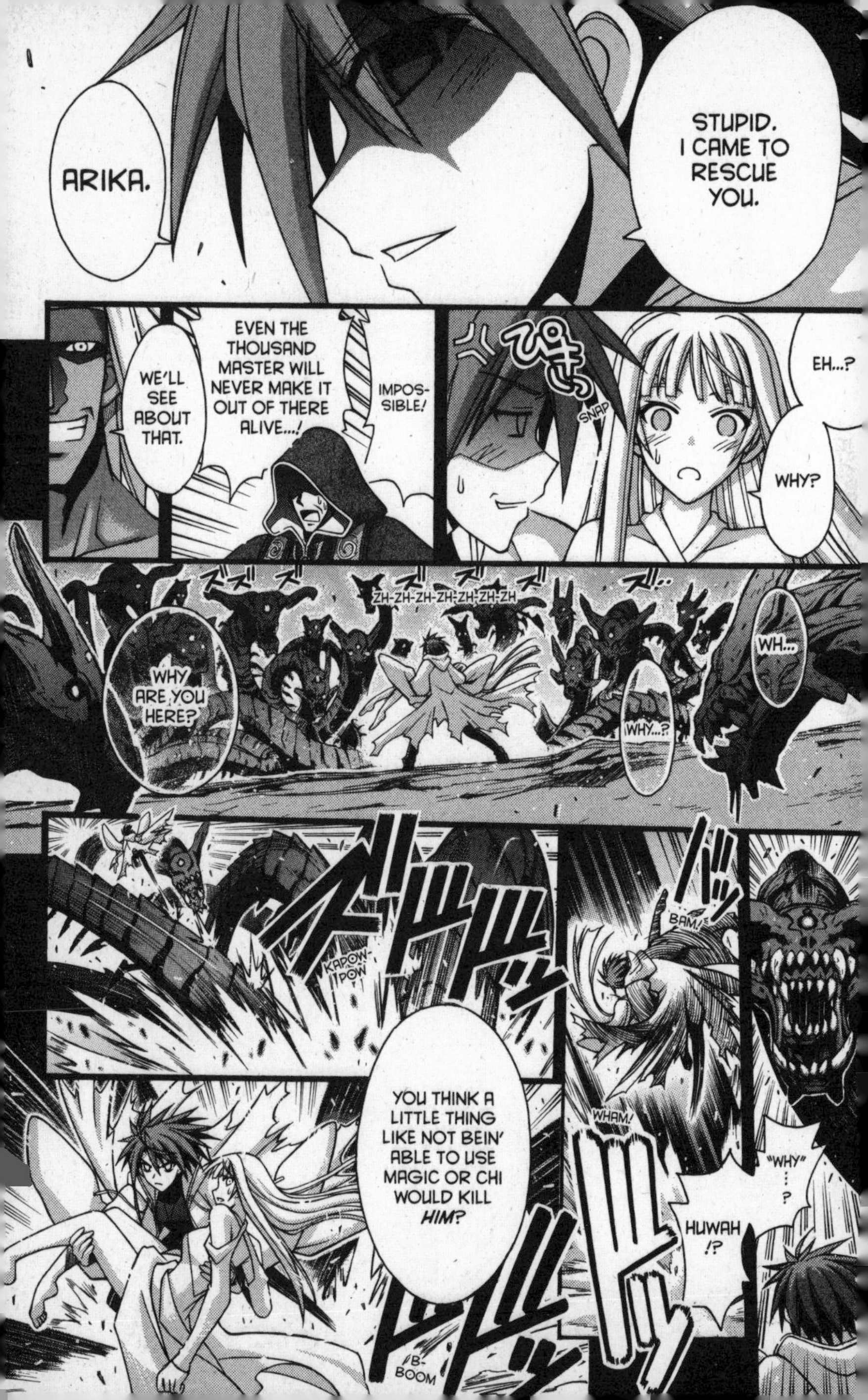
STUPID. I CAME TO RESCUE YOU.
ARIKA.
EH...?
SNAP
WHY?
IMPOS-SIBLE!
EVEN THE THOUSAND MASTER WILL NEVER MAKE IT OUT OF THERE ALIVE...!
WE'LL SEE ABOUT THAT.
WH...
WHY...?
ZH-ZH-ZH-ZH-ZH-ZH-ZH
WHY ARE YOU HERE?
BAM!
"WHY" ...?
WHAM!
HUWAH!?
KAPOW-POW
YOU THINK A LITTLE THING LIKE NOT BEIN' ABLE TO USE MAGIC OR CHI WOULD KILL *HIM*?
B-BOOM

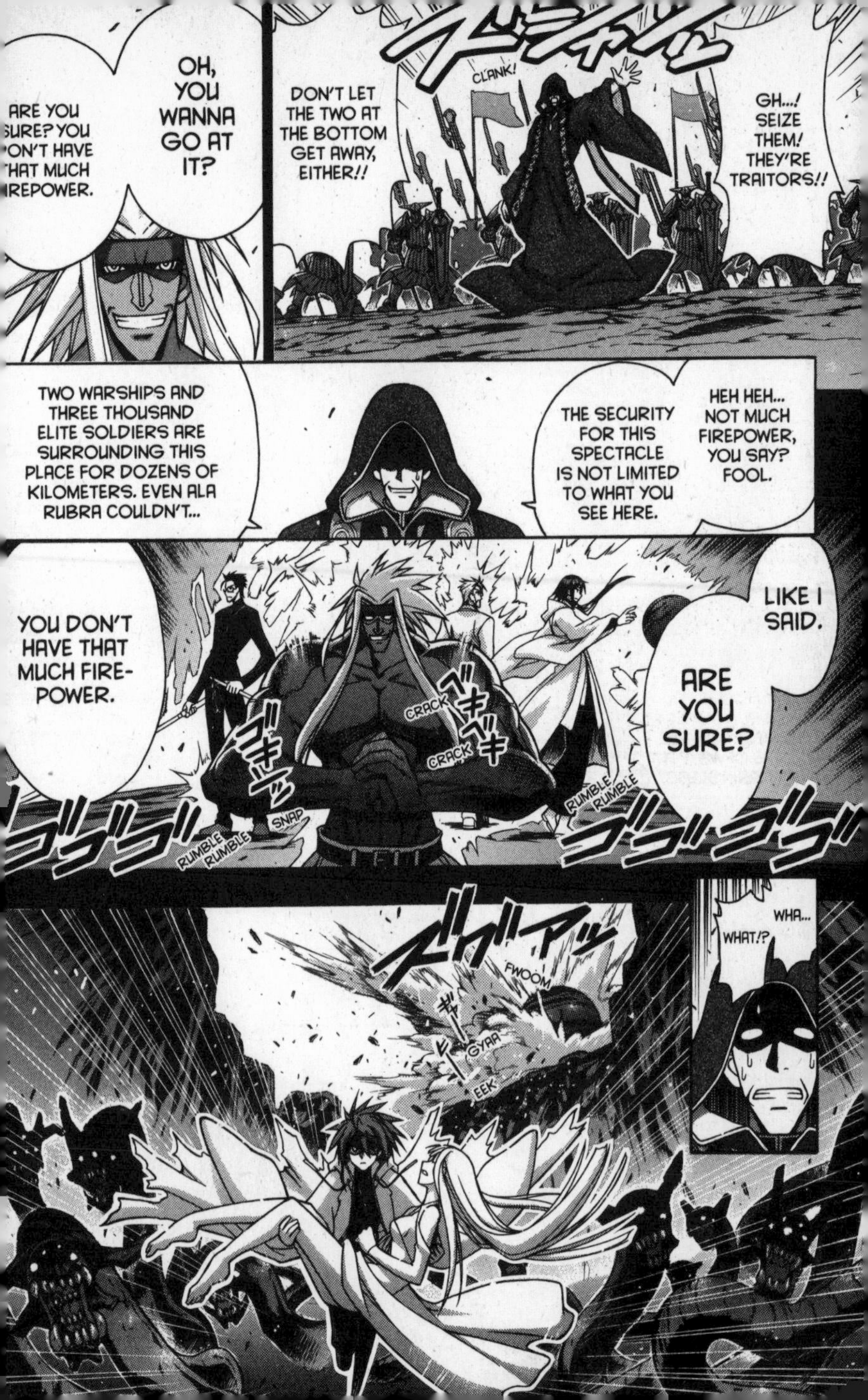

CLANK!
GH...! SEIZE THEM! THEY'RE TRAITORS!!
DON'T LET THE TWO AT THE BOTTOM GET AWAY, EITHER!!
OH, YOU WANNA GO AT IT?
ARE YOU SURE? YOU ON'T HAVE HAT MUCH IREPOWER.
HEH HEH... NOT MUCH FIREPOWER, YOU SAY? FOOL.
THE SECURITY FOR THIS SPECTACLE IS NOT LIMITED TO WHAT YOU SEE HERE.
TWO WARSHIPS AND THREE THOUSAND ELITE SOLDIERS ARE SURROUNDING THIS PLACE FOR DOZENS OF KILOMETERS. EVEN ALA RUBRA COULDN'T...
LIKE I SAID.
ARE YOU SURE?
RUMBLE RUMBLE
CRACK
CRACK
SNAP
YOU DON'T HAVE THAT MUCH FIRE-POWER.
RUMBLE RUMBLE
WHA...
WHAT!?
FWOOM
GYAA
EEK

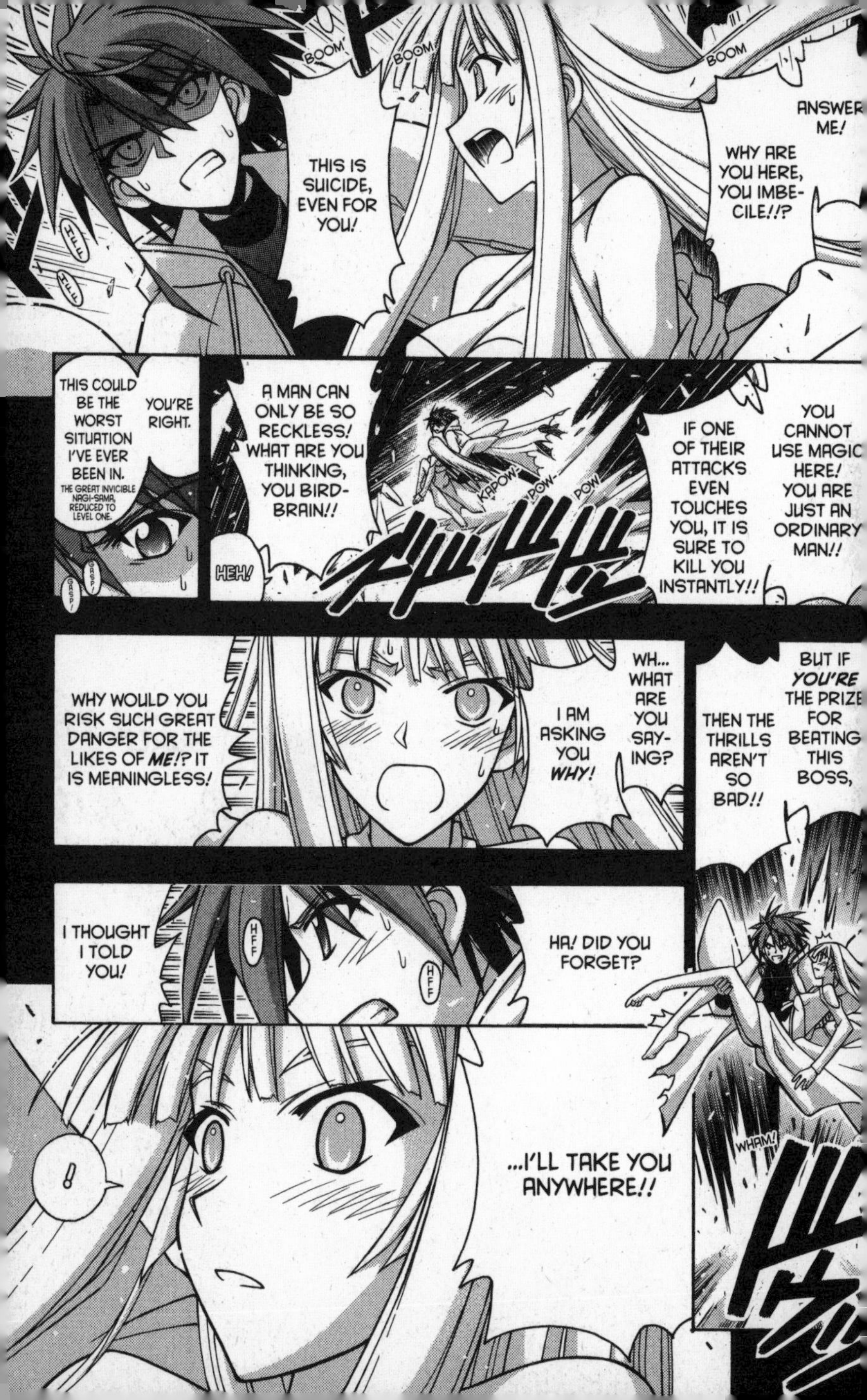
BOOM
BOOM
BOOM
ANSWER ME!
WHY ARE YOU HERE, YOU IMBECILE!!?
THIS IS SUICIDE, EVEN FOR YOU!
HFF
HFF
YOU CANNOT USE MAGIC HERE! YOU ARE JUST AN ORDINARY MAN!!
IF ONE OF THEIR ATTACKS EVEN TOUCHES YOU, IT IS SURE TO KILL YOU INSTANTLY!!
POW
POW
KAPOW
A MAN CAN ONLY BE SO RECKLESS! WHAT ARE YOU THINKING, YOU BIRD-BRAIN!!
HEH!
YOU'RE RIGHT.
THIS COULD BE THE WORST SITUATION I'VE EVER BEEN IN.
THE GREAT INVICIBLE NAGI-SAMA, REDUCED TO LEVEL ONE.
GASP!
GASP!
BUT IF *YOU'RE* THE PRIZE FOR BEATING THIS BOSS,
THEN THE THRILLS AREN'T SO BAD!!
WH... WHAT ARE YOU SAYING?
I AM ASKING YOU *WHY*!
WHY WOULD YOU RISK SUCH GREAT DANGER FOR THE LIKES OF *ME*!? IT IS MEANINGLESS!
WHAM!
HA! DID YOU FORGET?
HFF
HFF
I THOUGHT I TOLD YOU!
...I'LL TAKE YOU ANYWHERE!!
!

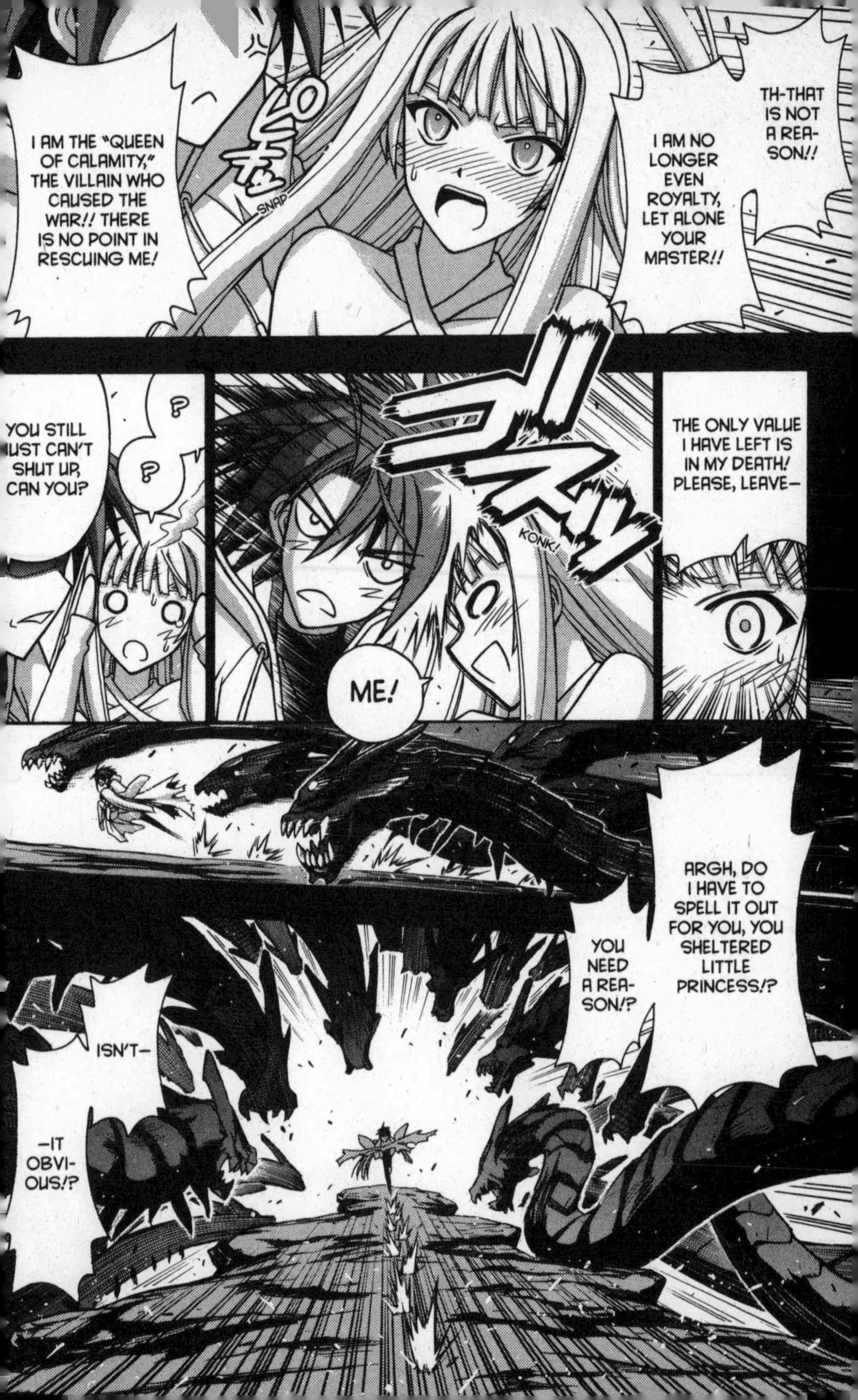
TH-THAT IS NOT A REA-SON!!
I AM NO LONGER EVEN ROYALTY, LET ALONE YOUR MASTER!!
SNAP
I AM THE "QUEEN OF CALAMITY," THE VILLAIN WHO CAUSED THE WAR!! THERE IS NO POINT IN RESCUING ME!
THE ONLY VALUE I HAVE LEFT IS IN MY DEATH! PLEASE, LEAVE—
KONK!
ME!
? ?
YOU STILL JUST CAN'T SHUT UP, CAN YOU?
ARGH, DO I HAVE TO SPELL IT OUT FOR YOU, YOU SHELTERED LITTLE PRINCESS!?
YOU NEED A REA-SON!?
ISN'T—
—IT OBVI-OUS!?

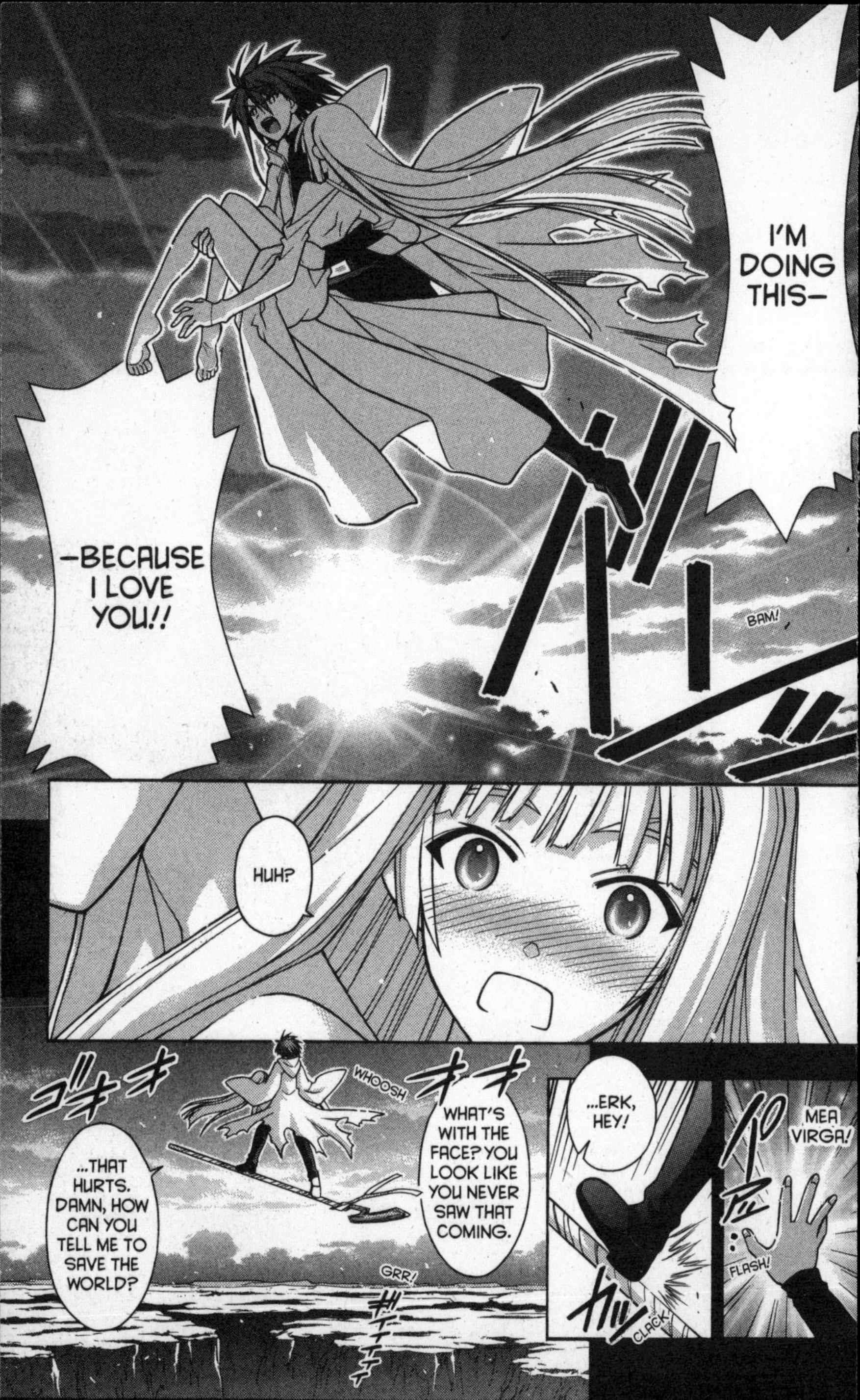
I'M DOING THIS—
—BECAUSE I LOVE YOU!!
BAM!
HUH?
MEA VIRGA!
FLASH!
...ERK, HEY!
CLACK
WHOOSH
WHAT'S WITH THE FACE? YOU LOOK LIKE YOU NEVER SAW THAT COMING.
...THAT HURTS. DAMN, HOW CAN YOU TELL ME TO SAVE THE WORLD?
GRR!

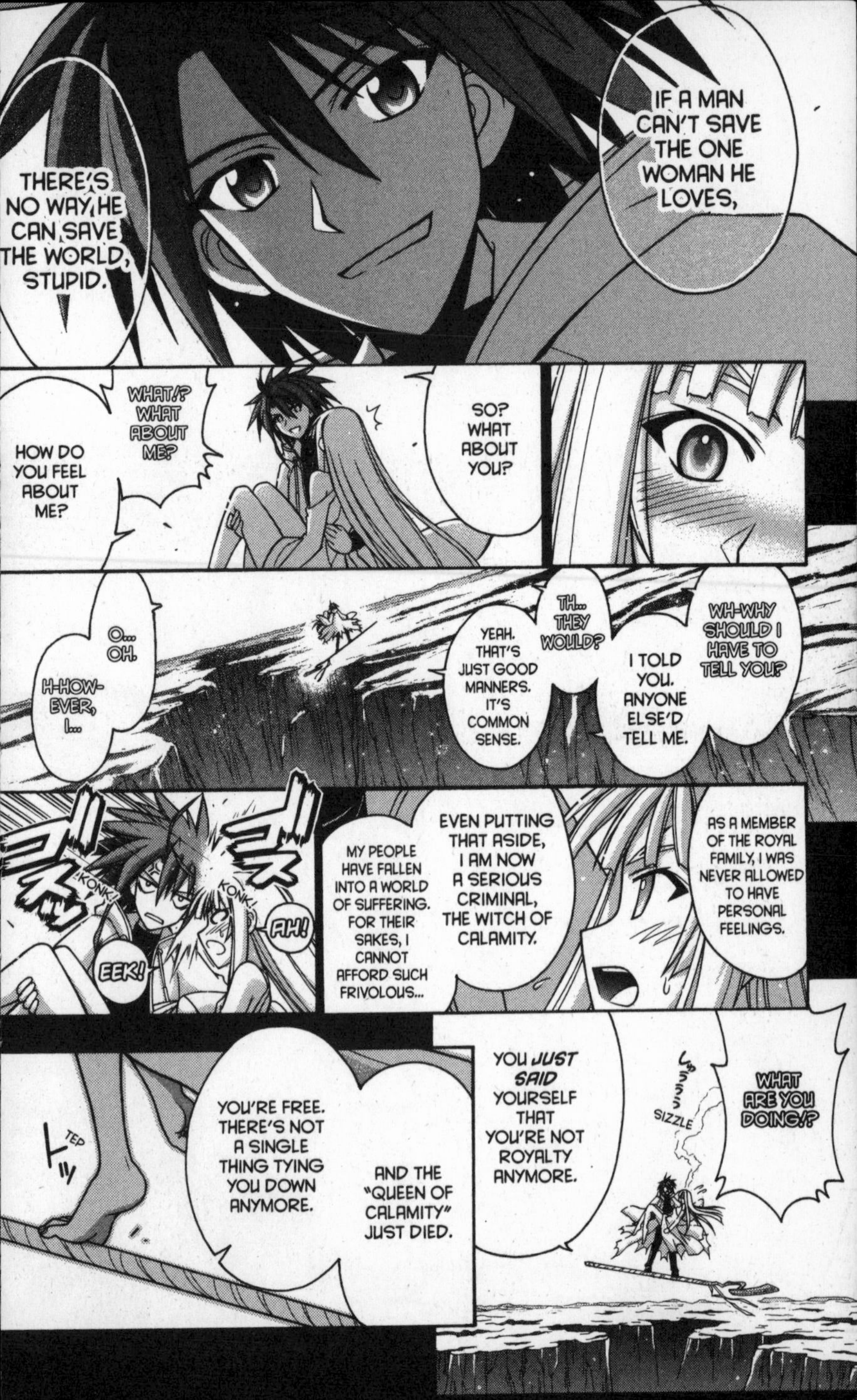
IF A MAN CAN'T SAVE THE ONE WOMAN HE LOVES,
THERE'S NO WAY HE CAN SAVE THE WORLD, STUPID.
SO? WHAT ABOUT YOU?
WHAT!? WHAT ABOUT ME?
HOW DO YOU FEEL ABOUT ME?
WH-WHY SHOULD I HAVE TO TELL YOU!?
I TOLD YOU. ANYONE ELSE'D TELL ME.
TH... THEY WOULD?
YEAH. THAT'S JUST GOOD MANNERS. IT'S COMMON SENSE.
O... OH.
H-HOW-EVER, I...
AS A MEMBER OF THE ROYAL FAMILY, I WAS NEVER ALLOWED TO HAVE PERSONAL FEELINGS.
EVEN PUTTING THAT ASIDE, I AM NOW A SERIOUS CRIMINAL, THE WITCH OF CALAMITY.
MY PEOPLE HAVE FALLEN INTO A WORLD OF SUFFERING. FOR THEIR SAKES, I CANNOT AFFORD SUCH FRIVOLOUS...
KONK!
KONK!
AH!
EEK!
WHAT ARE YOU DOING!?
SIZZLE
YOU *JUST SAID* YOURSELF THAT YOU'RE NOT ROYALTY ANYMORE.
AND THE "QUEEN OF CALAMITY" JUST DIED.
YOU'RE FREE. THERE'S NOT A SINGLE THING TYING YOU DOWN ANYMORE.
TEP

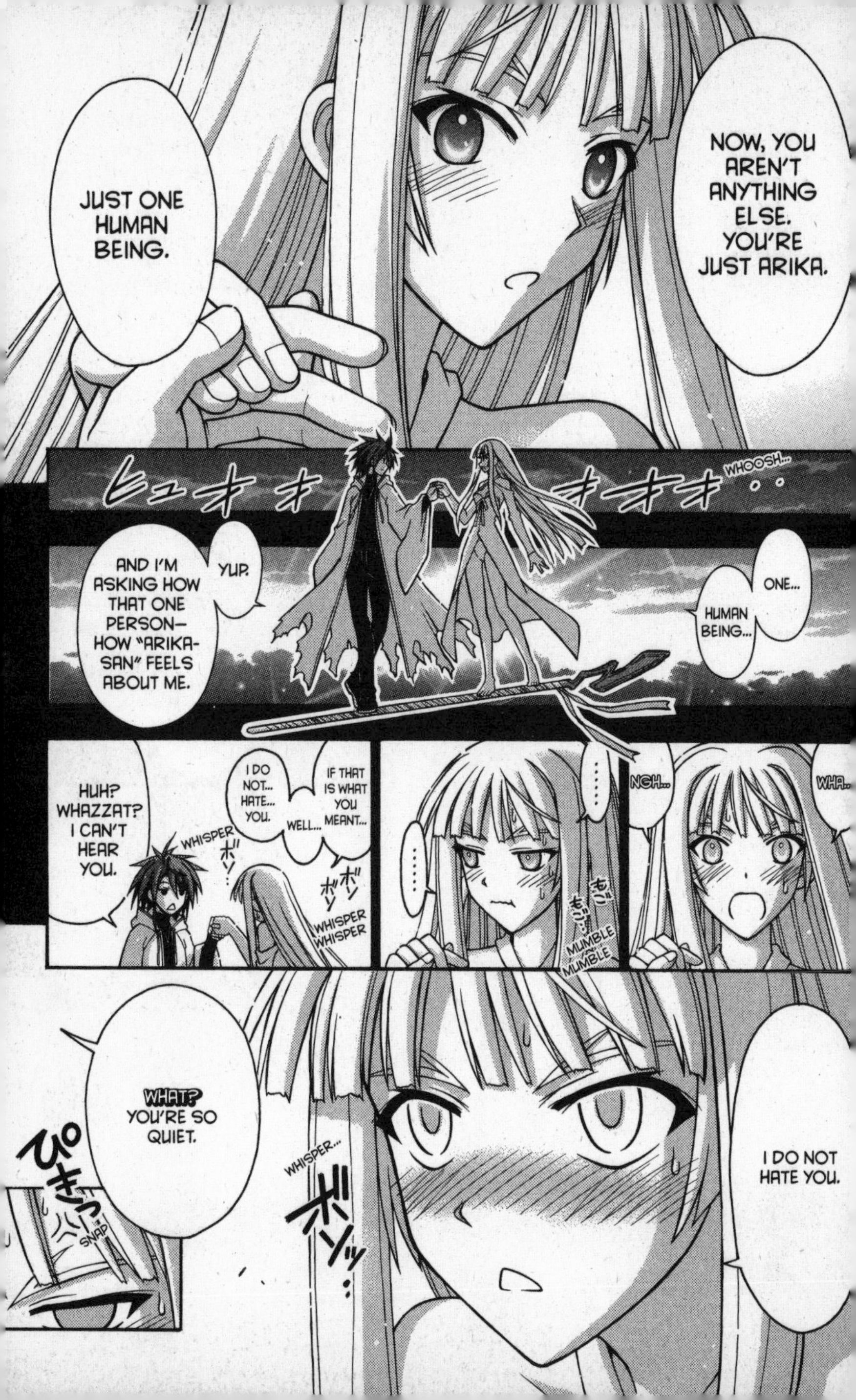
NOW, YOU AREN'T ANYTHING ELSE. YOU'RE JUST ARIKA.
JUST ONE HUMAN BEING.
ヒュオオ
オオオ
WHOOSH...
ONE...
HUMAN BEING...
YUP.
AND I'M ASKING HOW THAT ONE PERSON— HOW "ARIKA-SAN" FEELS ABOUT ME.
WHA...
NGH...
......
......
もごもご
MUMBLE MUMBLE
IF THAT IS WHAT YOU MEANT...
I DO NOT... HATE... YOU.
WELL...
ボソボソ
WHISPER WHISPER
ボソ
WHISPER
HUH? WHAZZAT? I CAN'T HEAR YOU.
I DO NOT HATE YOU.
ボソッ
WHISPER...
WHAT? YOU'RE SO QUIET.
ぴきっ
SNAP

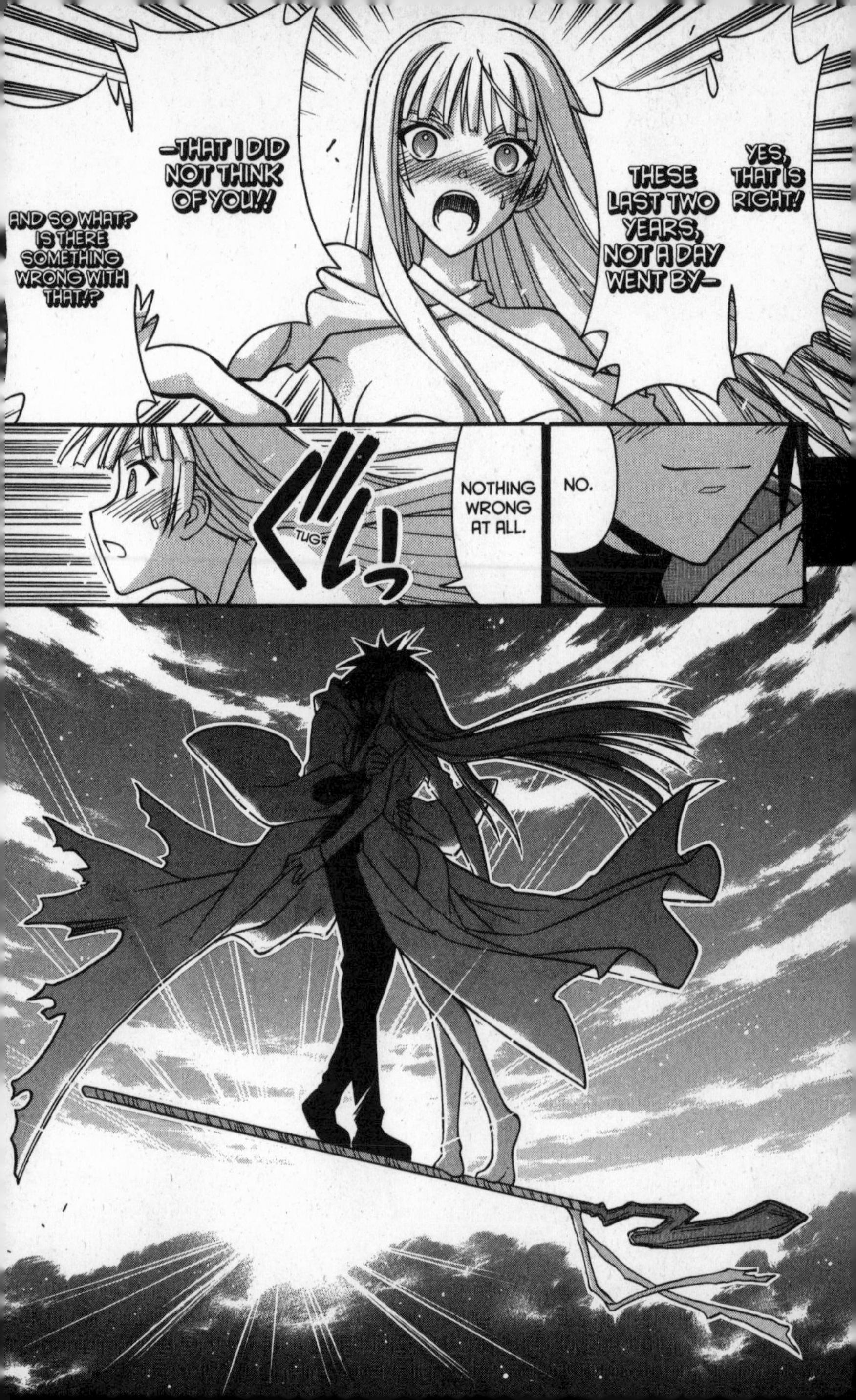
YES, THAT IS RIGHT!
THESE LAST TWO YEARS, NOT A DAY WENT BY—
—THAT I DID NOT THINK OF YOU!!
AND SO WHAT? IS THERE SOMETHING WRONG WITH THAT!?
NO.
NOTHING WRONG AT ALL.
TUG

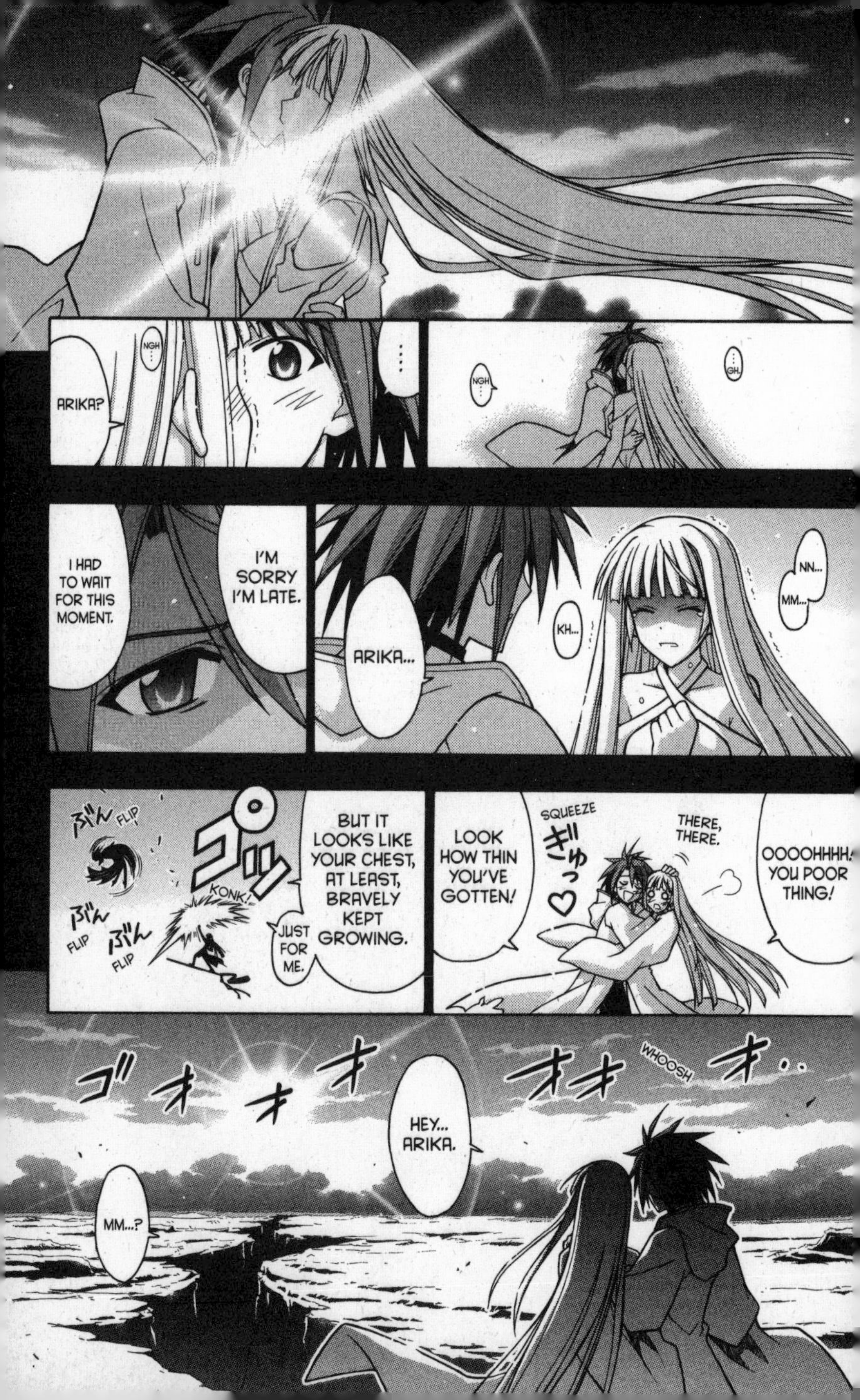

...GH...
NGH...
...
NGH...
ARIKA?
NN...
MM...
KH...
ARIKA...
I'M SORRY I'M LATE.
I HAD TO WAIT FOR THIS MOMENT.
OOOOHHHH! YOU POOR THING!
THERE, THERE.
ぎゅっ SQUEEZE
LOOK HOW THIN YOU'VE GOTTEN!
BUT IT LOOKS LIKE YOUR CHEST, AT LEAST, BRAVELY KEPT GROWING.
JUST FOR ME.
ポッ KONK!
ぶん FLIP
ぶん FLIP
ぶん FLIP
ゴォォォォォォ‥
WHOOSH
HEY... ARIKA.
MM...?

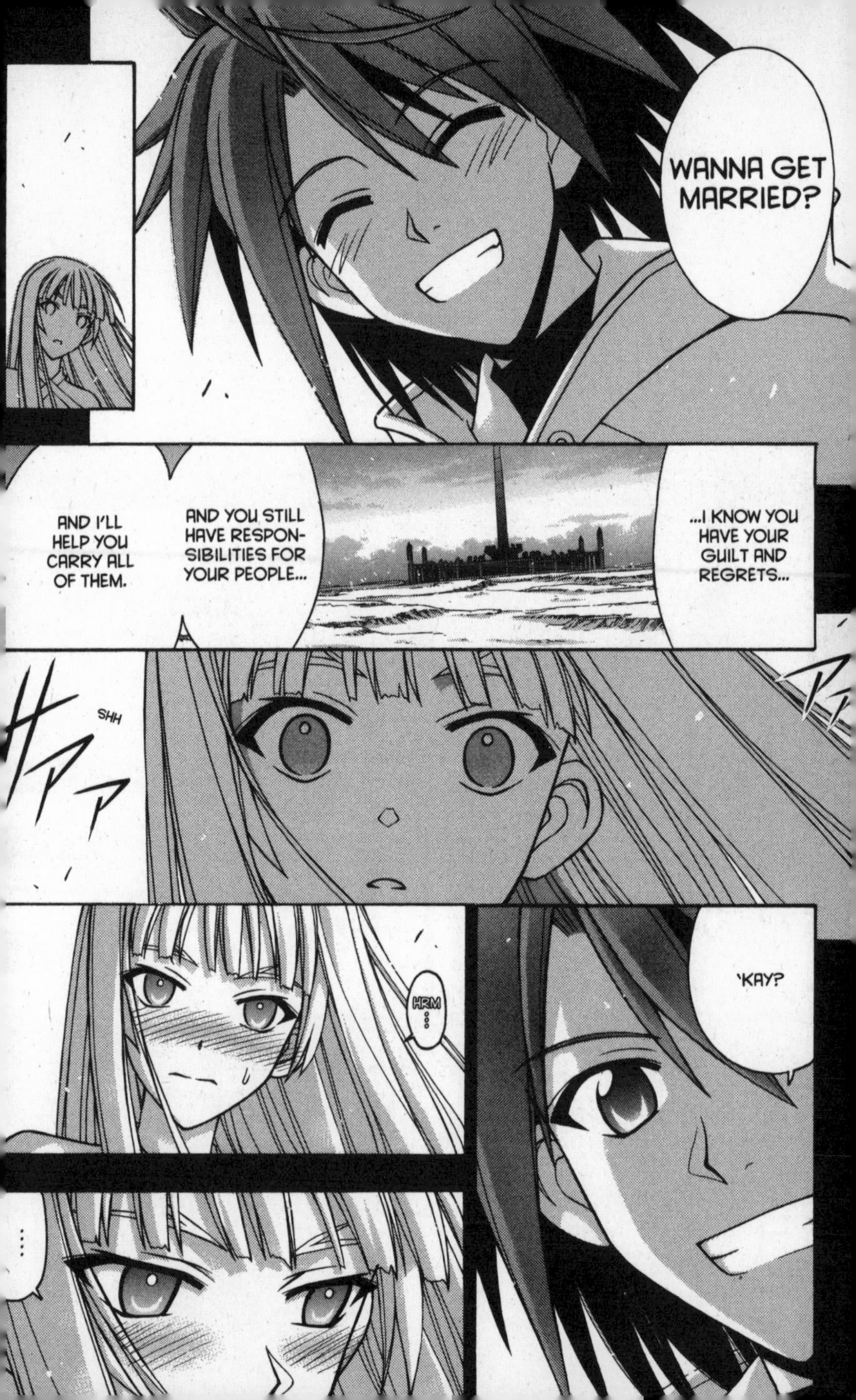
WANNA GET MARRIED?
...I KNOW YOU HAVE YOUR GUILT AND REGRETS...
AND YOU STILL HAVE RESPON-SIBILITIES FOR YOUR PEOPLE...
AND I'LL HELP YOU CARRY ALL OF THEM.
SHH
'KAY?
HRM...
....

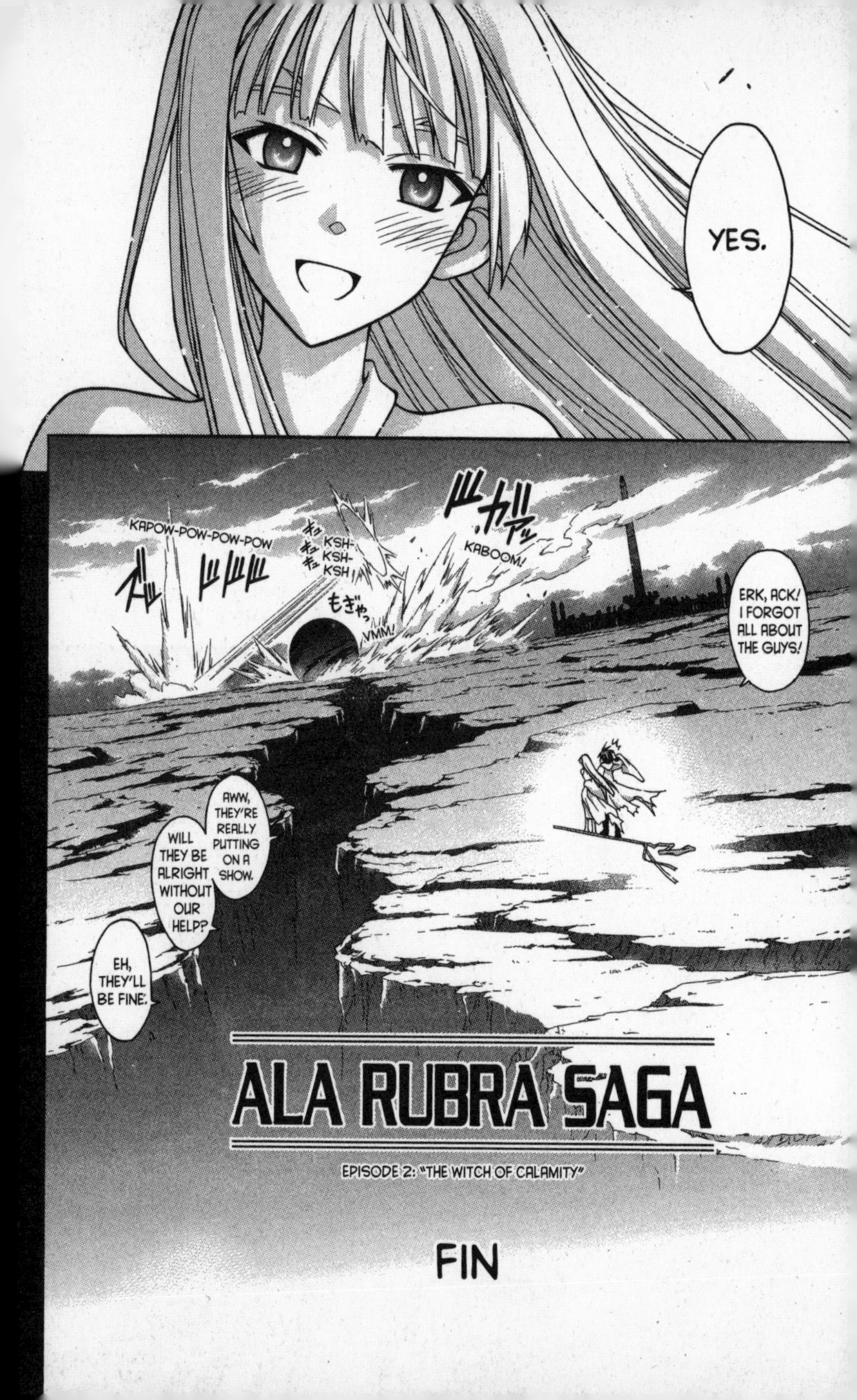
YES.
ERK, ACK! I FORGOT ALL ABOUT THE GUYS!
KABOOM!
KSH-KSH-KSH
KAPOW-POW-POW-POW
もぎゃっ
VMM!
AWW, THEY'RE REALLY PUTTING ON A SHOW.
WILL THEY BE ALRIGHT WITHOUT OUR HELP?
EH, THEY'LL BE FINE.
ALA RUBRA SAGA
EPISODE 2: "THE WITCH OF CALAMITY"
FIN

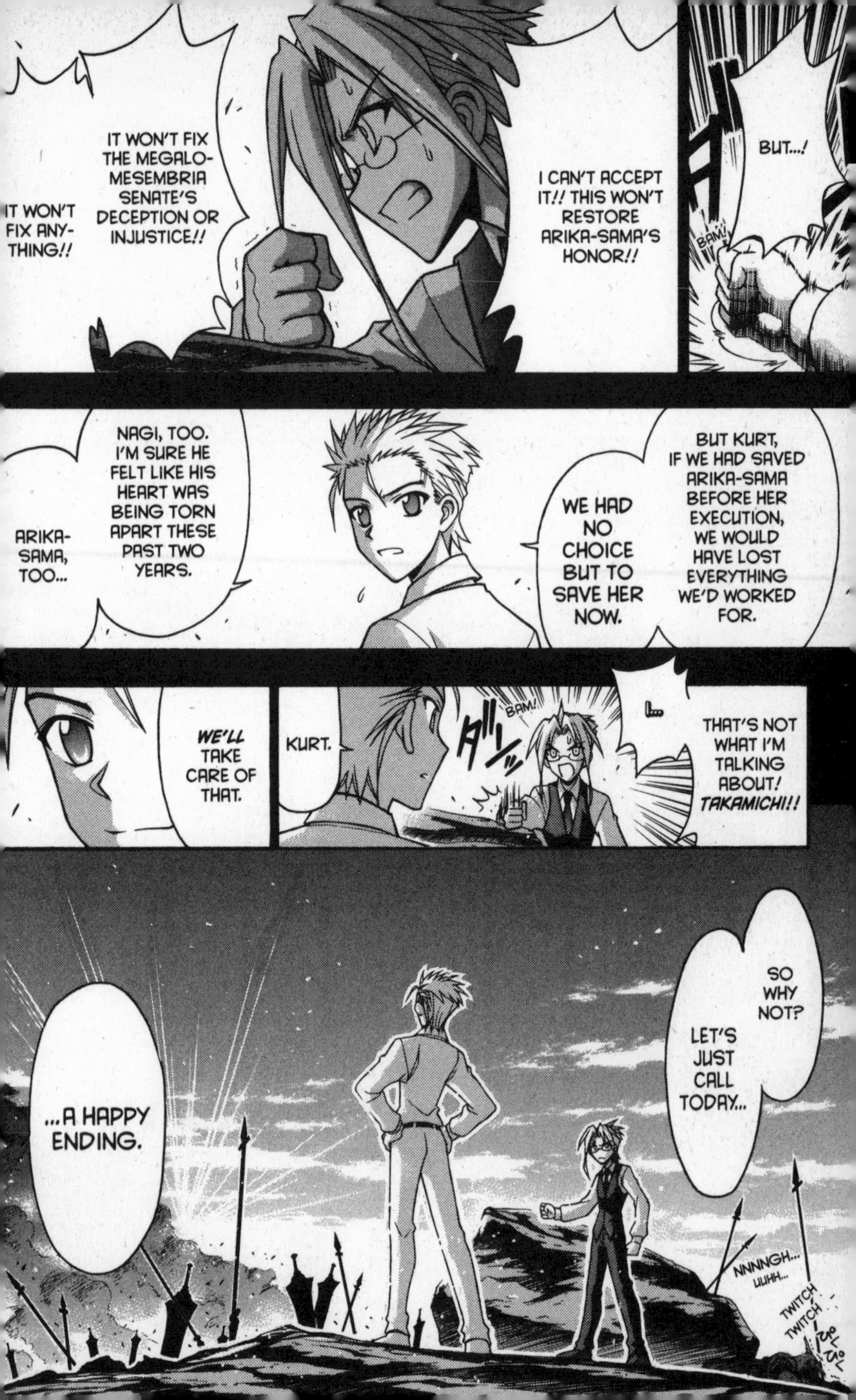

BUT...!
BAM!
I CAN'T ACCEPT IT!! THIS WON'T RESTORE ARIKA-SAMA'S HONOR!!
IT WON'T FIX THE MEGALO-MESEMBRIA SENATE'S DECEPTION OR INJUSTICE!!
IT WON'T FIX ANY-THING!!
BUT KURT, IF WE HAD SAVED ARIKA-SAMA BEFORE HER EXECUTION, WE WOULD HAVE LOST EVERYTHING WE'D WORKED FOR.
WE HAD NO CHOICE BUT TO SAVE HER NOW.
NAGI, TOO. I'M SURE HE FELT LIKE HIS HEART WAS BEING TORN APART THESE PAST TWO YEARS.
ARIKA-SAMA, TOO...
THAT'S NOT WHAT I'M TALKING ABOUT! *TAKAMICHI!!*
I...
BAM!
KURT.
WE'LL TAKE CARE OF THAT.
SO WHY NOT?
LET'S JUST CALL TODAY...
NNNNGH... UUHH...
TWITCH TWITCH
...A HAPPY ENDING.

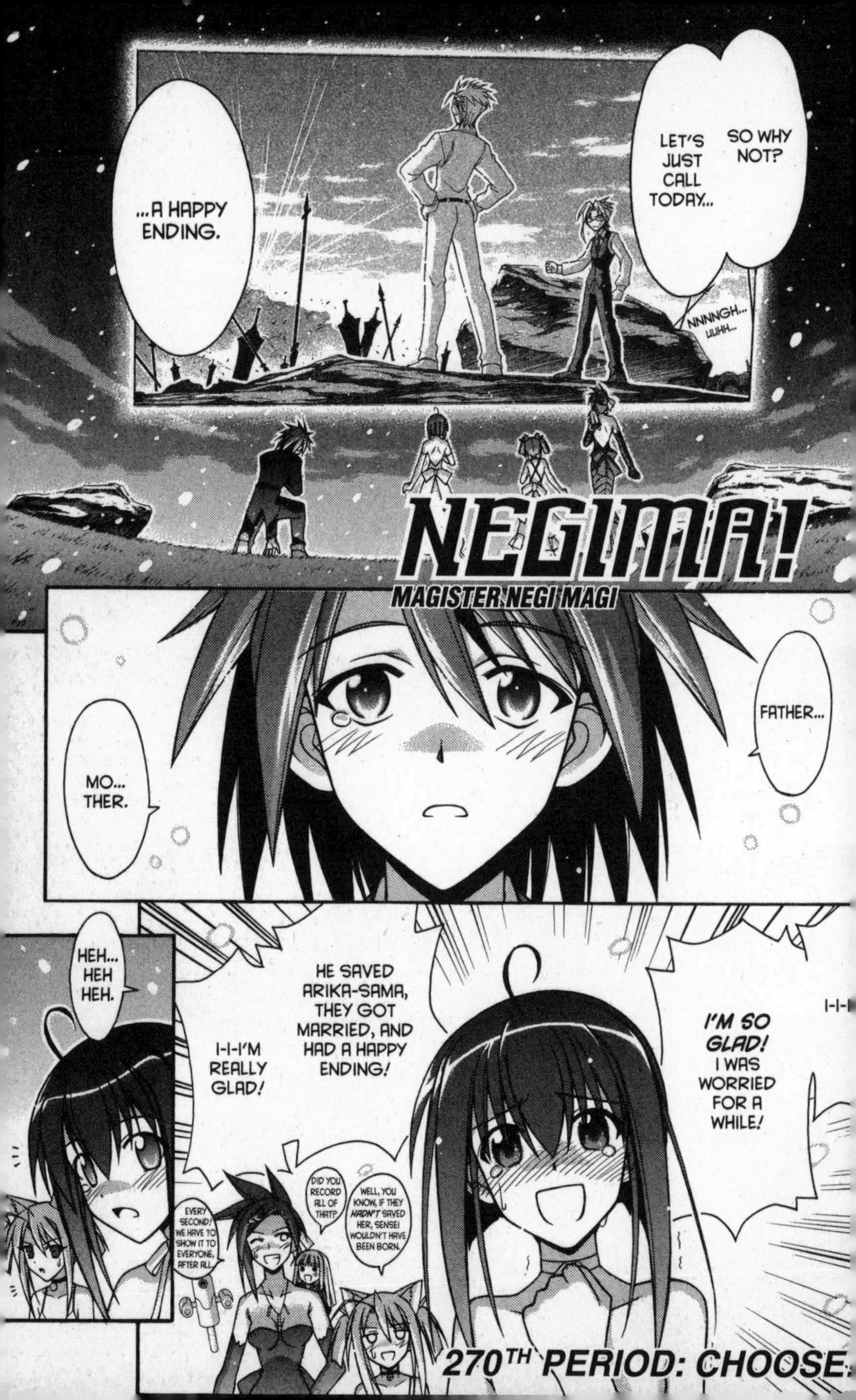
SO WHY NOT?
LET'S JUST CALL TODAY...
NNNNGH... UUHH...
...A HAPPY ENDING.
NEGIMA!
MAGISTER NEGI MAGI
FATHER...
MO... THER.
I-I-I
I'M SO GLAD! I WAS WORRIED FOR A WHILE!
HE SAVED ARIKA-SAMA, THEY GOT MARRIED, AND HAD A HAPPY ENDING!
I-I-I'M REALLY GLAD!
WELL, YOU KNOW, IF THEY HADN'T SAVED HER, SENSEI WOULDN'T HAVE BEEN BORN.
DID YOU RECORD ALL OF THAT?
EVERY SECOND! WE HAVE TO SHOW IT TO EVERYONE, AFTER ALL.
HEH... HEH HEH.
270TH PERIOD: CHOOSE.

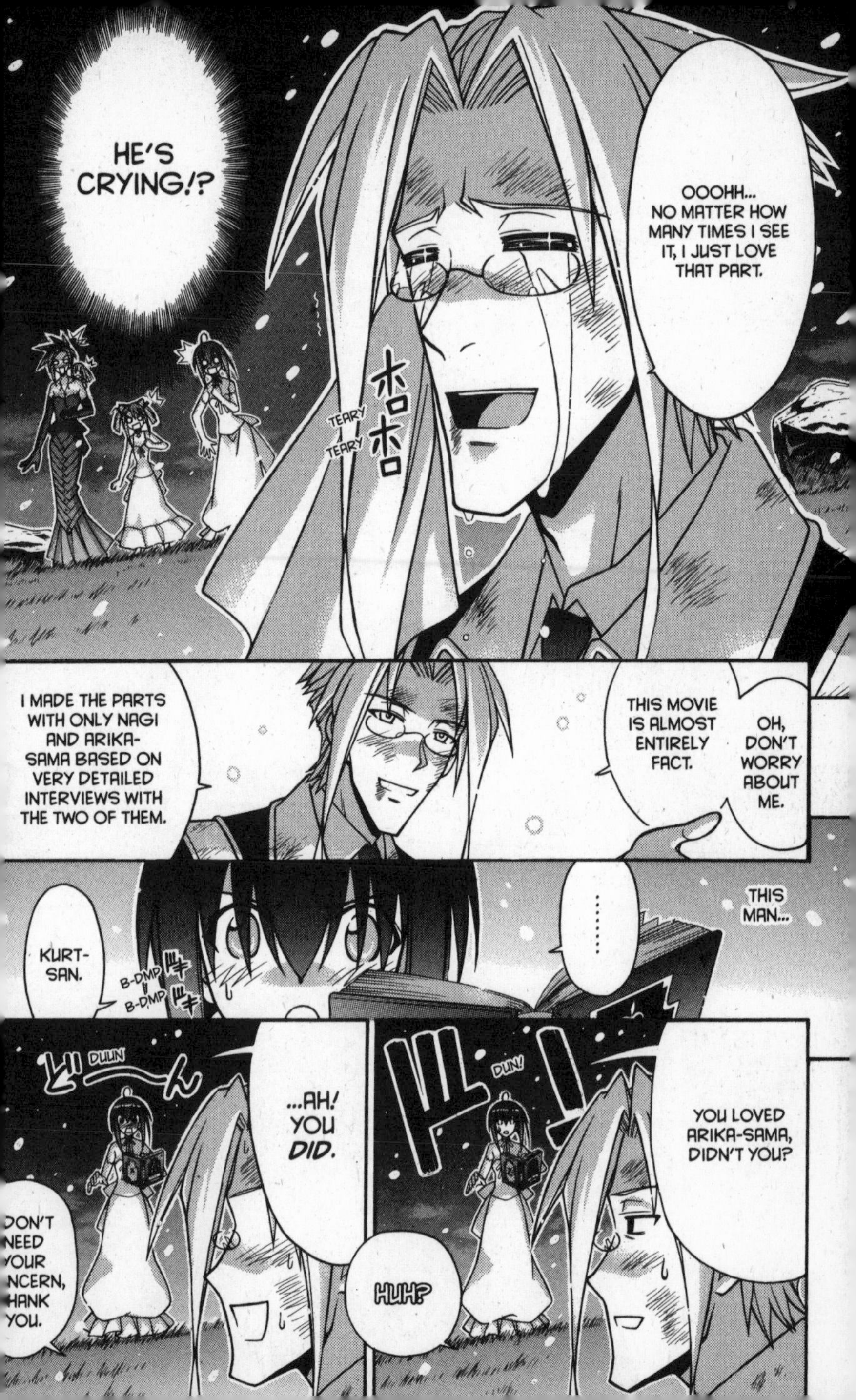
OOOHH... NO MATTER HOW MANY TIMES I SEE IT, I JUST LOVE THAT PART.
ホロホロ
TEARY TEARY
HE'S CRYING!?
OH, DON'T WORRY ABOUT ME.
THIS MOVIE IS ALMOST ENTIRELY FACT.
I MADE THE PARTS WITH ONLY NAGI AND ARIKA-SAMA BASED ON VERY DETAILED INTERVIEWS WITH THE TWO OF THEM.
THIS MAN...
......
ドキ ドキ
B-DMP B-DMP
KURT-SAN.
YOU LOVED ARIKA-SAMA, DIDN'T YOU?
ドン
DUN!
HUH?
...AH! YOU DID.
どーん
DUUN
DON'T NEED YOUR NCERN, HANK YOU.

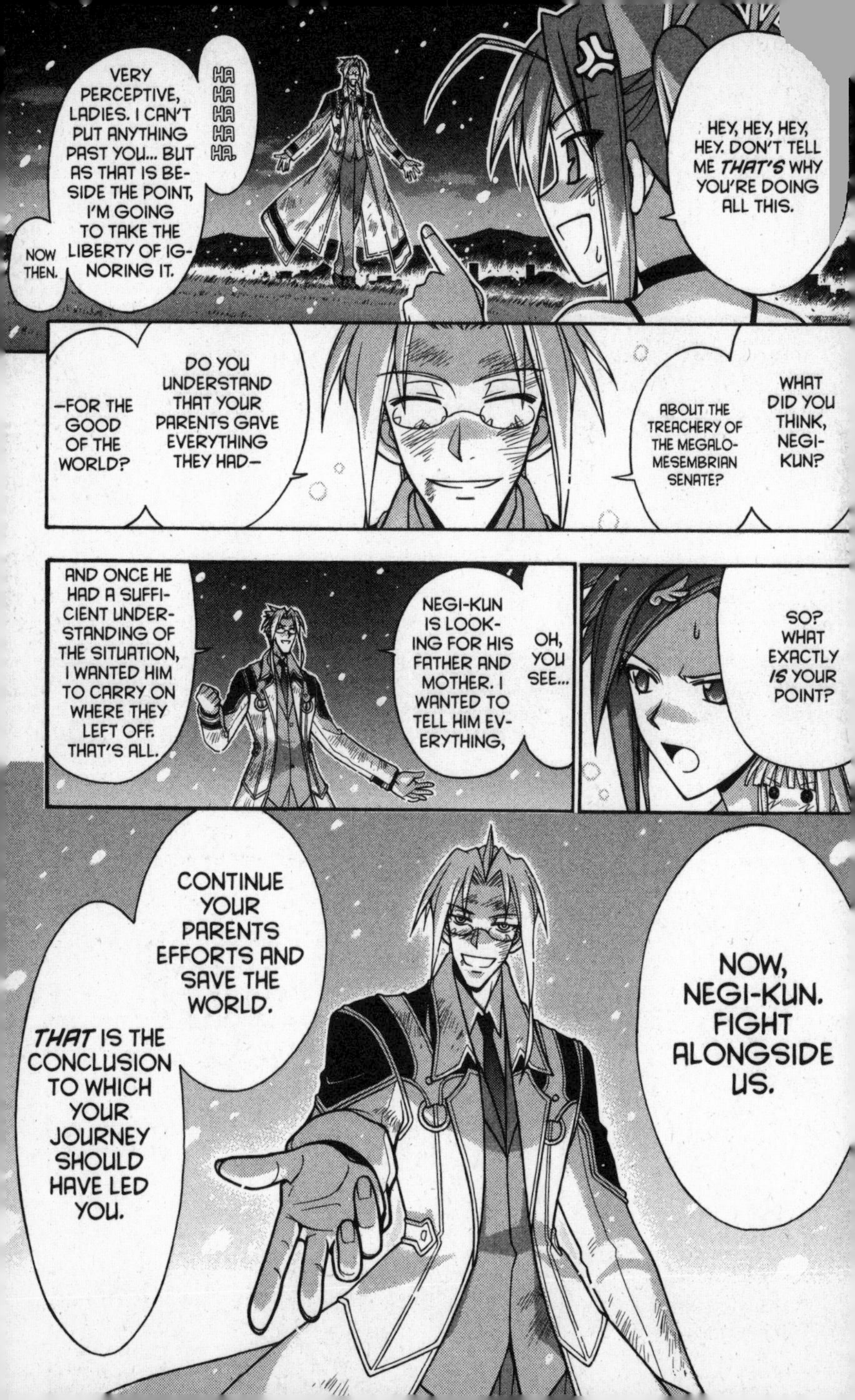
HEY, HEY, HEY, HEY. DON'T TELL ME *THAT'S* WHY YOU'RE DOING ALL THIS.
HA HA HA HA HA.
VERY PERCEPTIVE, LADIES. I CAN'T PUT ANYTHING PAST YOU... BUT AS THAT IS BESIDE THE POINT, I'M GOING TO TAKE THE LIBERTY OF IGNORING IT.
NOW THEN.
WHAT DID YOU THINK, NEGI-KUN?
ABOUT THE TREACHERY OF THE MEGALOMESEMBRIAN SENATE?
DO YOU UNDERSTAND THAT YOUR PARENTS GAVE EVERYTHING THEY HAD—
—FOR THE GOOD OF THE WORLD?
SO? WHAT EXACTLY *IS* YOUR POINT?
OH, YOU SEE...
NEGI-KUN IS LOOKING FOR HIS FATHER AND MOTHER. I WANTED TO TELL HIM EVERYTHING,
AND ONCE HE HAD A SUFFICIENT UNDERSTANDING OF THE SITUATION, I WANTED HIM TO CARRY ON WHERE THEY LEFT OFF. THAT'S ALL.
NOW, NEGI-KUN. FIGHT ALONGSIDE US.
CONTINUE YOUR PARENTS EFFORTS AND SAVE THE WORLD.
THAT IS THE CONCLUSION TO WHICH YOUR JOURNEY SHOULD HAVE LED YOU.

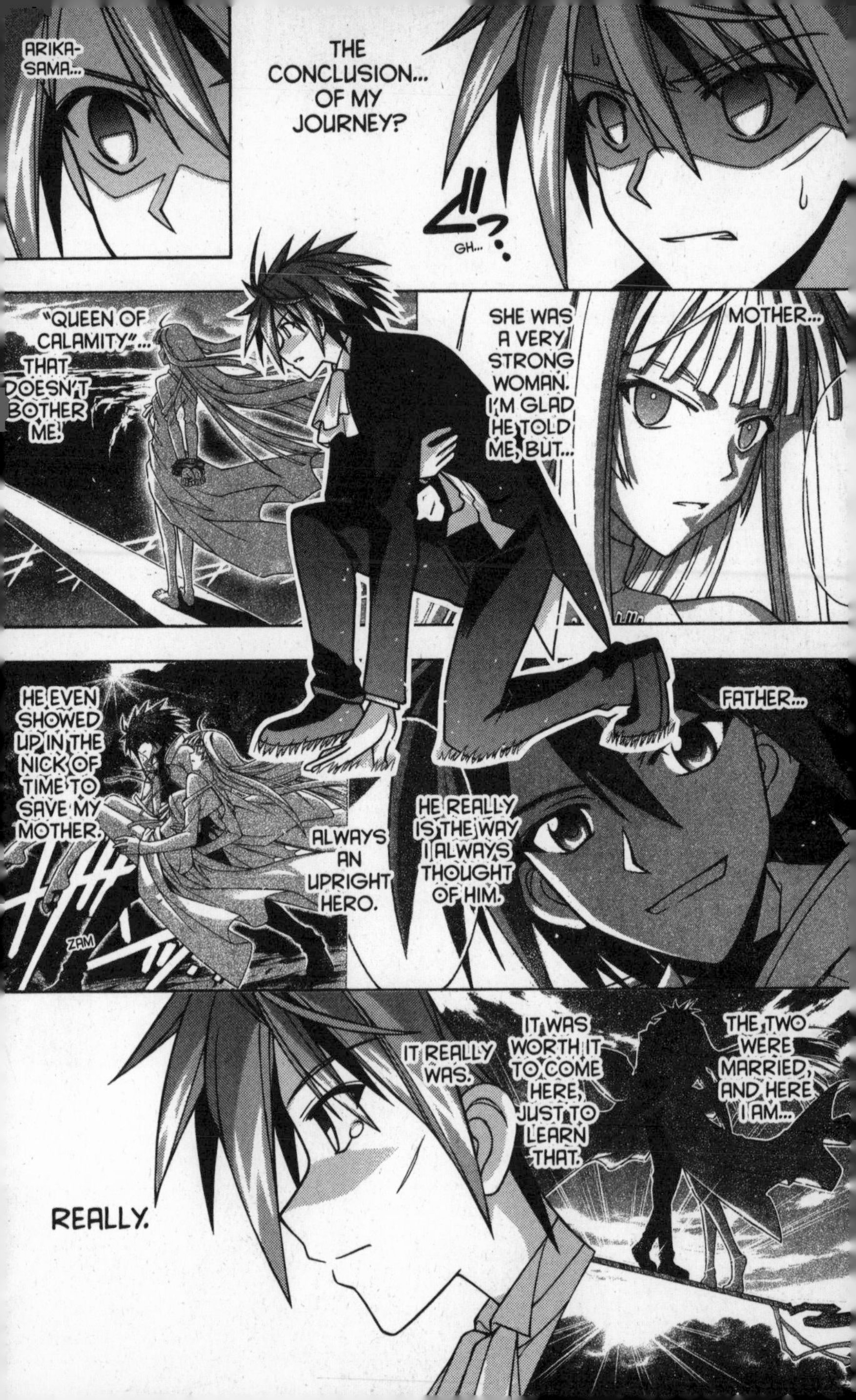
THE CONCLUSION... OF MY JOURNEY?
GH...
ARIKA-SAMA...
MOTHER...
SHE WAS A VERY STRONG WOMAN. I'M GLAD HE TOLD ME, BUT...
"QUEEN OF CALAMITY"... THAT DOESN'T BOTHER ME!
FATHER...
HE REALLY IS THE WAY I ALWAYS THOUGHT OF HIM.
ALWAYS AN UPRIGHT HERO.
HE EVEN SHOWED UP IN THE NICK OF TIME TO SAVE MY MOTHER.
ZAM
THE TWO WERE MARRIED, AND HERE I AM...
IT WAS WORTH IT TO COME HERE, JUST TO LEARN THAT.
IT REALLY WAS.
REALLY.

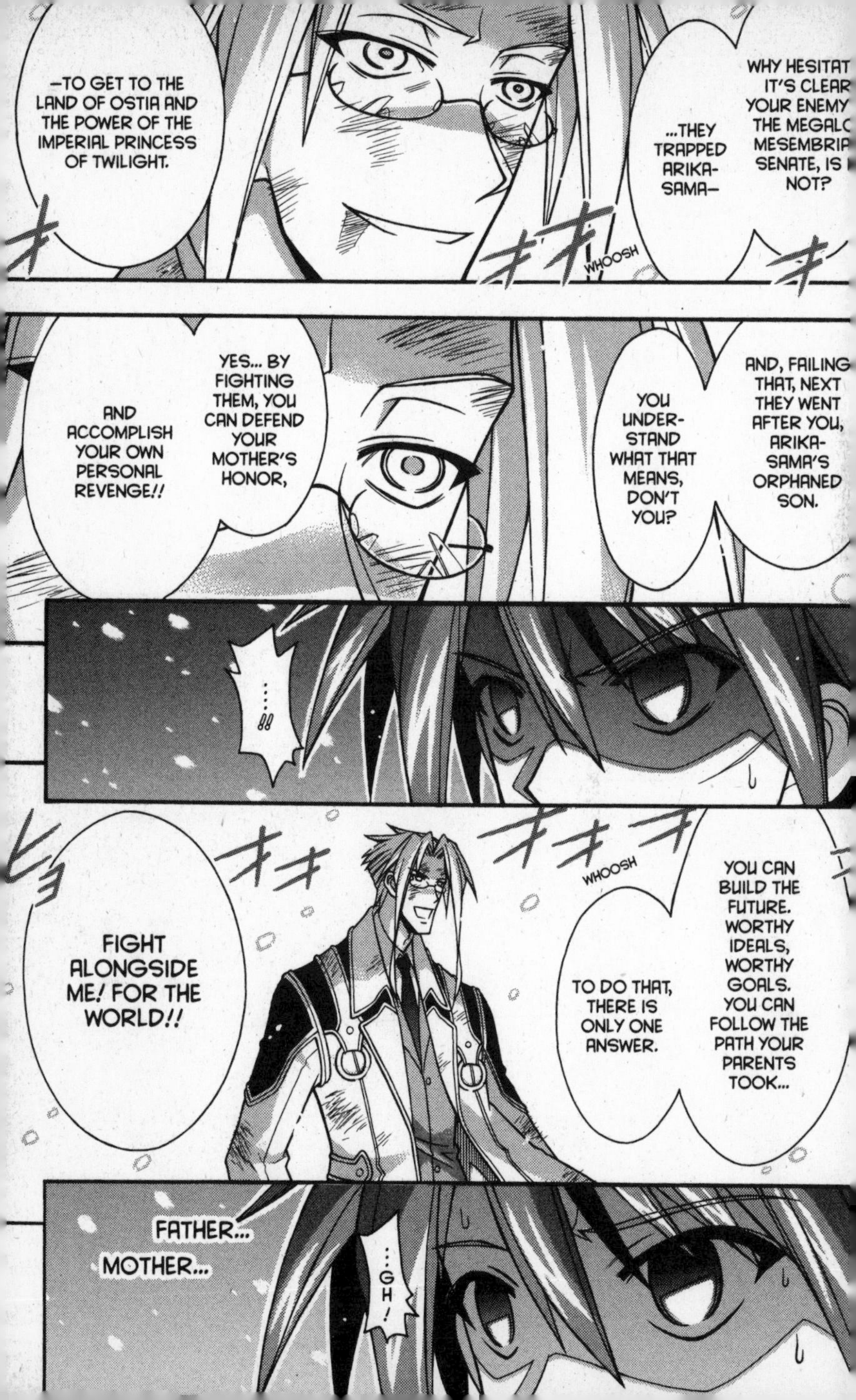
WHY HESITAT IT'S CLEAR YOUR ENEMY THE MEGALC MESEMBRIA SENATE, IS NOT?
WHOOSH
...THEY TRAPPED ARIKA-SAMA—
—TO GET TO THE LAND OF OSTIA AND THE POWER OF THE IMPERIAL PRINCESS OF TWILIGHT.
AND, FAILING THAT, NEXT THEY WENT AFTER YOU, ARIKA-SAMA'S ORPHANED SON.
YOU UNDER-STAND WHAT THAT MEANS, DON'T YOU?
YES... BY FIGHTING THEM, YOU CAN DEFEND YOUR MOTHER'S HONOR,
AND ACCOMPLISH YOUR OWN PERSONAL REVENGE!!
......!!
YOU CAN BUILD THE FUTURE. WORTHY IDEALS, WORTHY GOALS. YOU CAN FOLLOW THE PATH YOUR PARENTS TOOK...
TO DO THAT, THERE IS ONLY ONE ANSWER.
WHOOSH
FIGHT ALONGSIDE ME! FOR THE WORLD!!
...GH!
FATHER...
MOTHER...

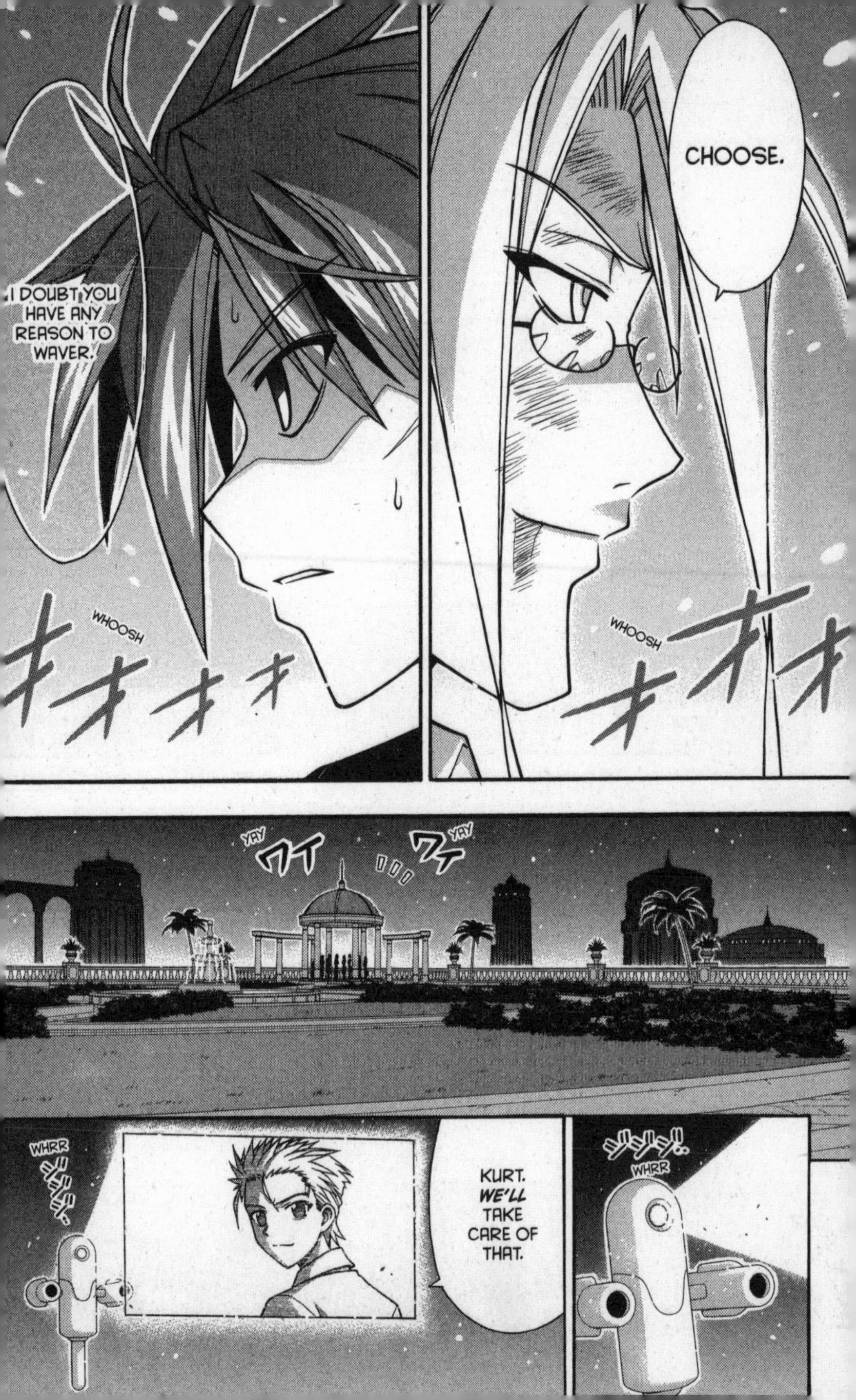
CHOOSE.
I DOUBT YOU HAVE ANY REASON TO WAVER.
WHOOSH
WHOOSH
YAY
YAY
WHRR
KURT. WE'LL TAKE CARE OF THAT.
WHRR

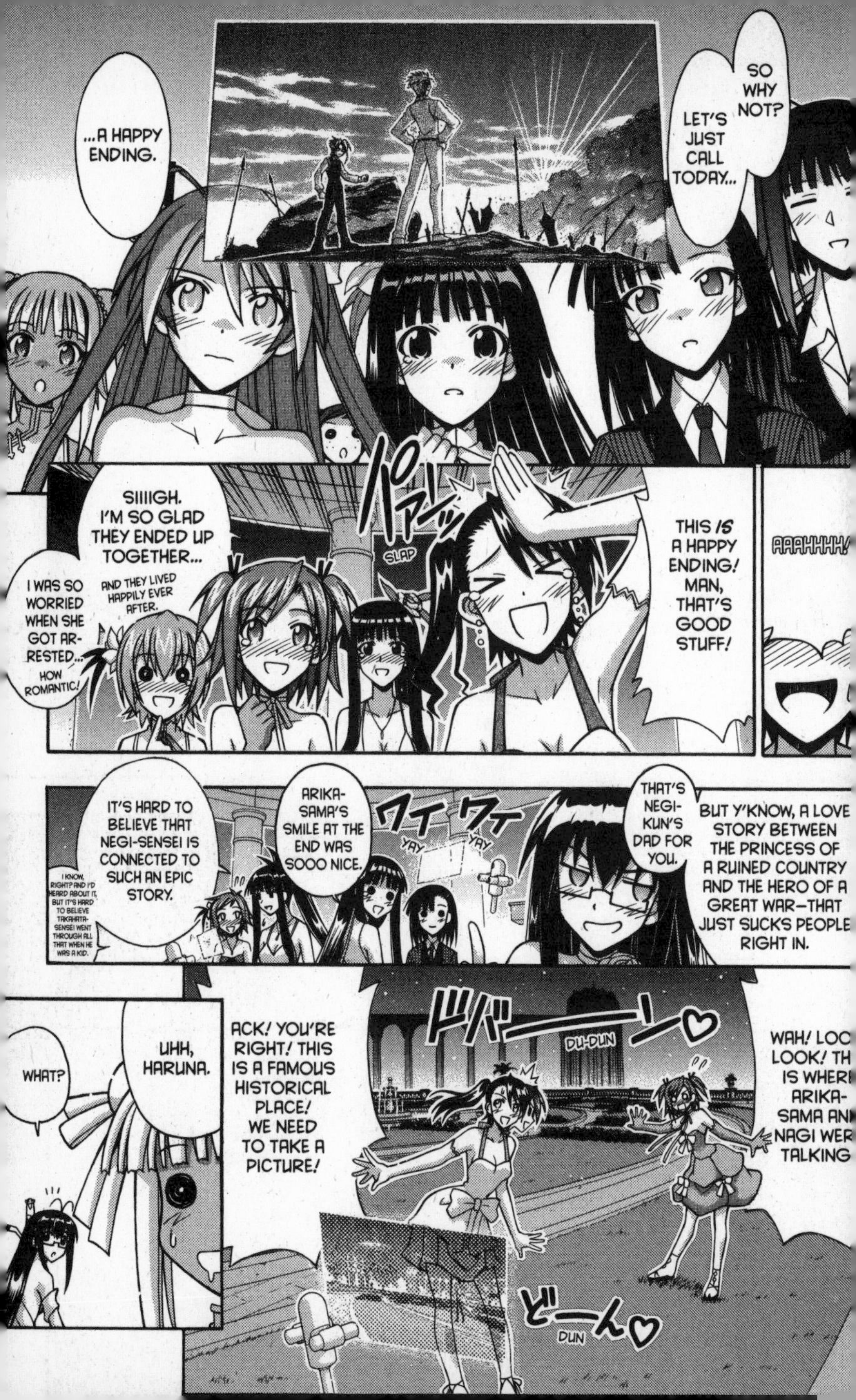

SO WHY NOT? LET'S JUST CALL TODAY...
...A HAPPY ENDING.
AAAHHHH!
THIS IS A HAPPY ENDING! MAN, THAT'S GOOD STUFF!
SLAP
SIIIGH. I'M SO GLAD THEY ENDED UP TOGETHER...
AND THEY LIVED HAPPILY EVER AFTER.
I WAS SO WORRIED WHEN SHE GOT AR-RESTED... HOW ROMANTIC!
BUT Y'KNOW, A LOVE STORY BETWEEN THE PRINCESS OF A RUINED COUNTRY AND THE HERO OF A GREAT WAR—THAT JUST SUCKS PEOPLE RIGHT IN.
THAT'S NEGI-KUN'S DAD FOR YOU.
YAY
YAY
ARIKA-SAMA'S SMILE AT THE END WAS SOOO NICE.
IT'S HARD TO BELIEVE THAT NEGI-SENSEI IS CONNECTED TO SUCH AN EPIC STORY.
I KNOW, RIGHT? AND I'D HEARD ABOUT IT, BUT IT'S HARD TO BELIEVE TAKAHATA-SENSEI WENT THROUGH ALL THAT WHEN HE WAS A KID.
WAH! LOO LOOK! TH IS WHER ARIKA-SAMA AN NAGI WER TALKING
DU-DUN
ACK! YOU'RE RIGHT! THIS IS A FAMOUS HISTORICAL PLACE! WE NEED TO TAKE A PICTURE!
DUN
UHH, HARUNA.
WHAT?

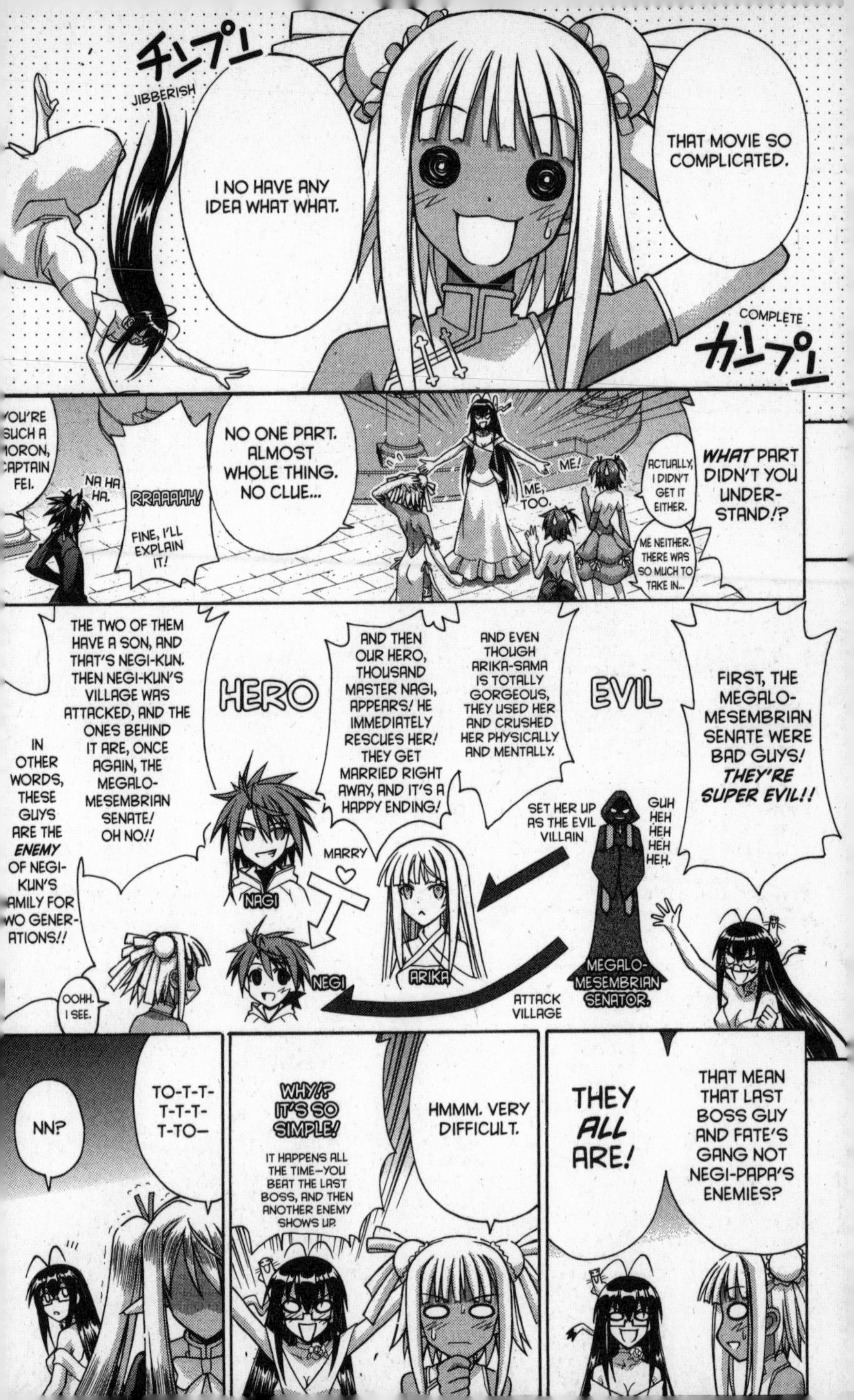
THAT MOVIE SO COMPLICATED.
I NO HAVE ANY IDEA WHAT WHAT.
チンプン
JIBBERISH
カンプン
COMPLETE
WHAT PART DIDN'T YOU UNDER-STAND!?
ACTUALLY, I DIDN'T GET IT EITHER.
ME NEITHER. THERE WAS SO MUCH TO TAKE IN...
ME!
ME, TOO.
NO ONE PART. ALMOST WHOLE THING. NO CLUE...
RRAAAAHH!
FINE, I'LL EXPLAIN IT!
NA HA HA.
OU'RE SUCH A ORON, APTAIN FEI.
FIRST, THE MEGALO-MESEMBRIAN SENATE WERE BAD GUYS! THEY'RE SUPER EVIL!!
EVIL
GUH HEH HEH HEH HEH.
SET HER UP AS THE EVIL VILLAIN
AND EVEN THOUGH ARIKA-SAMA IS TOTALLY GORGEOUS, THEY USED HER AND CRUSHED HER PHYSICALLY AND MENTALLY.
AND THEN OUR HERO, THOUSAND MASTER NAGI, APPEARS! HE IMMEDIATELY RESCUES HER! THEY GET MARRIED RIGHT AWAY, AND IT'S A HAPPY ENDING!
HERO
THE TWO OF THEM HAVE A SON, AND THAT'S NEGI-KUN. THEN NEGI-KUN'S VILLAGE WAS ATTACKED, AND THE ONES BEHIND IT ARE, ONCE AGAIN, THE MEGALO-MESEMBRIAN SENATE! OH NO!!
IN OTHER WORDS, THESE GUYS ARE THE ENEMY OF NEGI-KUN'S AMILY FOR WO GENER-ATIONS!!
MEGALO-MESEMBRIAN SENATOR
ARIKA
MARRY
NAGI
ATTACK VILLAGE
NEGI
OOHH. I SEE.
THAT MEAN THAT LAST BOSS GUY AND FATE'S GANG NOT NEGI-PAPA'S ENEMIES?
THEY ALL ARE!
HMMM. VERY DIFFICULT.
WHY!? IT'S SO SIMPLE!
IT HAPPENS ALL THE TIME—YOU BEAT THE LAST BOSS, AND THEN ANOTHER ENEMY SHOWS UP.
TO-T-T-T-T-T-T-T-TO—
NN?

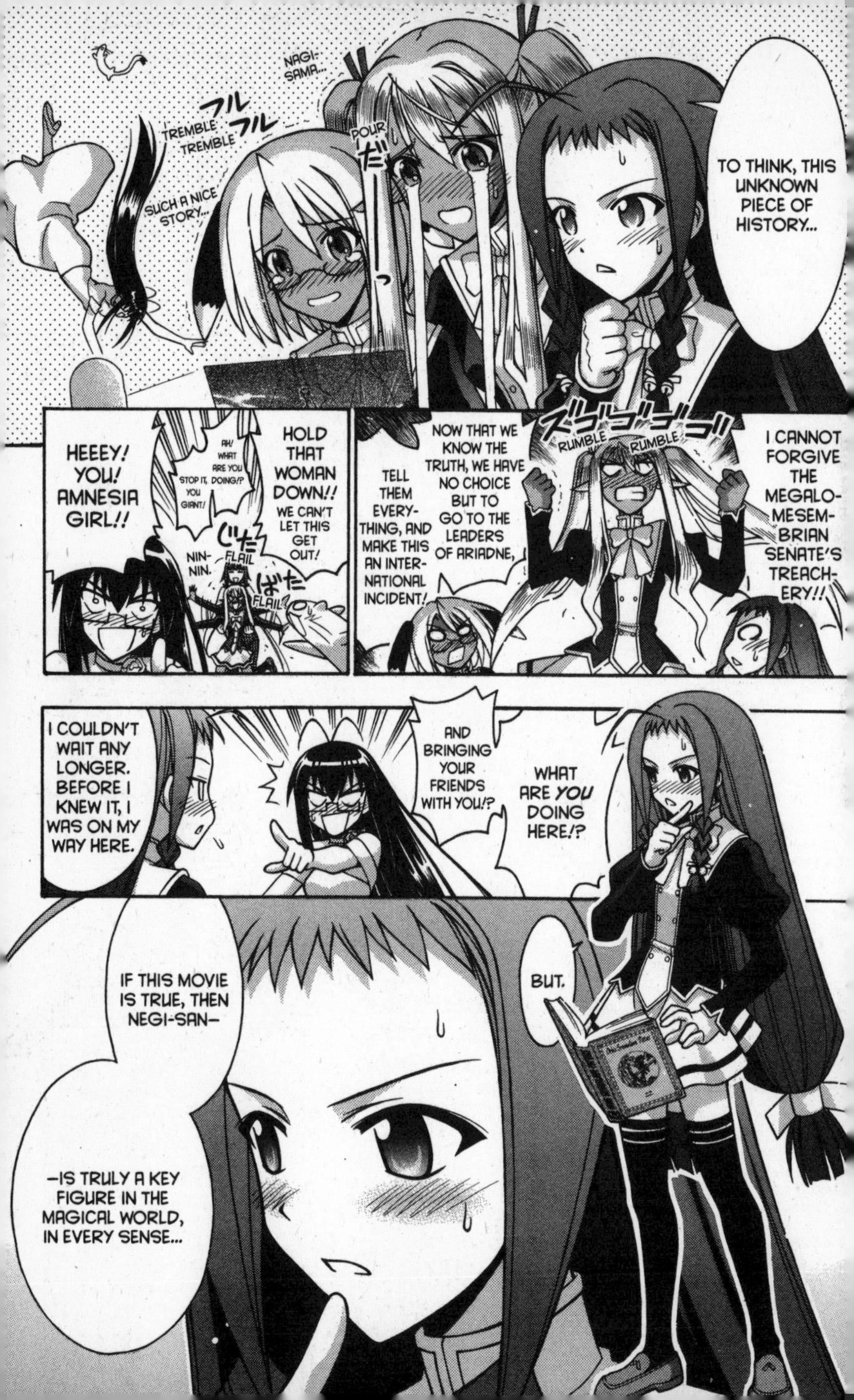
TO THINK, THIS UNKNOWN PIECE OF HISTORY...
NAGI-SAMA...
POUR だー
TREMBLE フル TREMBLE フル
SUCH A NICE STORY...
I CANNOT FORGIVE THE MEGALO-MESEMBRIAN SENATE'S TREACHERY!!
RUMBLE RUMBLE
NOW THAT WE KNOW THE TRUTH, WE HAVE NO CHOICE BUT TO GO TO THE LEADERS OF ARIADNE,
TELL THEM EVERYTHING, AND MAKE THIS AN INTERNATIONAL INCIDENT!
HOLD THAT WOMAN DOWN!! WE CAN'T LET THIS GET OUT!
AH! WHAT ARE YOU DOING!? STOP IT, YOU GIANT!
HEEEY! YOU! AMNESIA GIRL!!
FLAIL
NIN-NIN.
FLAIL
WHAT ARE YOU DOING HERE!?
AND BRINGING YOUR FRIENDS WITH YOU!?
I COULDN'T WAIT ANY LONGER. BEFORE I KNEW IT, I WAS ON MY WAY HERE.
BUT.
IF THIS MOVIE IS TRUE, THEN NEGI-SAN—
—IS TRULY A KEY FIGURE IN THE MAGICAL WORLD, IN EVERY SENSE...

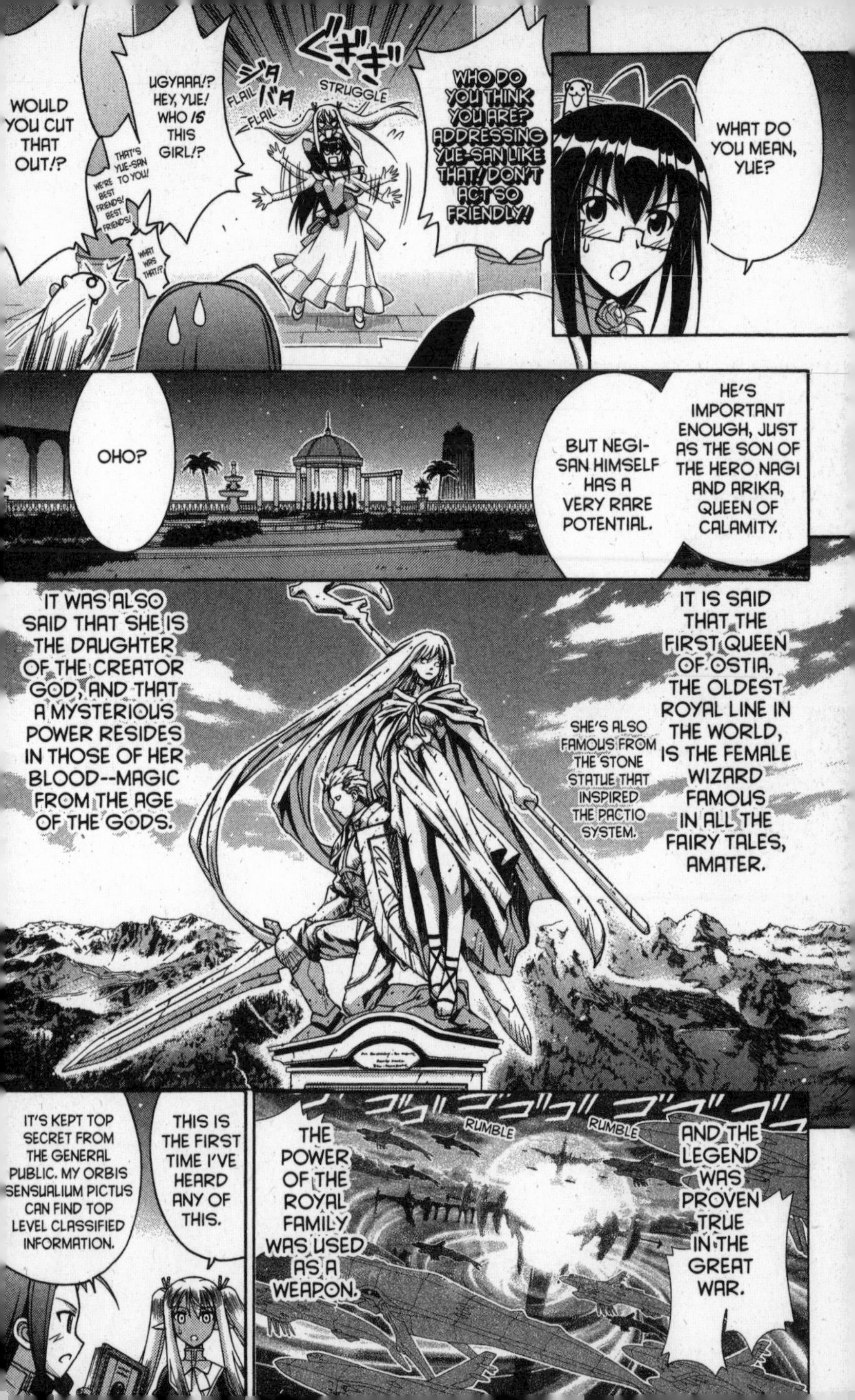
WHAT DO YOU MEAN, YUE?
WHO DO YOU THINK YOU ARE? ADDRESSING YUE-SAN LIKE THAT! DON'T ACT SO FRIENDLY!
ぐぎぎ
STRUGGLE
ジタ バタ
FLAIL FLAIL
UGYAAA!? HEY, YUE! WHO IS THIS GIRL!?
THAT'S YUE-SAN TO YOU!
WE'RE BEST FRIENDS! BEST FRIENDS!
WOULD YOU CUT THAT OUT!?
WHAT WAS THAT!?
HE'S IMPORTANT ENOUGH, JUST AS THE SON OF THE HERO NAGI AND ARIKA, QUEEN OF CALAMITY.
BUT NEGI-SAN HIMSELF HAS A VERY RARE POTENTIAL.
OHO?
IT IS SAID THAT THE FIRST QUEEN OF OSTIA, THE OLDEST ROYAL LINE IN THE WORLD, IS THE FEMALE WIZARD FAMOUS IN ALL THE FAIRY TALES, AMATER.
SHE'S ALSO FAMOUS FROM THE STONE STATUE THAT INSPIRED THE PACTIO SYSTEM.
IT WAS ALSO SAID THAT SHE IS THE DAUGHTER OF THE CREATOR GOD, AND THAT A MYSTERIOUS POWER RESIDES IN THOSE OF HER BLOOD--MAGIC FROM THE AGE OF THE GODS.
ゴゴゴゴゴゴ
RUMBLE
RUMBLE
AND THE LEGEND WAS PROVEN TRUE IN THE GREAT WAR.
THE POWER OF THE ROYAL FAMILY WAS USED AS A WEAPON.
THIS IS THE FIRST TIME I'VE HEARD ANY OF THIS.
IT'S KEPT TOP SECRET FROM THE GENERAL PUBLIC. MY ORBIS SENSUALIUM PICTUS CAN FIND TOP LEVEL CLASSIFIED INFORMATION.

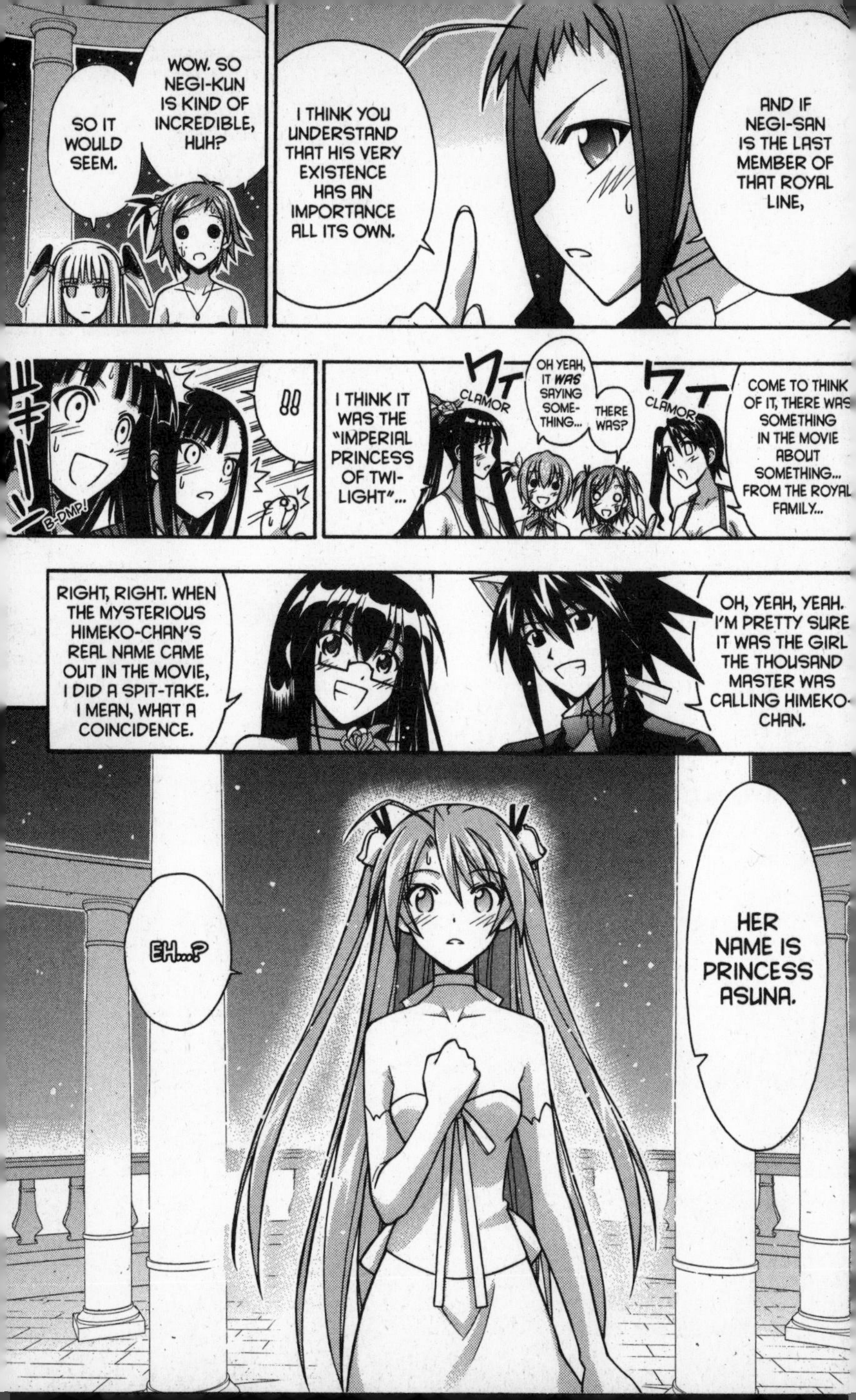
AND IF NEGI-SAN IS THE LAST MEMBER OF THAT ROYAL LINE,
I THINK YOU UNDERSTAND THAT HIS VERY EXISTENCE HAS AN IMPORTANCE ALL ITS OWN.
WOW. SO NEGI-KUN IS KIND OF INCREDIBLE, HUH?
SO IT WOULD SEEM.
COME TO THINK OF IT, THERE WAS SOMETHING IN THE MOVIE ABOUT SOMETHING... FROM THE ROYAL FAMILY...
CLAMOR
THERE WAS?
OH YEAH, IT *WAS* SAYING SOME-THING...
CLAMOR
I THINK IT WAS THE "IMPERIAL PRINCESS OF TWI-LIGHT"...
!!
B-DMP!
OH, YEAH, YEAH. I'M PRETTY SURE IT WAS THE GIRL THE THOUSAND MASTER WAS CALLING HIMEKO-CHAN.
RIGHT, RIGHT. WHEN THE MYSTERIOUS HIMEKO-CHAN'S REAL NAME CAME OUT IN THE MOVIE, I DID A SPIT-TAKE. I MEAN, WHAT A COINCIDENCE.
HER NAME IS PRINCESS ASUNA.
EH...?

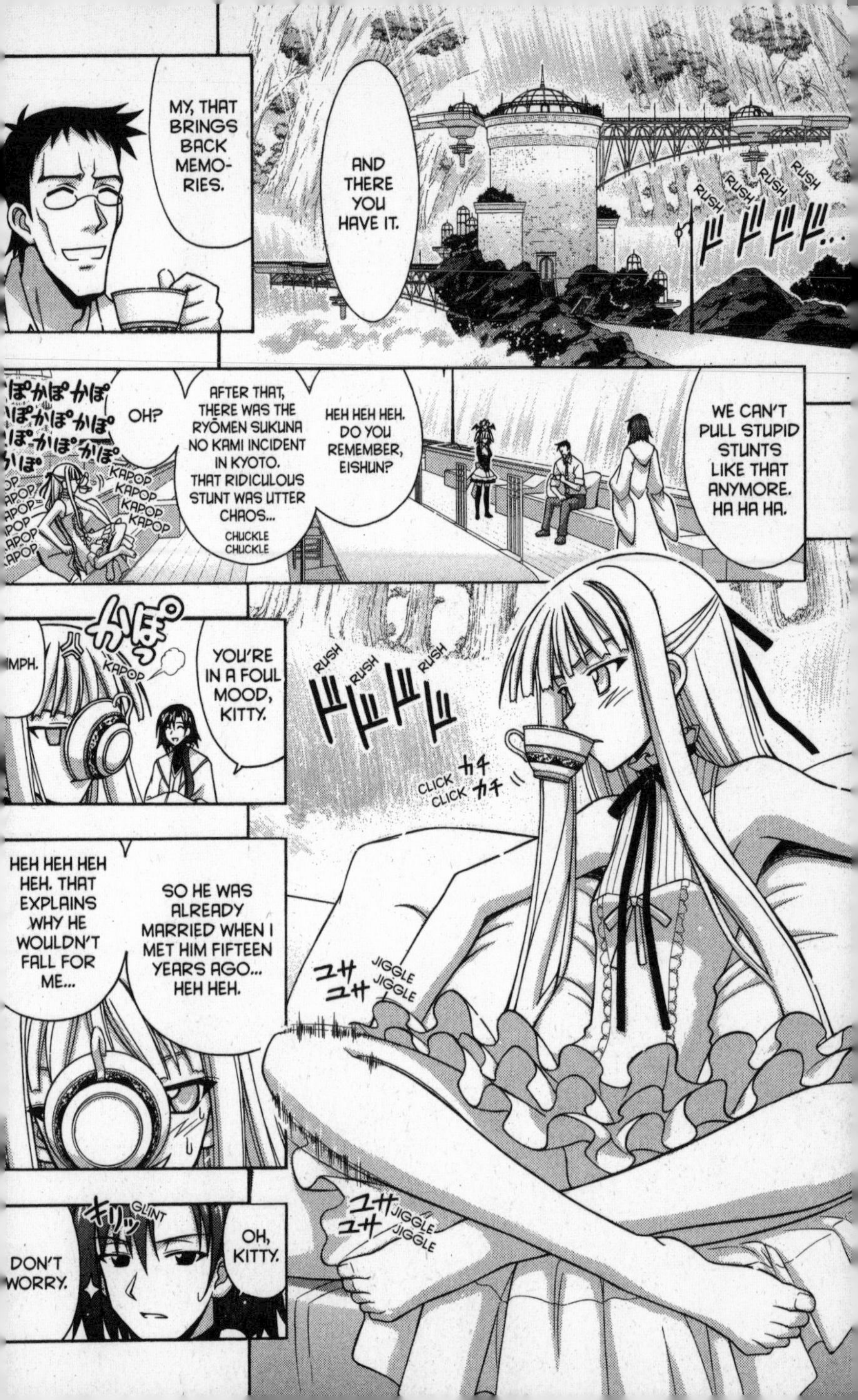
AND THERE YOU HAVE IT.
RUSH RUSH RUSH RUSH
ドドドド…
MY, THAT BRINGS BACK MEMORIES.
WE CAN'T PULL STUPID STUNTS LIKE THAT ANYMORE. HA HA HA.
HEH HEH HEH. DO YOU REMEMBER, EISHUN?
AFTER THAT, THERE WAS THE RYŌMEN SUKUNA NO KAMI INCIDENT IN KYOTO. THAT RIDICULOUS STUNT WAS UTTER CHAOS...
CHUCKLE CHUCKLE
OH?
かぽかぽかぽ かぽかぽかぽ かぽかぽかぽ
KAPOP KAPOP KAPOP KAPOP
RUSH RUSH RUSH
ドドドド
CLICK カチ CLICK カチ
JIGGLE ユサ JIGGLE ユサ
YOU'RE IN A FOUL MOOD, KITTY.
かぽっ
KAPOP
MPH.
SO HE WAS ALREADY MARRIED WHEN I MET HIM FIFTEEN YEARS AGO... HEH HEH.
HEH HEH HEH HEH. THAT EXPLAINS WHY HE WOULDN'T FALL FOR ME...
JIGGLE ユサ JIGGLE ユサ
OH, KITTY.
キリッ
GLINT
DON'T WORRY.

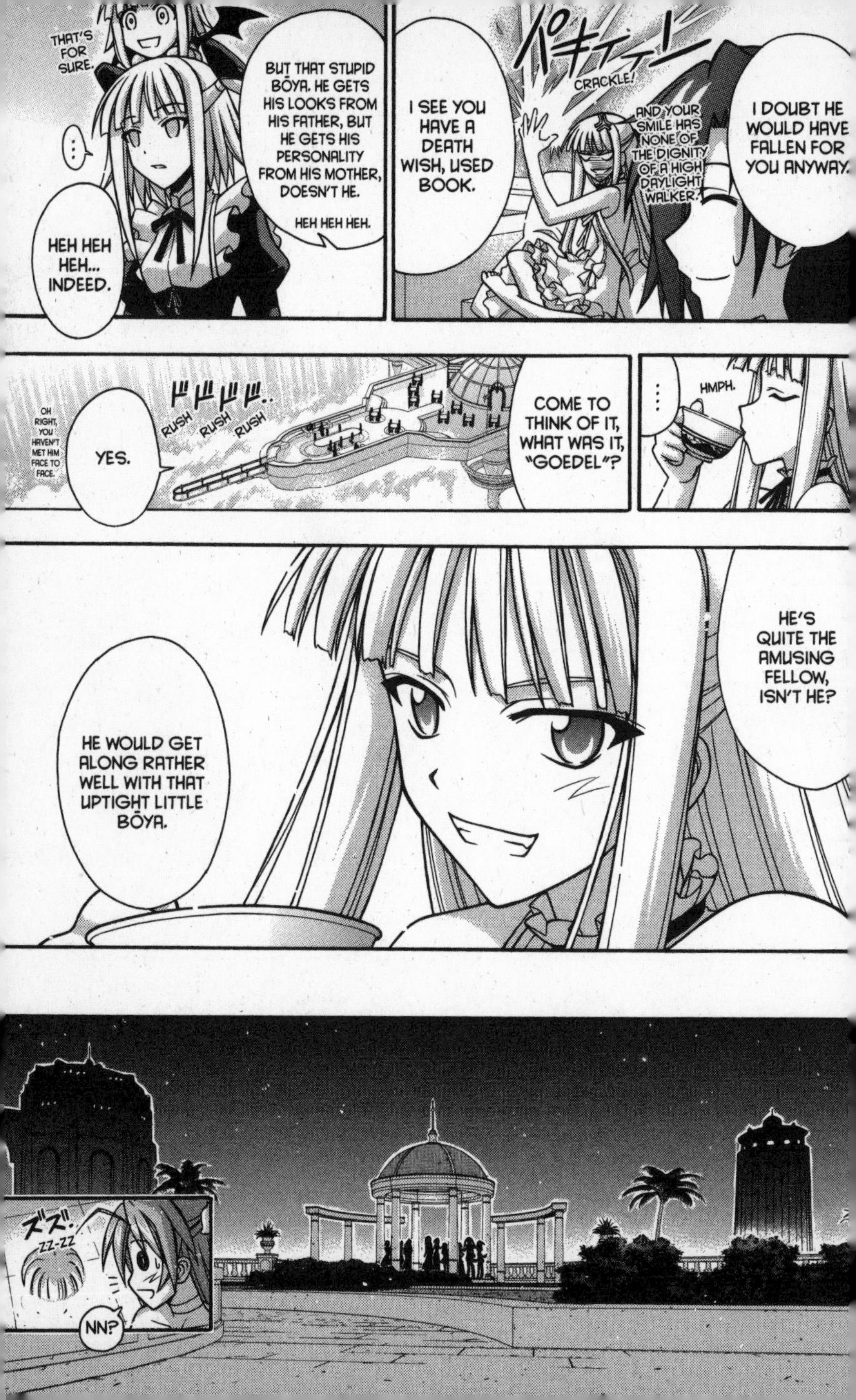
I DOUBT HE WOULD HAVE FALLEN FOR YOU ANYWAY.
AND YOUR SMILE HAS NONE OF THE DIGNITY OF A HIGH DAYLIGHT WALKER.
CRACKLE!
I SEE YOU HAVE A DEATH WISH, USED BOOK.
BUT THAT STUPID BŌYA. HE GETS HIS LOOKS FROM HIS FATHER, BUT HE GETS HIS PERSONALITY FROM HIS MOTHER, DOESN'T HE.
HEH HEH HEH.
THAT'S FOR SURE.
...
HEH HEH HEH... INDEED.
HMPH.
...
COME TO THINK OF IT, WHAT WAS IT, "GOEDEL"?
RUSH RUSH RUSH
YES.
OH RIGHT, YOU HAVEN'T MET HIM FACE TO FACE.
HE'S QUITE THE AMUSING FELLOW, ISN'T HE?
HE WOULD GET ALONG RATHER WELL WITH THAT UPTIGHT LITTLE BŌYA.
ZZ-ZZ
NN?

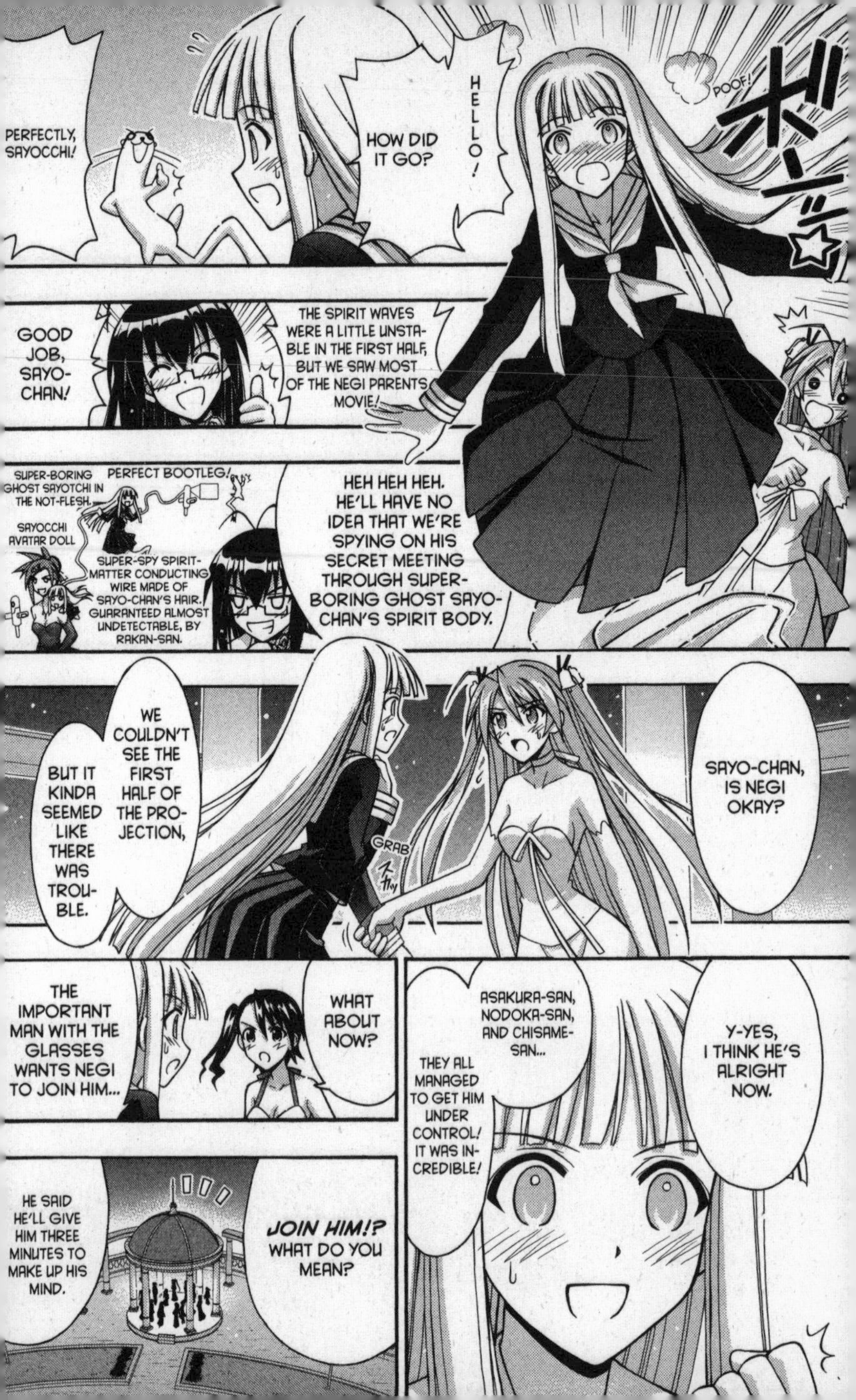

POOF!
HELLO!
HOW DID IT GO?
PERFECTLY, SAYOCCHI!
THE SPIRIT WAVES WERE A LITTLE UNSTABLE IN THE FIRST HALF, BUT WE SAW MOST OF THE NEGI PARENTS MOVIE!
GOOD JOB, SAYO-CHAN!
HEH HEH HEH. HE'LL HAVE NO IDEA THAT WE'RE SPYING ON HIS SECRET MEETING THROUGH SUPER-BORING GHOST SAYO-CHAN'S SPIRIT BODY.
PERFECT BOOTLEG!
SUPER-BORING GHOST SAYOTCHI IN THE NOT-FLESH.
SAYOCCHI AVATAR DOLL
SUPER-SPY SPIRIT-MATTER CONDUCTING WIRE MADE OF SAYO-CHAN'S HAIR. GUARANTEED ALMOST UNDETECTABLE, BY RAKAN-SAN.
SAYO-CHAN, IS NEGI OKAY?
WE COULDN'T SEE THE FIRST HALF OF THE PROJECTION,
BUT IT KINDA SEEMED LIKE THERE WAS TROUBLE.
GRAB
Y-YES, I THINK HE'S ALRIGHT NOW.
ASAKURA-SAN, NODOKA-SAN, AND CHISAME-SAN...
THEY ALL MANAGED TO GET HIM UNDER CONTROL! IT WAS INCREDIBLE!
WHAT ABOUT NOW?
THE IMPORTANT MAN WITH THE GLASSES WANTS NEGI TO JOIN HIM...
JOIN HIM!? WHAT DO YOU MEAN?
HE SAID HE'LL GIVE HIM THREE MINUTES TO MAKE UP HIS MIND.

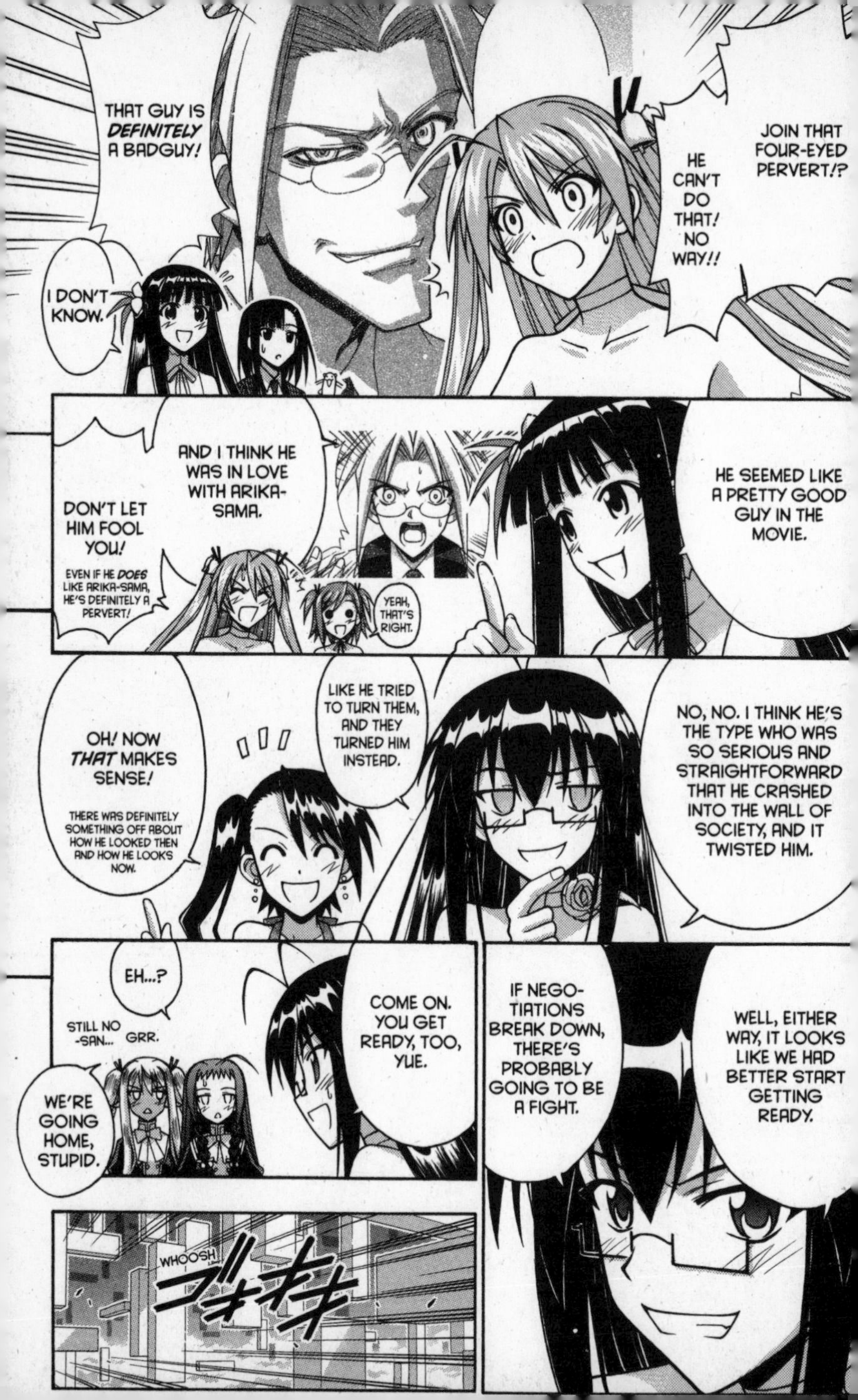
JOIN THAT FOUR-EYED PERVERT!?
HE CAN'T DO THAT! NO WAY!!
THAT GUY IS *DEFINITELY* A BADGUY!
I DON'T KNOW.
HE SEEMED LIKE A PRETTY GOOD GUY IN THE MOVIE.
AND I THINK HE WAS IN LOVE WITH ARIKA-SAMA.
DON'T LET HIM FOOL YOU!
EVEN IF HE *DOES* LIKE ARIKA-SAMA, HE'S DEFINITELY A PERVERT!
YEAH, THAT'S RIGHT.
NO, NO. I THINK HE'S THE TYPE WHO WAS SO SERIOUS AND STRAIGHTFORWARD THAT HE CRASHED INTO THE WALL OF SOCIETY, AND IT TWISTED HIM.
LIKE HE TRIED TO TURN THEM, AND THEY TURNED HIM INSTEAD.
OH! NOW *THAT* MAKES SENSE!
THERE WAS DEFINITELY SOMETHING OFF ABOUT HOW HE LOOKED THEN AND HOW HE LOOKS NOW.
WELL, EITHER WAY, IT LOOKS LIKE WE HAD BETTER START GETTING READY.
IF NEGO-TIATIONS BREAK DOWN, THERE'S PROBABLY GOING TO BE A FIGHT.
COME ON. YOU GET READY, TOO, YUE.
EH...?
STILL NO -SAN... GRR.
WE'RE GOING HOME, STUPID.
WHOOSH

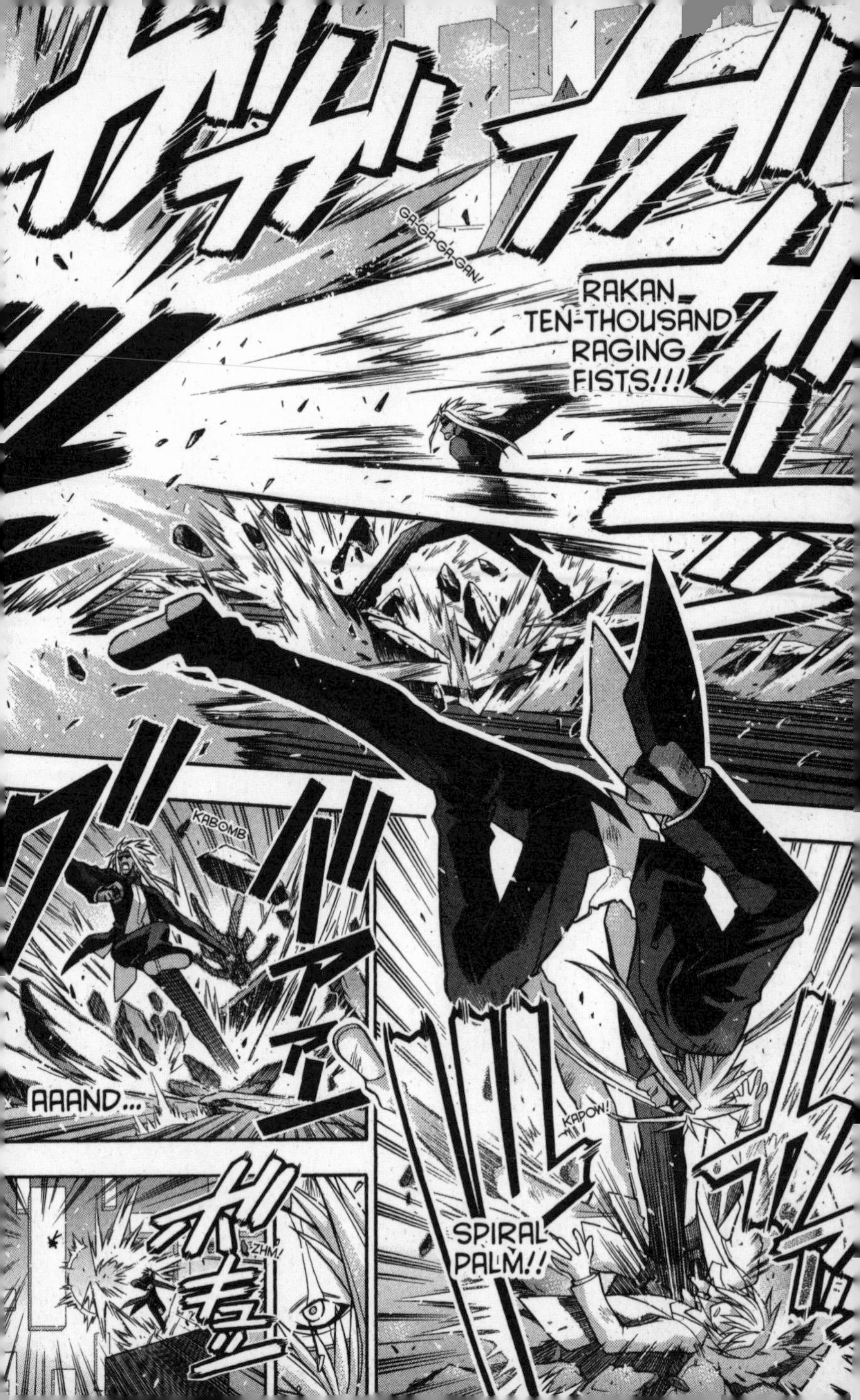
RAKAN TEN-THOUSAND RAGING FISTS!!!
GA-GA-GA-GAN!
KAPOW!
KABOMB
AAAND...
SPIRAL PALM!!
ZHM!

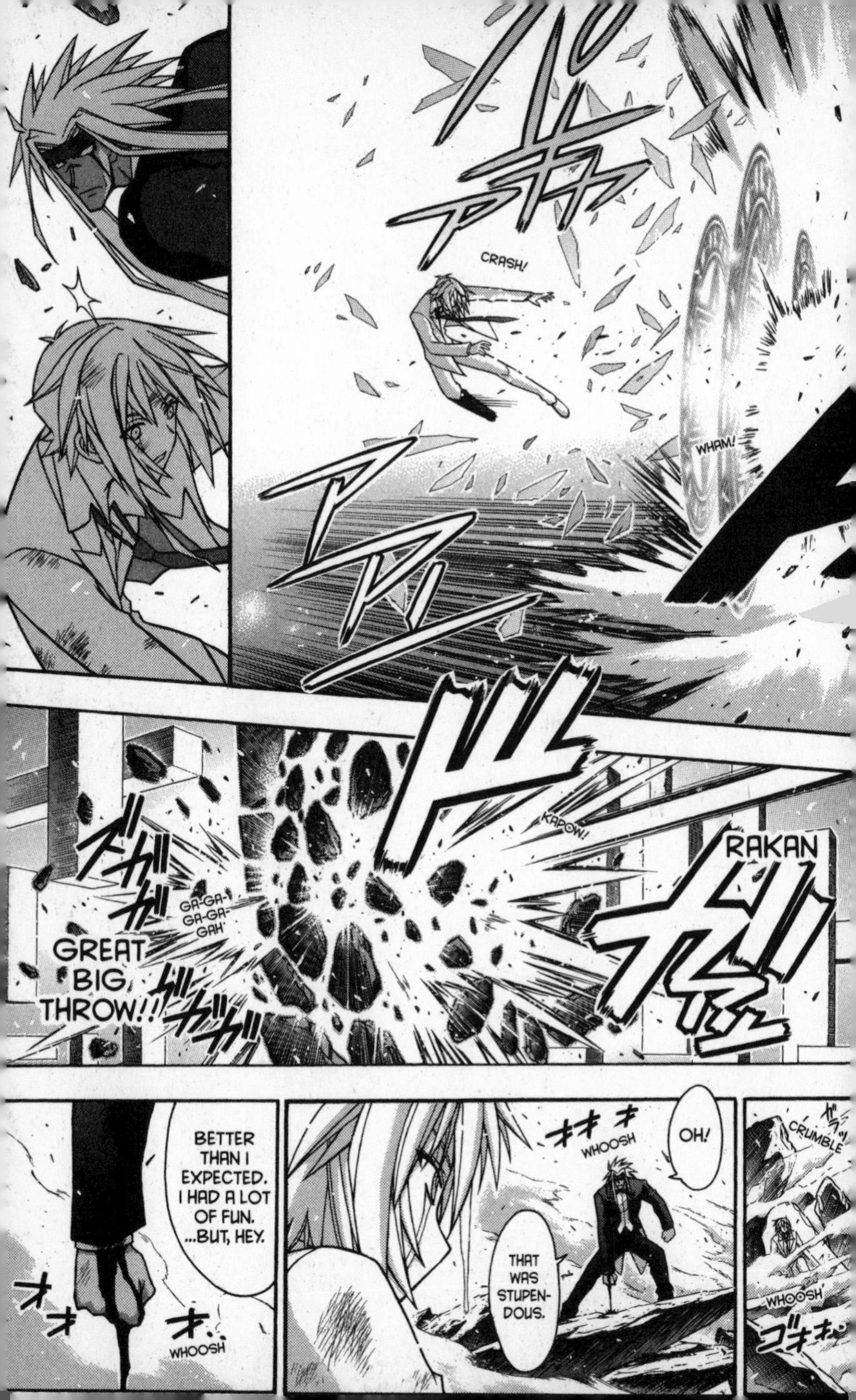
CRASH!
WHAM!
RAKAN
KAPOW!
GA-GA-GA-GA-GAH
GREAT BIG THROW!!
CRUMBLE
WHOOSH
OH!
WHOOSH
THAT WAS STUPENDOUS.
BETTER THAN I EXPECTED. I HAD A LOT OF FUN. ...BUT, HEY.
WHOOSH

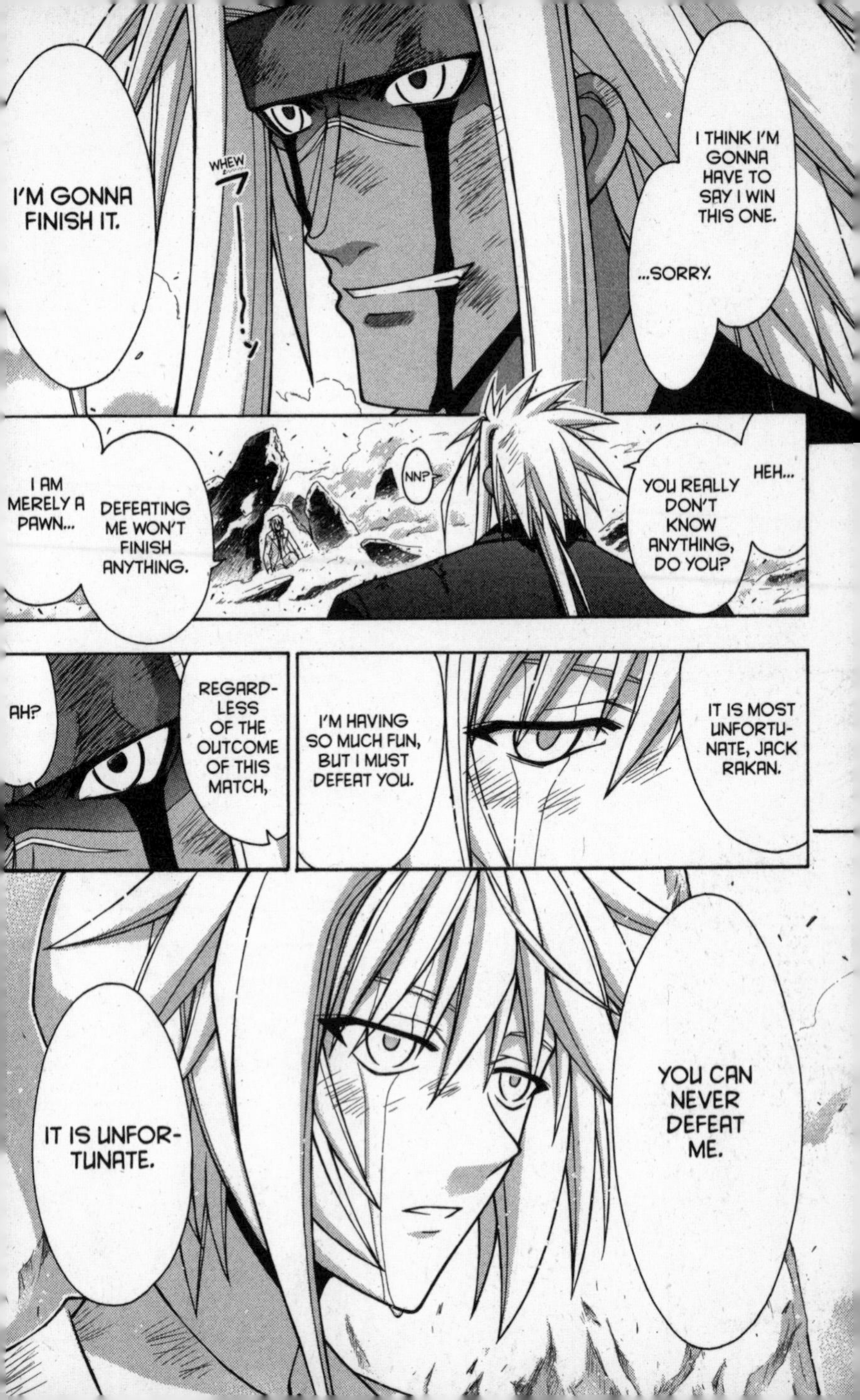
I THINK I'M GONNA HAVE TO SAY I WIN THIS ONE.
...SORRY.
WHEW
I'M GONNA FINISH IT.
HEH...
YOU REALLY DON'T KNOW ANYTHING, DO YOU?
NN?
I AM MERELY A PAWN...
DEFEATING ME WON'T FINISH ANYTHING.
IT IS MOST UNFORTU-NATE, JACK RAKAN.
I'M HAVING SO MUCH FUN, BUT I MUST DEFEAT YOU.
REGARD-LESS OF THE OUTCOME OF THIS MATCH,
AH?
YOU CAN NEVER DEFEAT ME.
IT IS UNFOR-TUNATE.

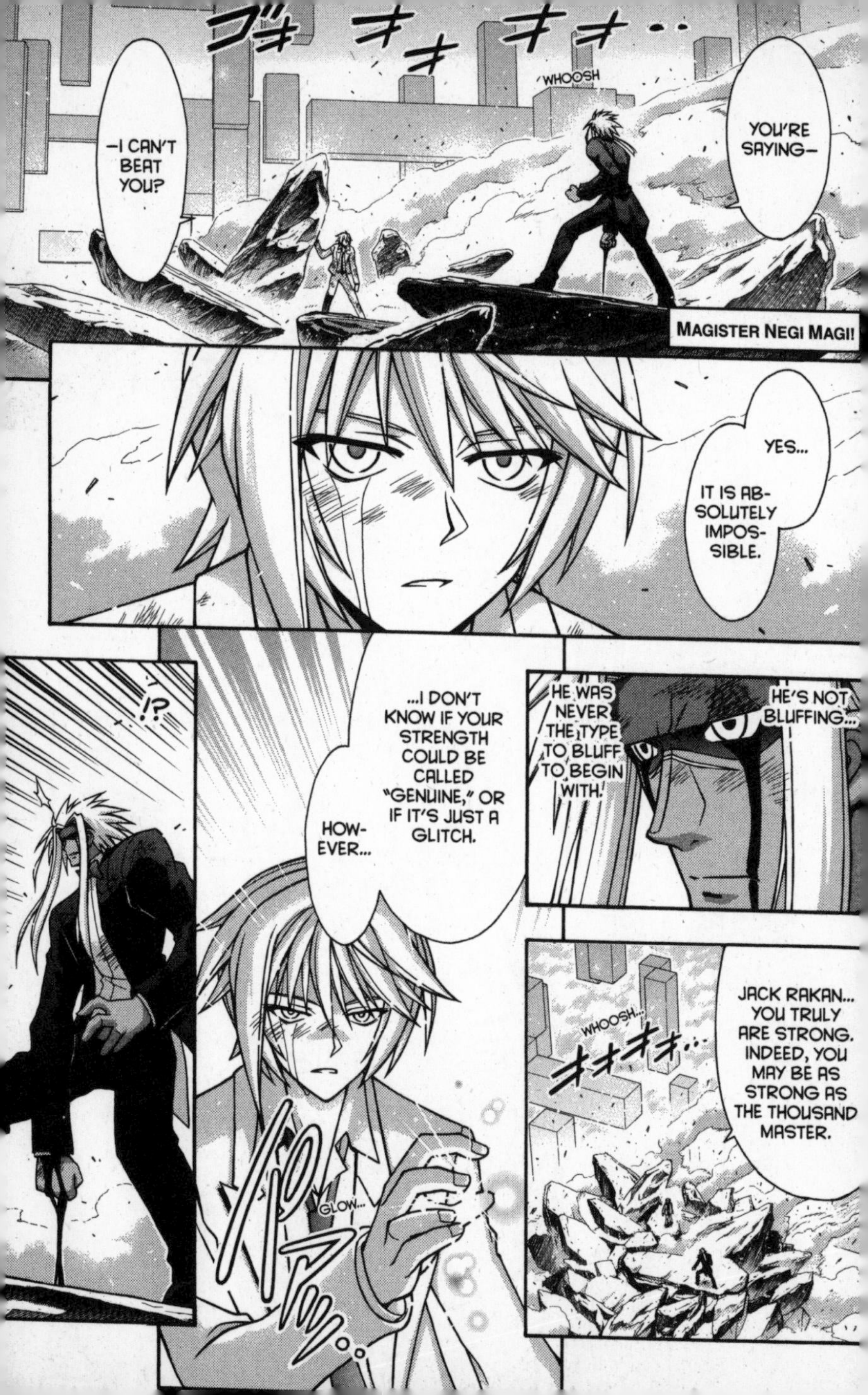
ゴォォォォ..
WHOOSH
YOU'RE SAYING—
—I CAN'T BEAT YOU?
MAGISTER NEGI MAGI!
YES... IT IS ABSOLUTELY IMPOSSIBLE.
HE'S NOT BLUFFING...
HE WAS NEVER THE TYPE TO BLUFF TO BEGIN WITH.
JACK RAKAN... YOU TRULY ARE STRONG. INDEED, YOU MAY BE AS STRONG AS THE THOUSAND MASTER.
WHOOSH...
...I DON'T KNOW IF YOUR STRENGTH COULD BE CALLED "GENUINE," OR IF IT'S JUST A GLITCH.
HOWEVER...
GLOW...
!?

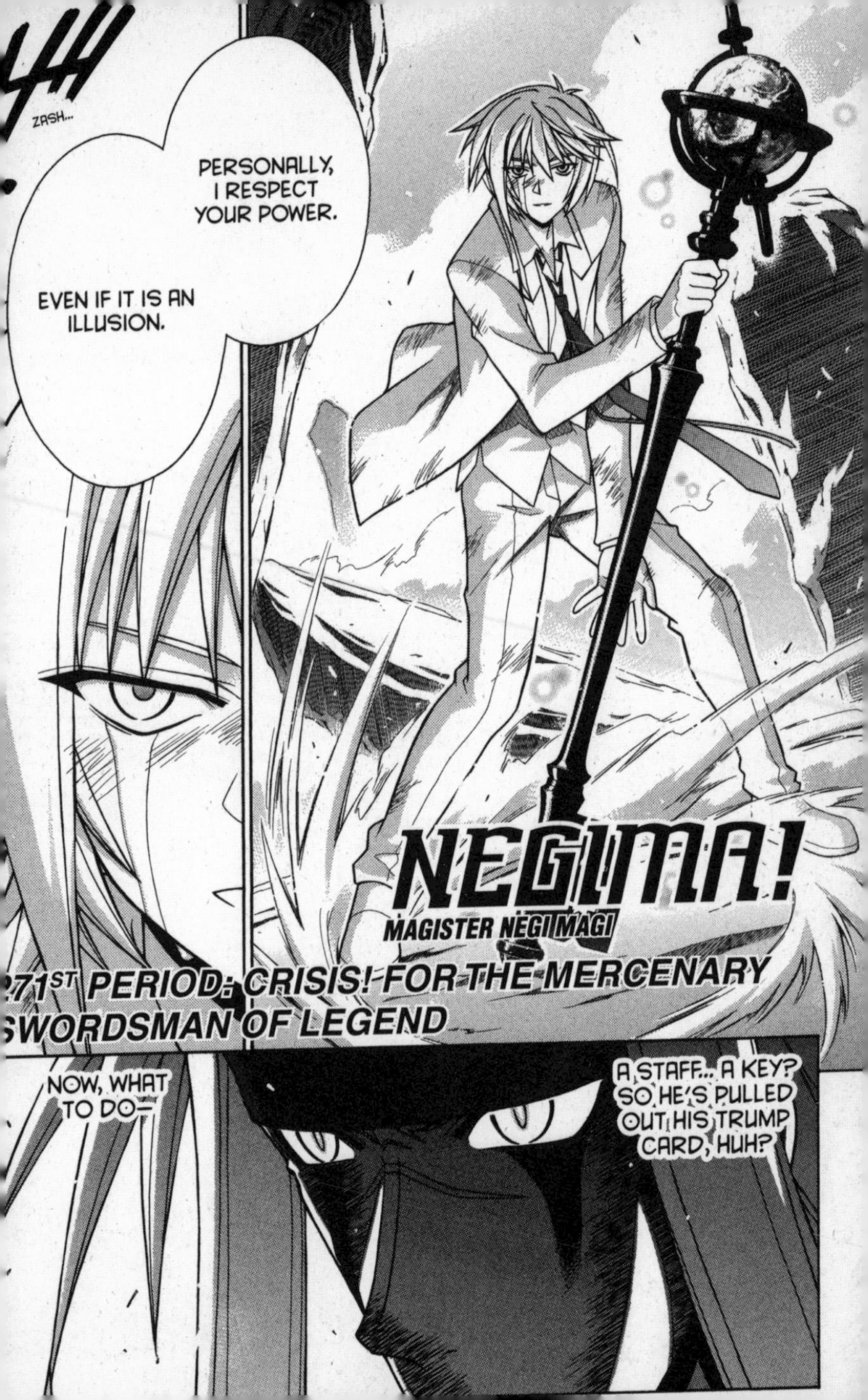
ZASH...
PERSONALLY, I RESPECT YOUR POWER.
EVEN IF IT IS AN ILLUSION.
NEGIMA!
MAGISTER NEGI MAGI
271ST PERIOD: CRISIS! FOR THE MERCENARY SWORDSMAN OF LEGEND
A STAFF... A KEY? SO HE'S PULLED OUT HIS TRUMP CARD, HUH?
NOW, WHAT TO DO—

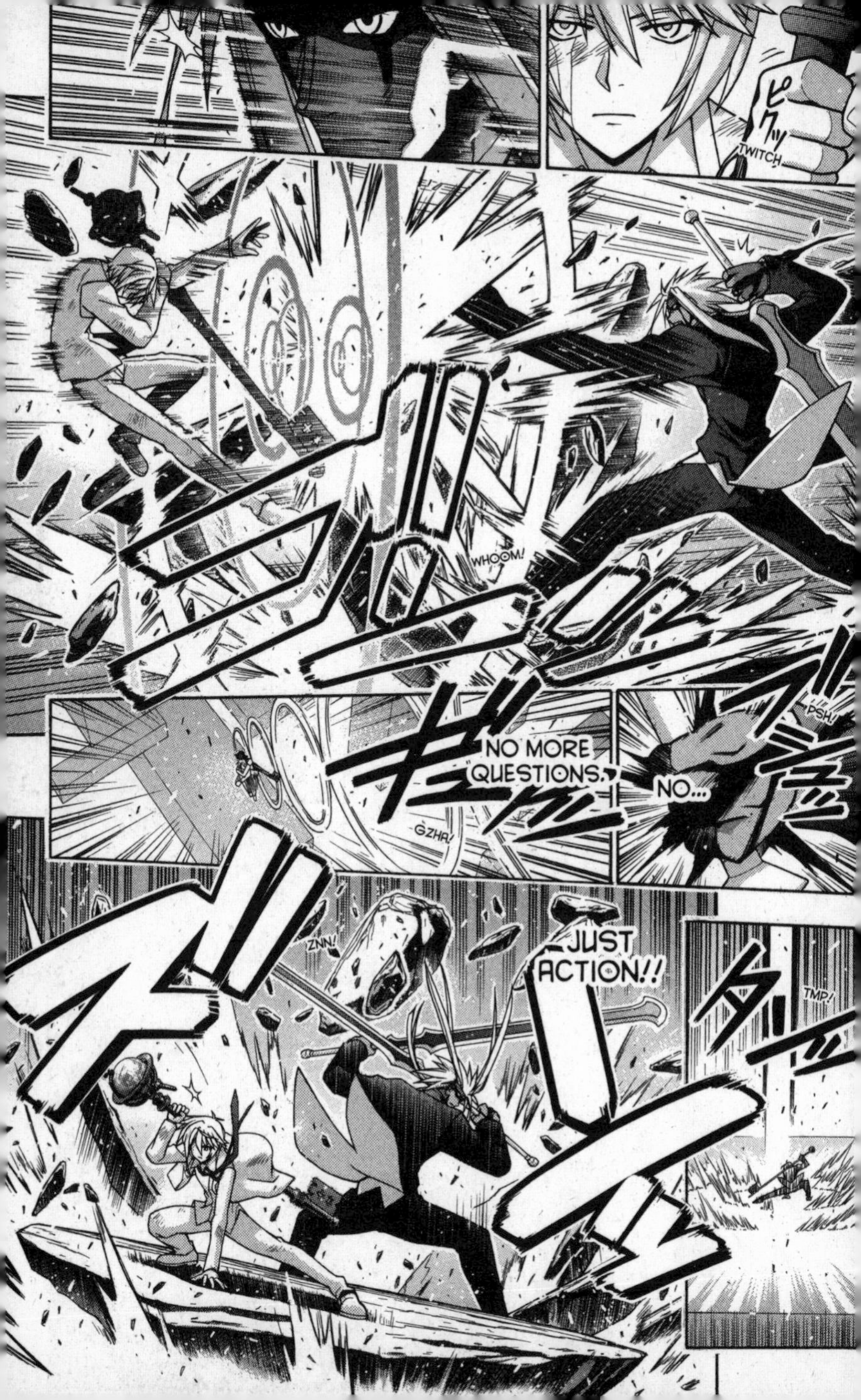
ピクッ
TWITCH
WHOOM!
PSH!
NO...
NO MORE QUESTIONS.
GZHA!
TMP!
JUST ACTION!!
ZNN!

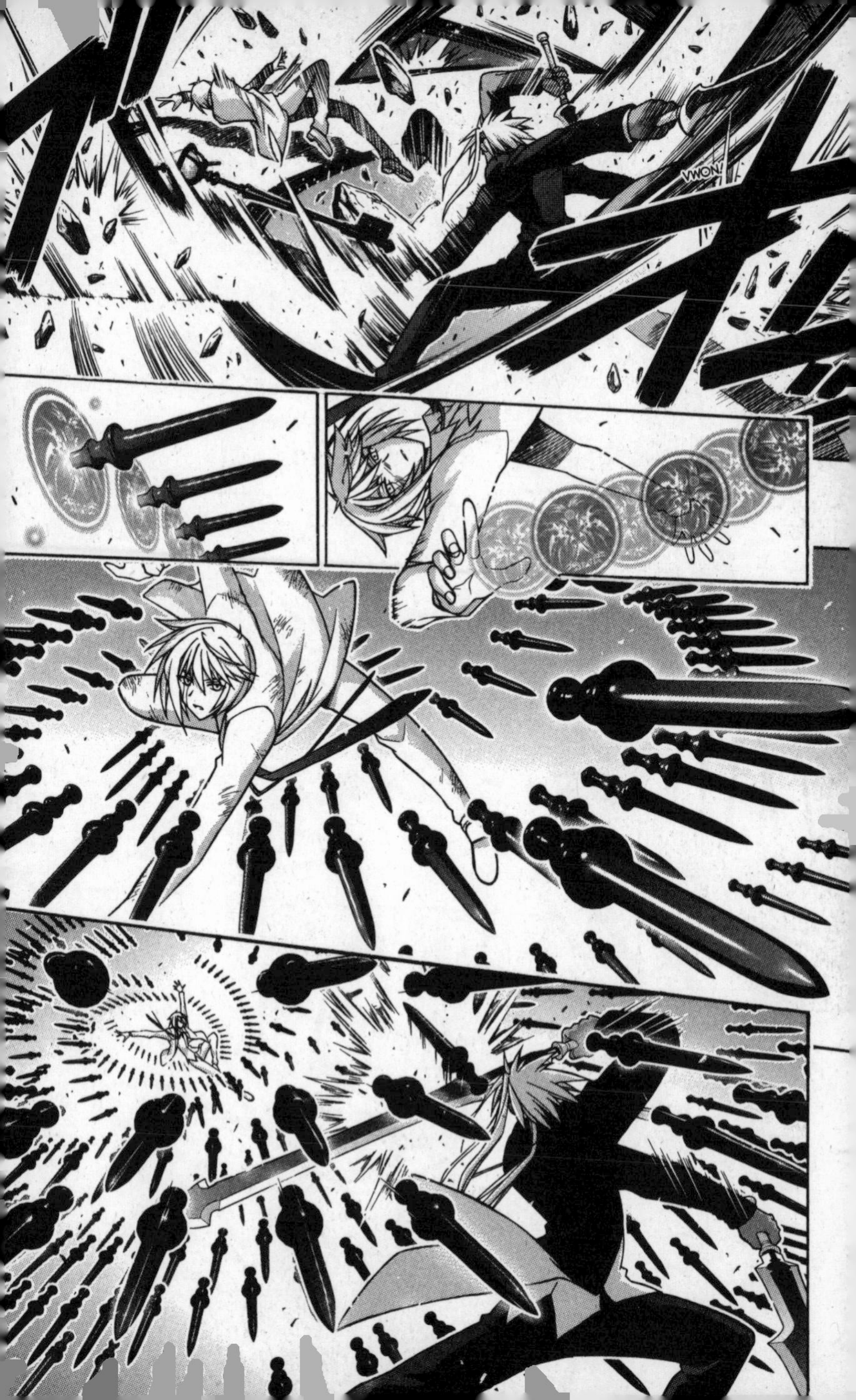
VWON!

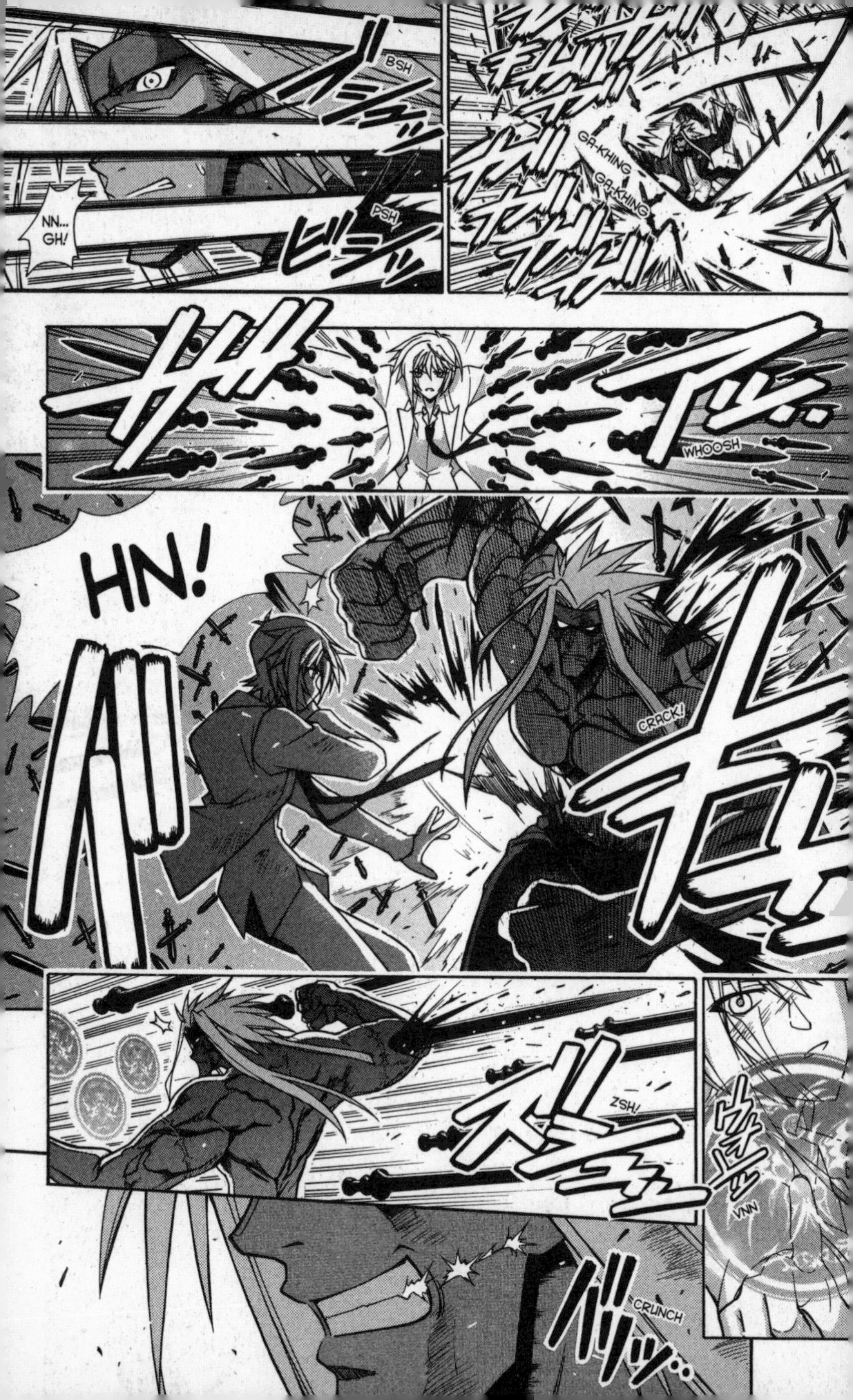
GA-KHING
GA-KHING
BSH
NN... GH!
PSH
WHOOSH
CRACK!
HN!
VNN
ZSH!
CRUNCH

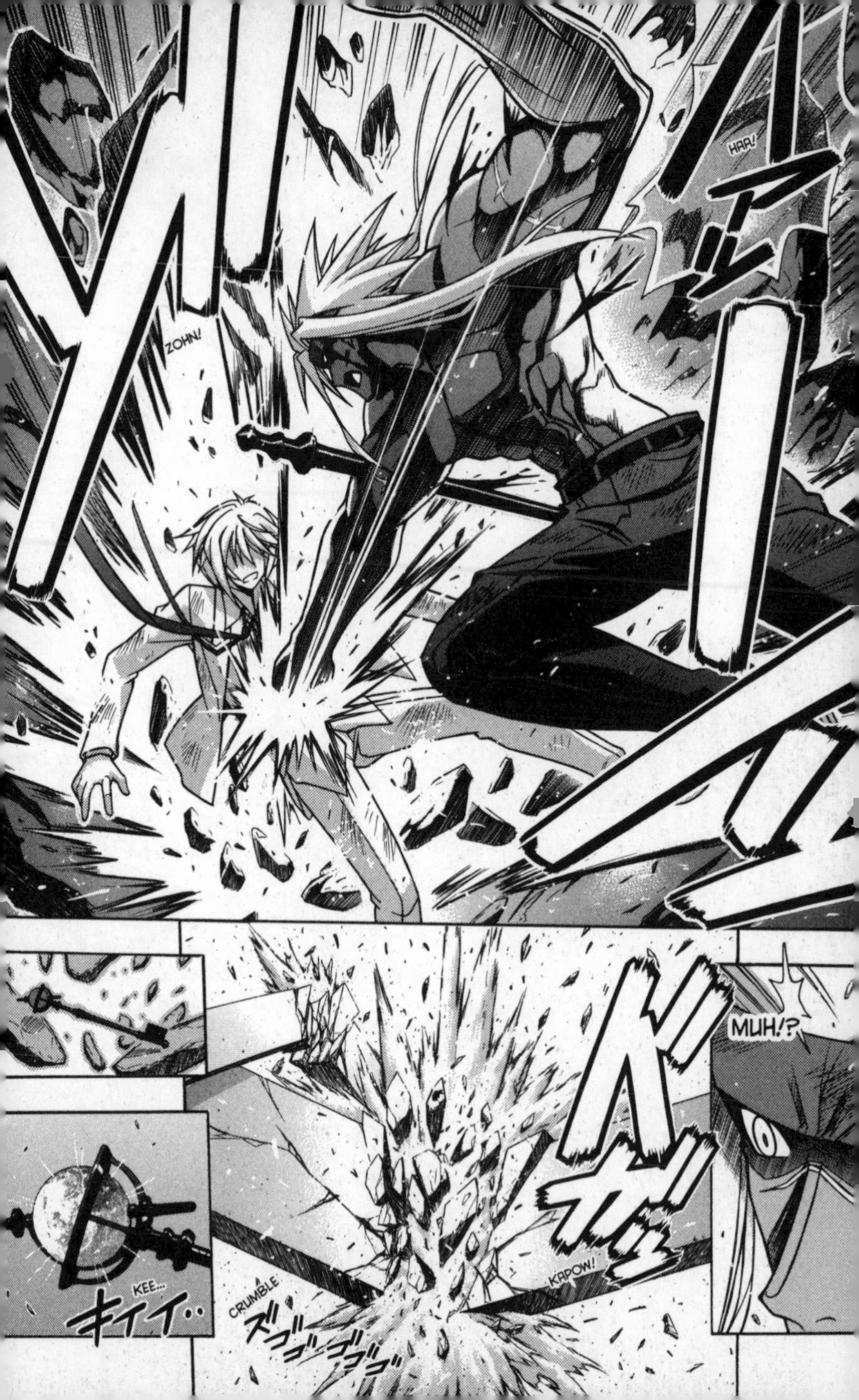
HAA!
ZOHN!
MUH!?
KAPOW!
CRUMBLE
ズゴゴゴゴ
KEE...
キイイ..

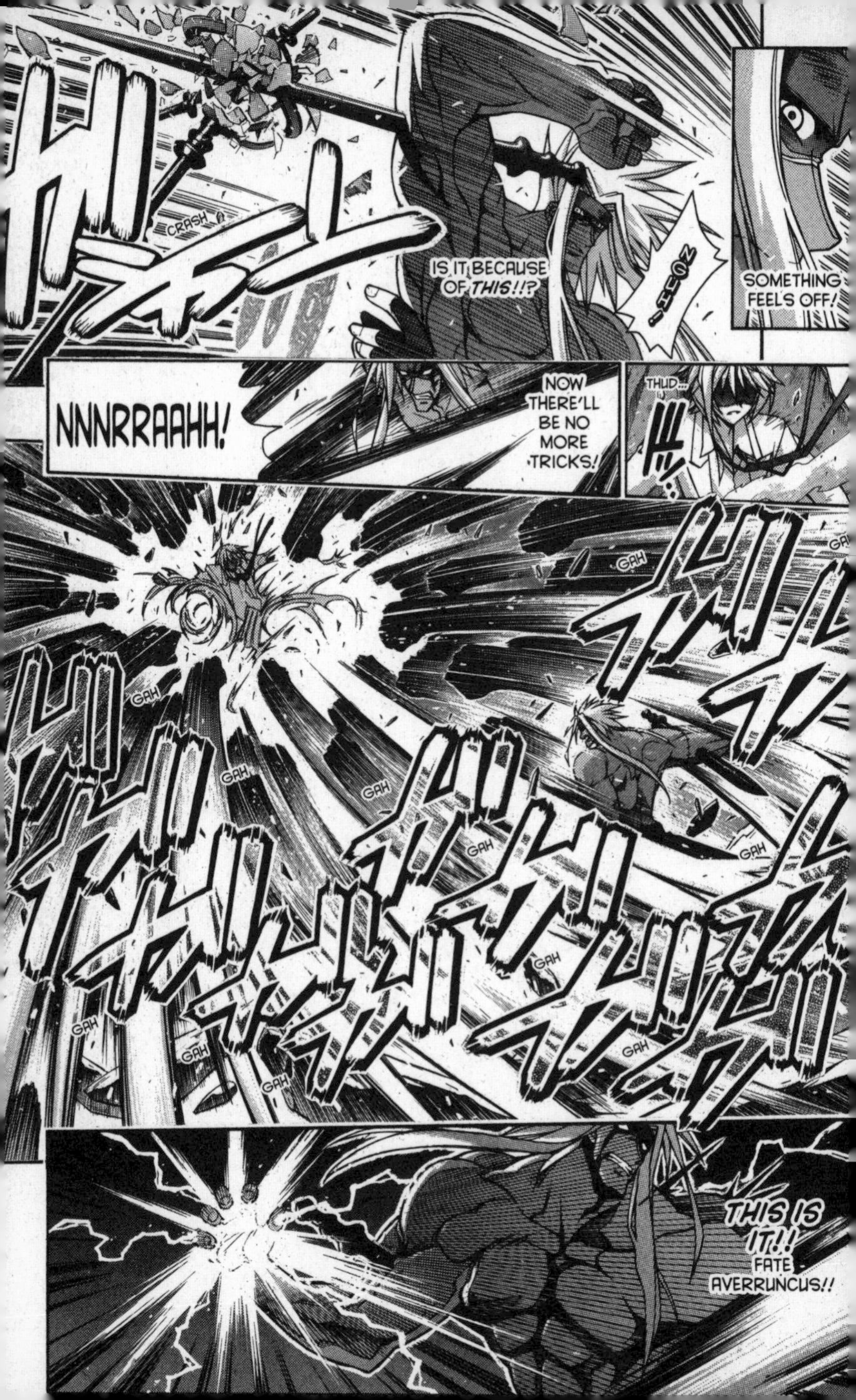
SOMETHING FEELS OFF!
NGH...!
IS IT BECAUSE OF THIS!!?
CRASH
THUD...
NOW THERE'LL BE NO MORE TRICKS!
NNNRRAAHH!
GAH
GAH
GAH
GAH
GAH
GAH
GAH
GAH
GAH
GAH
GAH
THIS IS IT!! FATE AVERRUNCUS!!

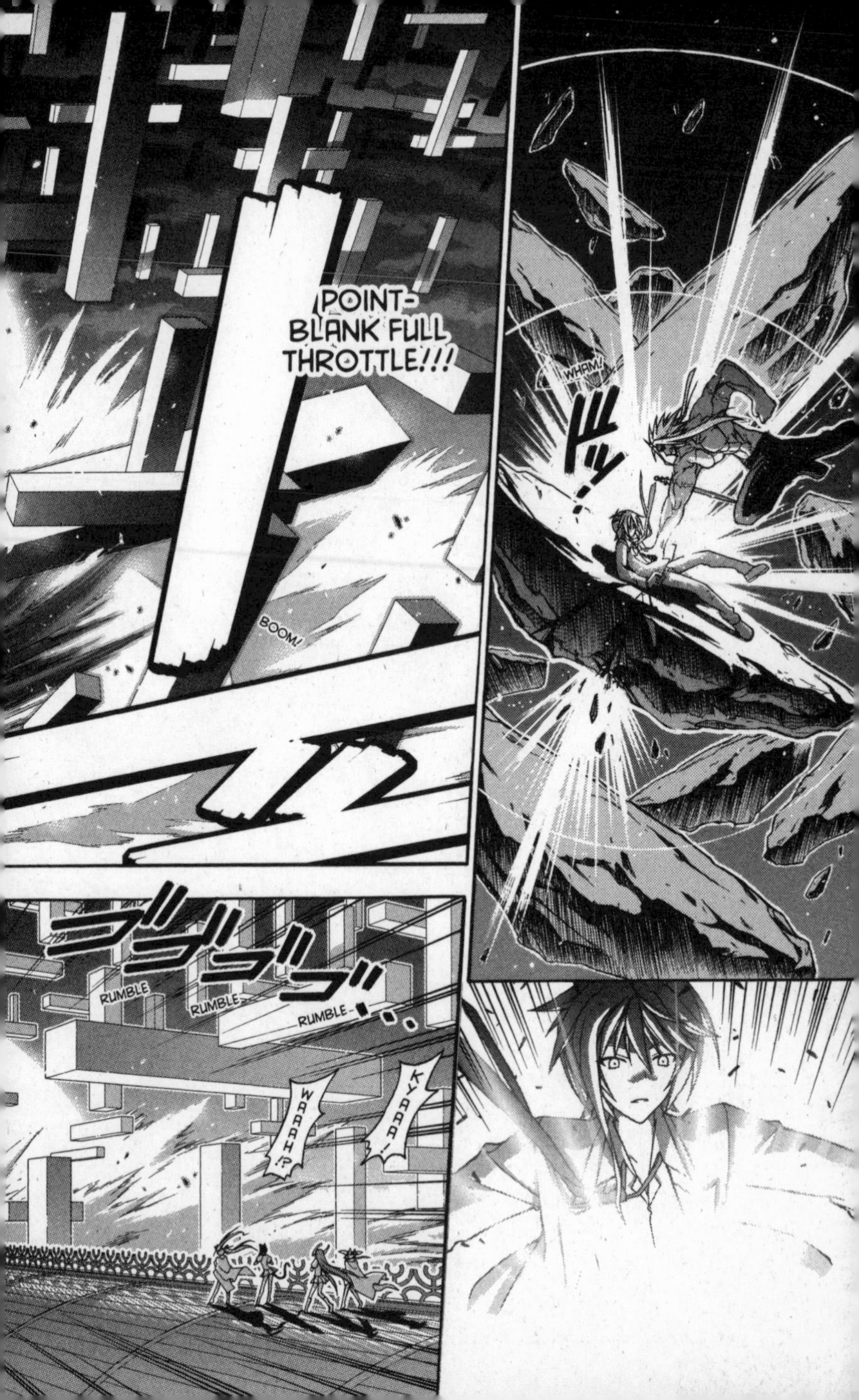
WHAM!
POINT-BLANK FULL THROTTLE!!!
BOOM!
RUMBLE
RUMBLE
RUMBLE
KYAAAA-!
WAAAAH!?

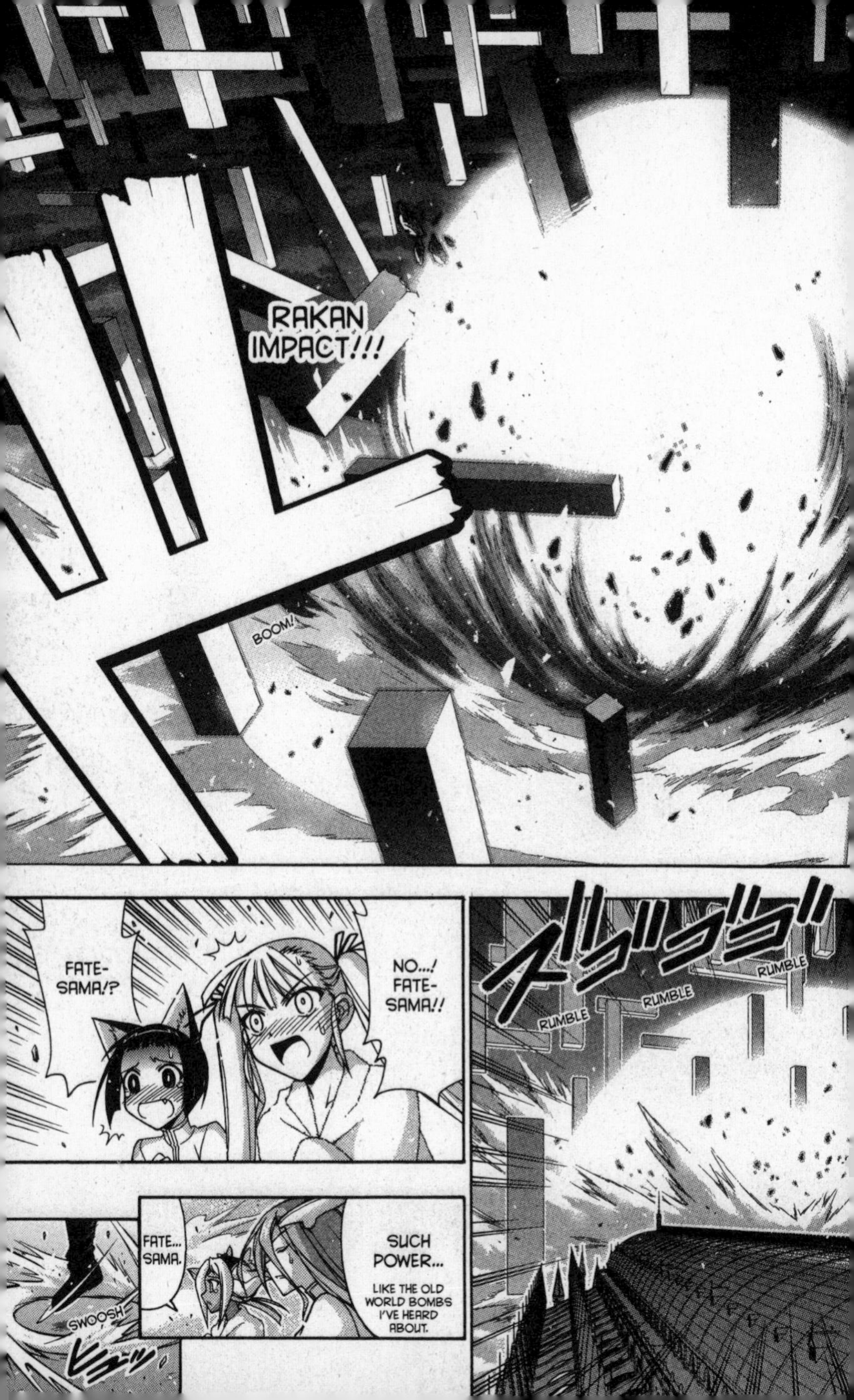
RAKAN IMPACT!!!
BOOM!
RUMBLE
RUMBLE
RUMBLE
NO...! FATE-SAMA!!
FATE-SAMA!?
SUCH POWER...
LIKE THE OLD WORLD BOMBS I'VE HEARD ABOUT.
FATE... SAMA.
SWOOSH

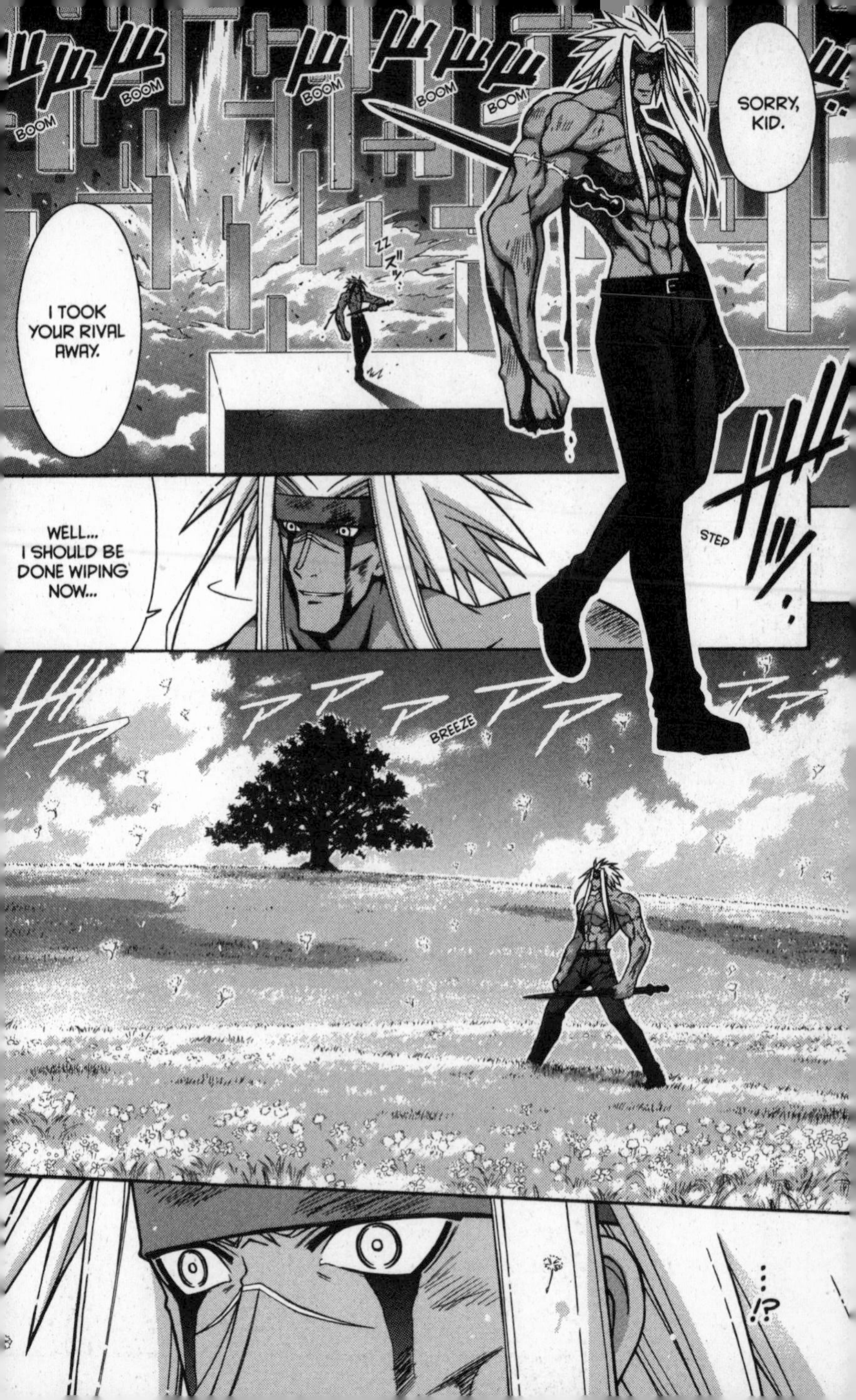
BOOM
BOOM
BOOM
BOOM
BOOM
SORRY, KID.
ZZ
I TOOK YOUR RIVAL AWAY.
STEP
WELL... I SHOULD BE DONE WIPING NOW...
BREEZE
...!?

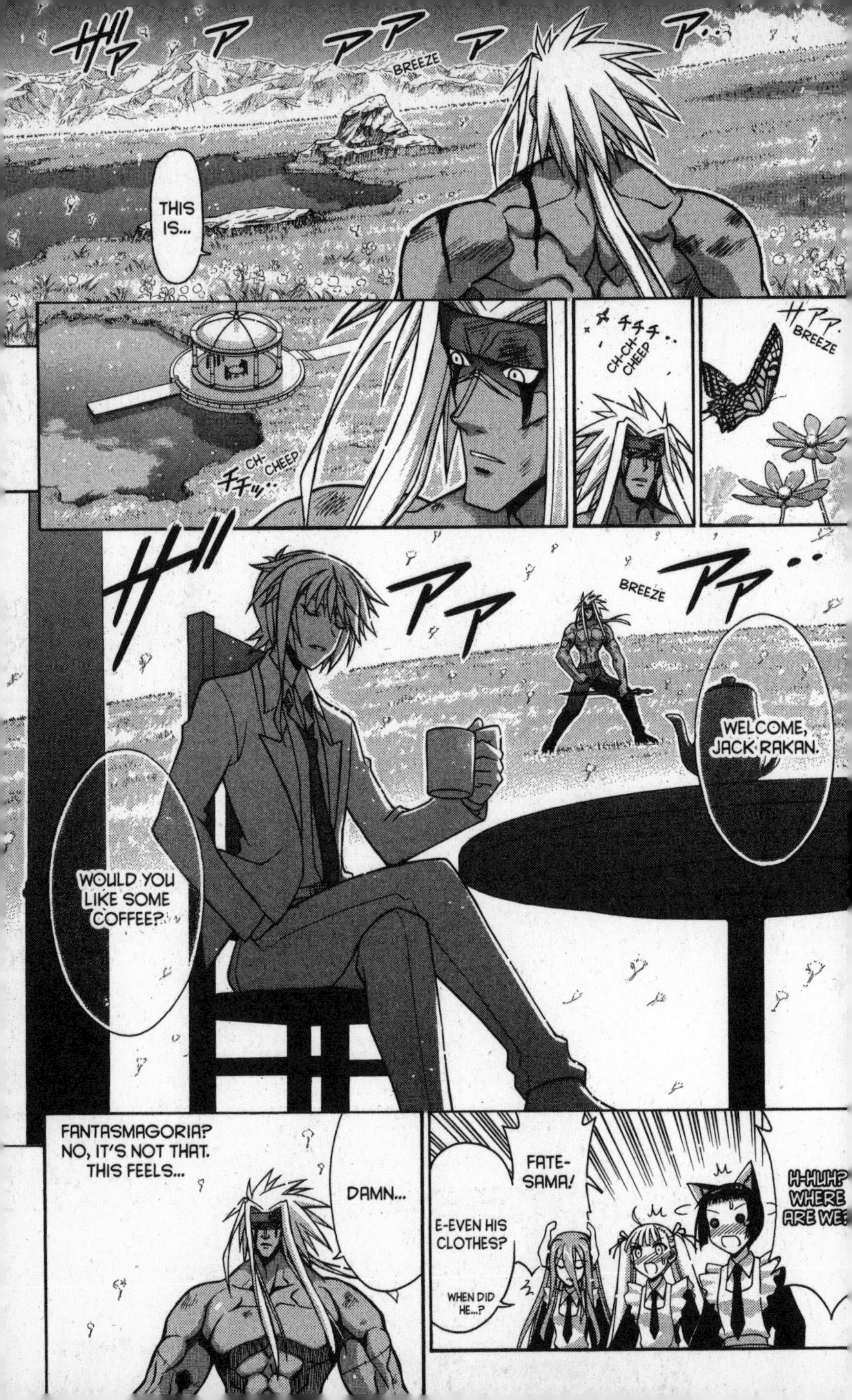
BREEZE
THIS IS...
BREEZE
CH-CH-CHEEP
CH-CHEEP
BREEZE
WELCOME, JACK RAKAN.
WOULD YOU LIKE SOME COFFEE?
H-HUH? WHERE ARE WE?
FATE-SAMA!
E-EVEN HIS CLOTHES?
WHEN DID HE...?
FANTASMAGORIA? NO, IT'S NOT THAT. THIS FEELS...
DAMN...

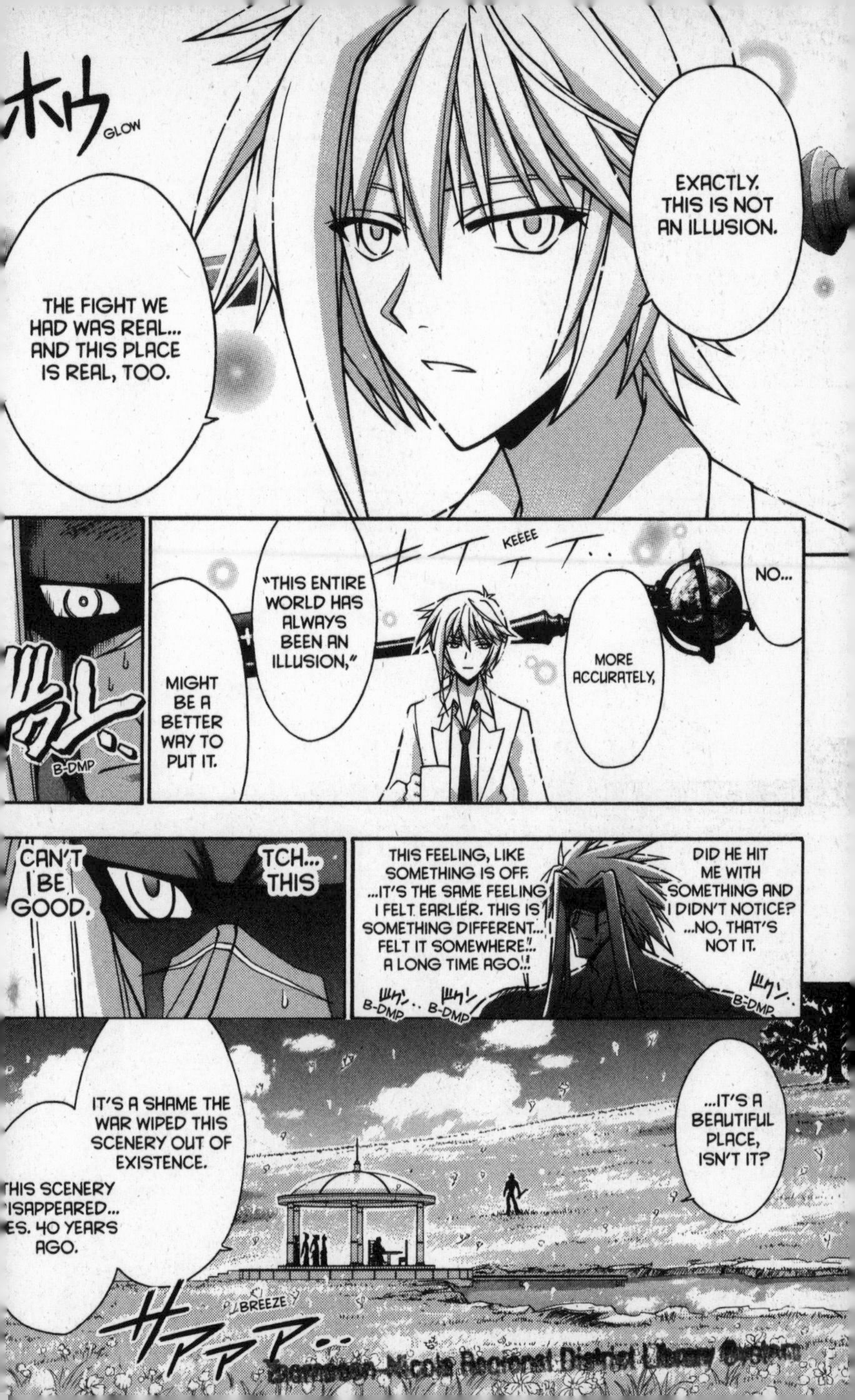
EXACTLY. THIS IS NOT AN ILLUSION.
ホウ GLOW
THE FIGHT WE HAD WAS REAL... AND THIS PLACE IS REAL, TOO.
NO...
キィィィ.. KEEEE
MORE ACCURATELY,
"THIS ENTIRE WORLD HAS ALWAYS BEEN AN ILLUSION,"
MIGHT BE A BETTER WAY TO PUT IT.
B-DMP
DID HE HIT ME WITH SOMETHING AND I DIDN'T NOTICE? ...NO, THAT'S NOT IT.
THIS FEELING, LIKE SOMETHING IS OFF. ...IT'S THE SAME FEELING I FELT EARLIER. THIS IS SOMETHING DIFFERENT... I FELT IT SOMEWHERE... A LONG TIME AGO...
B-DMP
B-DMP
B-DMP
TCH... THIS
CAN'T BE GOOD.
...IT'S A BEAUTIFUL PLACE, ISN'T IT?
IT'S A SHAME THE WAR WIPED THIS SCENERY OUT OF EXISTENCE.
THIS SCENERY ISAPPEARED... ES. 40 YEARS AGO.
BREEZE

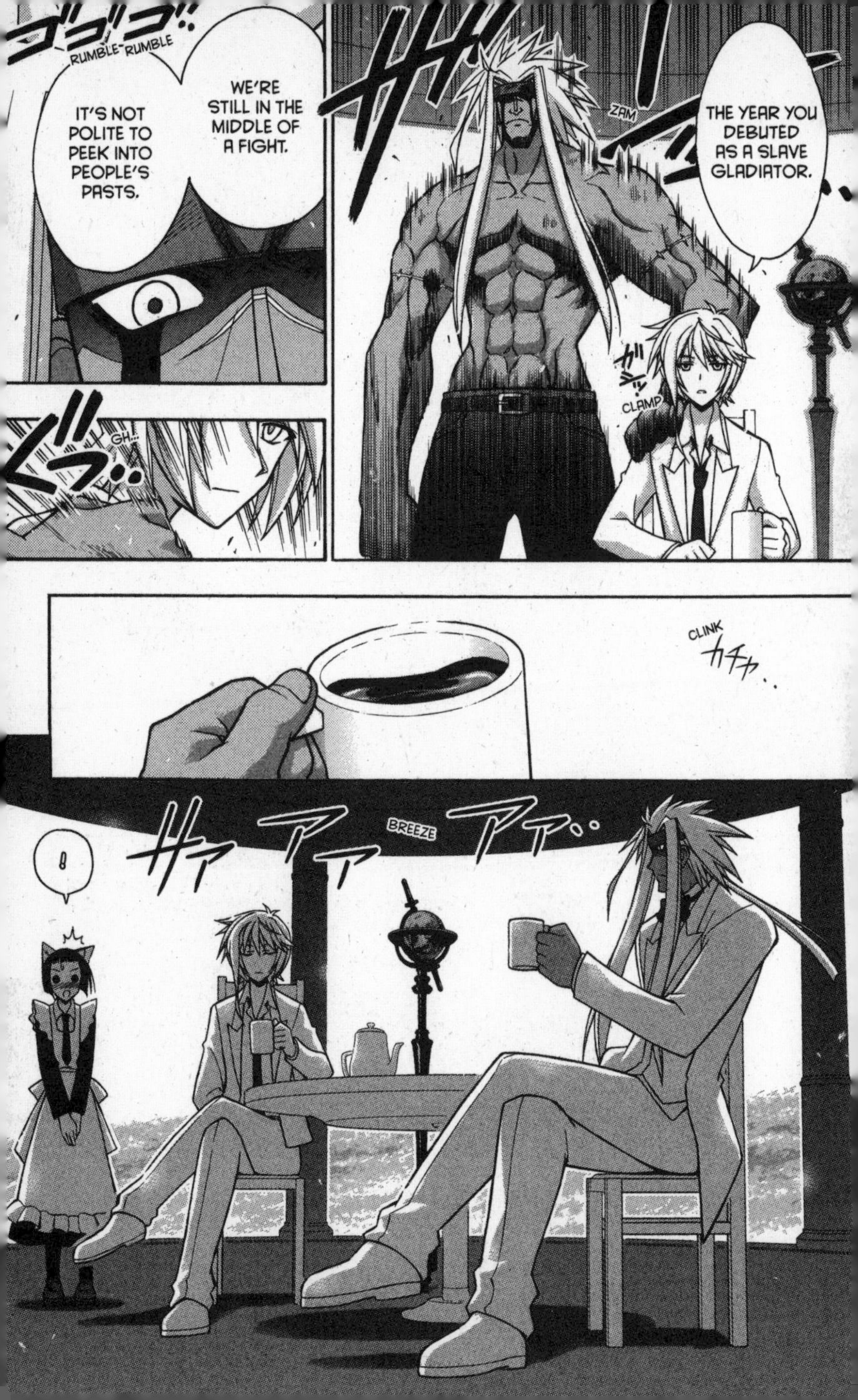
ZAM
THE YEAR YOU DEBUTED AS A SLAVE GLADIATOR.
CLAMP
RUMBLE RUMBLE
WE'RE STILL IN THE MIDDLE OF A FIGHT.
IT'S NOT POLITE TO PEEK INTO PEOPLE'S PASTS.
GH...
CLINK
BREEZE
!

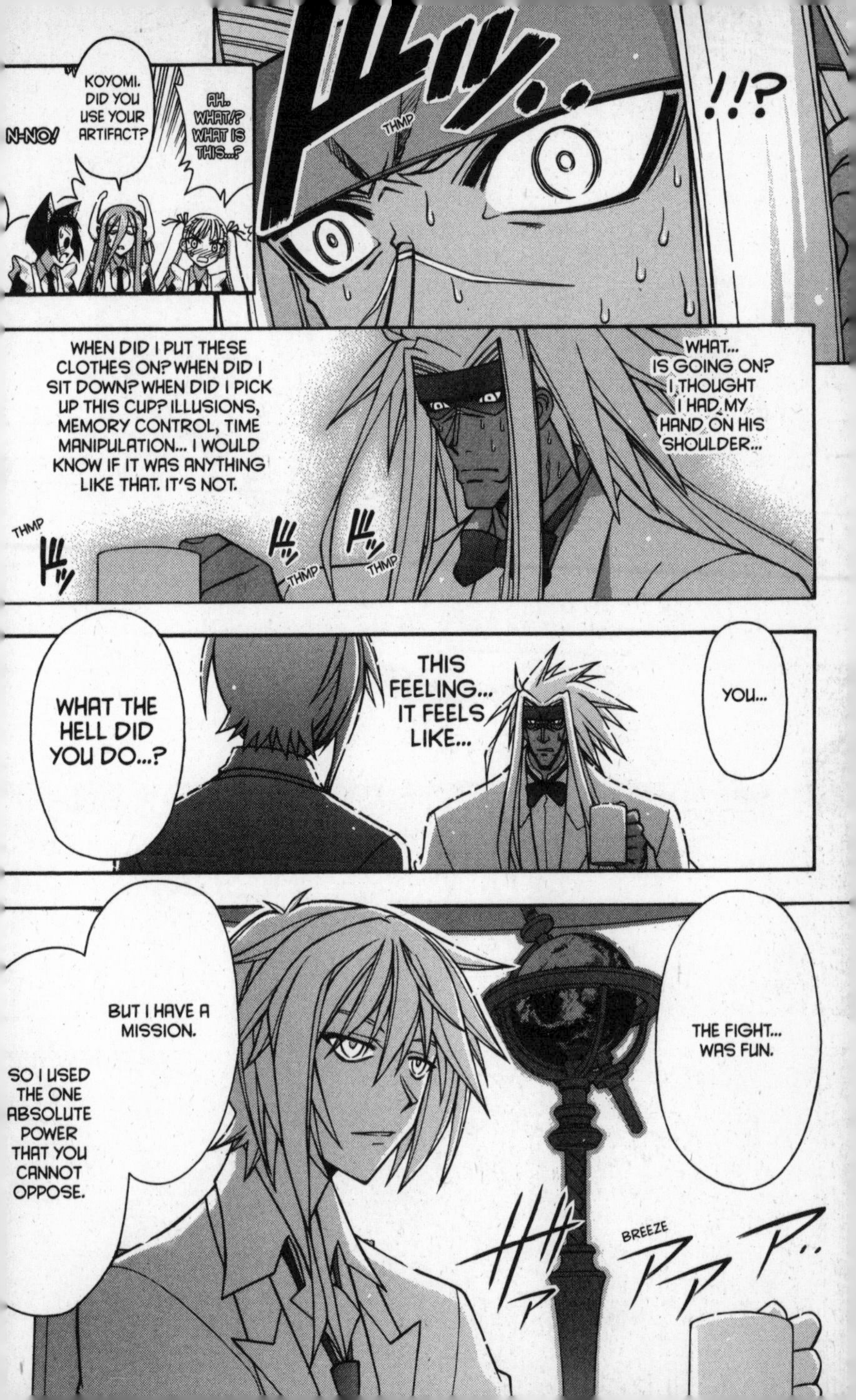
!!?
THMP
AH.. WHAT!? WHAT IS THIS...?
KOYOMI. DID YOU USE YOUR ARTIFACT?
N-NO!
WHAT... IS GOING ON? I THOUGHT I HAD MY HAND ON HIS SHOULDER...
WHEN DID I PUT THESE CLOTHES ON? WHEN DID I SIT DOWN? WHEN DID I PICK UP THIS CUP? ILLUSIONS, MEMORY CONTROL, TIME MANIPULATION... I WOULD KNOW IF IT WAS ANYTHING LIKE THAT. IT'S NOT.
THMP
THMP
THMP
YOU...
THIS FEELING... IT FEELS LIKE...
WHAT THE HELL DID YOU DO...?
THE FIGHT... WAS FUN.
BUT I HAVE A MISSION.
SO I USED THE ONE ABSOLUTE POWER THAT YOU CANNOT OPPOSE.
BREEZE

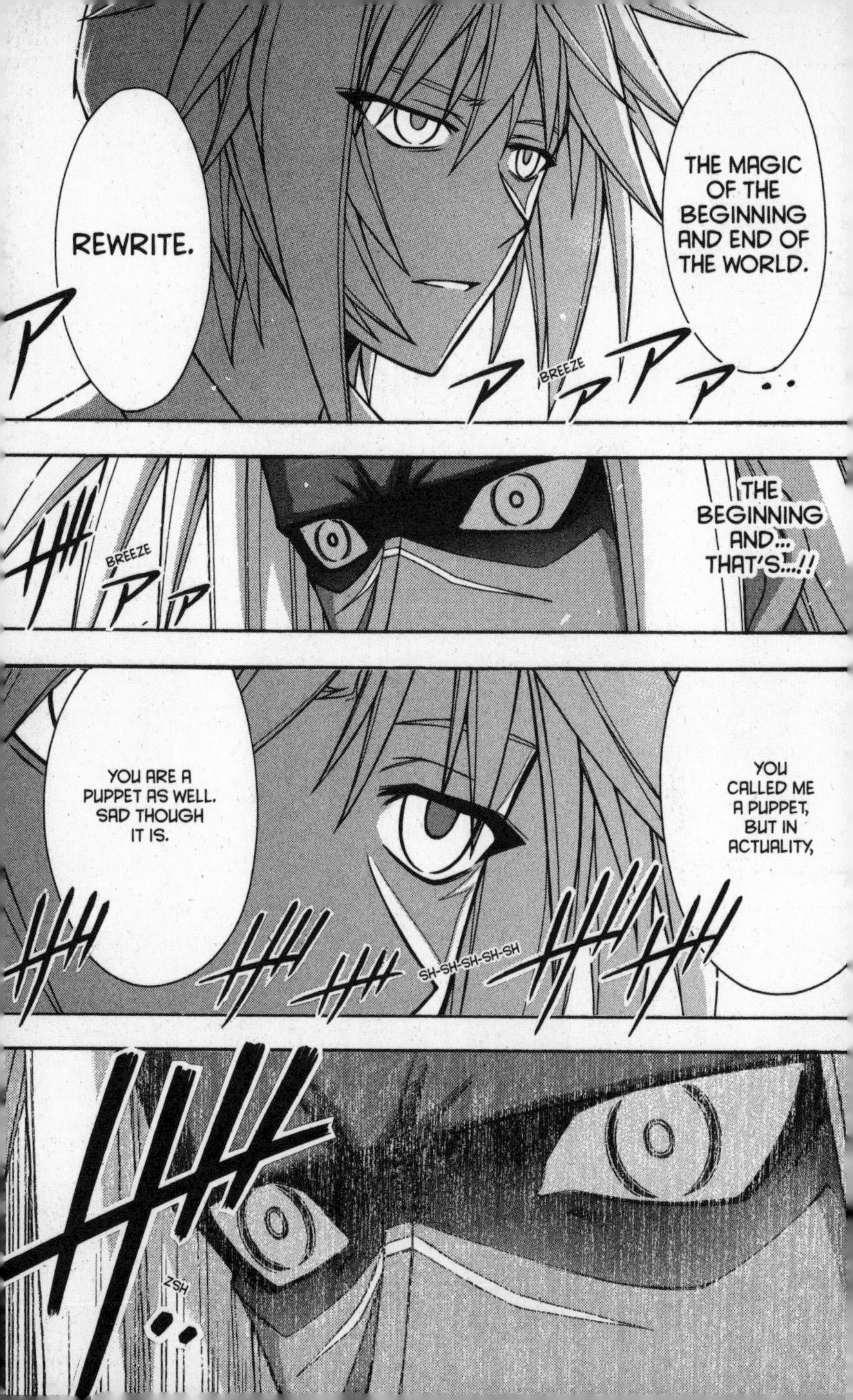
THE MAGIC OF THE BEGINNING AND END OF THE WORLD.
REWRITE.
BREEZE
THE BEGINNING AND... THAT'S...!!
BREEZE
YOU CALLED ME A PUPPET, BUT IN ACTUALITY,
YOU ARE A PUPPET AS WELL. SAD THOUGH IT IS.
SH-SH-SH-SH-SH
ZSH

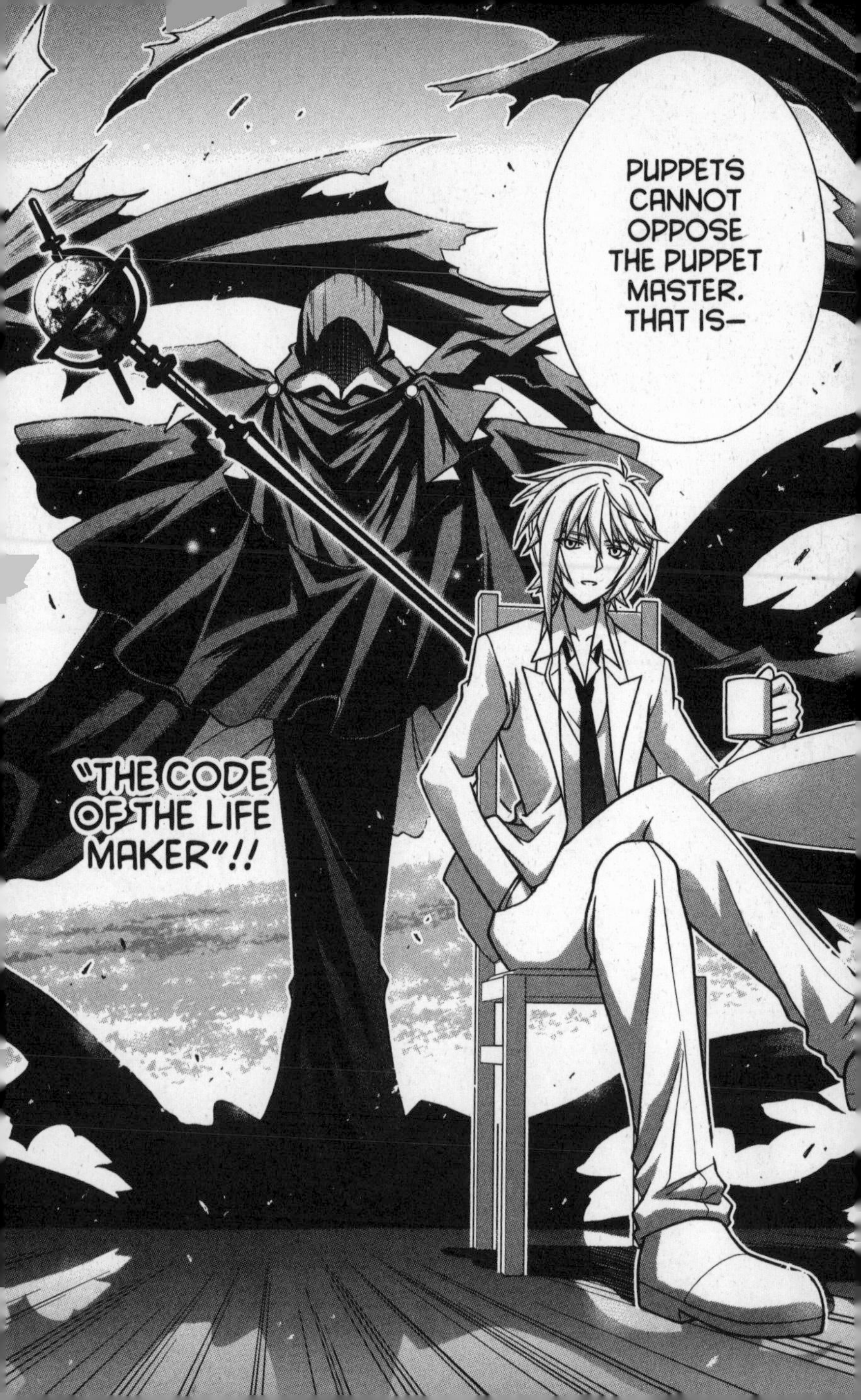
PUPPETS CANNOT OPPOSE THE PUPPET MASTER. THAT IS—
"THE CODE OF THE LIFE MAKER"!!

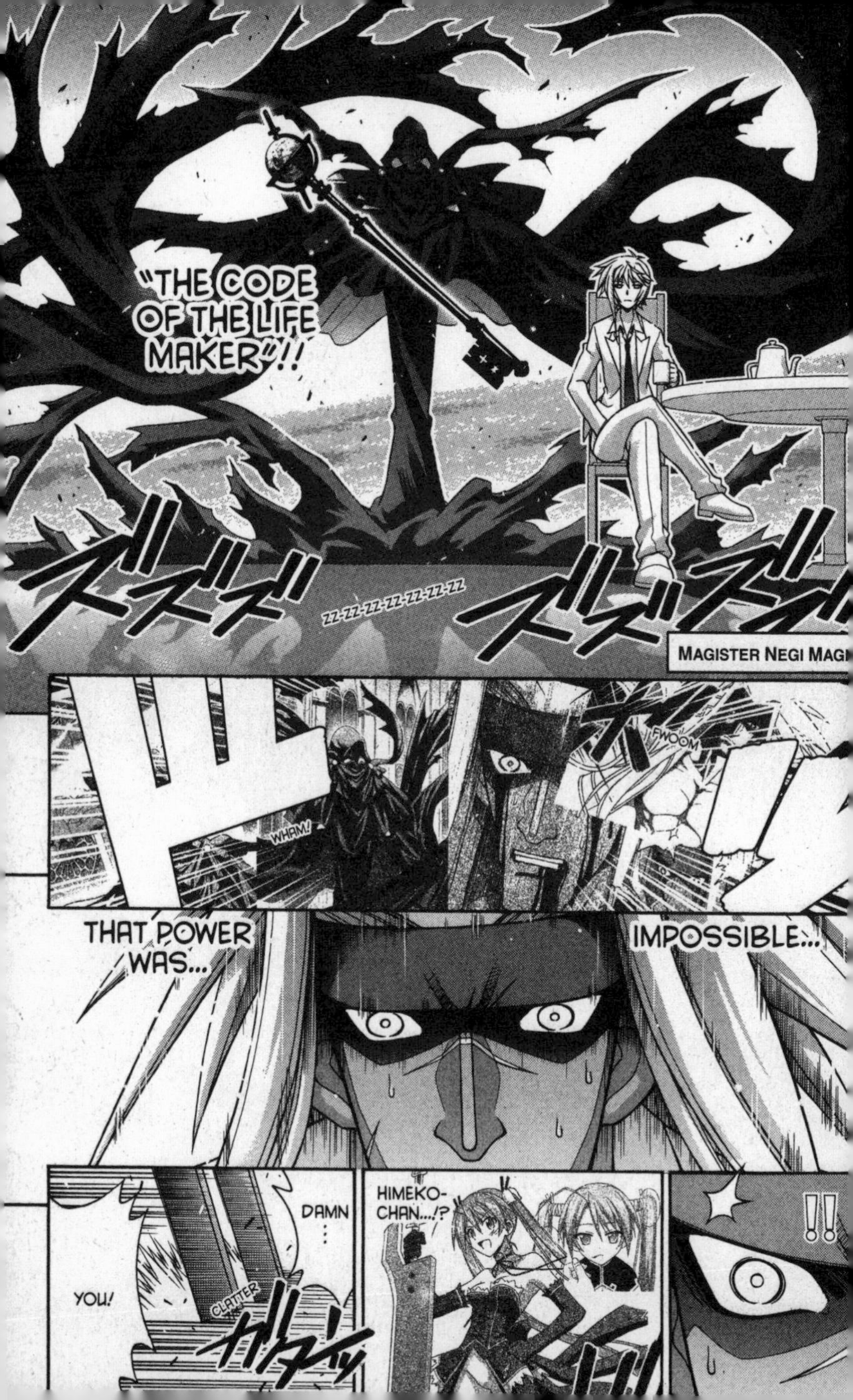
"THE CODE OF THE LIFE MAKER"!!
ZZ-ZZ-ZZ-ZZ-ZZ-ZZ-ZZ
MAGISTER NEGI MAG
FWOOM
WHAM!
IMPOSSIBLE...
THAT POWER WAS...
!!
HIMEKO-CHAN...!?
DAMN...
YOU!
CLATTER

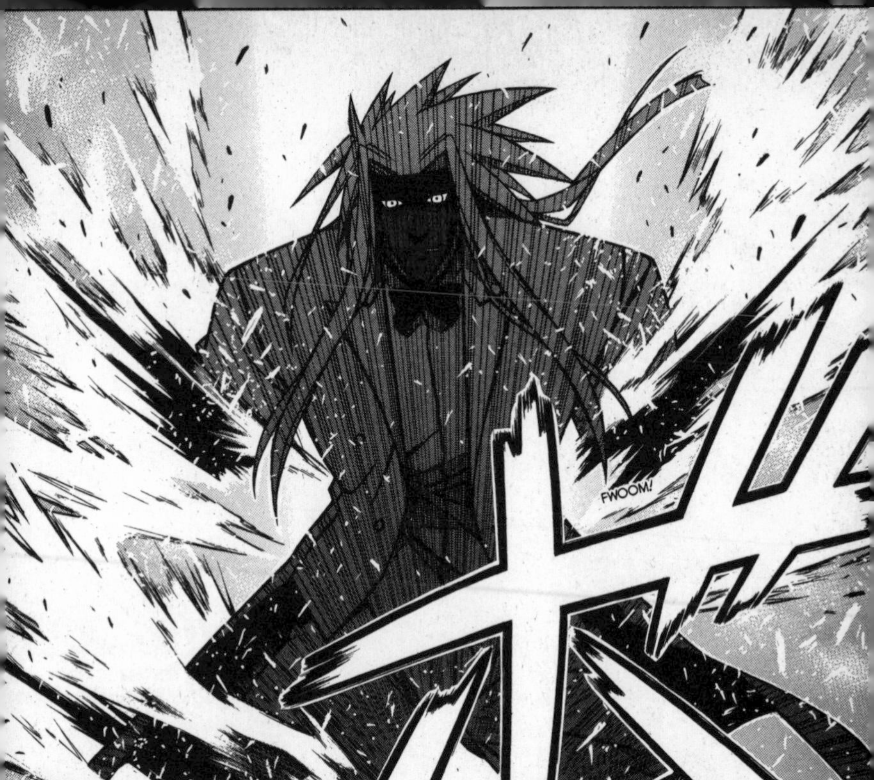
FWOOM!
NEGIMA!
MAGISTER NEGI MAGI

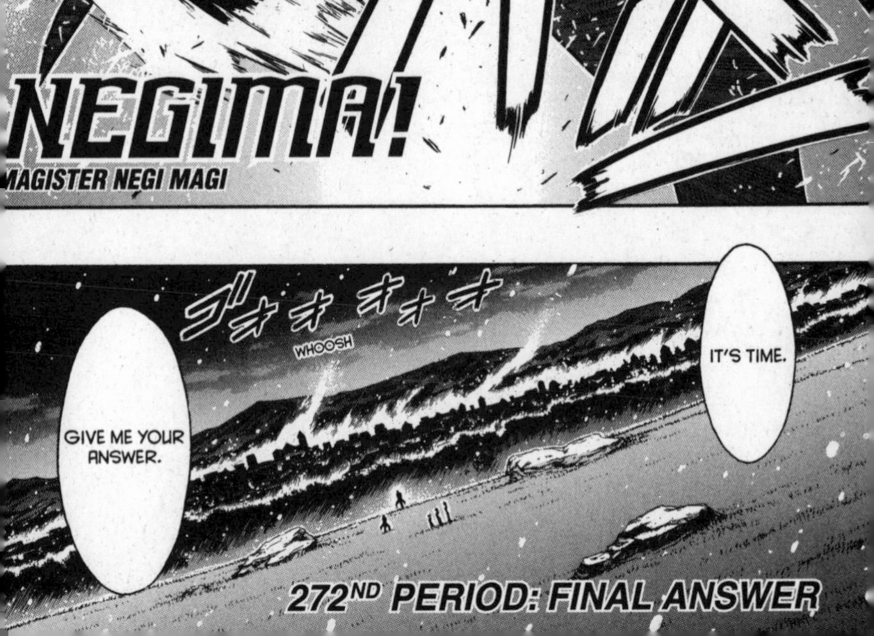
WHOOSH
IT'S TIME.
GIVE ME YOUR ANSWER.
272ND PERIOD: FINAL ANSWER

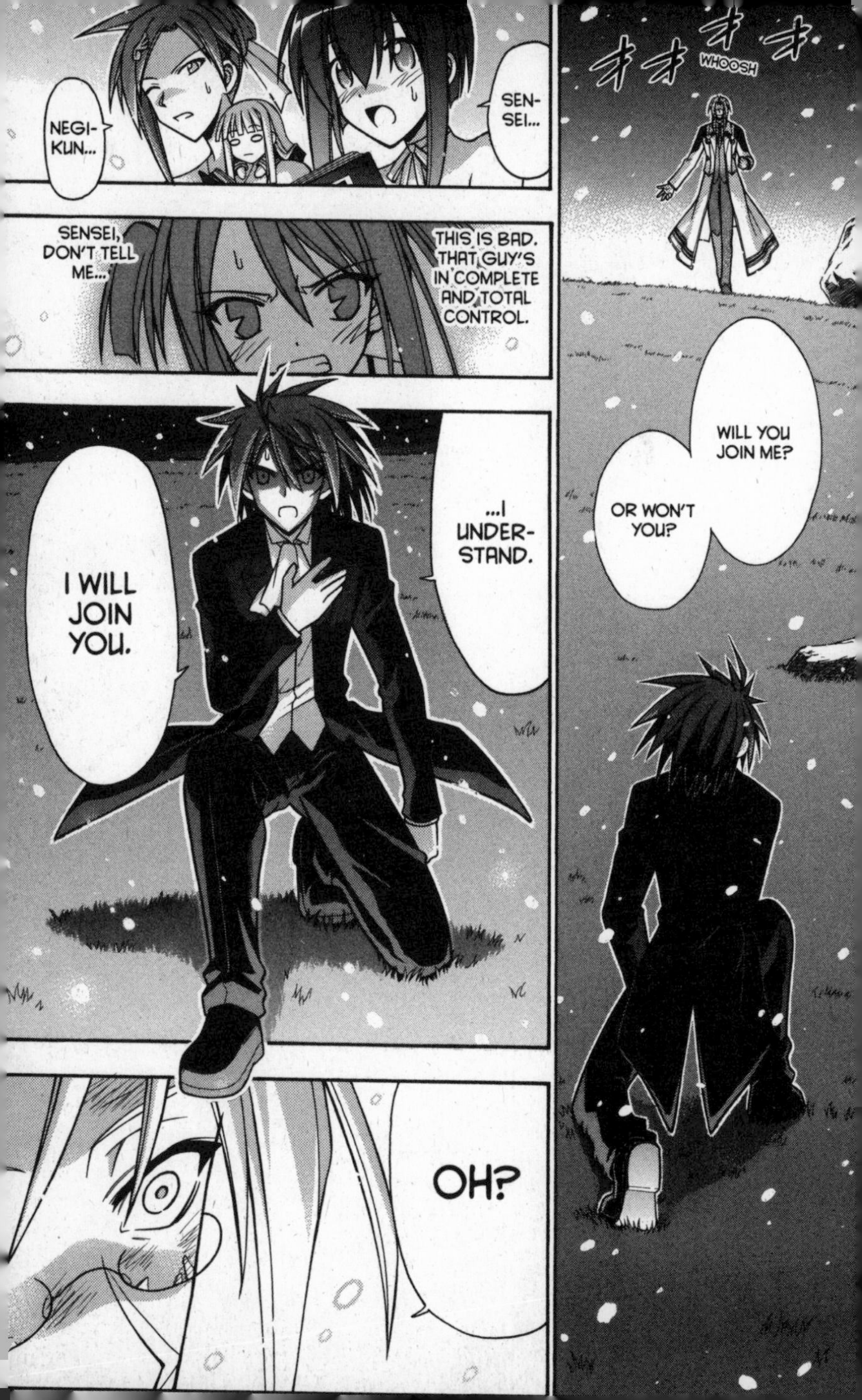

オオオオ
WHOOSH
WILL YOU JOIN ME?
OR WON'T YOU?
SEN-SEI...
NEGI-KUN...
THIS IS BAD. THAT GUY'S IN COMPLETE AND TOTAL CONTROL.
SENSEI, DON'T TELL ME...
...I UNDER-STAND.
I WILL JOIN YOU.
OH?

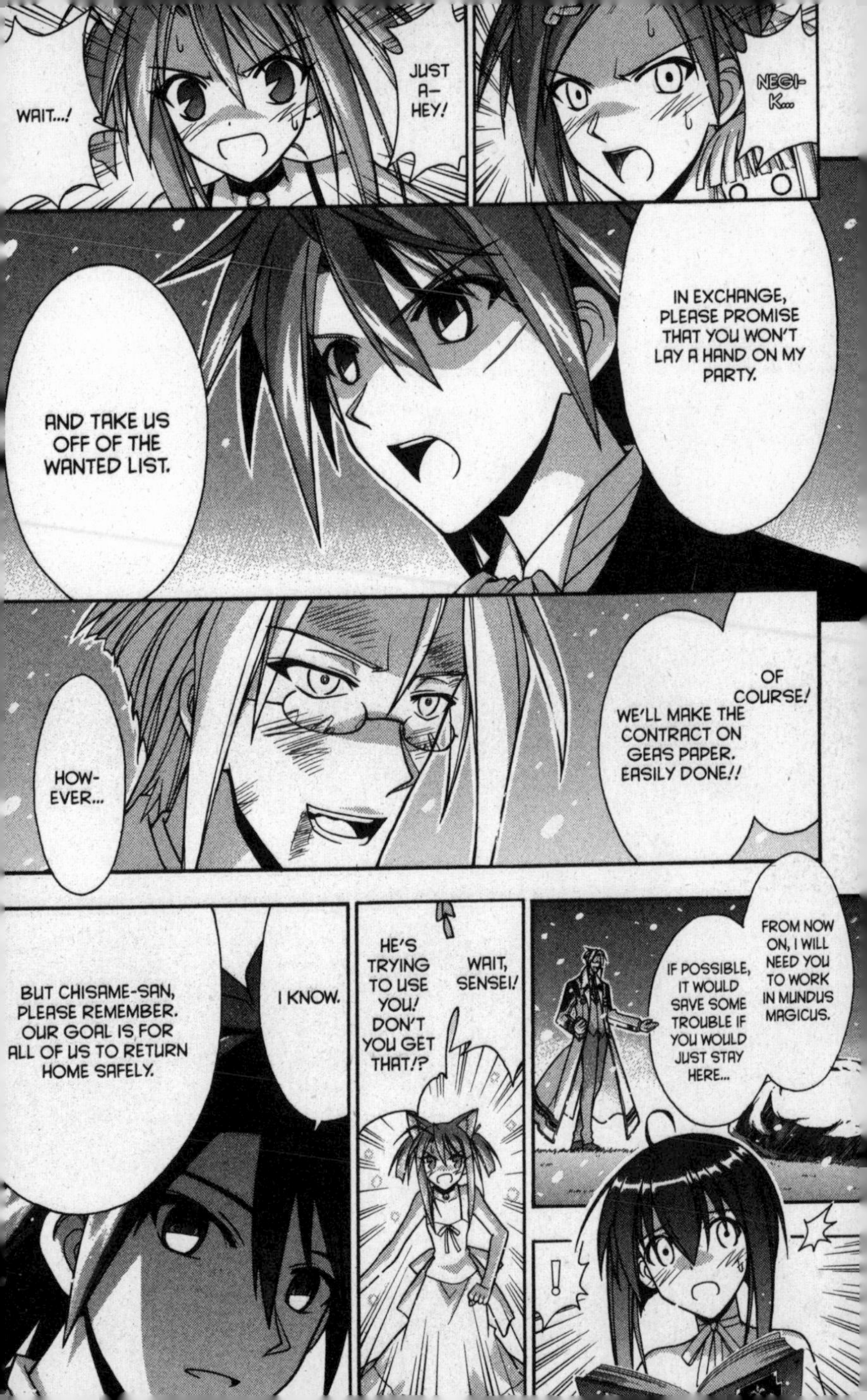
NEGI-K...
JUST A— HEY!
WAIT...!
IN EXCHANGE, PLEASE PROMISE THAT YOU WON'T LAY A HAND ON MY PARTY.
AND TAKE US OFF OF THE WANTED LIST.
OF COURSE! WE'LL MAKE THE CONTRACT ON GEAS PAPER. EASILY DONE!!
HOW-EVER...
FROM NOW ON, I WILL NEED YOU TO WORK IN MUNDUS MAGICUS.
IF POSSIBLE, IT WOULD SAVE SOME TROUBLE IF YOU WOULD JUST STAY HERE...
!
WAIT, SENSEI!
HE'S TRYING TO USE YOU! DON'T YOU GET THAT!?
I KNOW.
BUT CHISAME-SAN, PLEASE REMEMBER. OUR GOAL IS FOR ALL OF US TO RETURN HOME SAFELY.

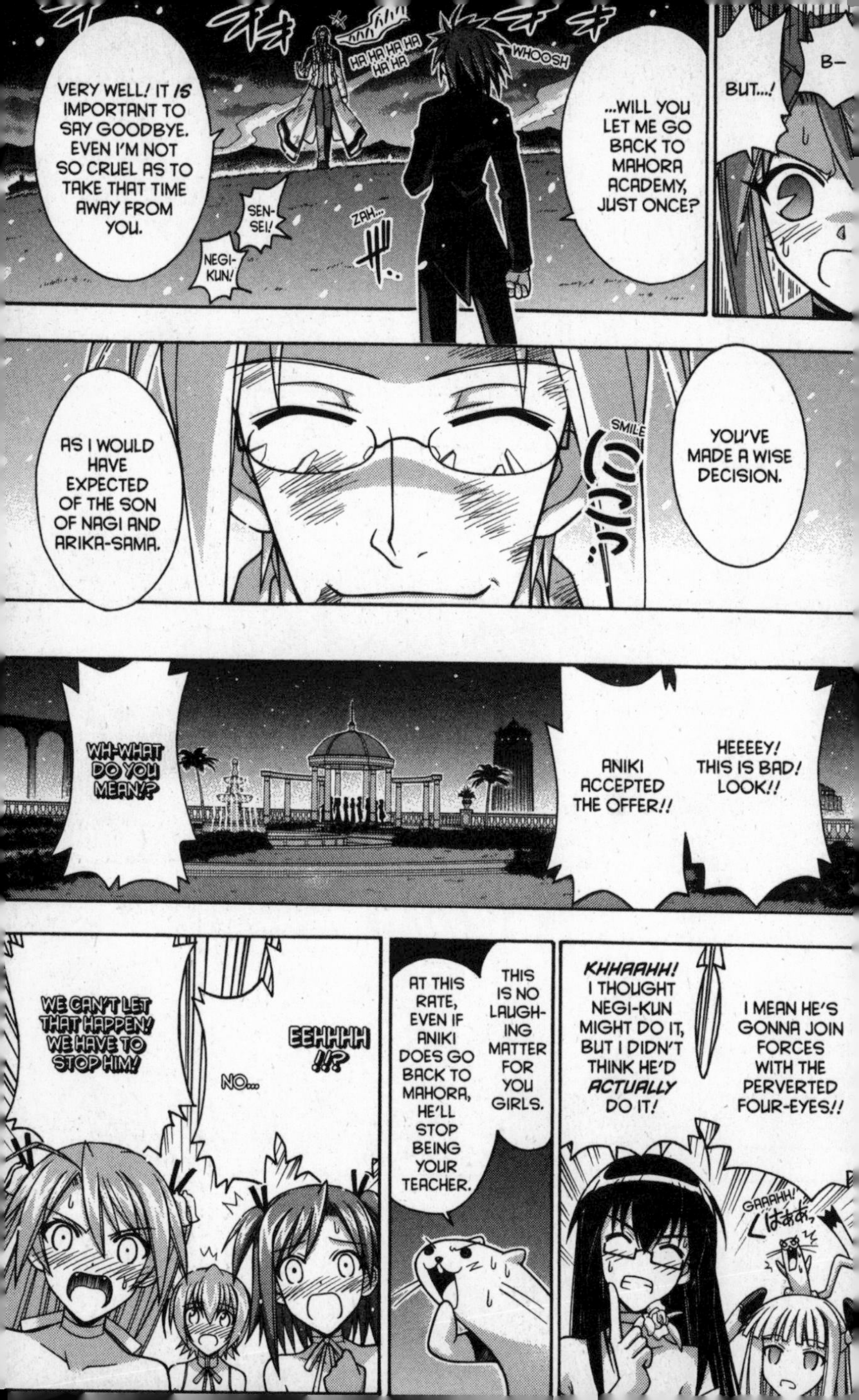
B—
BUT...!
...WILL YOU LET ME GO BACK TO MAHORA ACADEMY, JUST ONCE?
WHOOSH
HA HA HA HA HA HA
VERY WELL! IT *IS* IMPORTANT TO SAY GOODBYE. EVEN I'M NOT SO CRUEL AS TO TAKE THAT TIME AWAY FROM YOU.
SEN-SEI!
ZAH...
NEGI-KUN!
YOU'VE MADE A WISE DECISION.
SMILE
AS I WOULD HAVE EXPECTED OF THE SON OF NAGI AND ARIKA-SAMA.
HEEEEY! THIS IS BAD! LOOK!!
ANIKI ACCEPTED THE OFFER!!
WH-WHAT DO YOU MEAN!?
I MEAN HE'S GONNA JOIN FORCES WITH THE PERVERTED FOUR-EYES!!
KHHAAHH! I THOUGHT NEGI-KUN MIGHT DO IT, BUT I DIDN'T THINK HE'D *ACTUALLY* DO IT!
GAAAHH!
THIS IS NO LAUGH-ING MATTER FOR YOU GIRLS.
AT THIS RATE, EVEN IF ANIKI DOES GO BACK TO MAHORA, HE'LL STOP BEING YOUR TEACHER.
EEHHHH!!?
NO...
WE CAN'T LET THAT HAPPEN! WE HAVE TO STOP HIM!

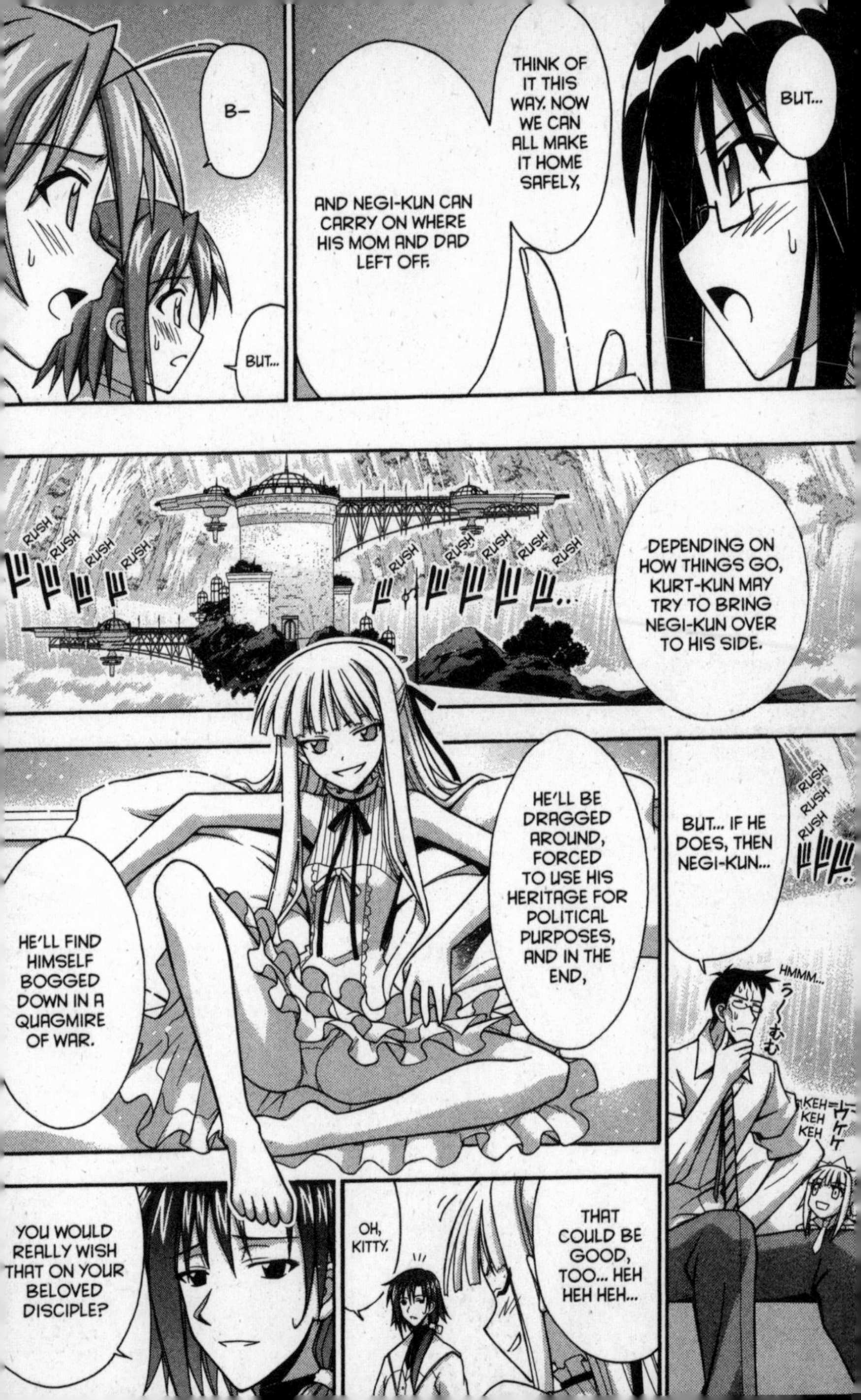
BUT...
THINK OF IT THIS WAY. NOW WE CAN ALL MAKE IT HOME SAFELY,
AND NEGI-KUN CAN CARRY ON WHERE HIS MOM AND DAD LEFT OFF.
B—
BUT...
RUSH RUSH RUSH RUSH RUSH
DEPENDING ON HOW THINGS GO, KURT-KUN MAY TRY TO BRING NEGI-KUN OVER TO HIS SIDE.
RUSH RUSH RUSH RUSH
BUT... IF HE DOES, THEN NEGI-KUN...
RUSH RUSH RUSH
HMMM...
KEH KEH KEH
HE'LL BE DRAGGED AROUND, FORCED TO USE HIS HERITAGE FOR POLITICAL PURPOSES, AND IN THE END,
HE'LL FIND HIMSELF BOGGED DOWN IN A QUAGMIRE OF WAR.
THAT COULD BE GOOD, TOO... HEH HEH HEH...
OH, KITTY.
YOU WOULD REALLY WISH THAT ON YOUR BELOVED DISCIPLE?

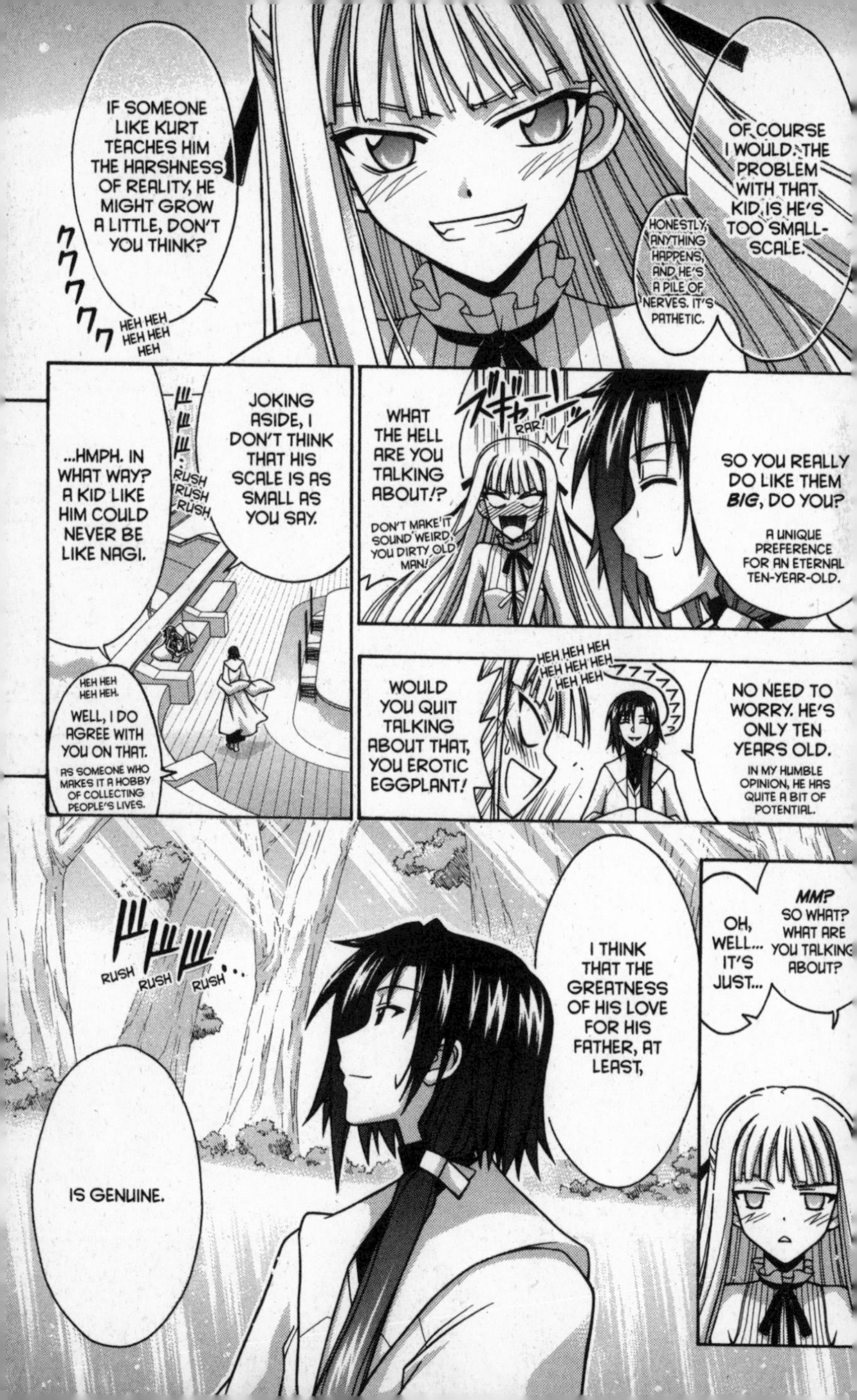
OF COURSE I WOULD. THE PROBLEM WITH THAT KID IS HE'S TOO SMALL-SCALE.
HONESTLY, ANYTHING HAPPENS, AND HE'S A PILE OF NERVES. IT'S PATHETIC.
IF SOMEONE LIKE KURT TEACHES HIM THE HARSHNESS OF REALITY, HE MIGHT GROW A LITTLE, DON'T YOU THINK?
HEH HEH HEH HEH HEH
SO YOU REALLY DO LIKE THEM *BIG*, DO YOU?
A UNIQUE PREFERENCE FOR AN ETERNAL TEN-YEAR-OLD.
RAR!
WHAT THE HELL ARE YOU TALKING ABOUT!?
DON'T MAKE IT SOUND WEIRD, YOU DIRTY OLD MAN!
NO NEED TO WORRY. HE'S ONLY TEN YEARS OLD.
IN MY HUMBLE OPINION, HE HAS QUITE A BIT OF POTENTIAL.
HEH HEH HEH HEH HEH HEH HEH HEH
WOULD YOU QUIT TALKING ABOUT THAT, YOU EROTIC EGGPLANT!
JOKING ASIDE, I DON'T THINK THAT HIS SCALE IS AS SMALL AS YOU SAY.
RUSH RUSH RUSH
...HMPH. IN WHAT WAY? A KID LIKE HIM COULD NEVER BE LIKE NAGI.
HEH HEH HEH HEH.
WELL, I DO AGREE WITH YOU ON THAT.
AS SOMEONE WHO MAKES IT A HOBBY OF COLLECTING PEOPLE'S LIVES.
MM? SO WHAT? WHAT ARE YOU TALKING ABOUT?
OH, WELL... IT'S JUST...
I THINK THAT THE GREATNESS OF HIS LOVE FOR HIS FATHER, AT LEAST,
RUSH RUSH RUSH...
IS GENUINE.

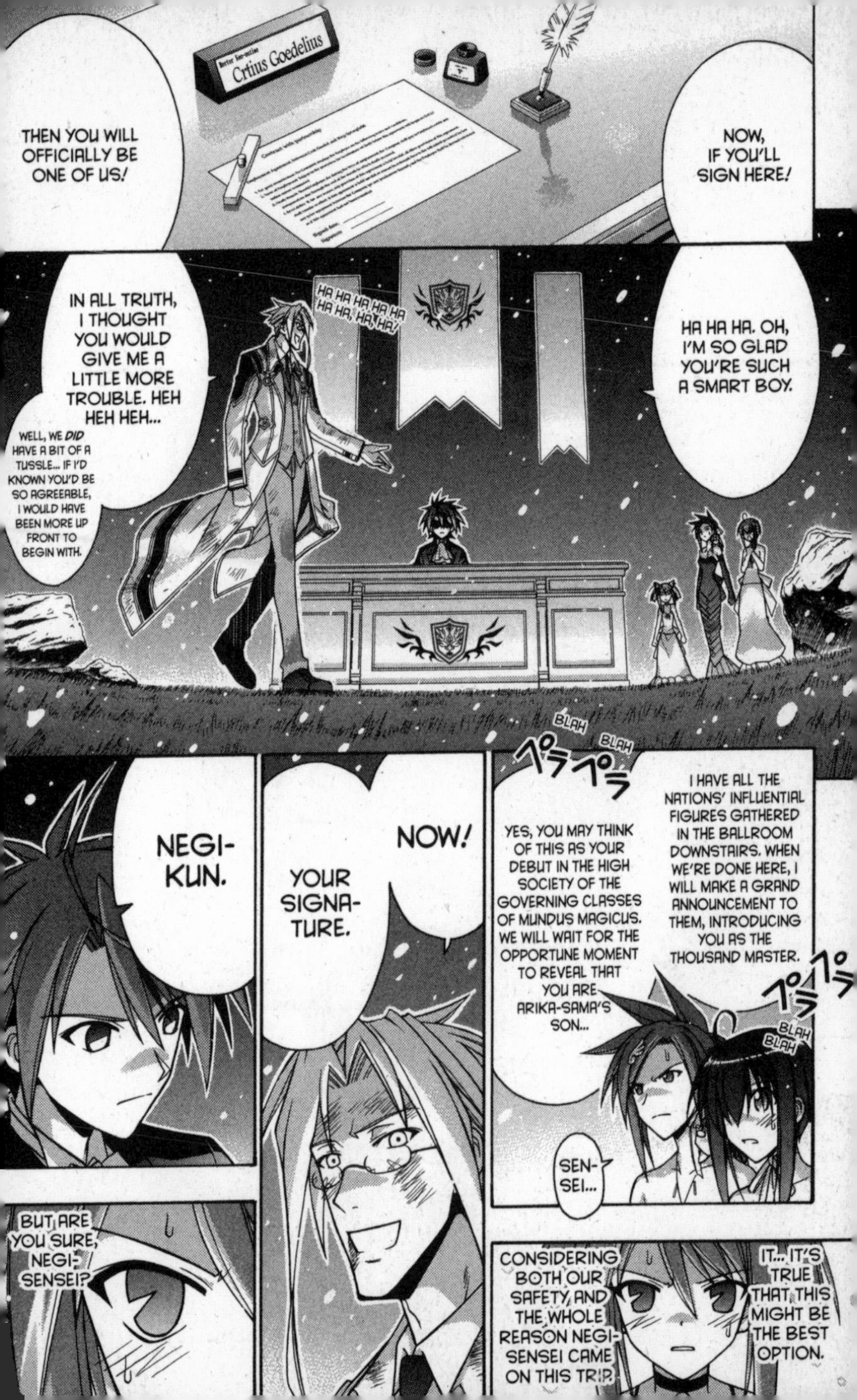
Crtius Goedelius
NOW, IF YOU'LL SIGN HERE!
THEN YOU WILL OFFICIALLY BE ONE OF US!
HA HA HA. OH, I'M SO GLAD YOU'RE SUCH A SMART BOY.
HA HA HA HA HA HA HA, HA, HA!
IN ALL TRUTH, I THOUGHT YOU WOULD GIVE ME A LITTLE MORE TROUBLE. HEH HEH HEH...
WELL, WE *DID* HAVE A BIT OF A TUSSLE... IF I'D KNOWN YOU'D BE SO AGREEABLE, I WOULD HAVE BEEN MORE UP FRONT TO BEGIN WITH.
BLAH BLAH
ペラペラ
I HAVE ALL THE NATIONS' INFLUENTIAL FIGURES GATHERED IN THE BALLROOM DOWNSTAIRS. WHEN WE'RE DONE HERE, I WILL MAKE A GRAND ANNOUNCEMENT TO THEM, INTRODUCING YOU AS THE THOUSAND MASTER.
YES, YOU MAY THINK OF THIS AS YOUR DEBUT IN THE HIGH SOCIETY OF THE GOVERNING CLASSES OF MUNDUS MAGICUS. WE WILL WAIT FOR THE OPPORTUNE MOMENT TO REVEAL THAT YOU ARE ARIKA-SAMA'S SON...
ペラペラ
BLAH BLAH
SEN-SEI...
NOW!
YOUR SIGNA-TURE.
NEGI-KUN.
IT... IT'S TRUE THAT THIS MIGHT BE THE BEST OPTION.
CONSIDERING BOTH OUR SAFETY AND THE WHOLE REASON NEGI-SENSEI CAME ON THIS TRIP.
BUT ARE YOU SURE, NEGI-SENSEI?

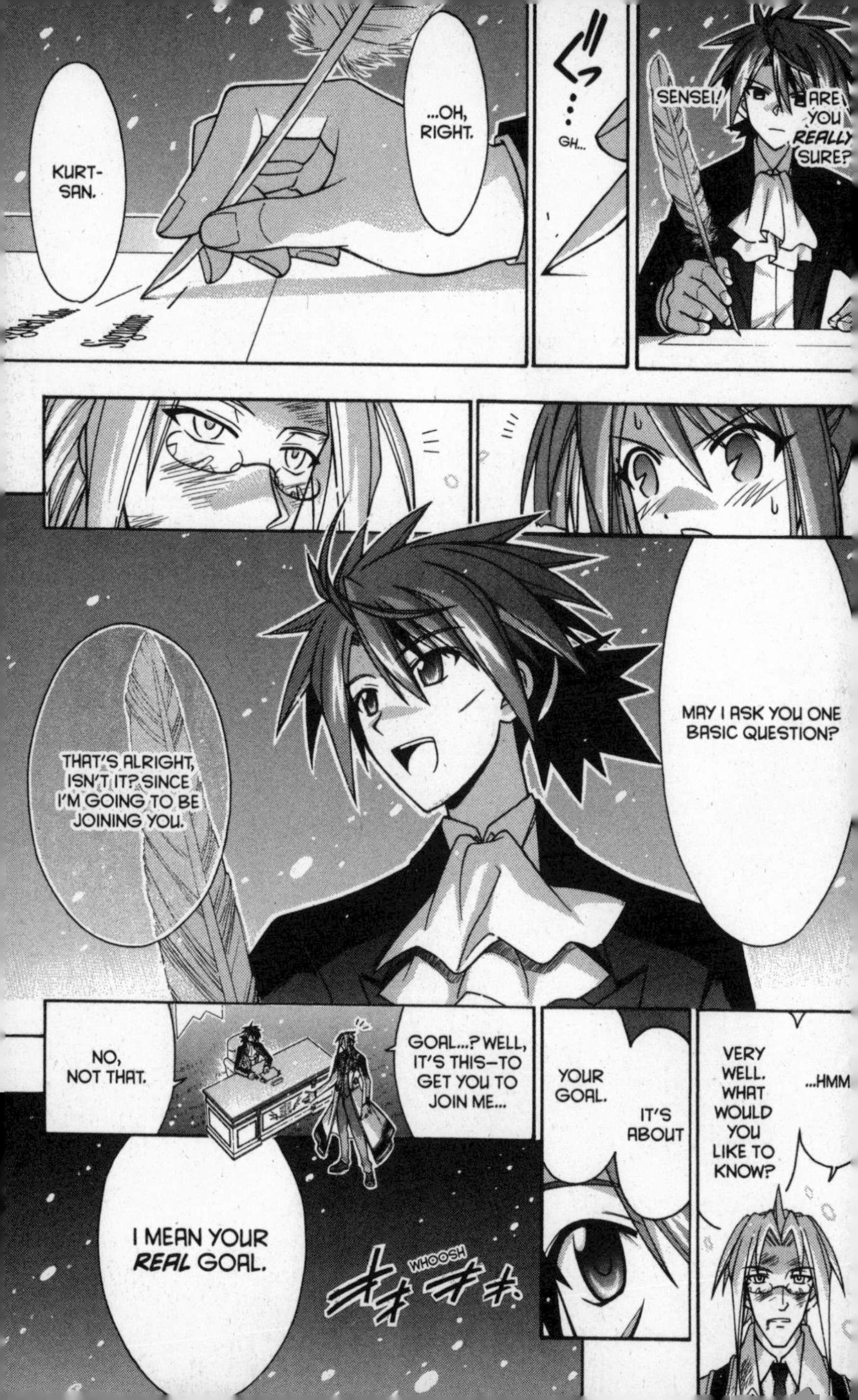
SENSEI!
ARE YOU *REALLY* SURE?
GH...
...OH, RIGHT.
KURT-SAN.
MAY I ASK YOU ONE BASIC QUESTION?
THAT'S ALRIGHT, ISN'T IT? SINCE I'M GOING TO BE JOINING YOU.
...HMM
VERY WELL. WHAT WOULD YOU LIKE TO KNOW?
IT'S ABOUT
YOUR GOAL.
GOAL...? WELL, IT'S THIS—TO GET YOU TO JOIN ME...
NO, NOT THAT.
I MEAN YOUR *REAL* GOAL.
WHOOSH

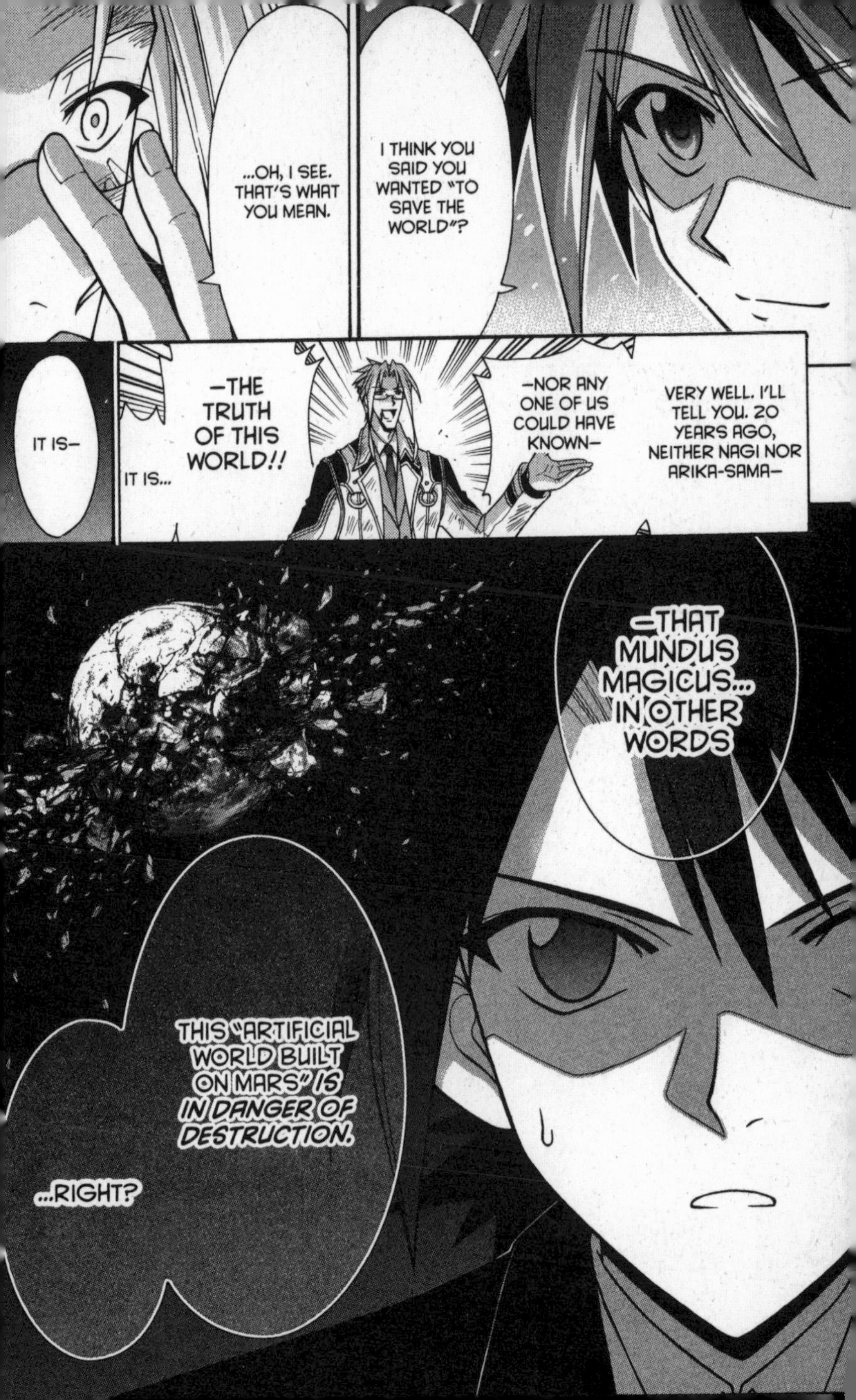
I THINK YOU SAID YOU WANTED "TO SAVE THE WORLD"?
...OH, I SEE. THAT'S WHAT YOU MEAN.
VERY WELL. I'LL TELL YOU. 20 YEARS AGO, NEITHER NAGI NOR ARIKA-SAMA—
—NOR ANY ONE OF US COULD HAVE KNOWN—
—THE TRUTH OF THIS WORLD!!
IT IS...
IT IS—
—THAT MUNDUS MAGICUS... IN OTHER WORDS
THIS "ARTIFICIAL WORLD BUILT ON MARS" IS IN DANGER OF DESTRUCTION.
...RIGHT?

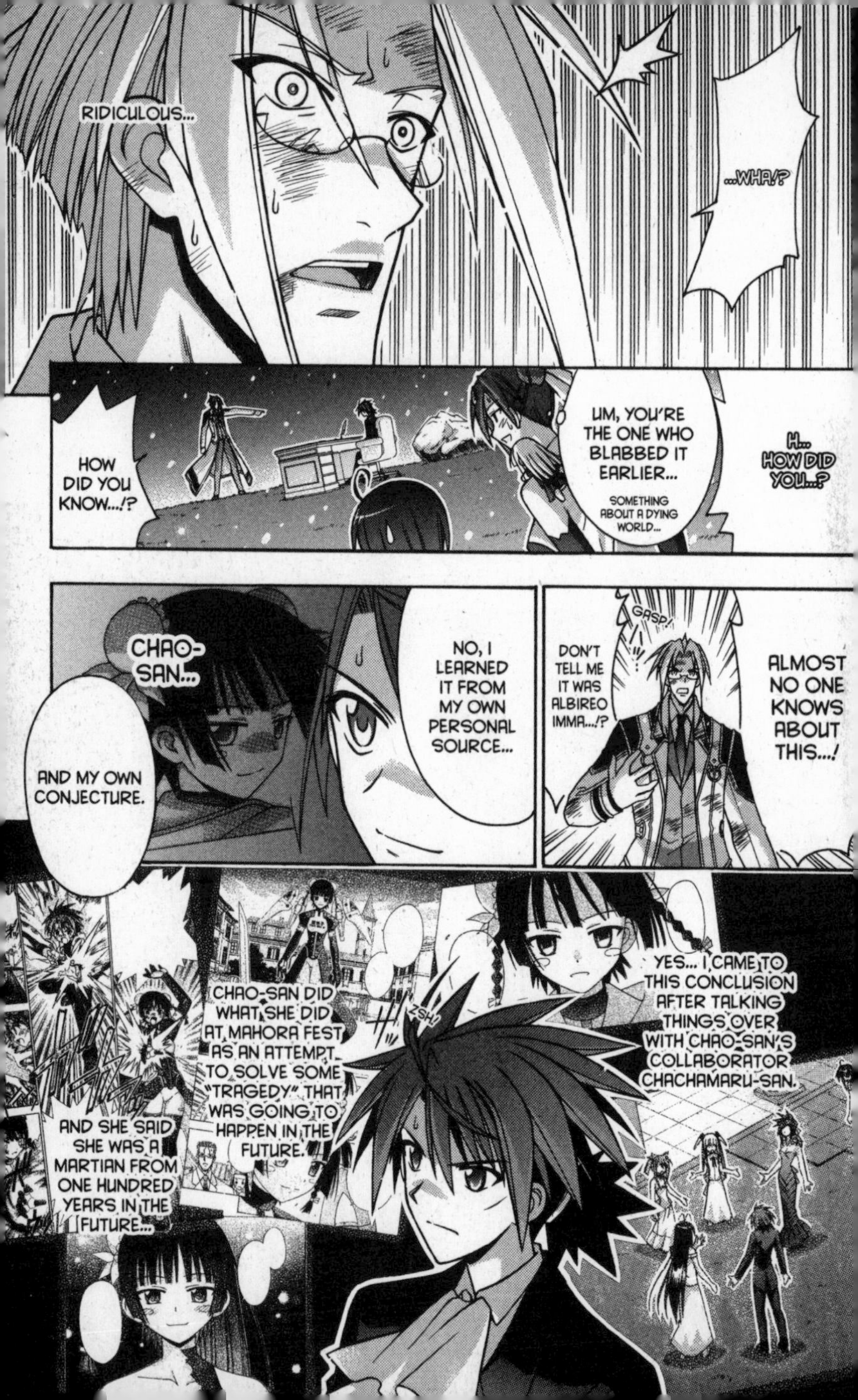
...WHA!?
RIDICULOUS...
H... HOW DID YOU...?
UM, YOU'RE THE ONE WHO BLABBED IT EARLIER...
SOMETHING ABOUT A DYING WORLD...
HOW DID YOU KNOW...!?
ALMOST NO ONE KNOWS ABOUT THIS...!
GASP!
DON'T TELL ME IT WAS ALBIREO IMMA...!?
NO, I LEARNED IT FROM MY OWN PERSONAL SOURCE...
CHAO-SAN...
AND MY OWN CONJECTURE.
YES... I CAME TO THIS CONCLUSION AFTER TALKING THINGS OVER WITH CHAO-SAN'S COLLABORATOR CHACHAMARU-SAN.
ZSH!
CHAO-SAN DID WHAT SHE DID AT MAHORA FEST AS AN ATTEMPT TO SOLVE SOME "TRAGEDY" THAT WAS GOING TO HAPPEN IN THE FUTURE.
AND SHE SAID SHE WAS A MARTIAN FROM ONE HUNDRED YEARS IN THE FUTURE...

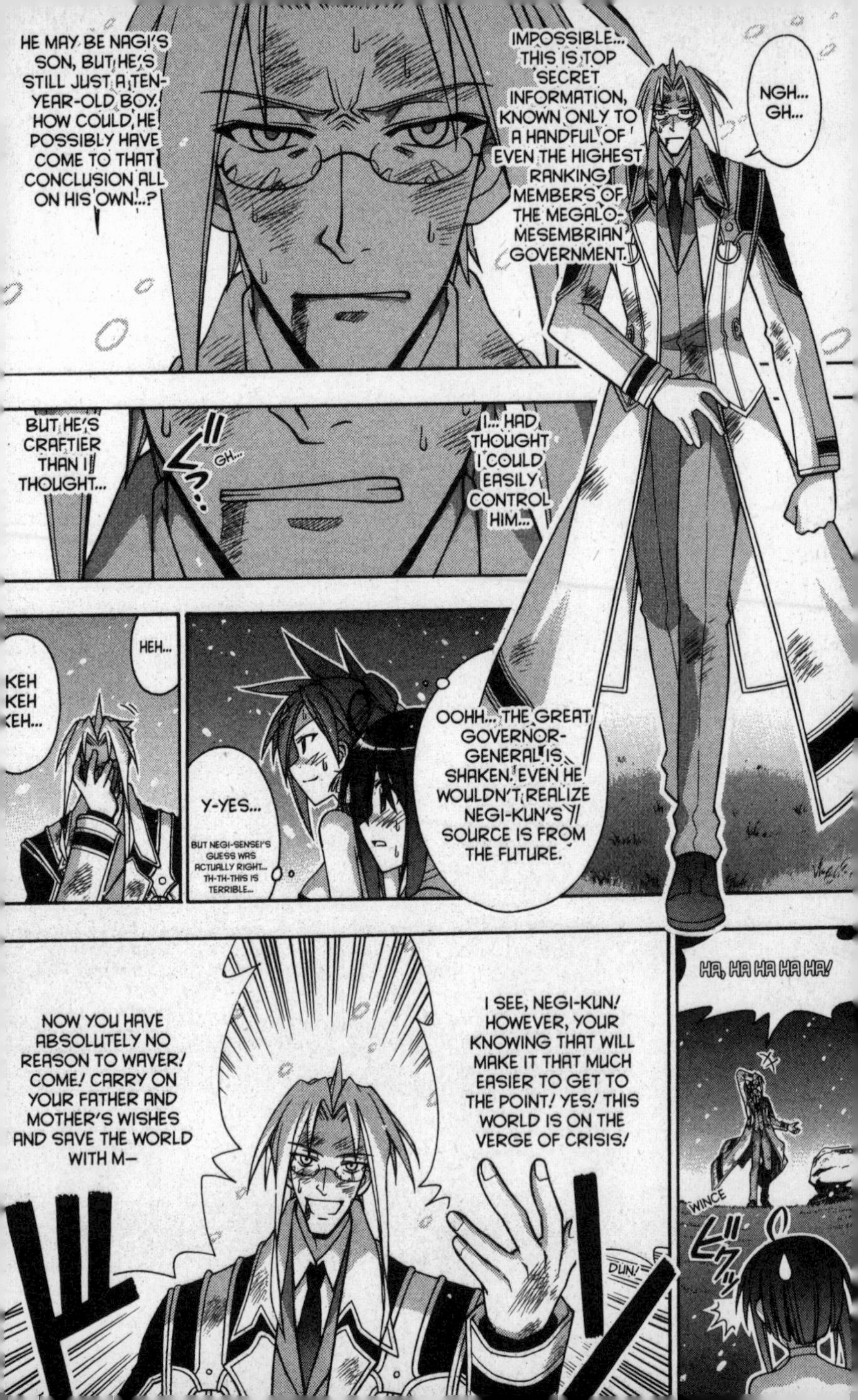
NGH... GH...
IMPOSSIBLE... THIS IS TOP SECRET INFORMATION, KNOWN ONLY TO A HANDFUL OF EVEN THE HIGHEST RANKING MEMBERS OF THE MEGALO-MESEMBRIAN GOVERNMENT.
HE MAY BE NAGI'S SON, BUT HE'S STILL JUST A TEN-YEAR-OLD BOY! HOW COULD HE POSSIBLY HAVE COME TO THAT CONCLUSION ALL ON HIS OWN...?
I... HAD THOUGHT I COULD EASILY CONTROL HIM...
GH...
BUT HE'S CRAFTIER THAN I THOUGHT...
OOHH... THE GREAT GOVERNOR-GENERAL IS SHAKEN. EVEN HE WOULDN'T REALIZE NEGI-KUN'S SOURCE IS FROM THE FUTURE.
Y-YES...
BUT NEGI-SENSEI'S GUESS WAS ACTUALLY RIGHT... TH-TH-THIS IS TERRIBLE...
HEH...
KEH KEH KEH...
HA, HA HA HA HA!
WINCE
I SEE, NEGI-KUN! HOWEVER, YOUR KNOWING THAT WILL MAKE IT THAT MUCH EASIER TO GET TO THE POINT! YES! THIS WORLD IS ON THE VERGE OF CRISIS!
NOW YOU HAVE ABSOLUTELY NO REASON TO WAVER! COME! CARRY ON YOUR FATHER AND MOTHER'S WISHES AND SAVE THE WORLD WITH M—
DUN!

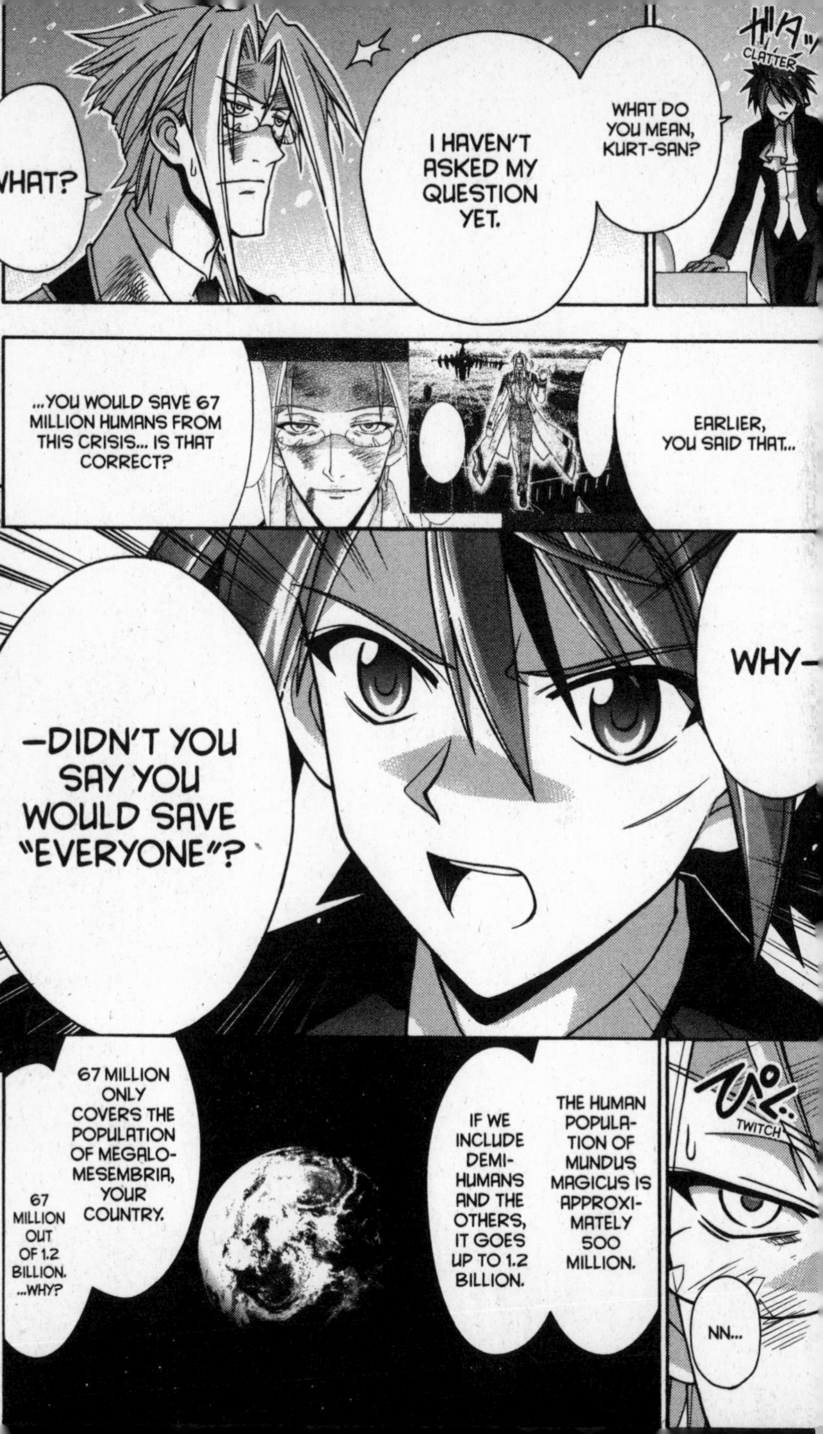
ガタッ
CLATTER
WHAT DO YOU MEAN, KURT-SAN?
I HAVEN'T ASKED MY QUESTION YET.
WHAT?
EARLIER, YOU SAID THAT...
...YOU WOULD SAVE 67 MILLION HUMANS FROM THIS CRISIS... IS THAT CORRECT?
WHY-
-DIDN'T YOU SAY YOU WOULD SAVE "EVERYONE"?
ぴくっ
TWITCH
NN...
THE HUMAN POPULATION OF MUNDUS MAGICUS IS APPROXIMATELY 500 MILLION.
IF WE INCLUDE DEMI-HUMANS AND THE OTHERS, IT GOES UP TO 1.2 BILLION.
67 MILLION ONLY COVERS THE POPULATION OF MEGALO-MESEMBRIA, YOUR COUNTRY.
67 MILLION OUT OF 1.2 BILLION. ...WHY?

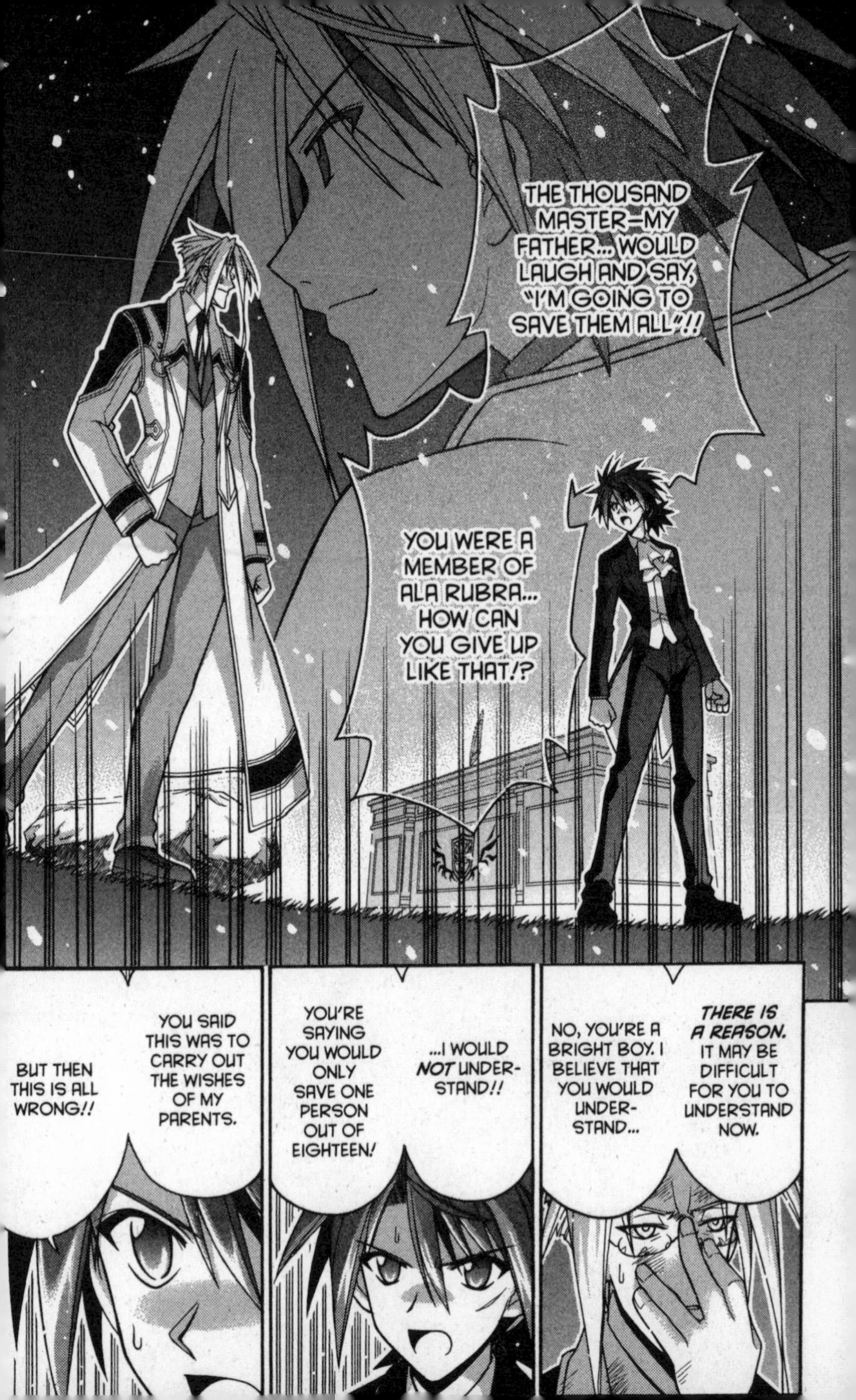
THE THOUSAND MASTER—MY FATHER... WOULD LAUGH AND SAY, "I'M GOING TO SAVE THEM ALL"!!
YOU WERE A MEMBER OF ALA RUBRA... HOW CAN YOU GIVE UP LIKE THAT!?
THERE IS A REASON. IT MAY BE DIFFICULT FOR YOU TO UNDERSTAND NOW.
NO, YOU'RE A BRIGHT BOY. I BELIEVE THAT YOU WOULD UNDER-STAND...
...I WOULD *NOT* UNDER-STAND!!
YOU'RE SAYING YOU WOULD ONLY SAVE ONE PERSON OUT OF EIGHTEEN!
YOU SAID THIS WAS TO CARRY OUT THE WISHES OF MY PARENTS.
BUT THEN THIS IS ALL WRONG!!

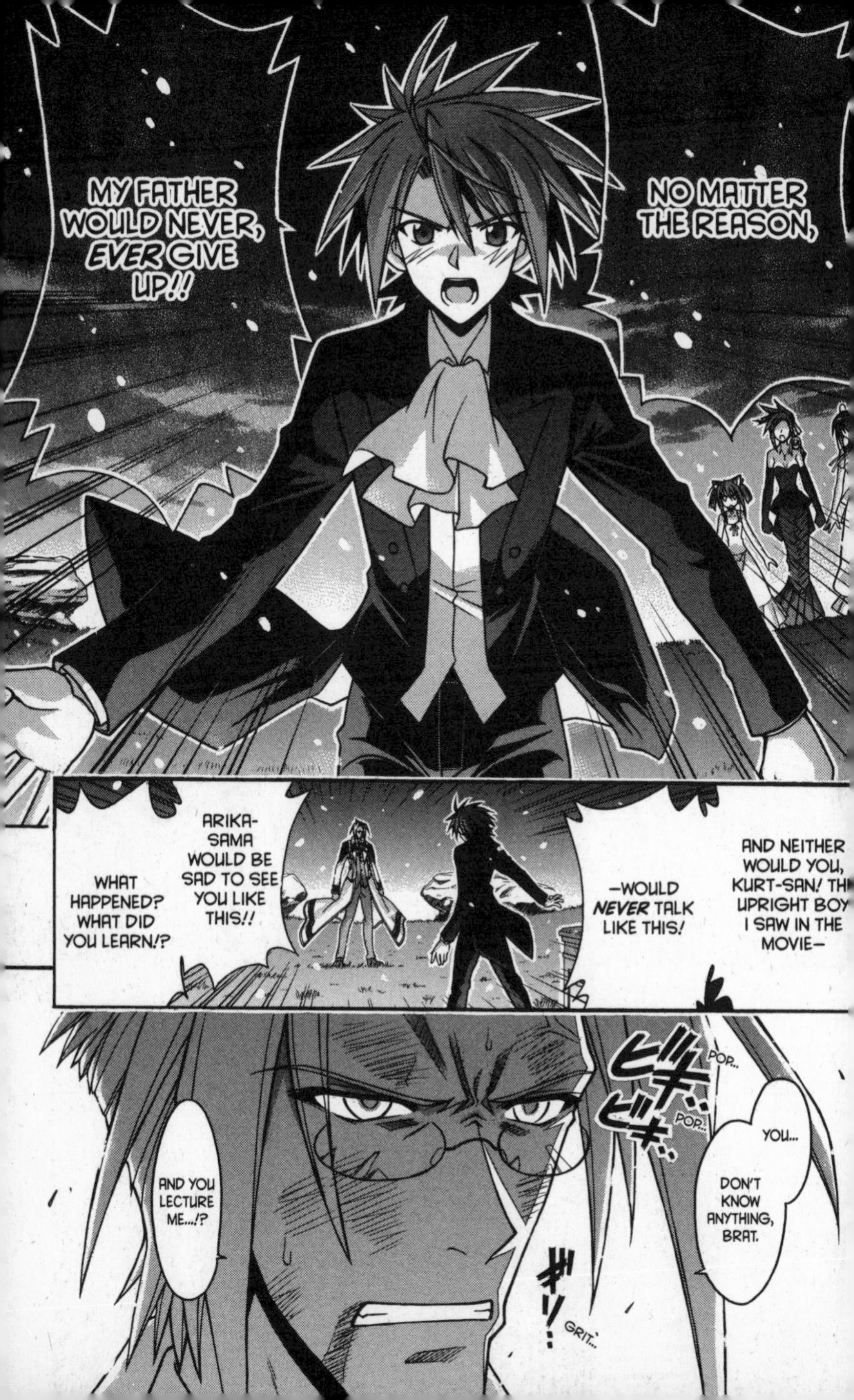
NO MATTER THE REASON,
MY FATHER WOULD NEVER, EVER GIVE UP!!
AND NEITHER WOULD YOU, KURT-SAN! TH UPRIGHT BOY I SAW IN THE MOVIE—
—WOULD NEVER TALK LIKE THIS!
ARIKA-SAMA WOULD BE SAD TO SEE YOU LIKE THIS!!
WHAT HAPPENED? WHAT DID YOU LEARN!?
POP...
POP...
YOU...
DON'T KNOW ANYTHING, BRAT.
GRIT...
AND YOU LECTURE ME...!?

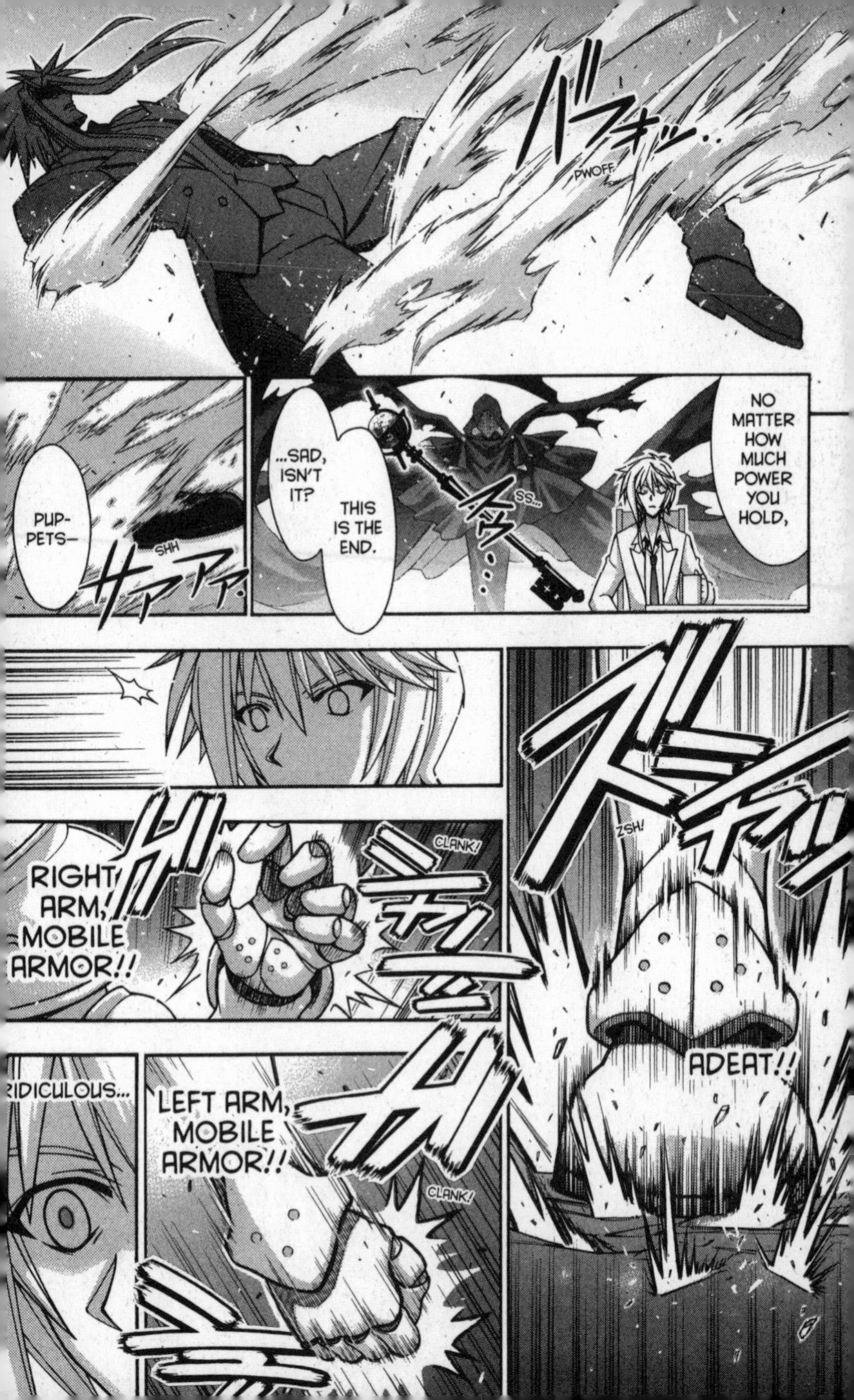
PWOFF
NO MATTER HOW MUCH POWER YOU HOLD,
SS...
...SAD, ISN'T IT?
THIS IS THE END.
PUP-PETS—
SHH
ZSH!
ADEAT!!
CLANK!
RIGHT ARM, MOBILE ARMOR!!
LEFT ARM, MOBILE ARMOR!!
CLANK!
RIDICULOUS...

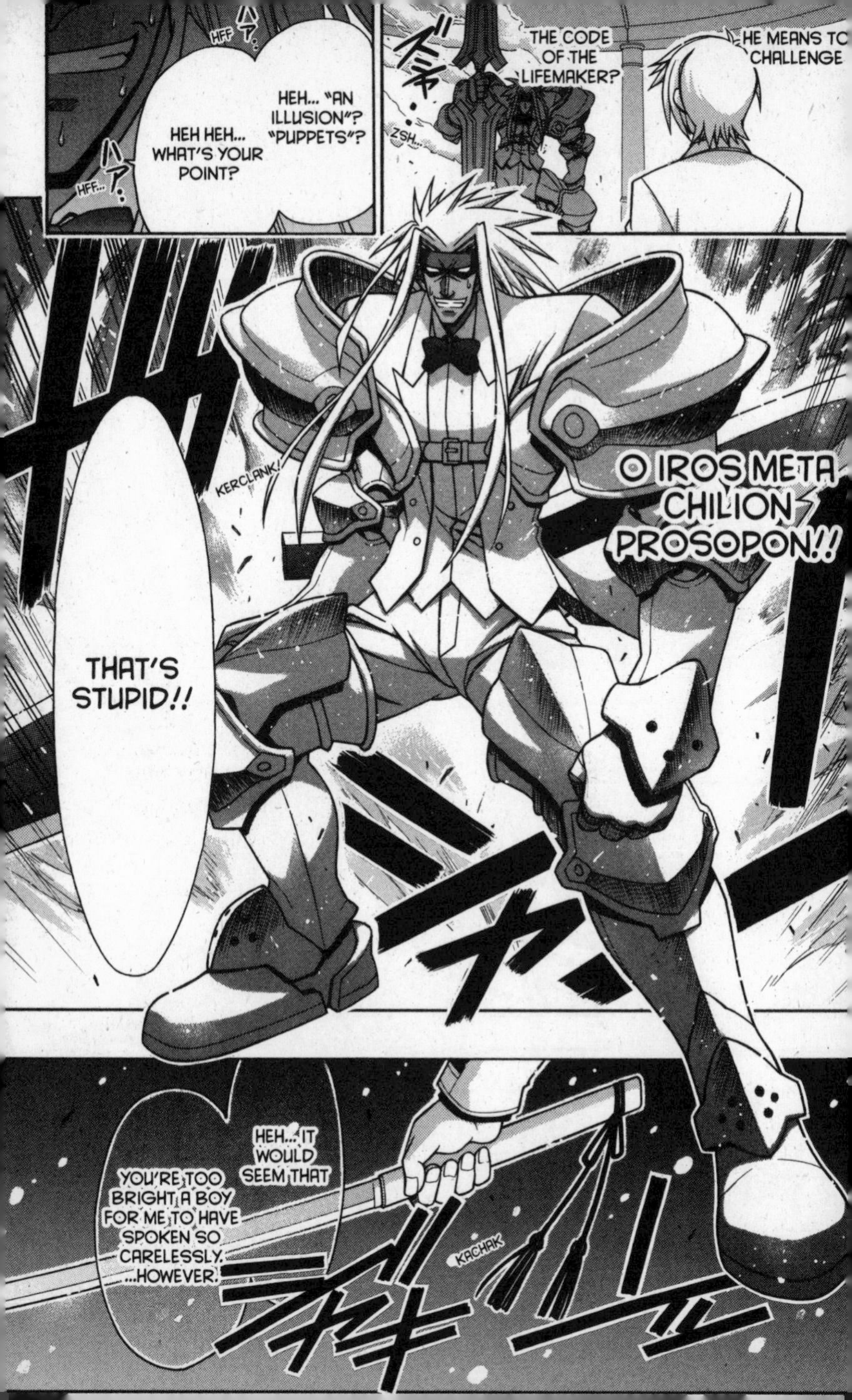
HE MEANS TO CHALLENGE
THE CODE OF THE LIFEMAKER?
ZSH...
HFF
HEH... "AN ILLUSION"? "PUPPETS"?
HEH HEH... WHAT'S YOUR POINT?
HFF...
O IROS META CHILION PROSOPON!!
KERCLANK!
THAT'S STUPID!!
KACHAK
HEH... IT WOULD SEEM THAT YOU'RE TOO BRIGHT A BOY FOR ME TO HAVE SPOKEN SO CARELESSLY. ...HOWEVER.

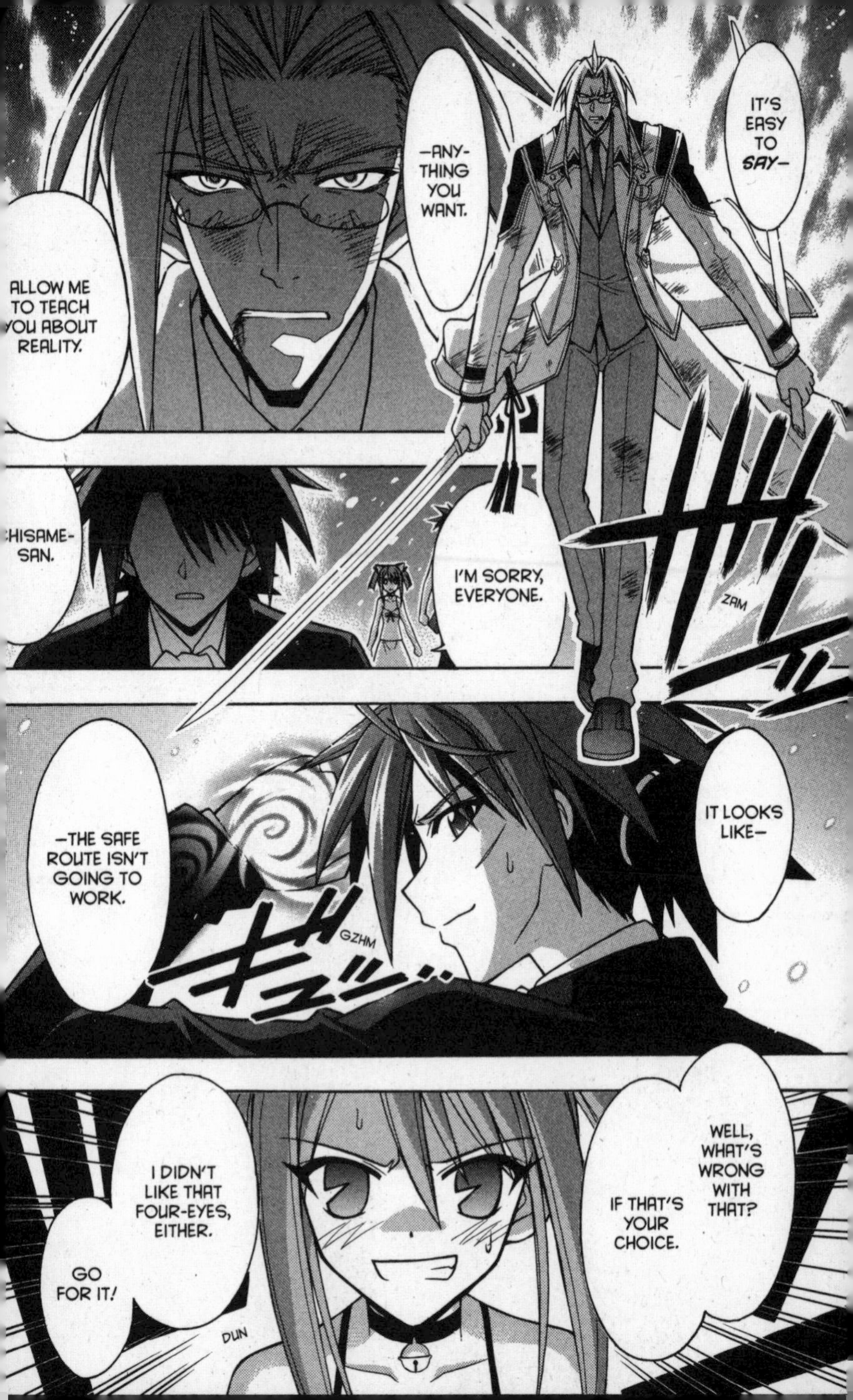

IT'S EASY TO SAY—
—ANYTHING YOU WANT.
ALLOW ME TO TEACH YOU ABOUT REALITY.
ZAM
I'M SORRY, EVERYONE.
CHISAME-SAN.
IT LOOKS LIKE—
—THE SAFE ROUTE ISN'T GOING TO WORK.
GZHM
WELL, WHAT'S WRONG WITH THAT?
IF THAT'S YOUR CHOICE.
I DIDN'T LIKE THAT FOUR-EYES, EITHER.
GO FOR IT!
DUN

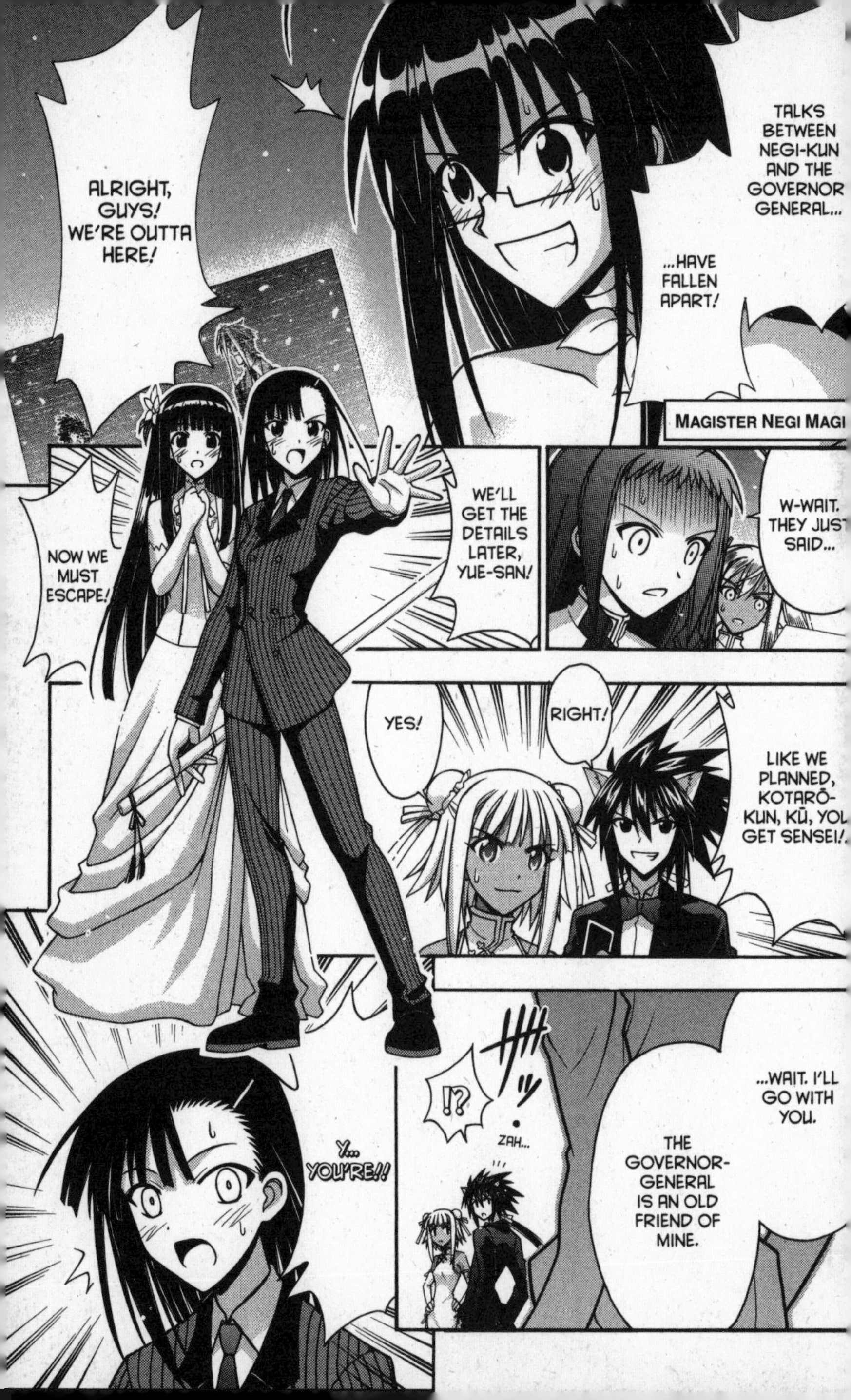
TALKS BETWEEN NEGI-KUN AND THE GOVERNOR GENERAL...
...HAVE FALLEN APART!
ALRIGHT, GUYS! WE'RE OUTTA HERE!
W-WAIT. THEY JUST SAID...
WE'LL GET THE DETAILS LATER, YUE-SAN!
NOW WE MUST ESCAPE!
LIKE WE PLANNED, KOTARŌ-KUN, KŪ, YOU GET SENSEI!
RIGHT!
YES!
...WAIT. I'LL GO WITH YOU.
THE GOVERNOR-GENERAL IS AN OLD FRIEND OF MINE.
!?
ZAH...
Y... YOU'RE!!

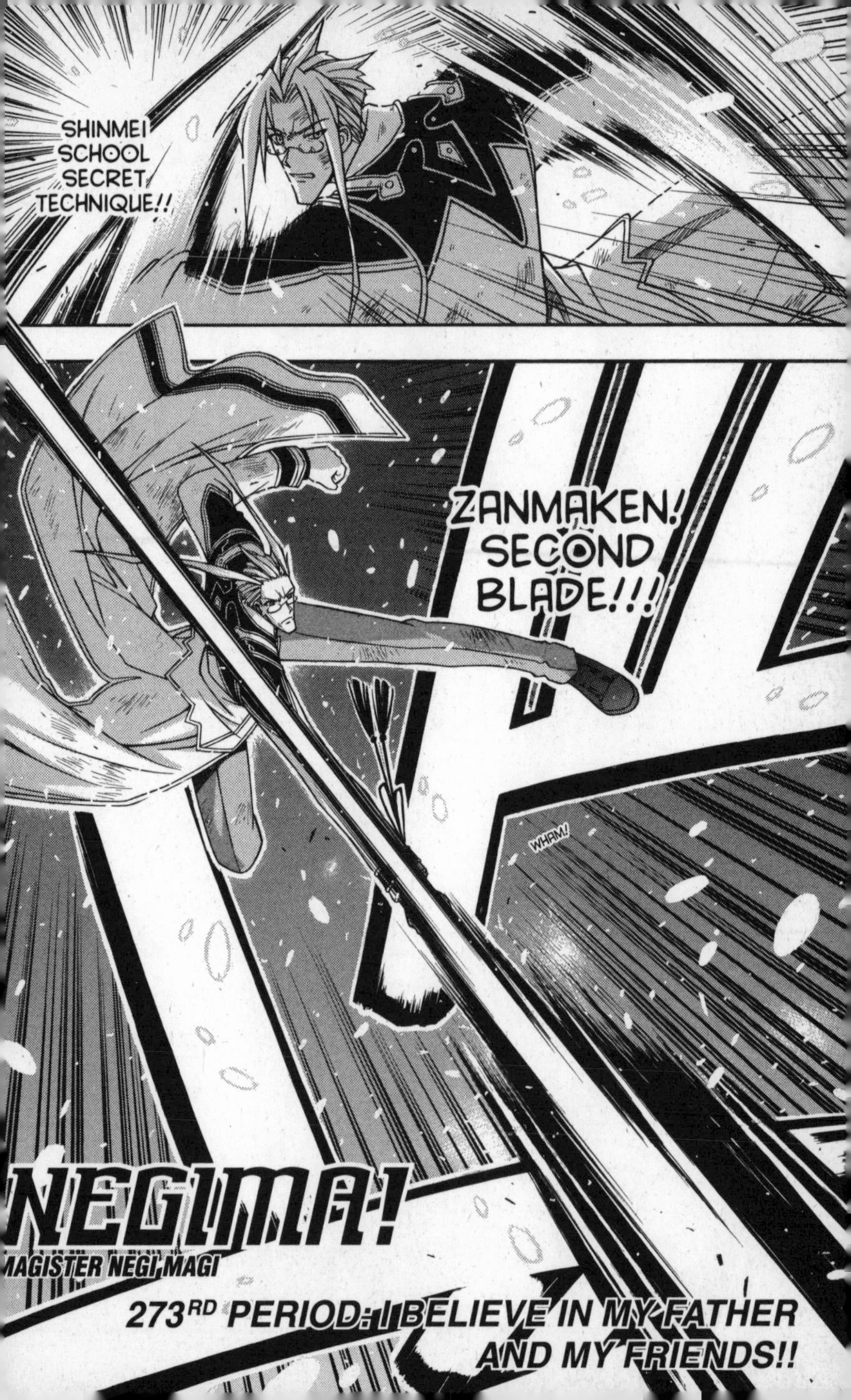
SHINMEI SCHOOL SECRET TECHNIQUE!!
ZANMAKEN! SECOND BLADE!!!
WHAM!
NEGIMA!
MAGISTER NEGI MAGI
273RD PERIOD: I BELIEVE IN MY FATHER AND MY FRIENDS!!

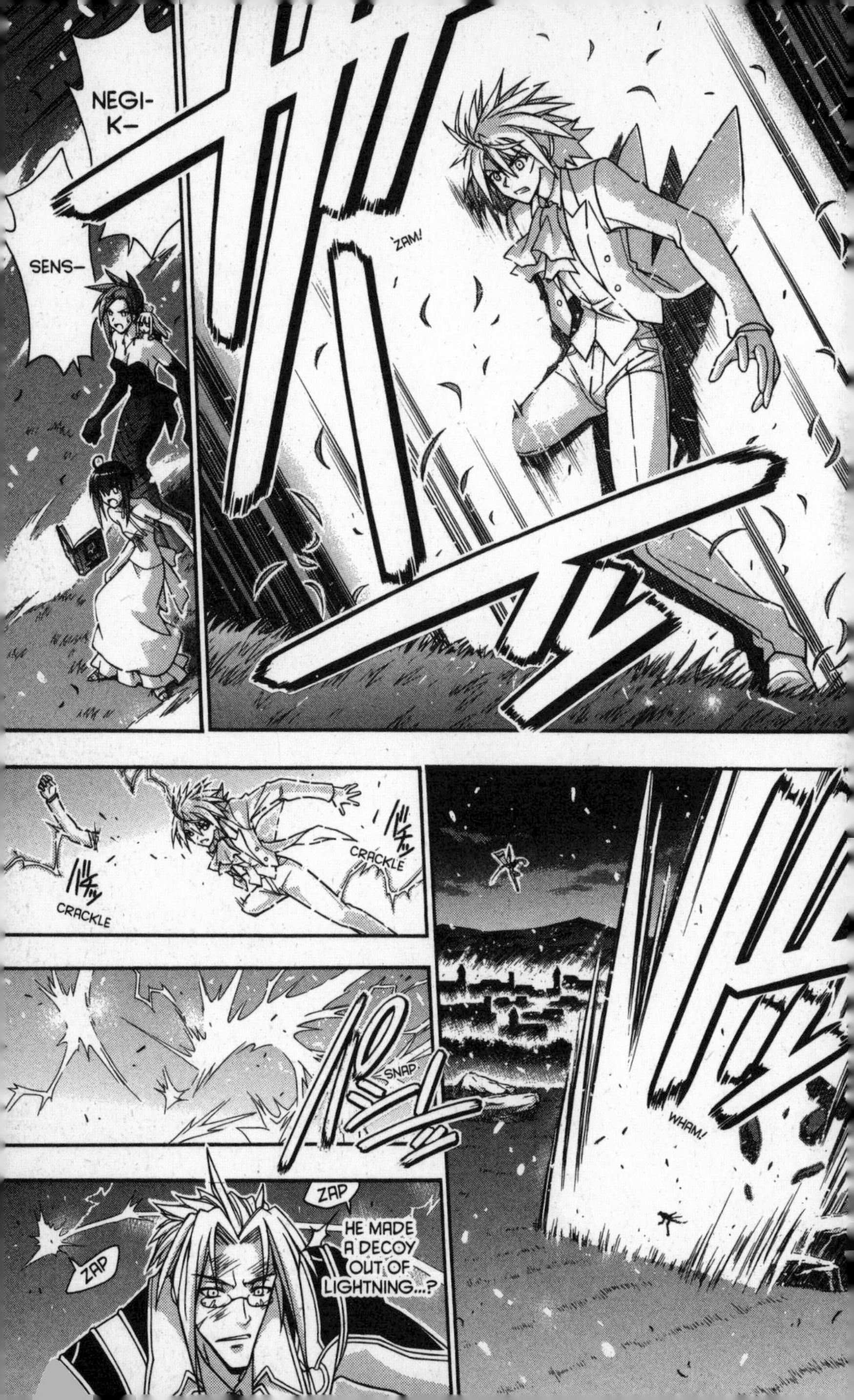
ZAM!
NEGI-K–
SENS–
WHAM!
CRACKLE
CRACKLE
SNAP
ZAP
HE MADE A DECOY OUT OF LIGHTNING...?
ZAP

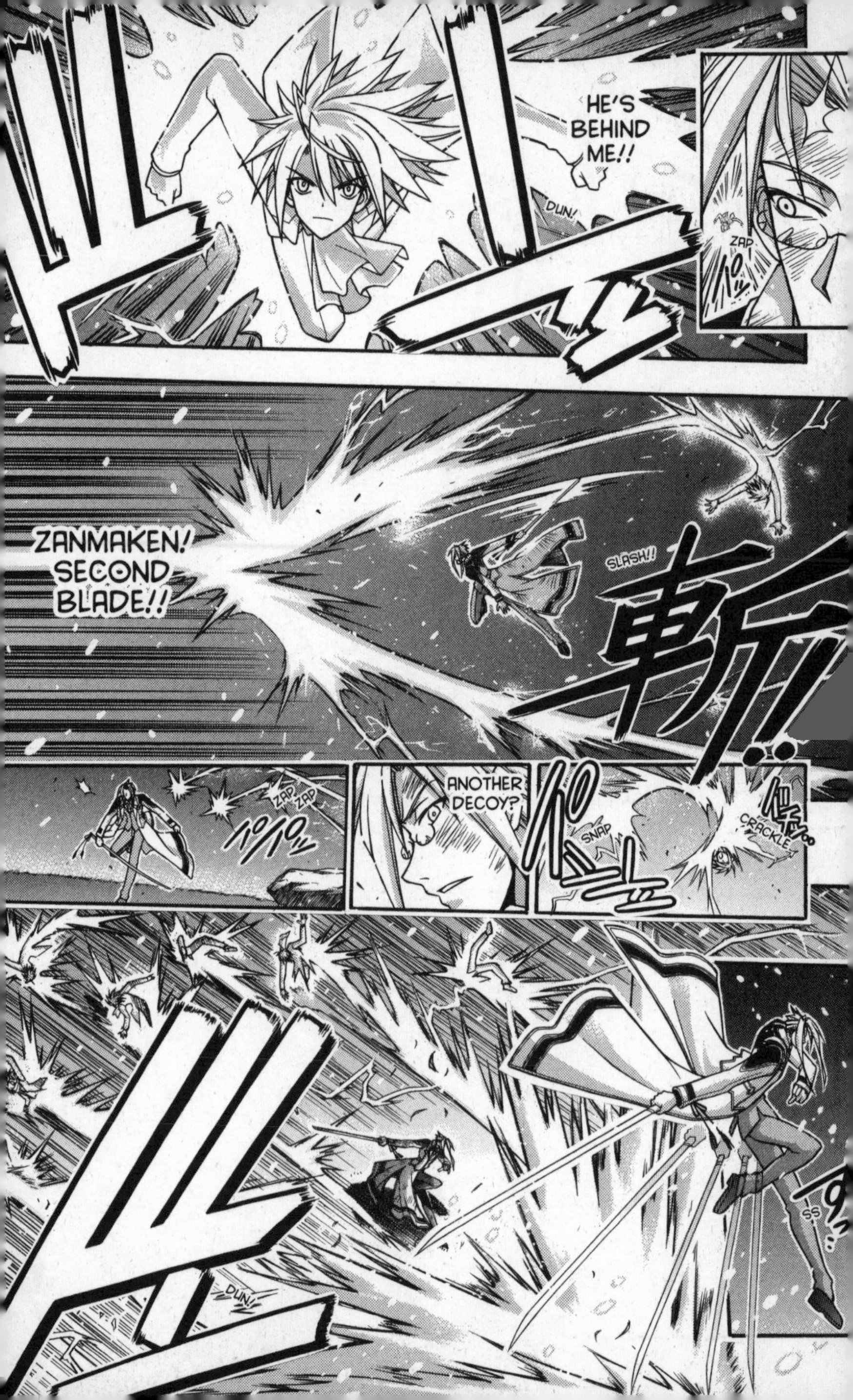
ZAP
HE'S BEHIND ME!!
DUN!
SLASH!!
ZANMAKEN! SECOND BLADE!!
CRACKLE
SNAP
ANOTHER DECOY?
ZAP ZAP
SS
DUN!

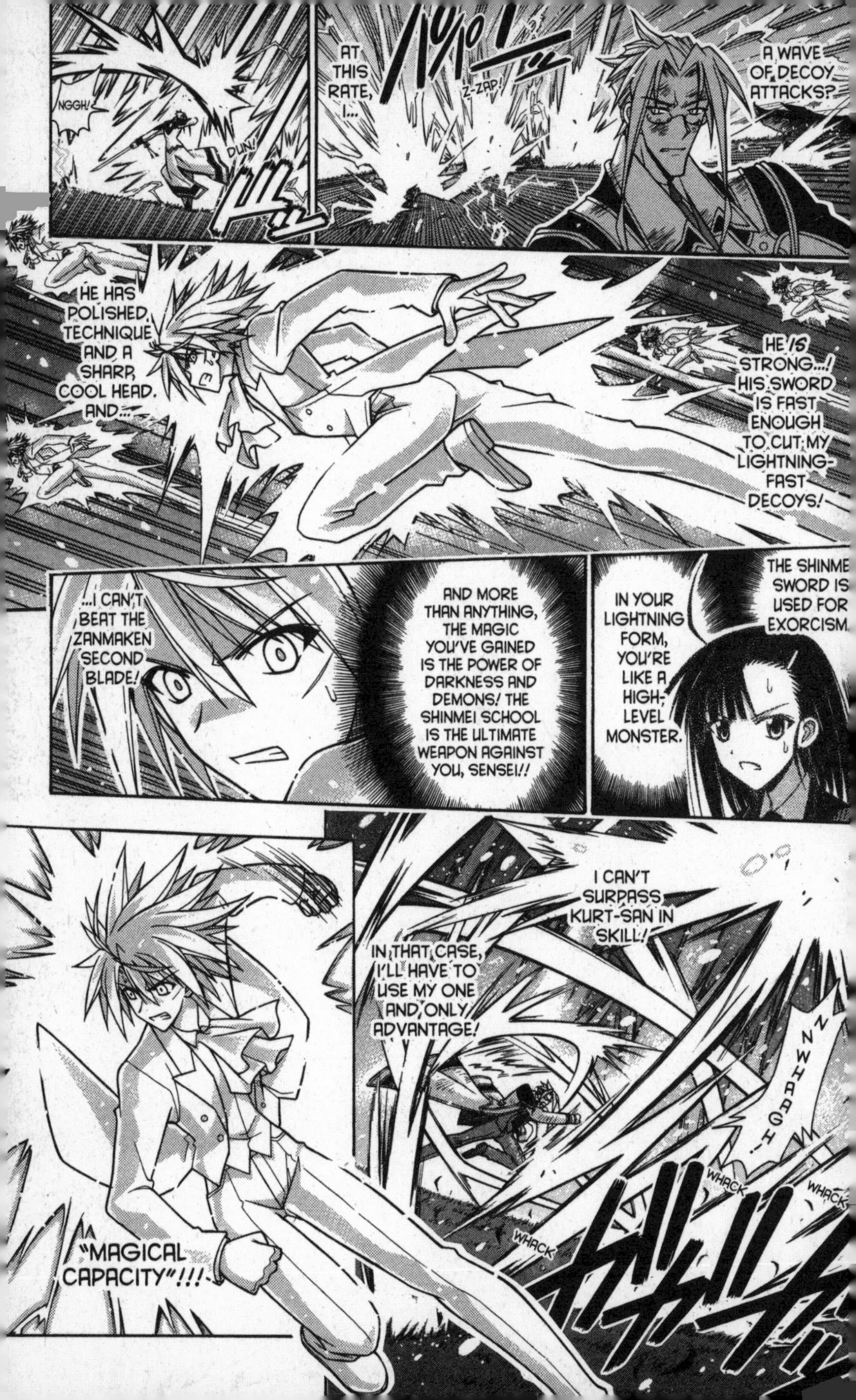
A WAVE OF DECOY ATTACKS?
AT THIS RATE, I...
Z-ZAP!
NGGH!
DUN!
HE IS STRONG...! HIS SWORD IS FAST ENOUGH TO CUT MY LIGHTNING-FAST DECOYS!
HE HAS POLISHED TECHNIQUE AND A SHARP, COOL HEAD. AND...
THE SHINME SWORD IS USED FOR EXORCISM.
IN YOUR LIGHTNING FORM, YOU'RE LIKE A HIGH-LEVEL MONSTER.
AND MORE THAN ANYTHING, THE MAGIC YOU'VE GAINED IS THE POWER OF DARKNESS AND DEMONS! THE SHINMEI SCHOOL IS THE ULTIMATE WEAPON AGAINST YOU, SENSEI!!
...I CAN'T BEAT THE ZANMAKEN SECOND BLADE!
I CAN'T SURPASS KURT-SAN IN SKILL!
IN THAT CASE, I'LL HAVE TO USE MY ONE AND ONLY ADVANTAGE!
NNWHAAGH...!
WHACK
WHACK
WHACK
"MAGICAL CAPACITY"!!!

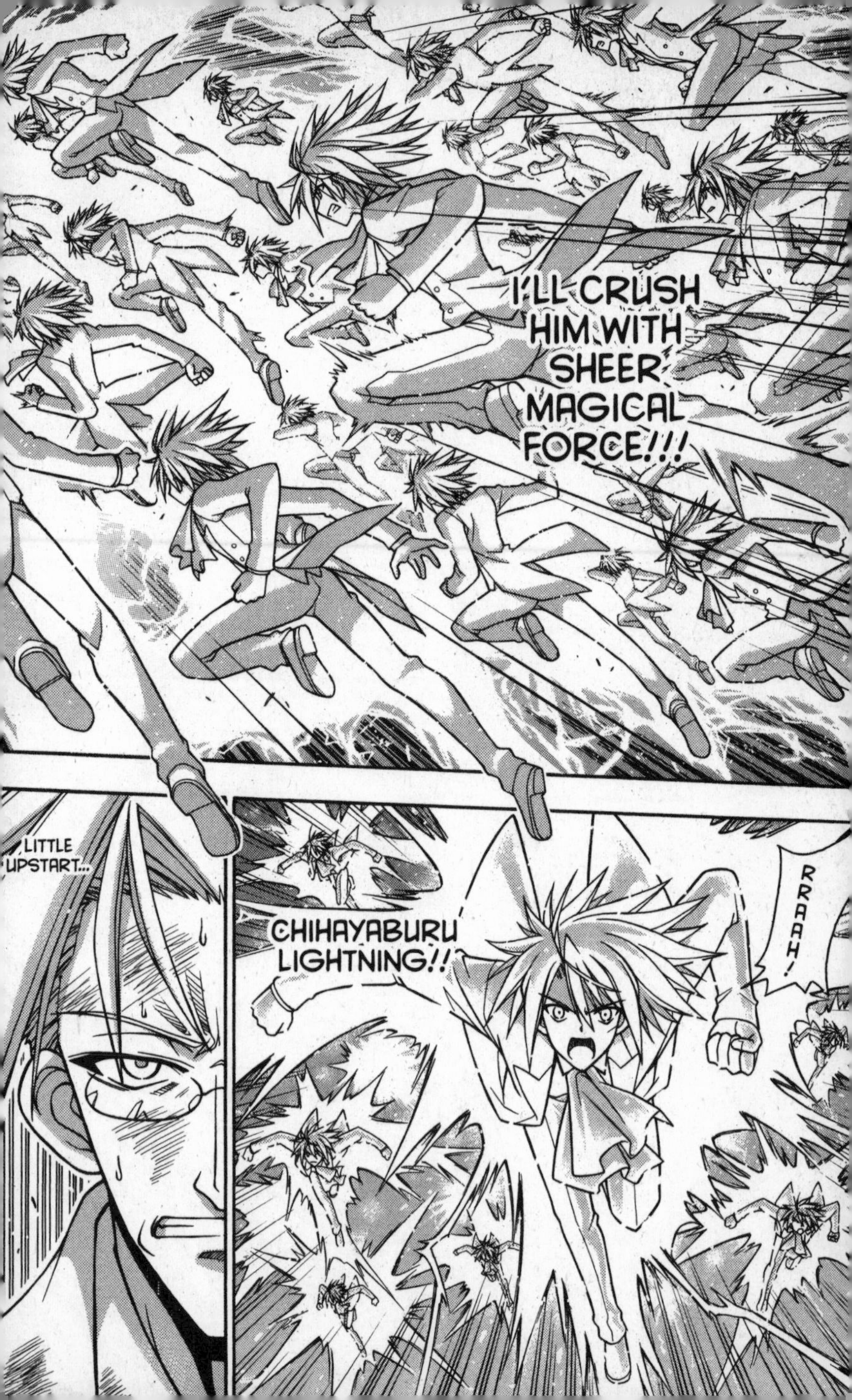
I'LL CRUSH HIM WITH SHEER MAGICAL FORCE!!!
RRAAH!
CHIHAYABURU LIGHTNING!!
LITTLE UPSTART...

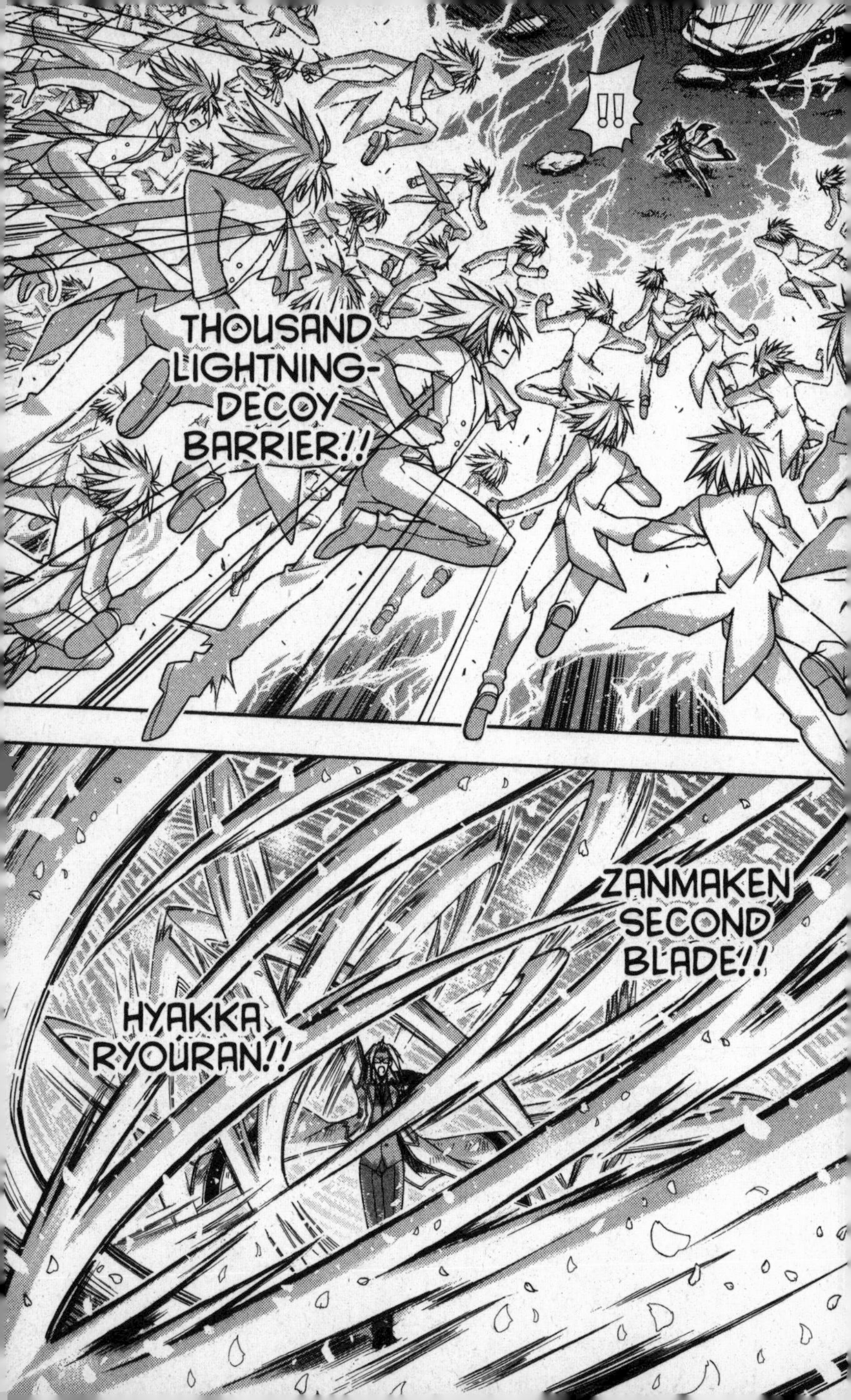
!!
THOUSAND LIGHTNING-DECOY BARRIER!!
ZANMAKEN SECOND BLADE!!
HYAKKA RYOURAN!!

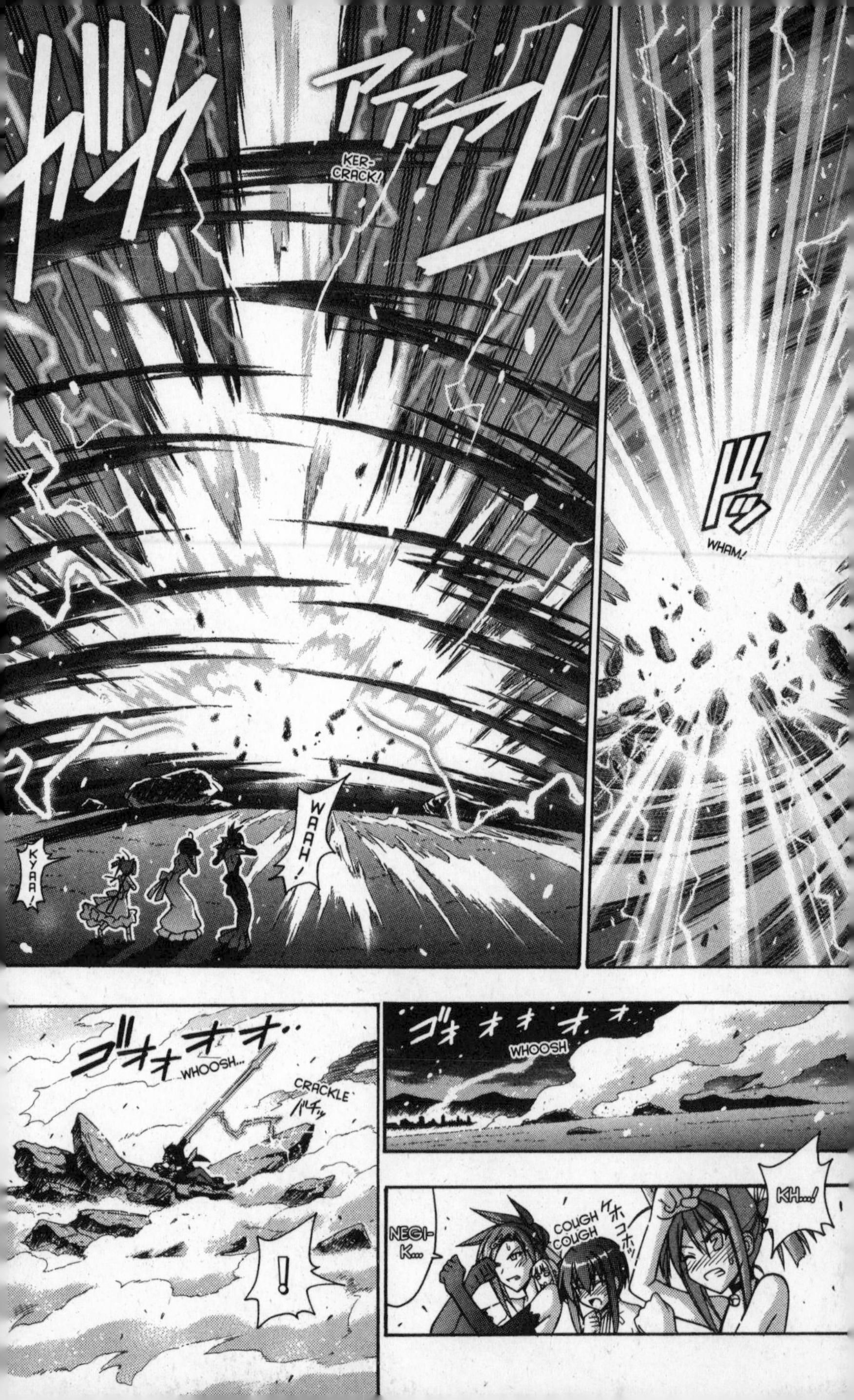
ドッ
WHAM!
KER-CRACK!
WAAH!
KYAA!
ゴオオオオ
WHOOSH
KH...!
ケホコホッ
COUGH COUGH
NEGI-K...
ゴオオオォ
WHOOSH...
CRACKLE
バチッ
!

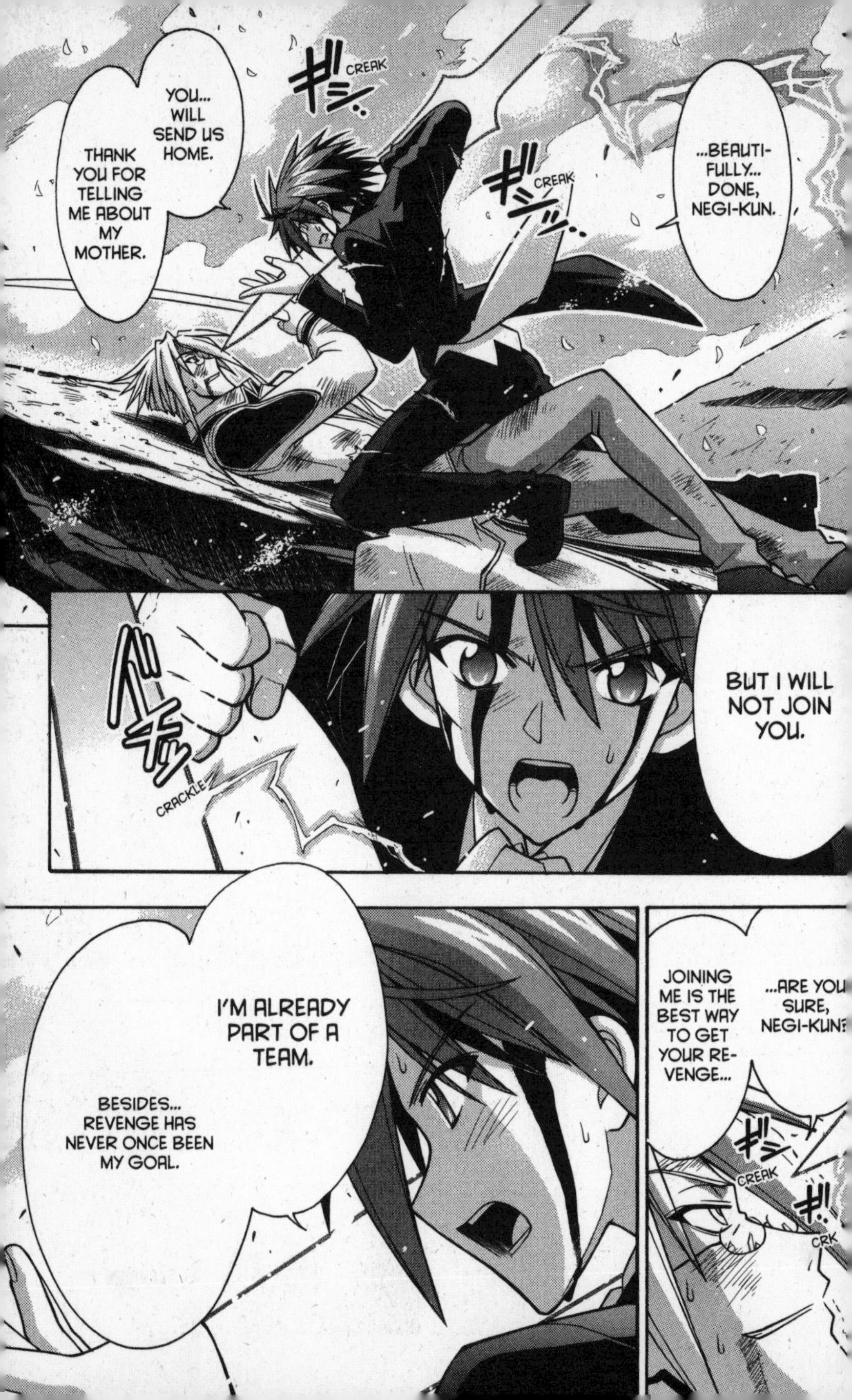
...BEAUTI-FULLY... DONE, NEGI-KUN.
CREAK
CREAK
YOU... WILL SEND US HOME.
THANK YOU FOR TELLING ME ABOUT MY MOTHER.
BUT I WILL NOT JOIN YOU.
CRACKLE
...ARE YOU SURE, NEGI-KUN?
JOINING ME IS THE BEST WAY TO GET YOUR RE-VENGE...
CREAK
CRK
I'M ALREADY PART OF A TEAM.
BESIDES... REVENGE HAS NEVER ONCE BEEN MY GOAL.

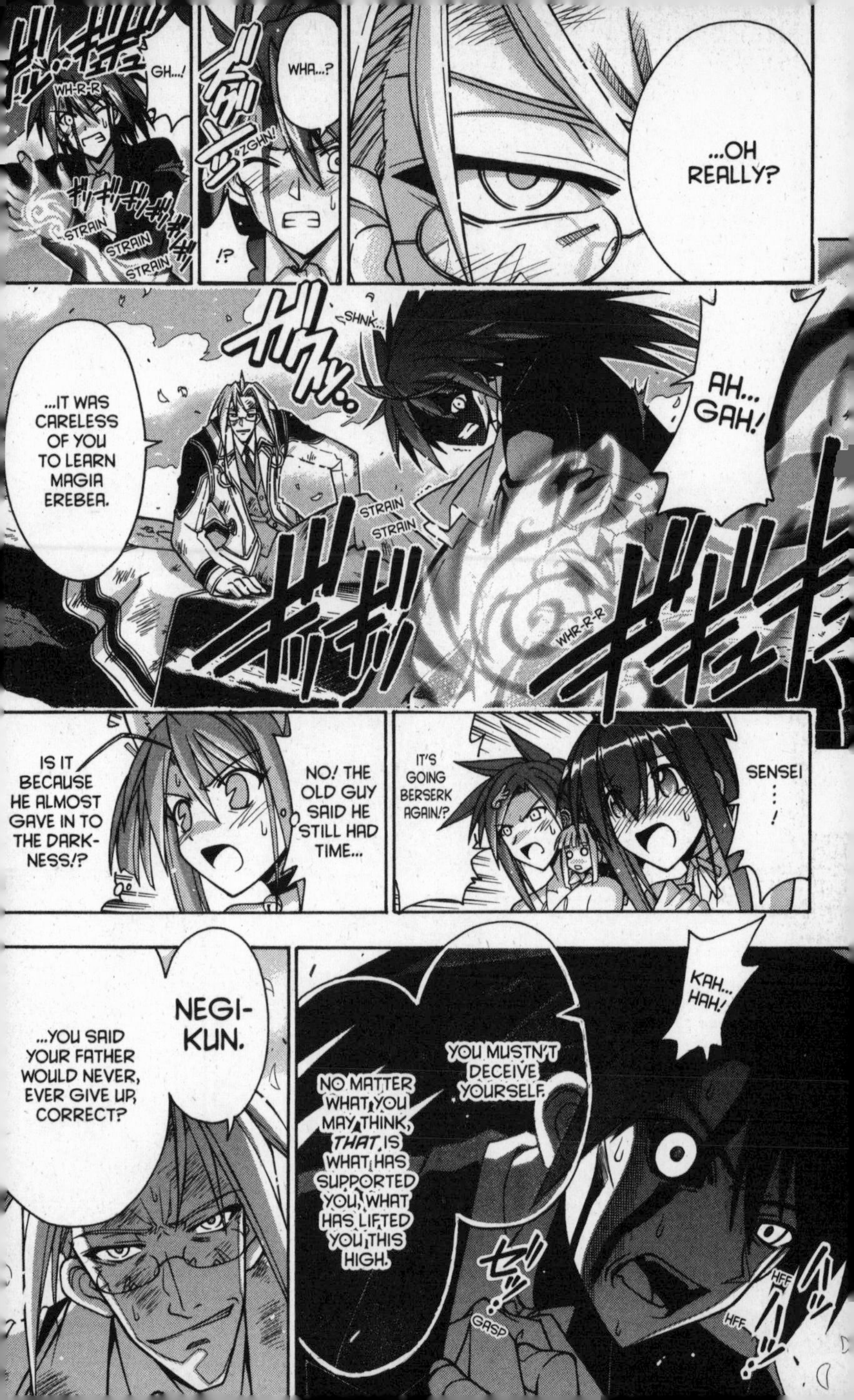
...OH REALLY?
WHA...?
ZGHN!
!?
GH...!
WH-R-R
STRAIN
STRAIN
STRAIN
AH... GAH!
SHNK...
...IT WAS CARELESS OF YOU TO LEARN MAGIA EREBEA.
STRAIN
STRAIN
WHR-R-R
SENSEI...!
IT'S GOING BERSERK AGAIN!?
NO! THE OLD GUY SAID HE STILL HAD TIME...
IS IT BECAUSE HE ALMOST GAVE IN TO THE DARKNESS!?
KAH... HAH!
YOU MUSTN'T DECEIVE YOURSELF.
NO MATTER WHAT YOU MAY THINK, *THAT* IS WHAT HAS SUPPORTED YOU, WHAT HAS LIFTED YOU THIS HIGH.
HFF
HFF
GASP
NEGI-KUN.
...YOU SAID YOUR FATHER WOULD NEVER, EVER GIVE UP, CORRECT?

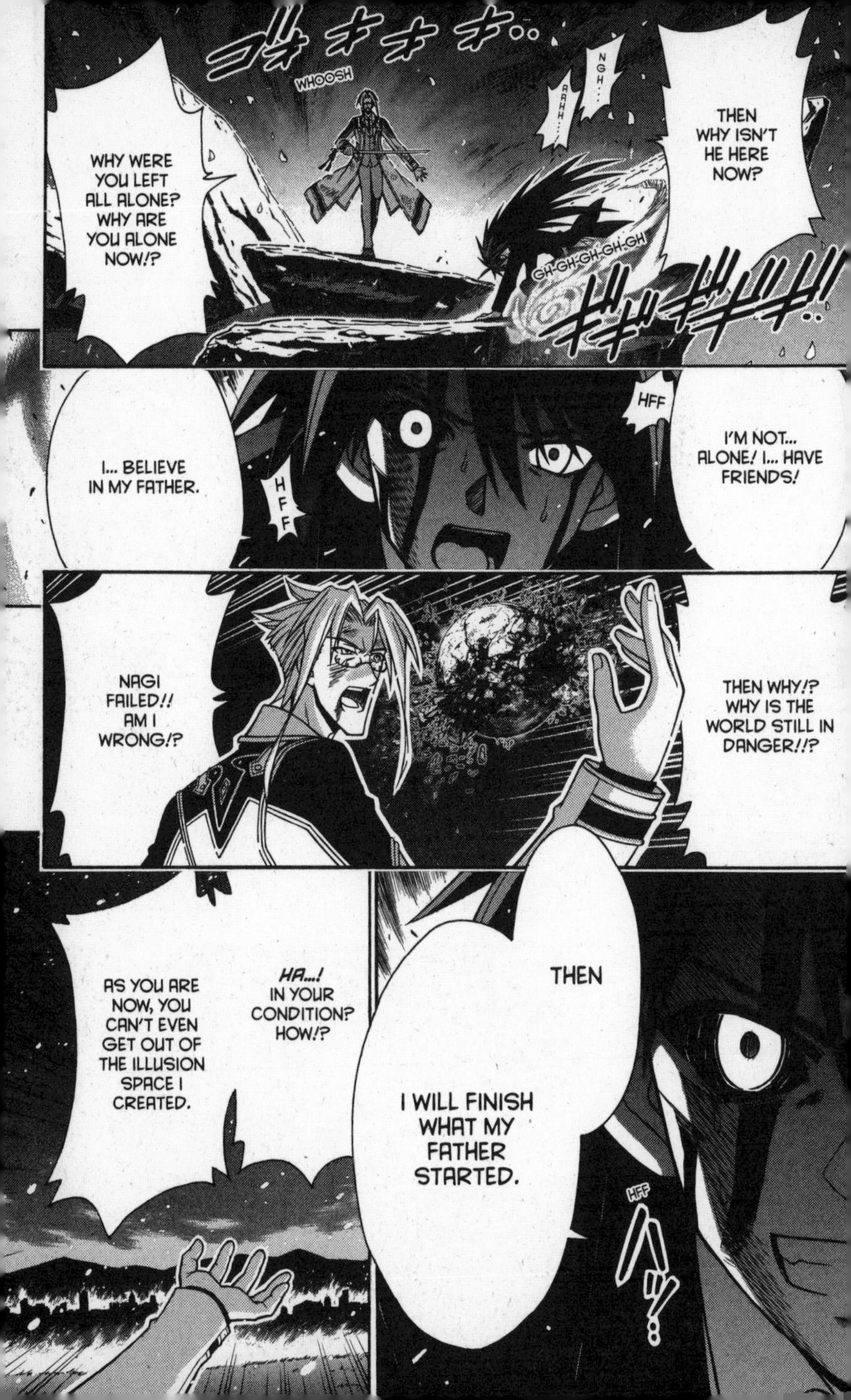
THEN WHY ISN'T HE HERE NOW?
NGH...
AAHH...
WHOOSH
GH-GH-GH-GH-GH
WHY WERE YOU LEFT ALL ALONE? WHY ARE YOU ALONE NOW!?
HFF
I'M NOT... ALONE! I... HAVE FRIENDS!
HFF
I... BELIEVE IN MY FATHER.
THEN WHY!? WHY IS THE WORLD STILL IN DANGER!!?
NAGI FAILED!! AM I WRONG!?
THEN
I WILL FINISH WHAT MY FATHER STARTED.
HFF
HA...! IN YOUR CONDITION? HOW!?
AS YOU ARE NOW, YOU CAN'T EVEN GET OUT OF THE ILLUSION SPACE I CREATED.

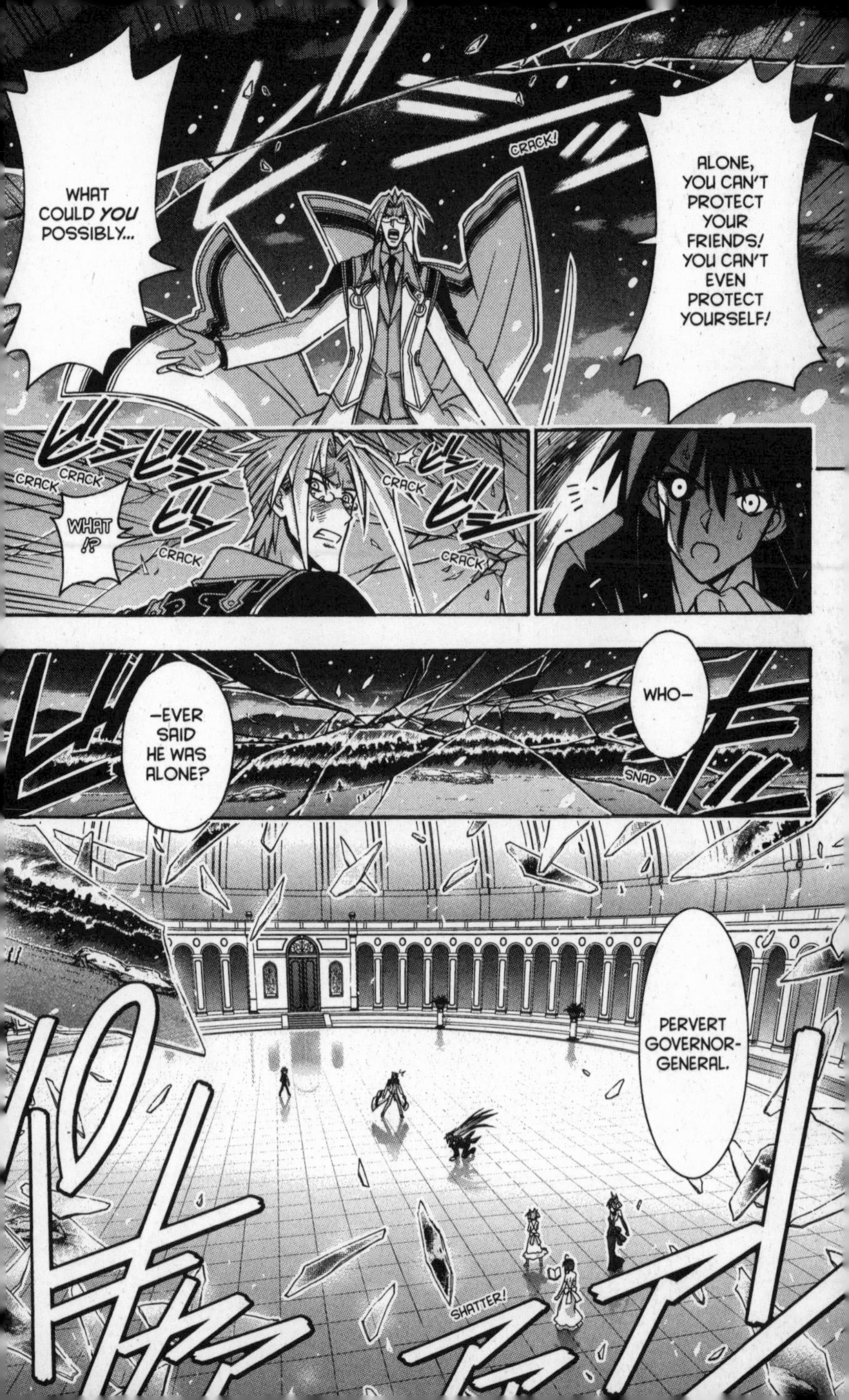
ALONE, YOU CAN'T PROTECT YOUR FRIENDS! YOU CAN'T EVEN PROTECT YOURSELF!
CRACK!
WHAT COULD *YOU* POSSIBLY...
CRACK
CRACK
CRACK
CRACK
WHAT !?
CRACK
WHO—
SNAP
—EVER SAID HE WAS ALONE?
PERVERT GOVERNOR-GENERAL.
SHATTER!

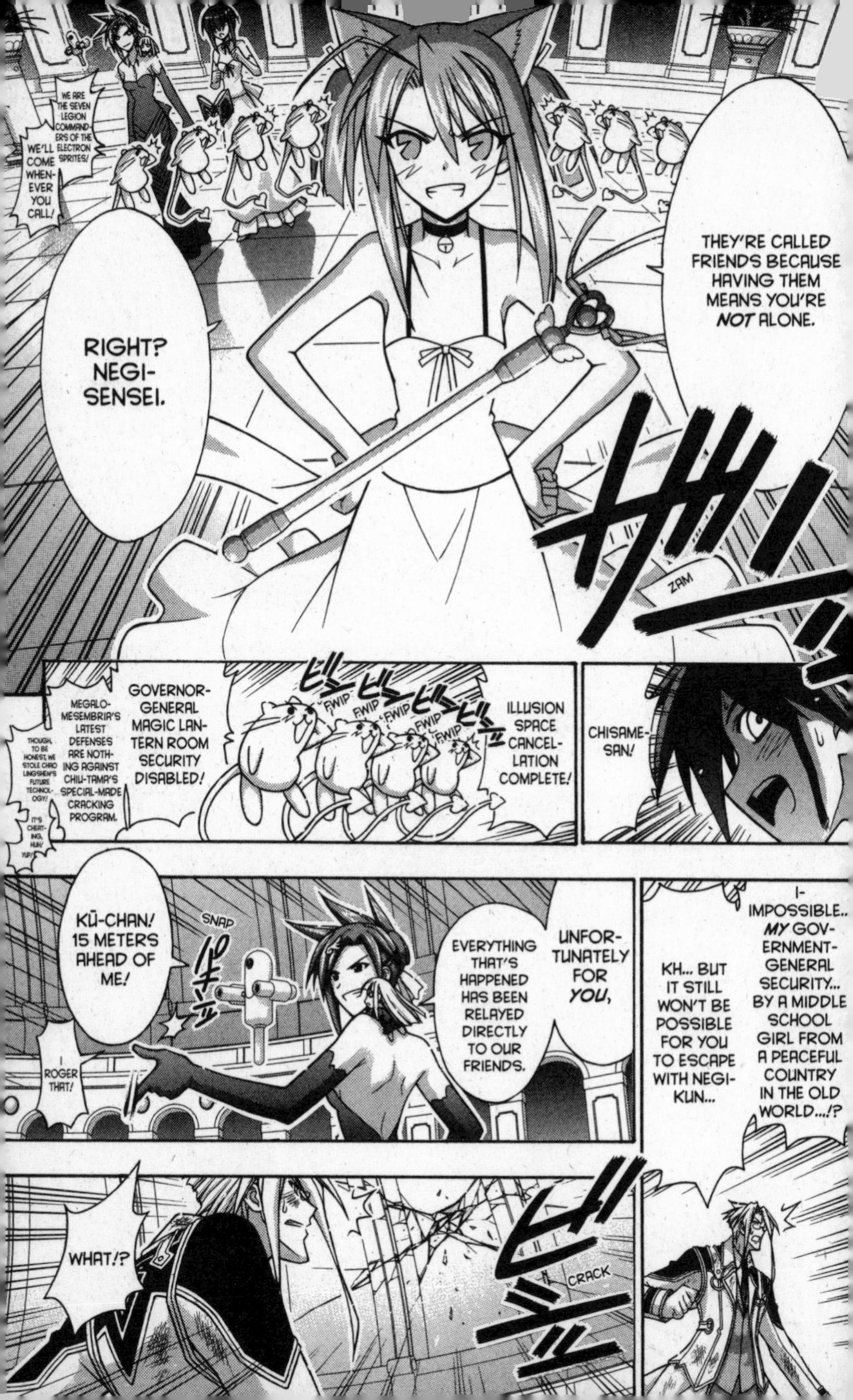
THEY'RE CALLED FRIENDS BECAUSE HAVING THEM MEANS YOU'RE NOT ALONE.
RIGHT? NEGI-SENSEI.
WE ARE THE SEVEN LEGION COMMANDERS OF THE ELECTRON SPRITES!
WE'LL COME WHENEVER YOU CALL!
ZAM
CHISAME-SAN!
ILLUSION SPACE CANCELLATION COMPLETE!
FWIP FWIP FWIP FWIP FWIP
GOVERNOR-GENERAL MAGIC LANTERN ROOM SECURITY DISABLED!
MEGALO-MESEMBRIA'S LATEST DEFENSES ARE NOTHING AGAINST CHIU-TAMA'S SPECIAL-MADE CRACKING PROGRAM.
THOUGH, TO BE HONEST, WE STOLE CHAO LINGSHEN'S FUTURE TECHNOLOGY!
IT'S CHEATING, HUH! YUP!
I-IMPOSSIBLE.. MY GOVERNMENT-GENERAL SECURITY... BY A MIDDLE SCHOOL GIRL FROM A PEACEFUL COUNTRY IN THE OLD WORLD...!?
KH... BUT IT STILL WON'T BE POSSIBLE FOR YOU TO ESCAPE WITH NEGI-KUN...
UNFORTUNATELY FOR YOU,
EVERYTHING THAT'S HAPPENED HAS BEEN RELAYED DIRECTLY TO OUR FRIENDS.
SNAP
KŪ-CHAN! 15 METERS AHEAD OF ME!
I ROGER THAT!
CRACK
WHAT!?

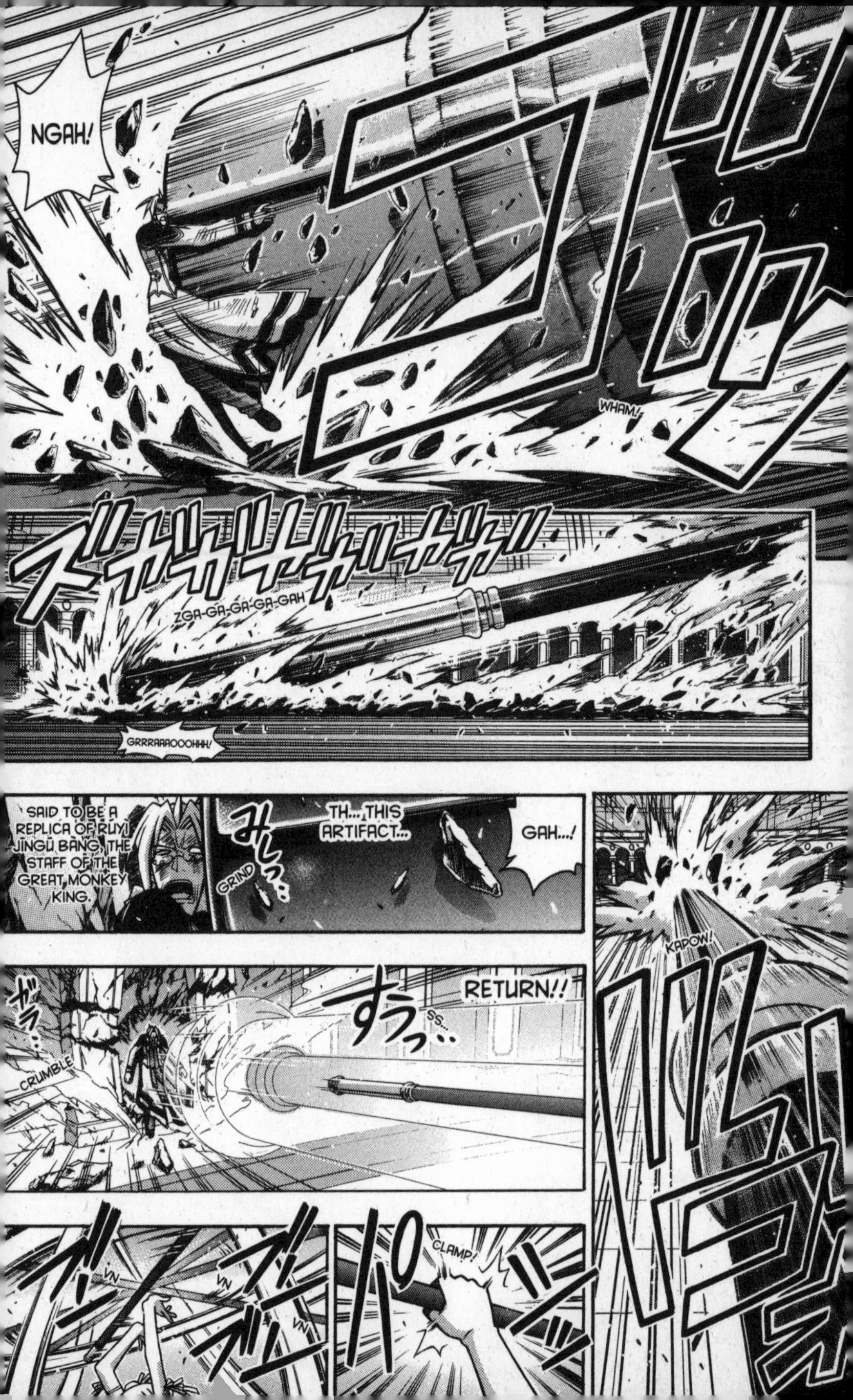
NGAH!
WHAM!
ZGA-GA-GA-GA-GAH
GRRRAAAOOOHHH!
KAPOW!
GAH...!
TH... THIS ARTIFACT...
GRIND
SAID TO BE A REPLICA OF RUYI JINGU BANG, THE STAFF OF THE GREAT MONKEY KING.
RETURN!!
SS...
CRUMBLE
CLAMP!
VN
VN
VN

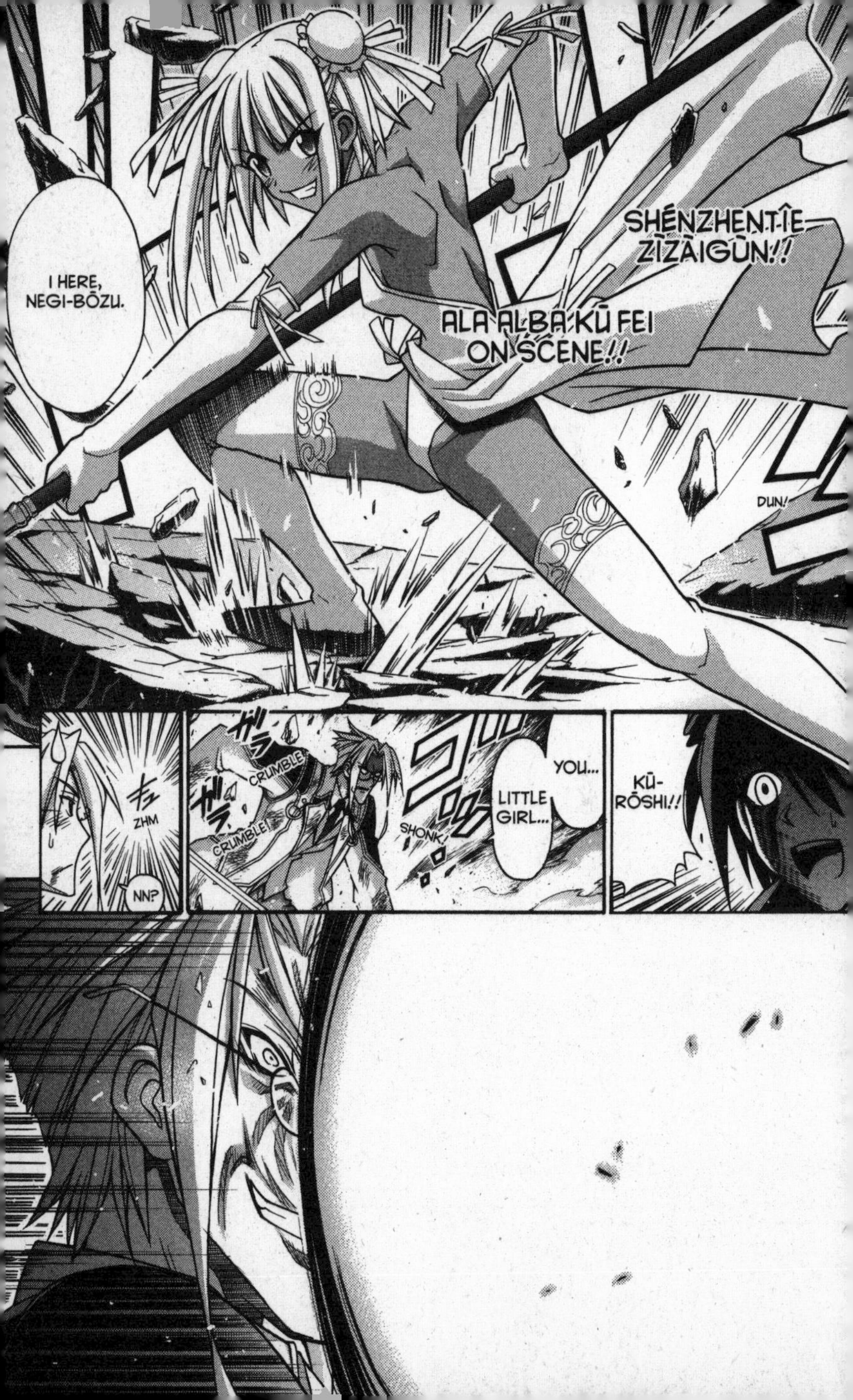
SHÉNZHENTÎE ZÌZÀIGÙN!!
ALA ALBA KŪ FEI ON SCENE!!
I HERE, NEGI-BŌZU.
DUN!
KŪ-RŌSHI!!
YOU... LITTLE GIRL...
SHONK!
CRUMBLE
CRUMBLE
ZHM
NN?

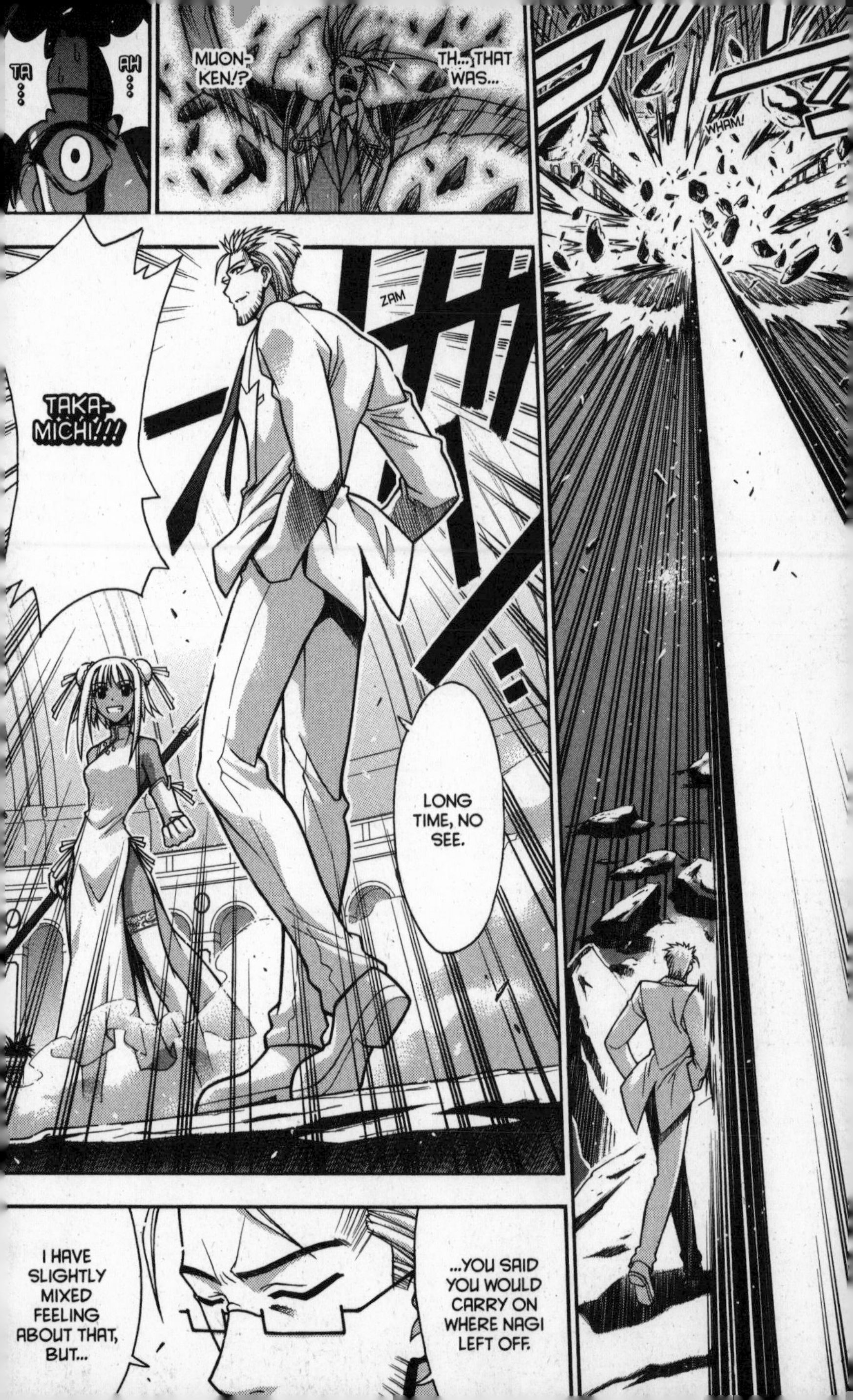
WHAM!
TH... THAT WAS...
MUON-KEN!?
AH...
TA...
ZAM
TAKA-MICHI!!!
LONG TIME, NO SEE.
...YOU SAID YOU WOULD CARRY ON WHERE NAGI LEFT OFF.
I HAVE SLIGHTLY MIXED FEELING ABOUT THAT, BUT...

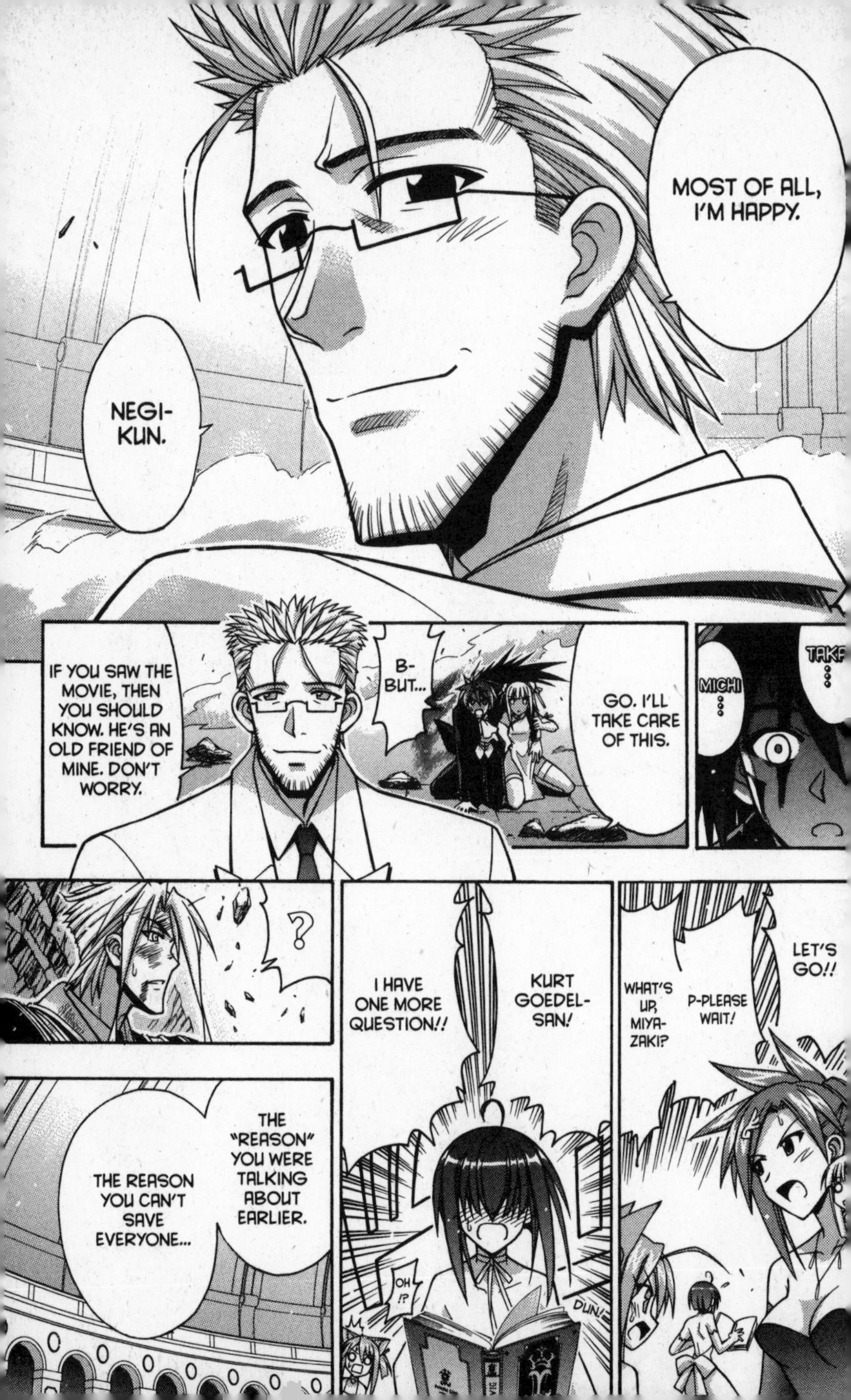
MOST OF ALL, I'M HAPPY.
NEGI-KUN.
TAKA...
MICHI...
GO. I'LL TAKE CARE OF THIS.
B-BUT...
IF YOU SAW THE MOVIE, THEN YOU SHOULD KNOW. HE'S AN OLD FRIEND OF MINE. DON'T WORRY.
LET'S GO!!
P-PLEASE WAIT!
WHAT'S UP, MIYAZAKI?
KURT GOEDEL-SAN!
I HAVE ONE MORE QUESTION!!
OH !?
DUN!
?
THE "REASON" YOU WERE TALKING ABOUT EARLIER.
THE REASON YOU CAN'T SAVE EVERYONE...

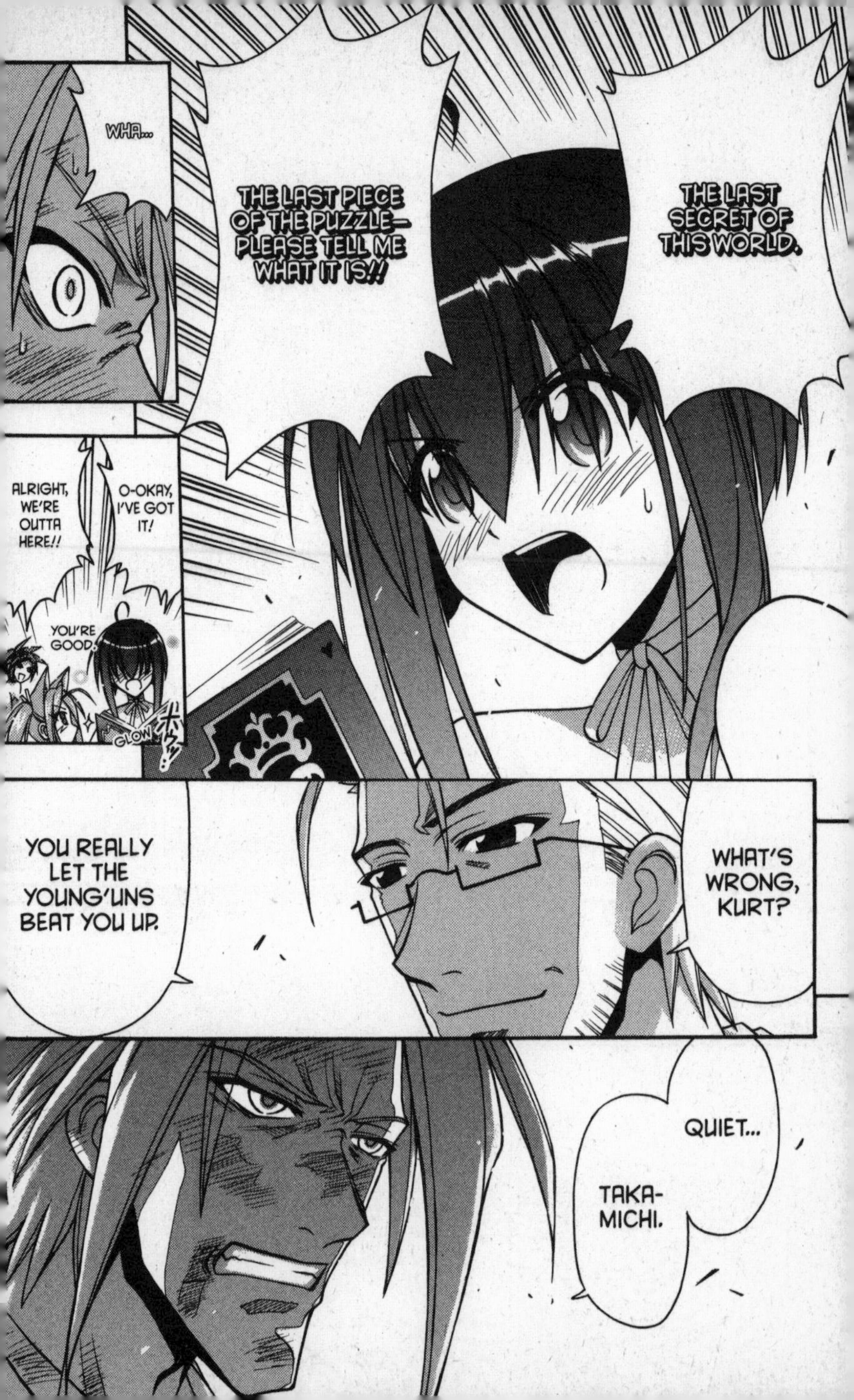

THE LAST SECRET OF THIS WORLD.
THE LAST PIECE OF THE PUZZLE—PLEASE TELL ME WHAT IT IS!!
WHA...
O-OKAY, I'VE GOT IT!
ALRIGHT, WE'RE OUTTA HERE!!
YOU'RE GOOD.
GLOW
WHAT'S WRONG, KURT?
YOU REALLY LET THE YOUNG'UNS BEAT YOU UP.
QUIET...
TAKA-MICHI.

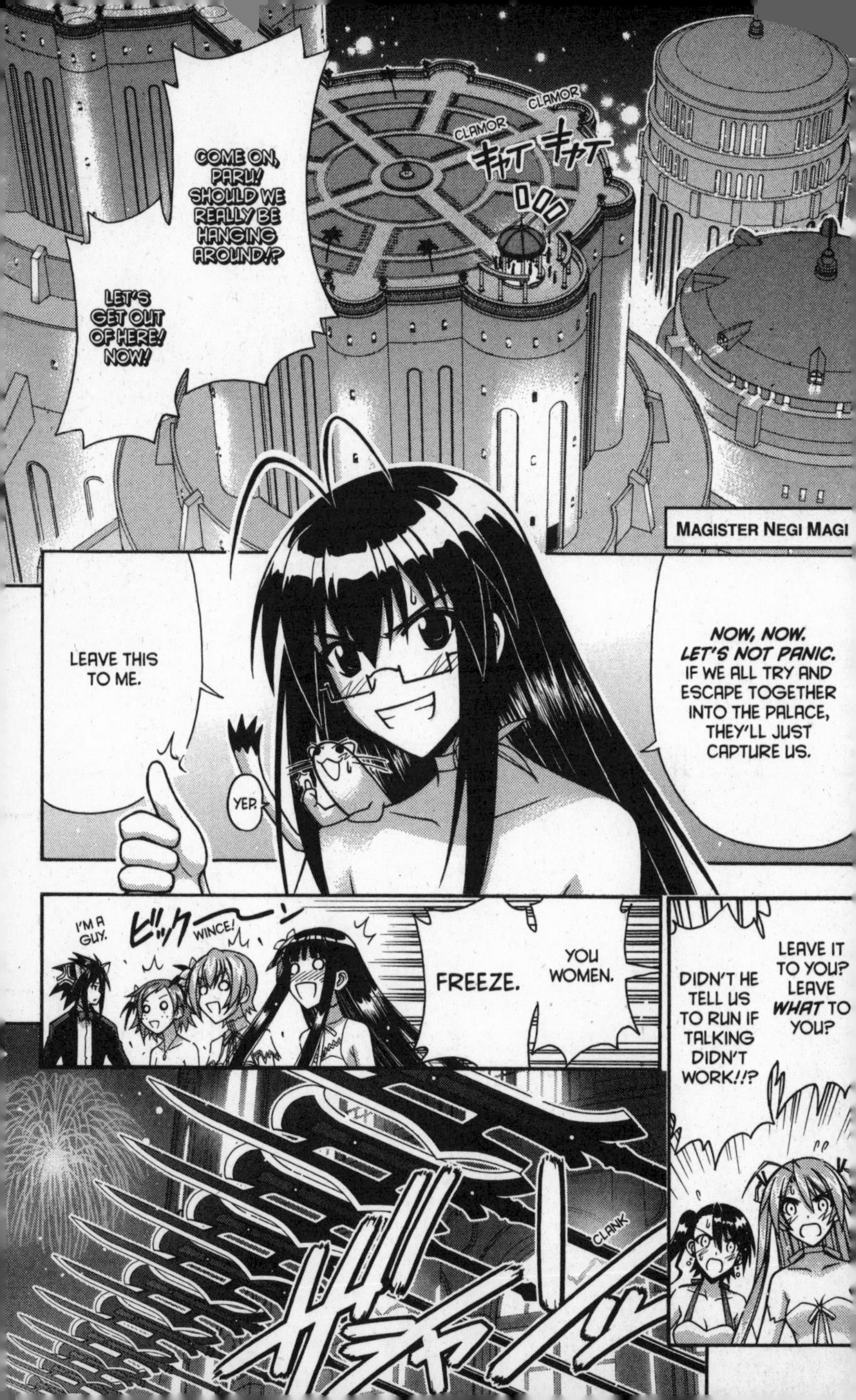
CLAMOR
CLAMOR
キャア キャア
ooo
COME ON, PARU!! SHOULD WE REALLY BE HANGING AROUND!?
LET'S GET OUT OF HERE! NOW!
MAGISTER NEGI MAGI
NOW, NOW. LET'S NOT PANIC. IF WE ALL TRY AND ESCAPE TOGETHER INTO THE PALACE, THEY'LL JUST CAPTURE US.
LEAVE THIS TO ME.
YEP.
LEAVE IT TO YOU? LEAVE *WHAT* TO YOU?
DIDN'T HE TELL US TO RUN IF TALKING DIDN'T WORK!!?
YOU WOMEN.
FREEZE.
WINCE!
I'M A GUY.
CLANK

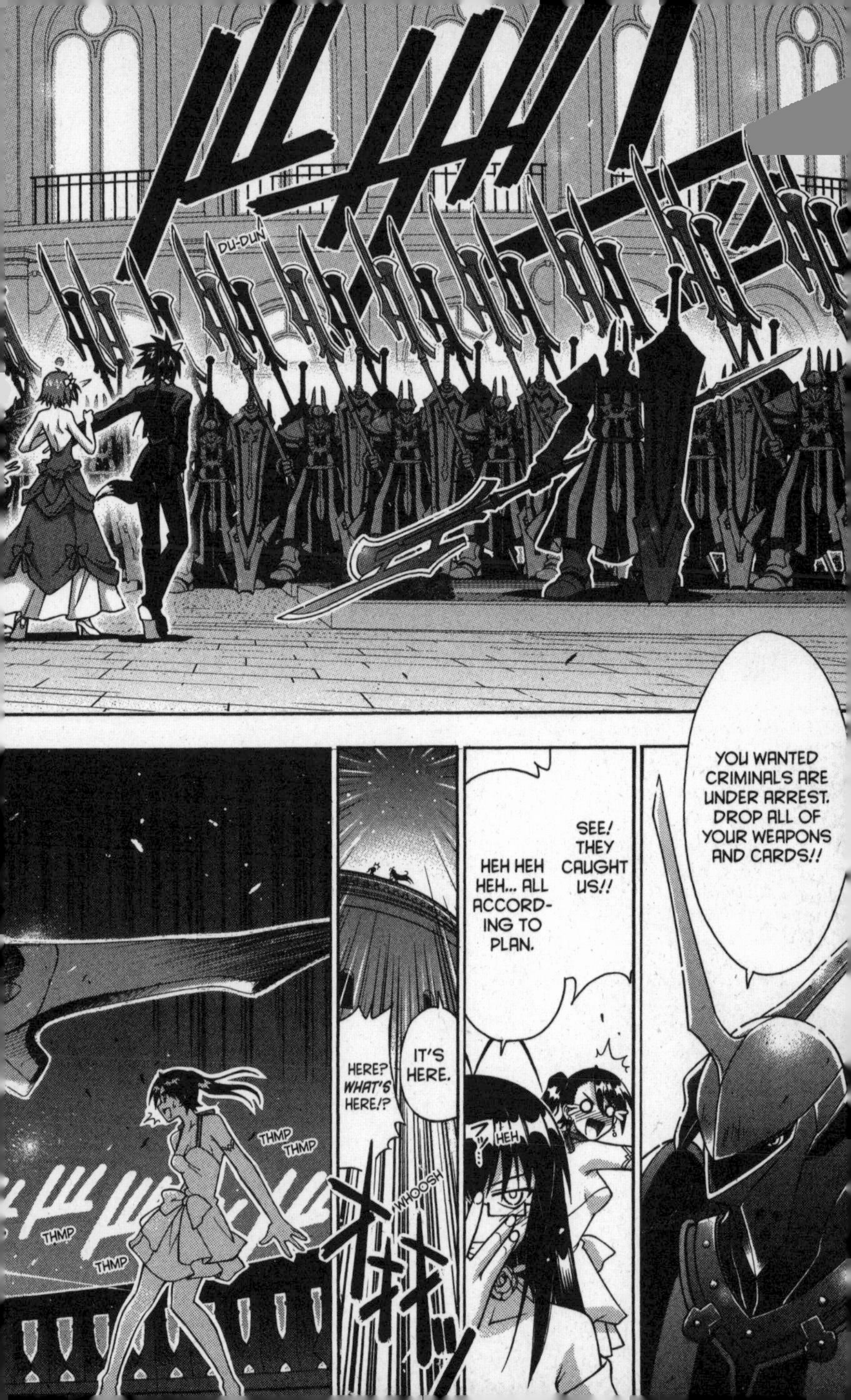
DU-DUN
YOU WANTED CRIMINALS ARE UNDER ARREST. DROP ALL OF YOUR WEAPONS AND CARDS!!
SEE! THEY CAUGHT US!!
HEH HEH HEH... ALL ACCORDING TO PLAN.
HEH
IT'S HERE.
HERE? WHAT'S HERE!?
WHOOSH
THMP THMP
THMP
THMP

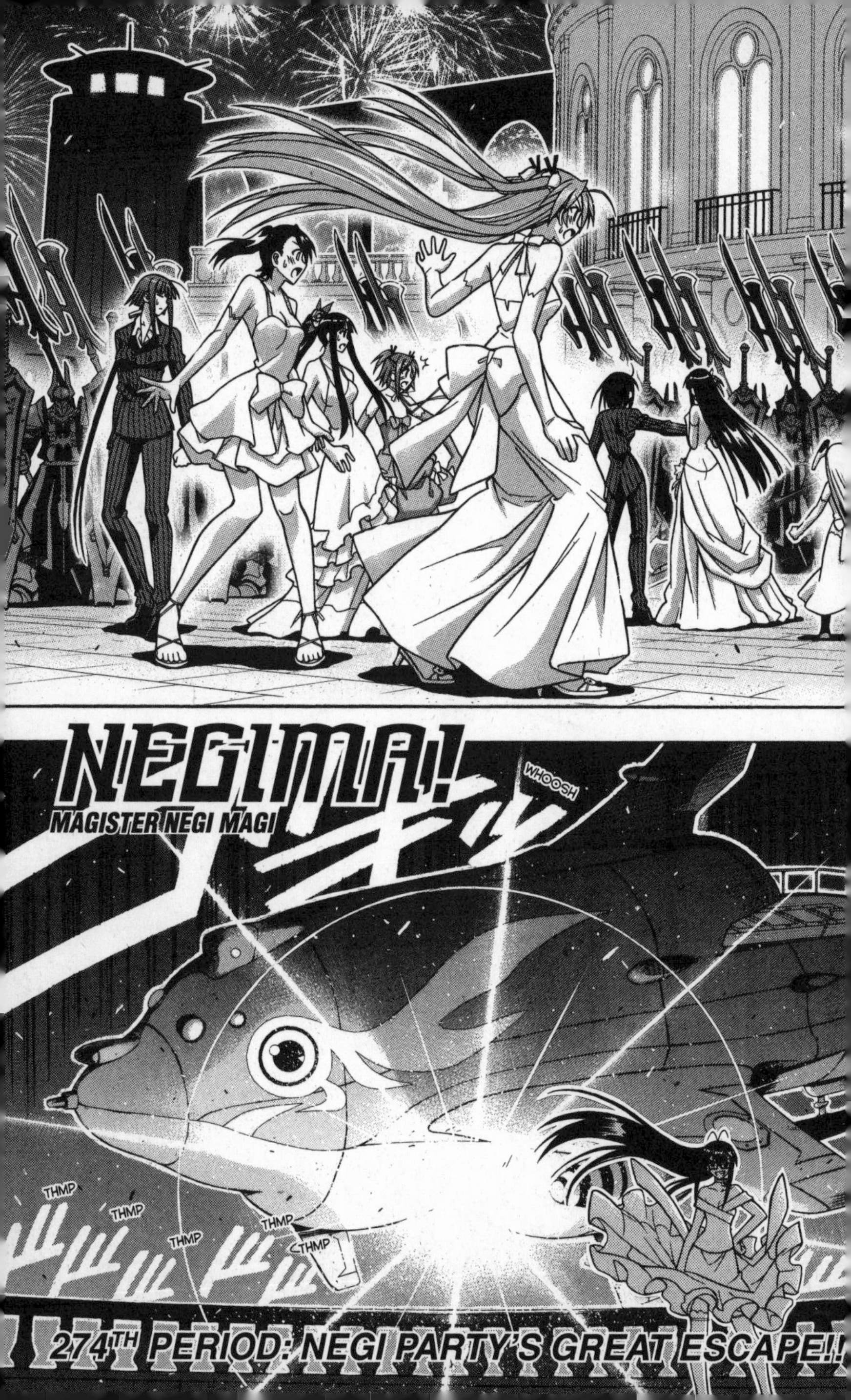
WHOOSH
NEGIMA!
MAGISTER NEGI MAGI
THMP
THMP
THMP
THMP
THMP
274TH PERIOD: NEGI PARTY'S GREAT ESCAPE!!

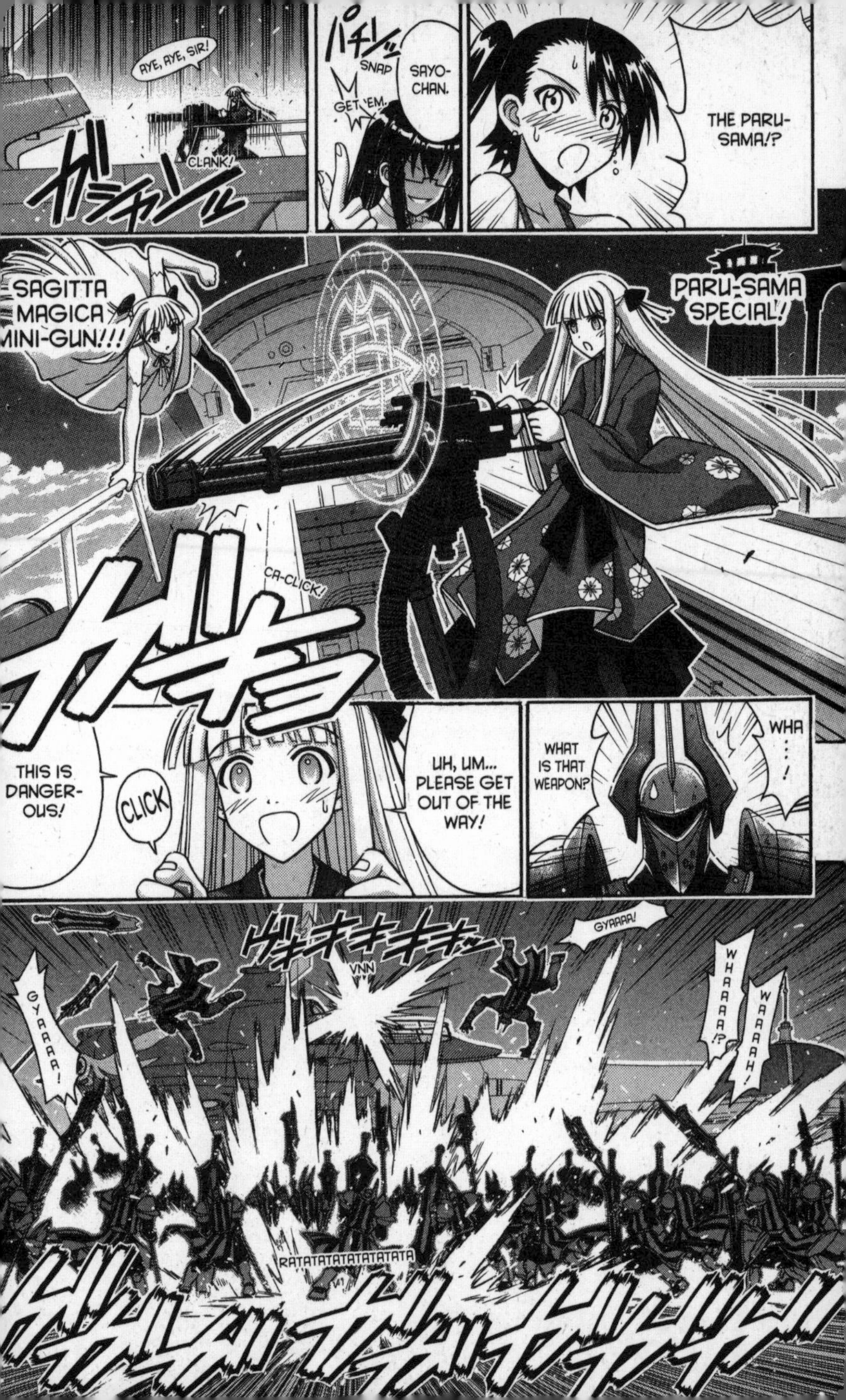

THE PARU-SAMA!?
SAYO-CHAN.
SNAP
GET 'EM.
AYE, AYE, SIR!
CLANK!
PARU-SAMA SPECIAL!
SAGITTA MAGICA MINI-GUN!!!
CA-CLICK!
WHA...!
WHAT IS THAT WEAPON?
UH, UM... PLEASE GET OUT OF THE WAY!
CLICK
THIS IS DANGER-OUS!
WAAAAAH!
WHAAAAA!?
GYAAAA!
VNN
GYAAAAA!
RATATATATATATATATA

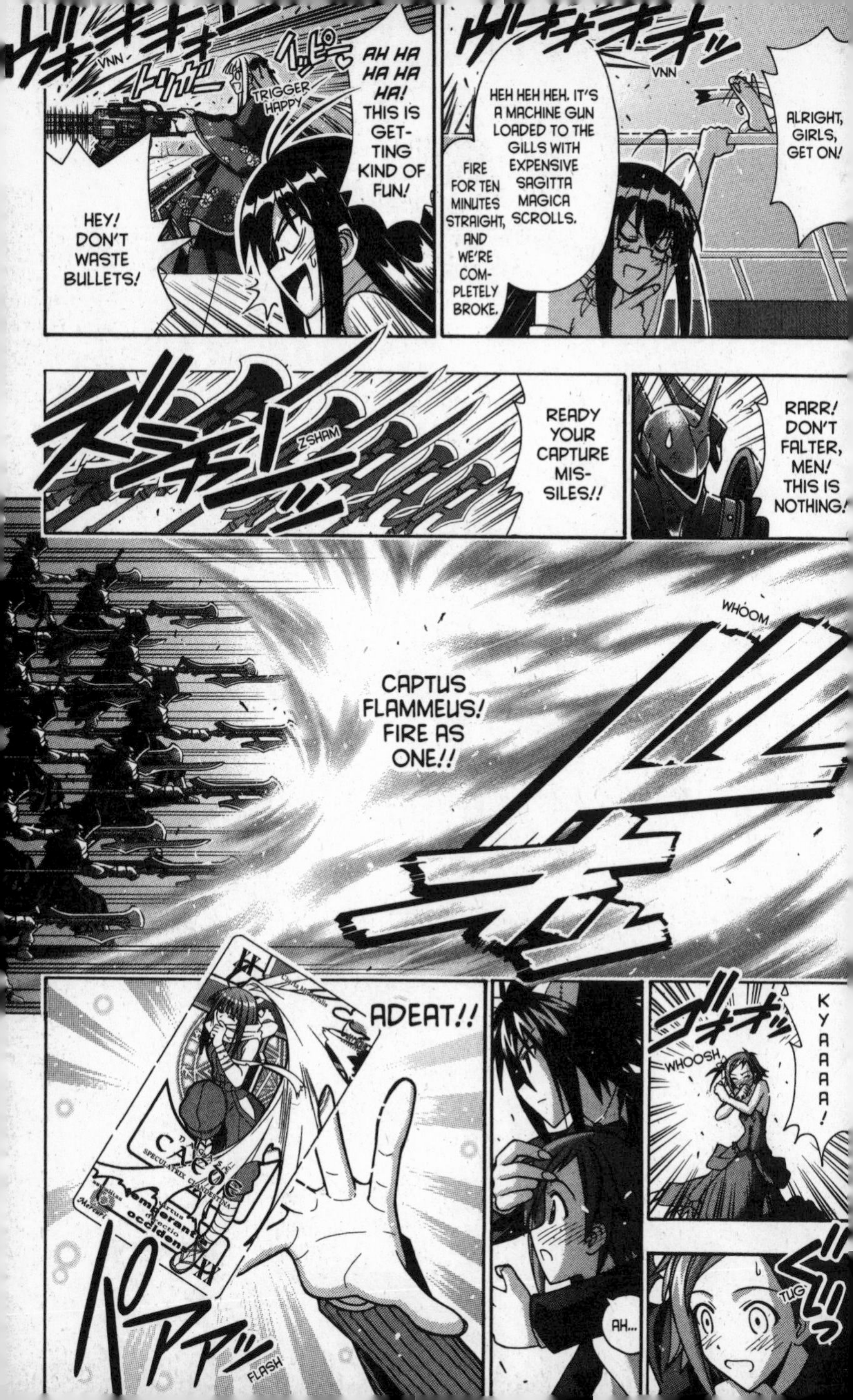
VNN
ALRIGHT, GIRLS, GET ON!
HEH HEH HEH. IT'S A MACHINE GUN LOADED TO THE GILLS WITH EXPENSIVE SAGITTA MAGICA SCROLLS.
FIRE FOR TEN MINUTES STRAIGHT, AND WE'RE COMPLETELY BROKE.
VNN
TRIGGER HAPPY
AH HA HA HA HA! THIS IS GET-TING KIND OF FUN!
HEY! DON'T WASTE BULLETS!
RARR! DON'T FALTER, MEN! THIS IS NOTHING!
READY YOUR CAPTURE MIS-SILES!!
ZSHAM
WHOOM
CAPTUS FLAMMEUS! FIRE AS ONE!!
KYAAAAA!
WHOOSH
TUG
AH...
ADEAT!!
FLASH

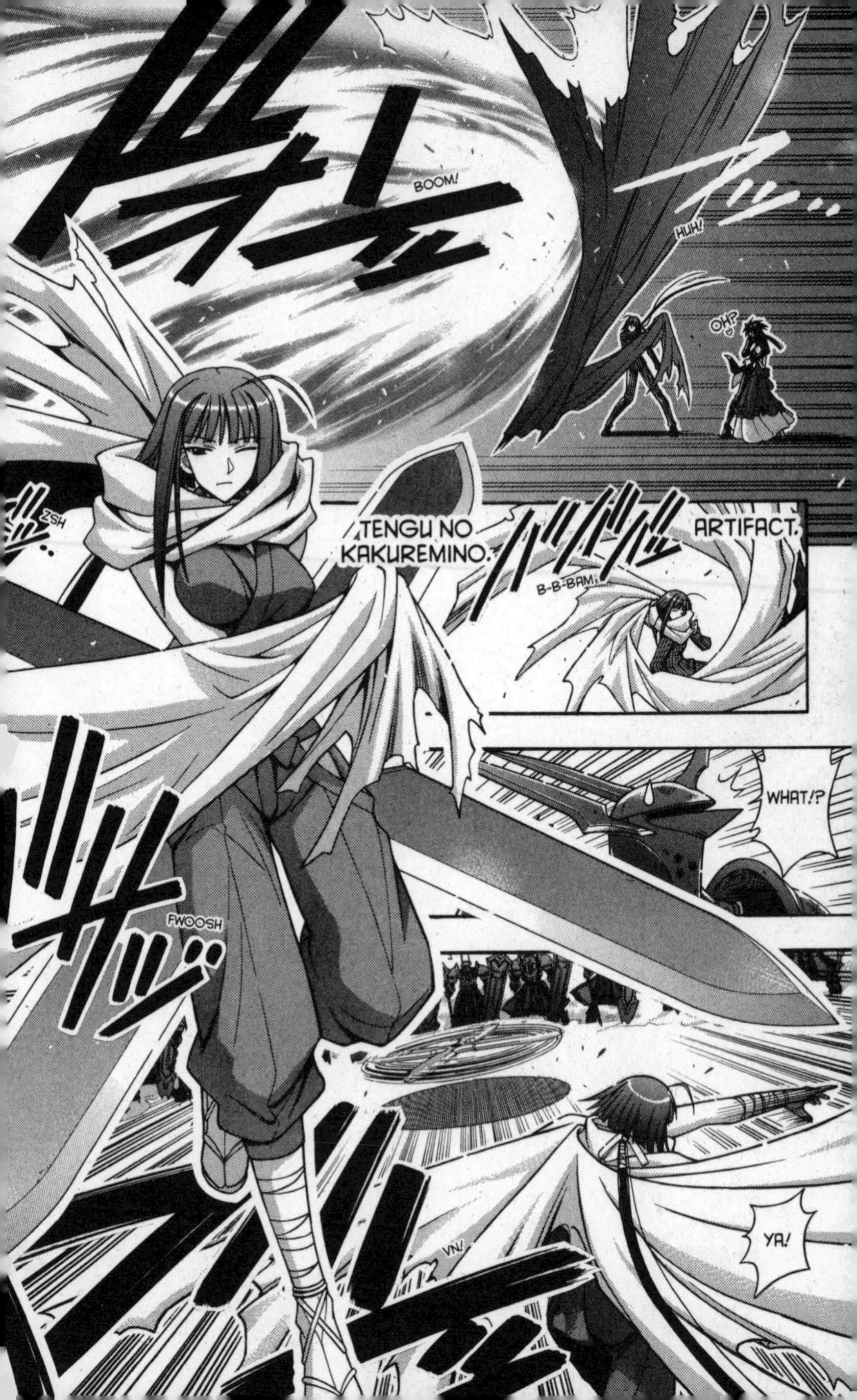
HUH!
OH? ♥
BOOM!
ARTIFACT.
B-B-BAM!
TENGU NO KAKUREMINO.
ZSH
WHAT!?
YA!
VN!
FWOOSH

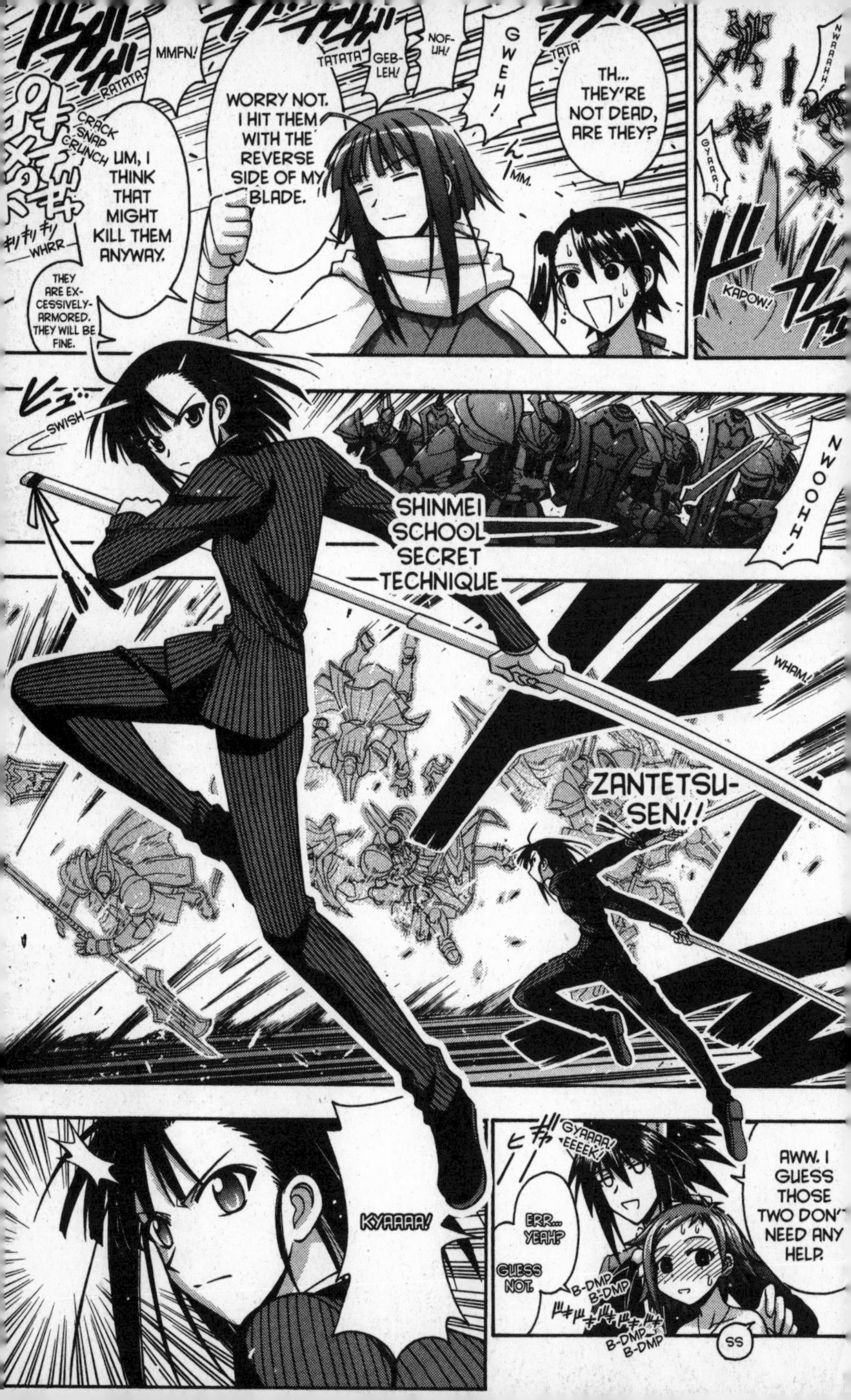
NWAAAHH!
GYAAA!
KAPOW!
TH... THEY'RE NOT DEAD, ARE THEY?
TATA
GWEH!
MM.
NOF-UH!
GEB-LEH!
TATATA
WORRY NOT. I HIT THEM WITH THE REVERSE SIDE OF MY BLADE.
MMFN!
RATATA
CRACK SNAP CRUNCH
UM, I THINK THAT MIGHT KILL THEM ANYWAY.
WHRR
THEY ARE EX-CESSIVELY-ARMORED. THEY WILL BE FINE.
NWOOHH!
SWISH
SHINMEI SCHOOL SECRET TECHNIQUE
WHAM!
ZANTETSU-SEN!!
AWW. I GUESS THOSE TWO DON'T NEED ANY HELP.
GYAAAA! EEEEK!
ERR... YEAH?
GUESS NOT.
B-DMP B-DMP
B-DMP B-DMP
SS
KYAAAA!

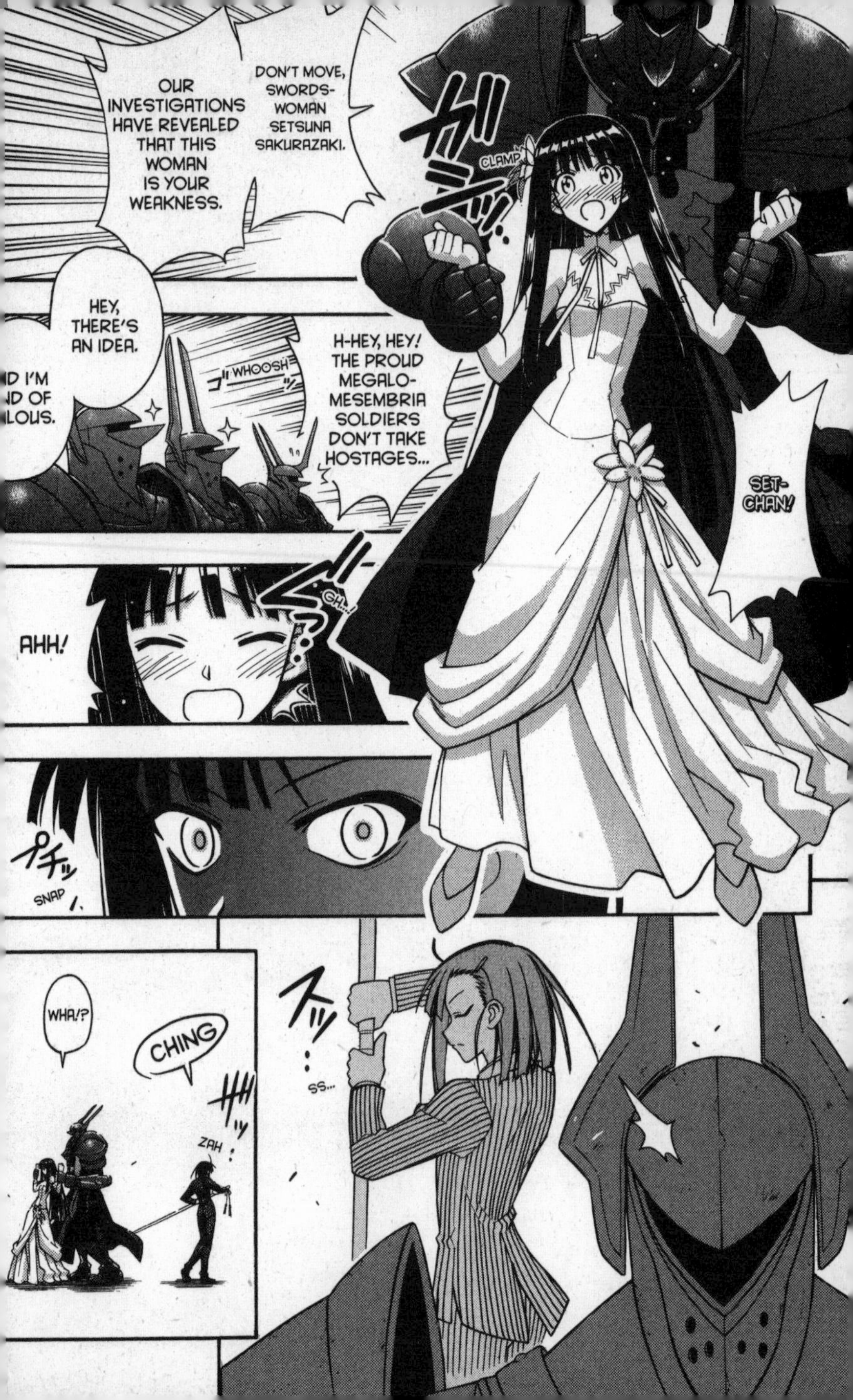
DON'T MOVE, SWORDSWOMAN SETSUNA SAKURAZAKI.
OUR INVESTIGATIONS HAVE REVEALED THAT THIS WOMAN IS YOUR WEAKNESS.
CLAMP
H-HEY, HEY! THE PROUD MEGALOMESEMBRIA SOLDIERS DON'T TAKE HOSTAGES...
WHOOSH
HEY, THERE'S AN IDEA.
SET-CHAN!
GH...
AHH!
SNAP
SS...
CHING
WHA!?
ZAH

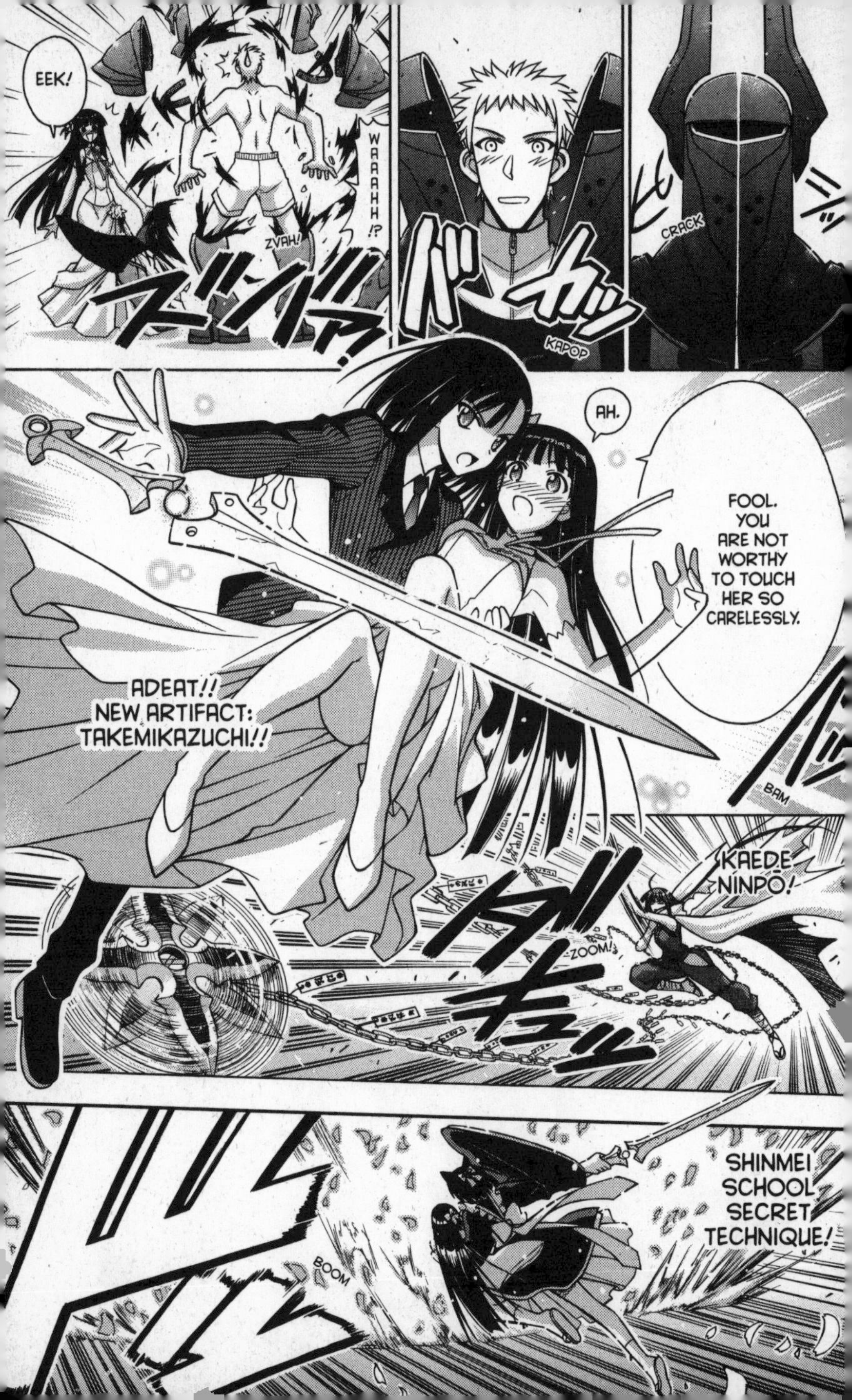
CRACK
KAPOP
WAAAAHH!?
EEK!
ZVAH!
FOOL. YOU ARE NOT WORTHY TO TOUCH HER SO CARELESSLY.
AH.
ADEAT!! NEW ARTIFACT: TAKEMIKAZUCHI!!
BAM
KAEDE NINPŌ!
ZOOM!
SHINMEI SCHOOL SECRET TECHNIQUE!
BOOM

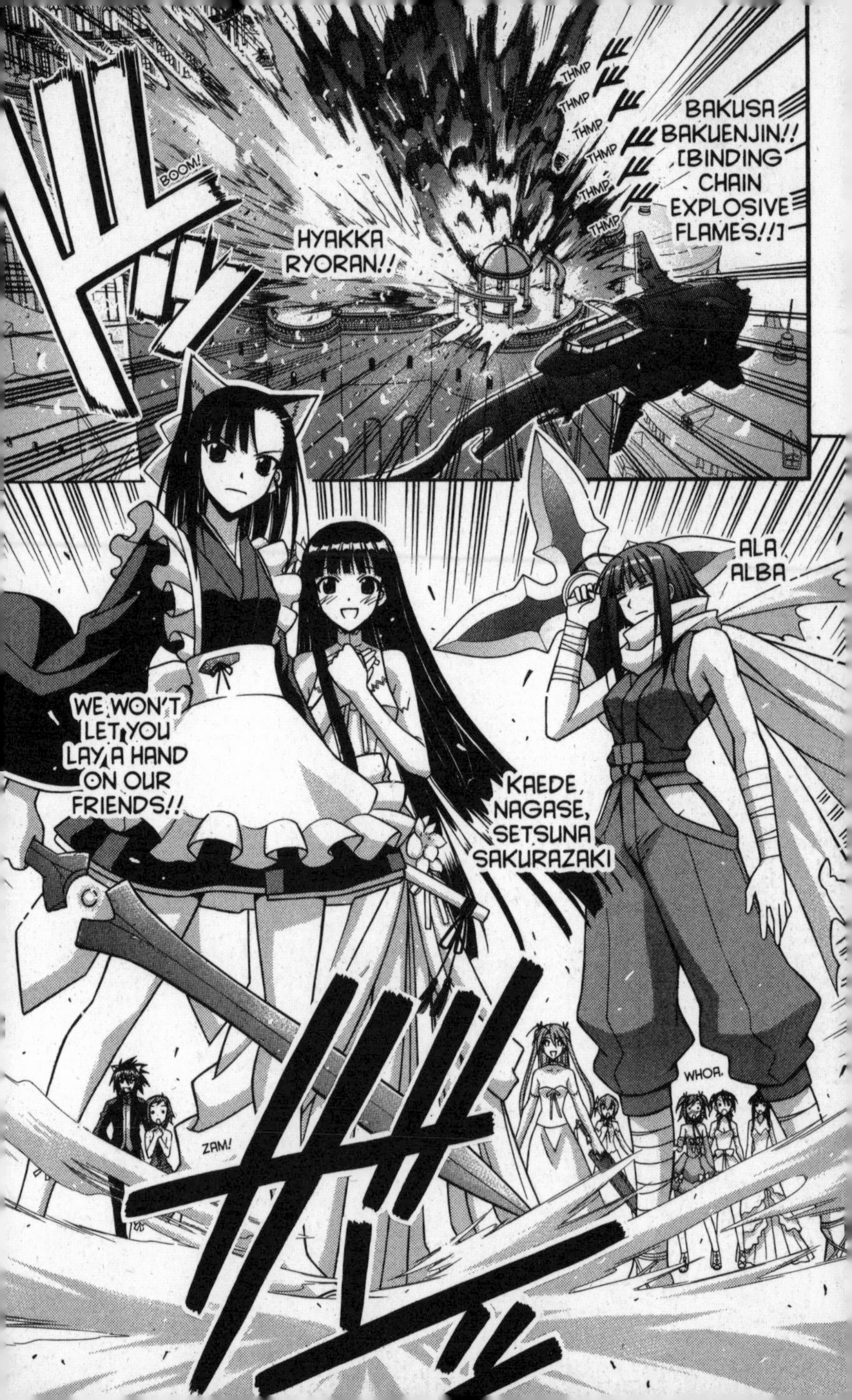
THMP
THMP
THMP
THMP
THMP
THMP
BAKUSA BAKUENJIN!! [BINDING CHAIN EXPLOSIVE FLAMES!!]
HYAKKA RYORAN!!
BOOM!
ALA ALBA
KAEDE NAGASE, SETSUNA SAKURAZAKI
WE WON'T LET YOU LAY A HAND ON OUR FRIENDS!!
WHOA.
ZAM!

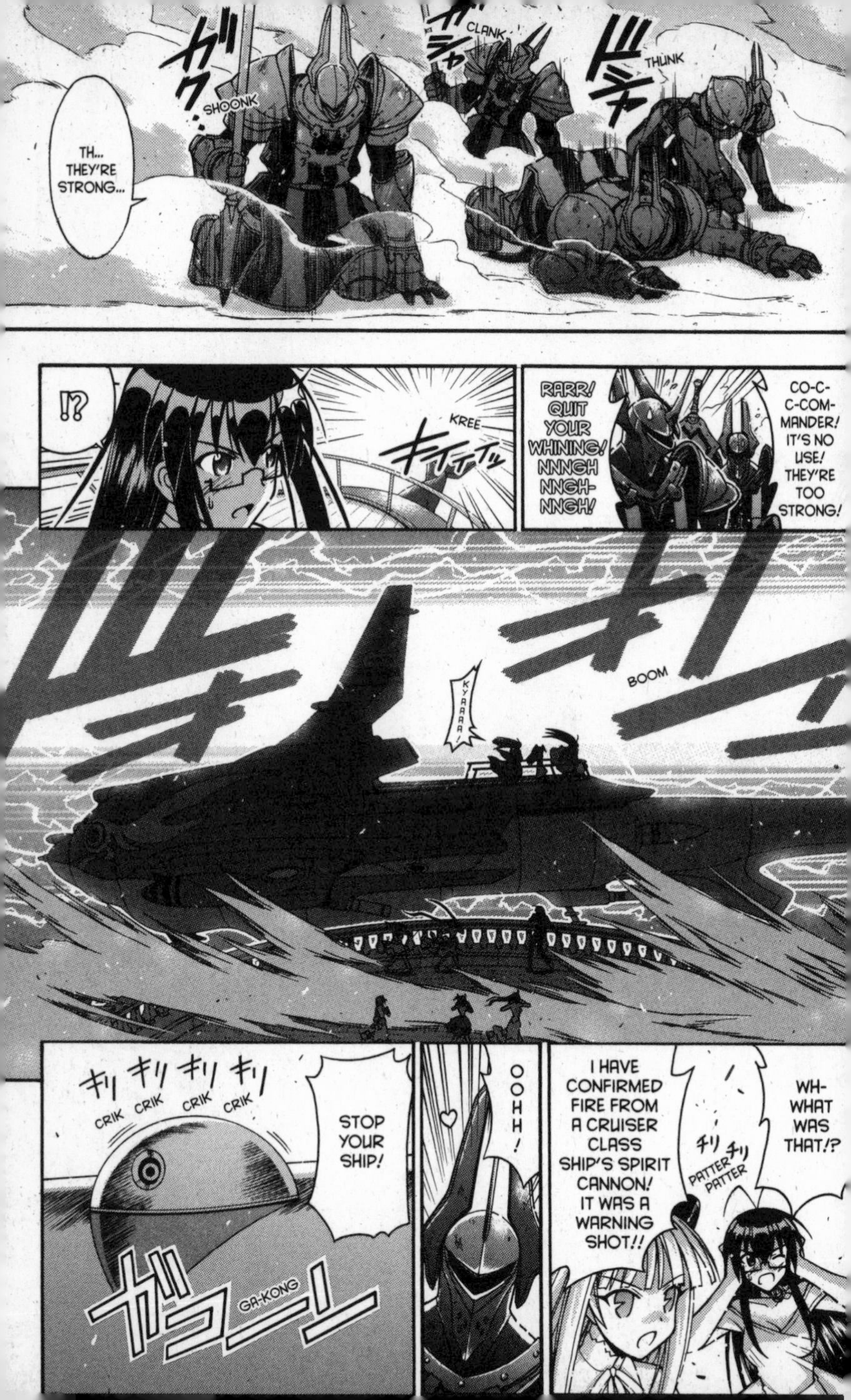
THUNK
CLANK
SHOONK
TH... THEY'RE STRONG...
CO-C-C-COM-MANDER! IT'S NO USE! THEY'RE TOO STRONG!
RARR! QUIT YOUR WHINING! NNNGH NNGH-NNGH!
KREE
!?
BOOM
KYAAAA!
WH-WHAT WAS THAT!?
PATTER PATTER
I HAVE CONFIRMED FIRE FROM A CRUISER CLASS SHIP'S SPIRIT CANNON! IT WAS A WARNING SHOT!!
OOHH!
STOP YOUR SHIP!
CRIK CRIK CRIK CRIK
GA-KONG

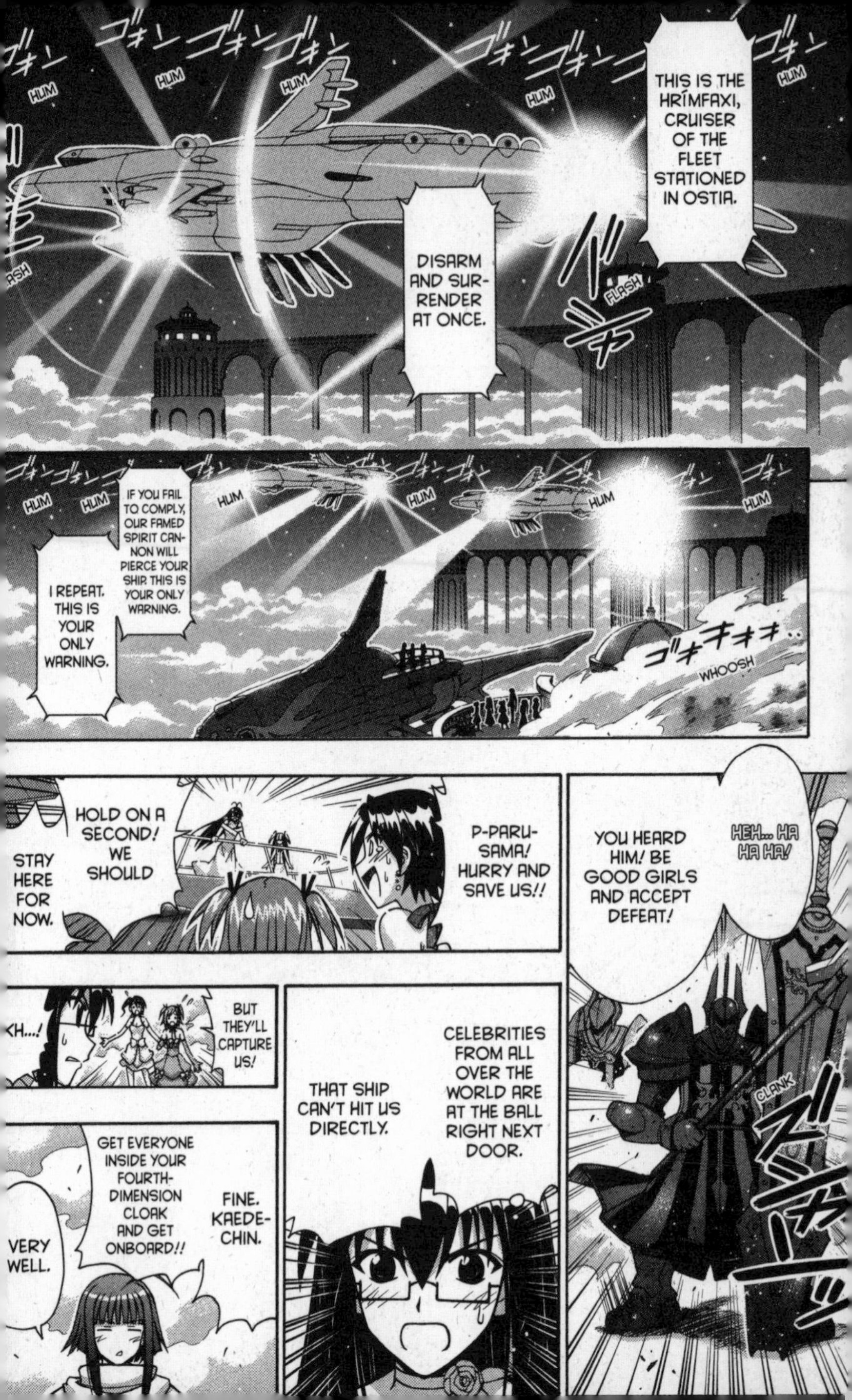
HUM
HUM
HUM
HUM
HUM
THIS IS THE HRÍMFAXI, CRUISER OF THE FLEET STATIONED IN OSTIA.
FLASH
DISARM AND SUR-RENDER AT ONCE.
FLASH
HUM
HUM
HUM
HUM
HUM
HUM
IF YOU FAIL TO COMPLY, OUR FAMED SPIRIT CAN-NON WILL PIERCE YOUR SHIP. THIS IS YOUR ONLY WARNING.
I REPEAT. THIS IS YOUR ONLY WARNING.
WHOOSH
HEH... HA HA HA!
YOU HEARD HIM! BE GOOD GIRLS AND ACCEPT DEFEAT!
CLANK
P-PARU-SAMA! HURRY AND SAVE US!!
HOLD ON A SECOND! WE SHOULD
STAY HERE FOR NOW.
CELEBRITIES FROM ALL OVER THE WORLD ARE AT THE BALL RIGHT NEXT DOOR.
THAT SHIP CAN'T HIT US DIRECTLY.
BUT THEY'LL CAPTURE US!
KH...!
GET EVERYONE INSIDE YOUR FOURTH-DIMENSION CLOAK AND GET ONBOARD!!
FINE. KAEDE-CHIN.
VERY WELL.

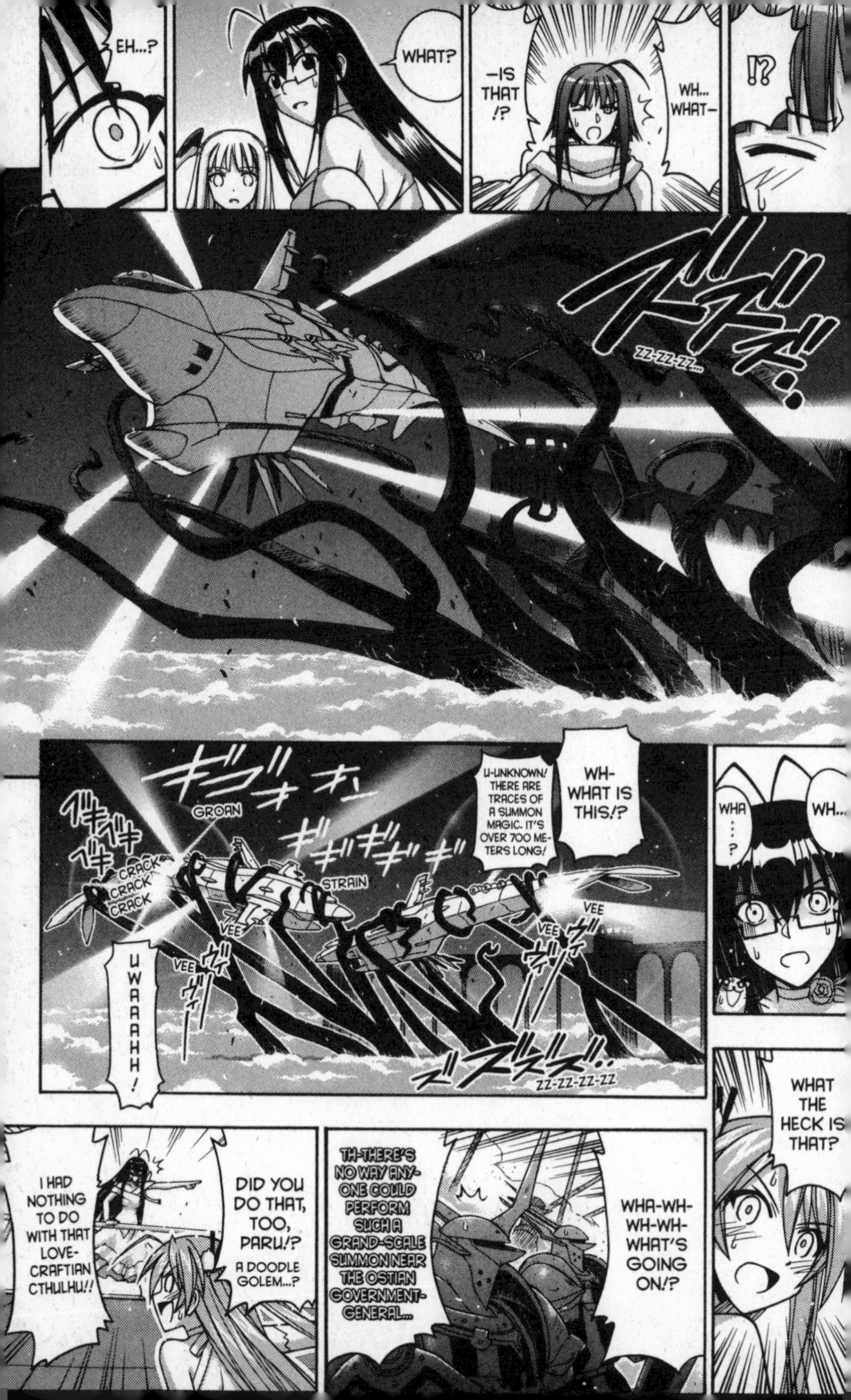
!?
WH... WHAT—
—IS THAT !?
WHAT?
EH...?
ZZ-ZZ-ZZ...
WH...
WHA...?
WH- WHAT IS THIS!?
U-UNKNOWN! THERE ARE TRACES OF A SUMMON MAGIC. IT'S OVER 700 METERS LONG!
GROAN
STRAIN
CRACK CRACK CRACK
VEE
VEE
VEE
UWAAAAHH!
ZZ-ZZ-ZZ-ZZ
WHAT THE HECK IS THAT?
WHA-WH-WH-WH-WHAT'S GOING ON!?
TH-THERE'S NO WAY ANYONE COULD PERFORM SUCH A GRAND-SCALE SUMMON NEAR THE OSTIAN GOVERNMENT-GENERAL...
DID YOU DO THAT, TOO, PARU!?
A DOODLE GOLEM...?
I HAD NOTHING TO DO WITH THAT LOVE-CRAFTIAN CTHULHU!!

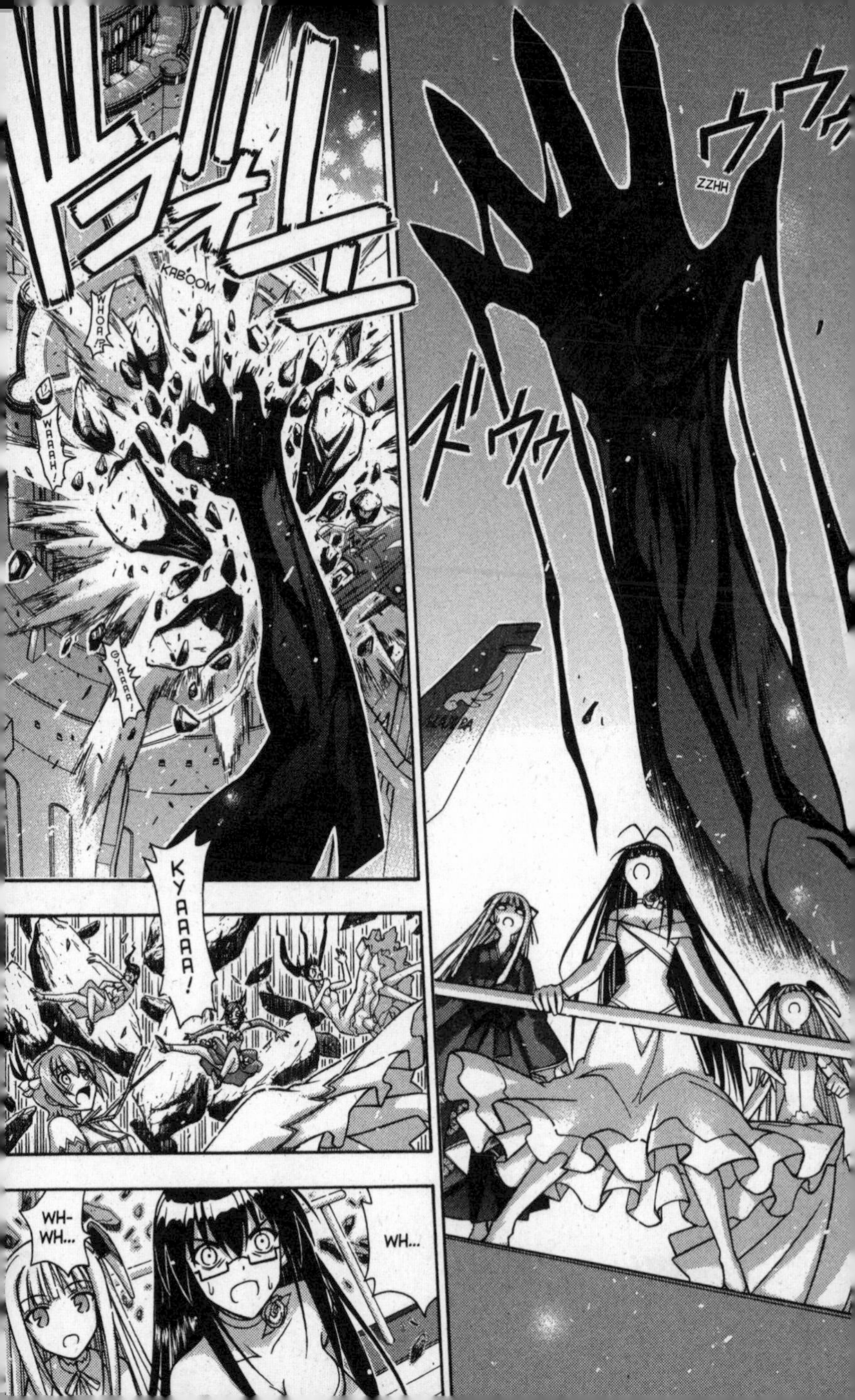
ZZHH
KABOOM
WHOA!?
WAAAH!
GYAAAA!
KYAAAAA!
WH...
WH-WH...

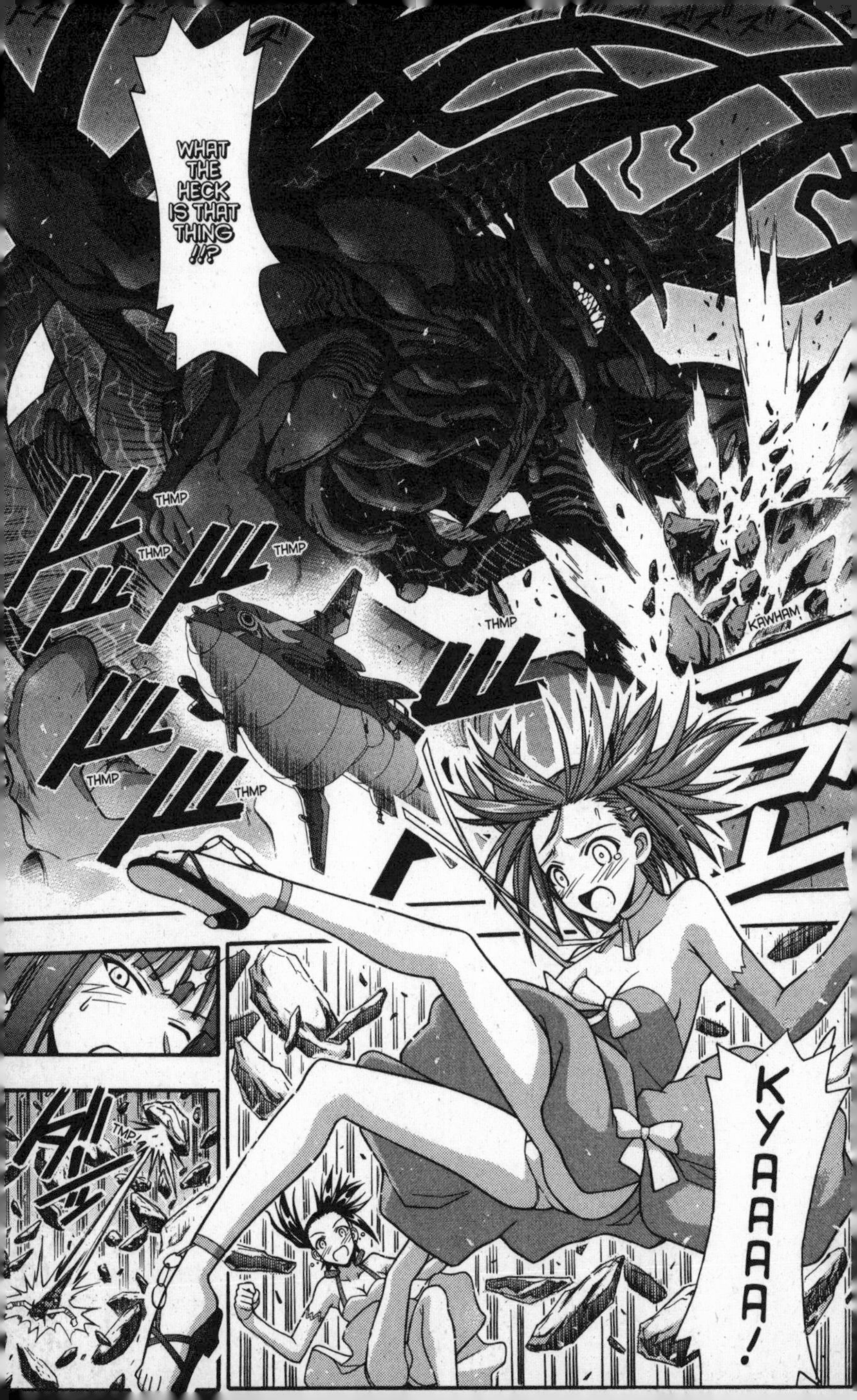
WHAT THE HECK IS THAT THING!!?
KAWHAM
THMP
THMP
THMP
THMP
THMP
THMP
KYAAAAA!
TMP!

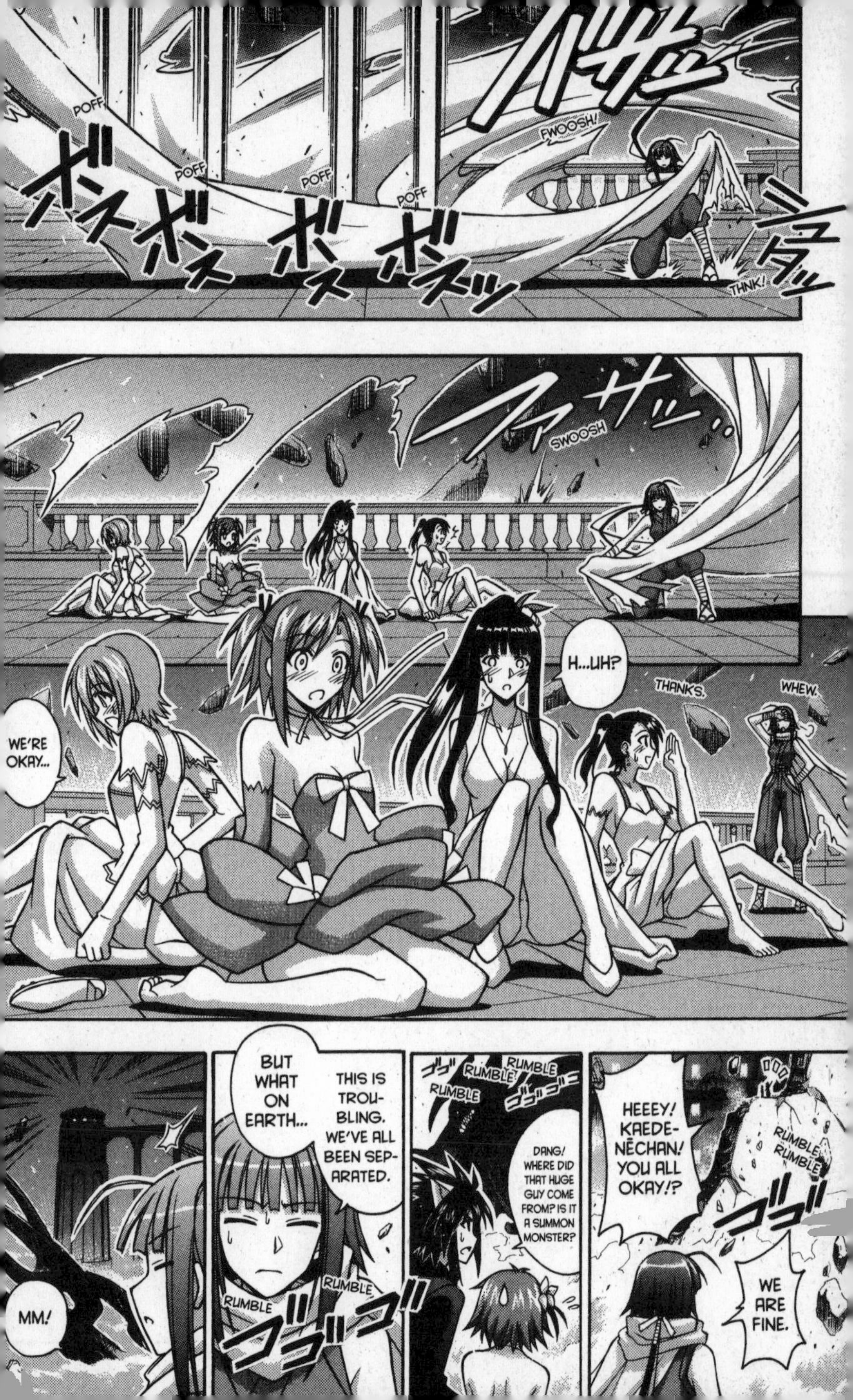

FWOOSH!
THNK!
POFF
POFF
POFF
POFF
SWOOSH
WHEW.
THANKS.
H...UH?
WE'RE OKAY...
HEEEY! KAEDE-NĒCHAN! YOU ALL OKAY!?
RUMBLE RUMBLE
WE ARE FINE.
RUMBLE
RUMBLE
RUMBLE
DANG! WHERE DID THAT HUGE GUY COME FROM? IS IT A SUMMON MONSTER?
THIS IS TROU-BLING. WE'VE ALL BEEN SEP-ARATED.
BUT WHAT ON EARTH...
RUMBLE
RUMBLE
MM!

THAT'S....!

SO, *THEY* HAVE COME TO US...

WHOOSH

THIS IS NOT GOOD.

THE ENEMY HAS ARRIVED IN SWARMS.

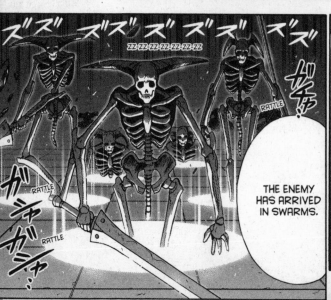

RATTLE

RATTLE

RATTLE

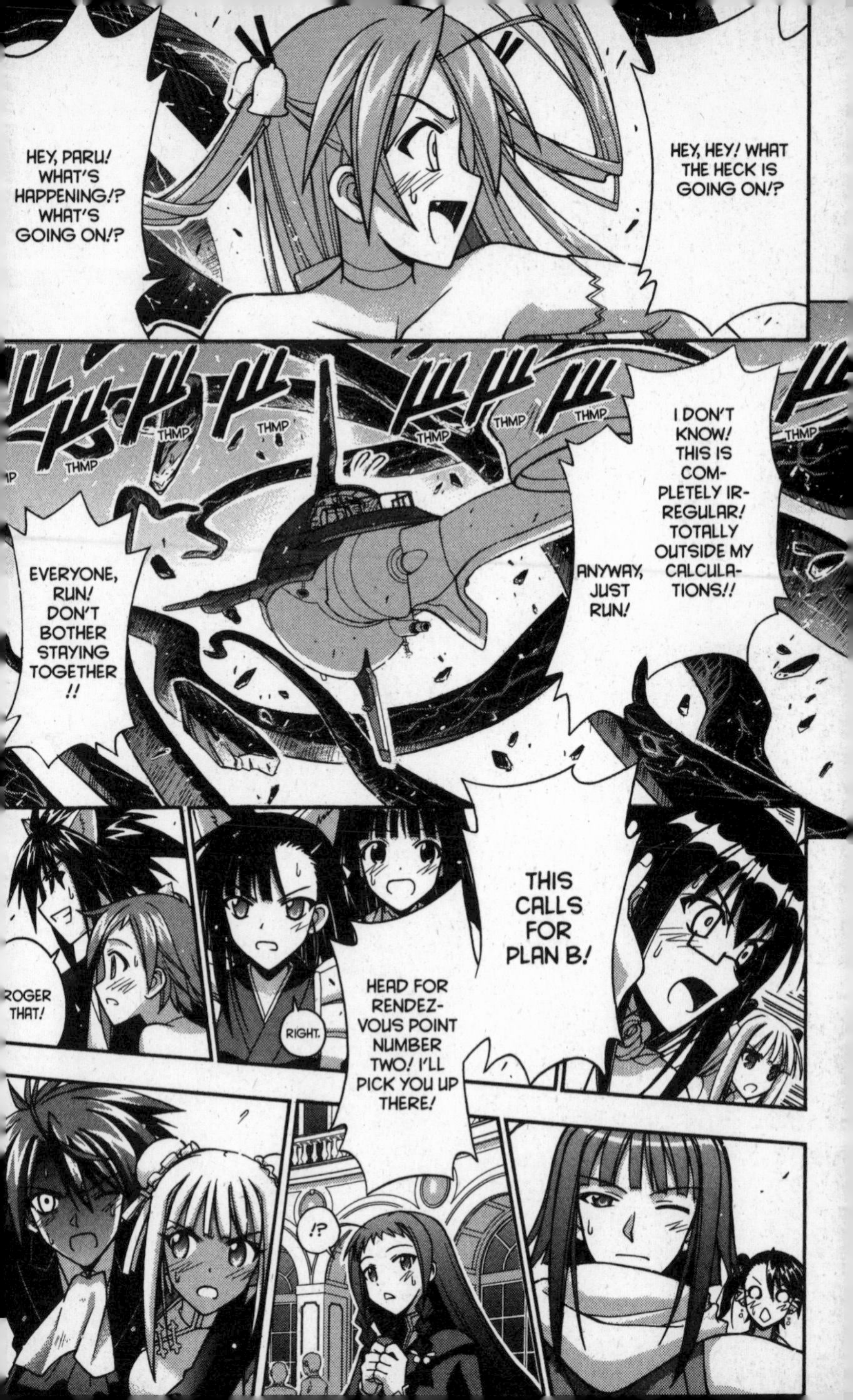
HEY, HEY! WHAT THE HECK IS GOING ON!?
HEY, PARU! WHAT'S HAPPENING!? WHAT'S GOING ON!?
THMP THMP THMP THMP THMP THMP THMP
I DON'T KNOW! THIS IS COM-PLETELY IR-REGULAR! TOTALLY OUTSIDE MY CALCULA-TIONS!!
ANYWAY, JUST RUN!
EVERYONE, RUN! DON'T BOTHER STAYING TOGETHER!!
THIS CALLS FOR PLAN B!
HEAD FOR RENDEZ-VOUS POINT NUMBER TWO! I'LL PICK YOU UP THERE!
RIGHT.
ROGER THAT!
!?

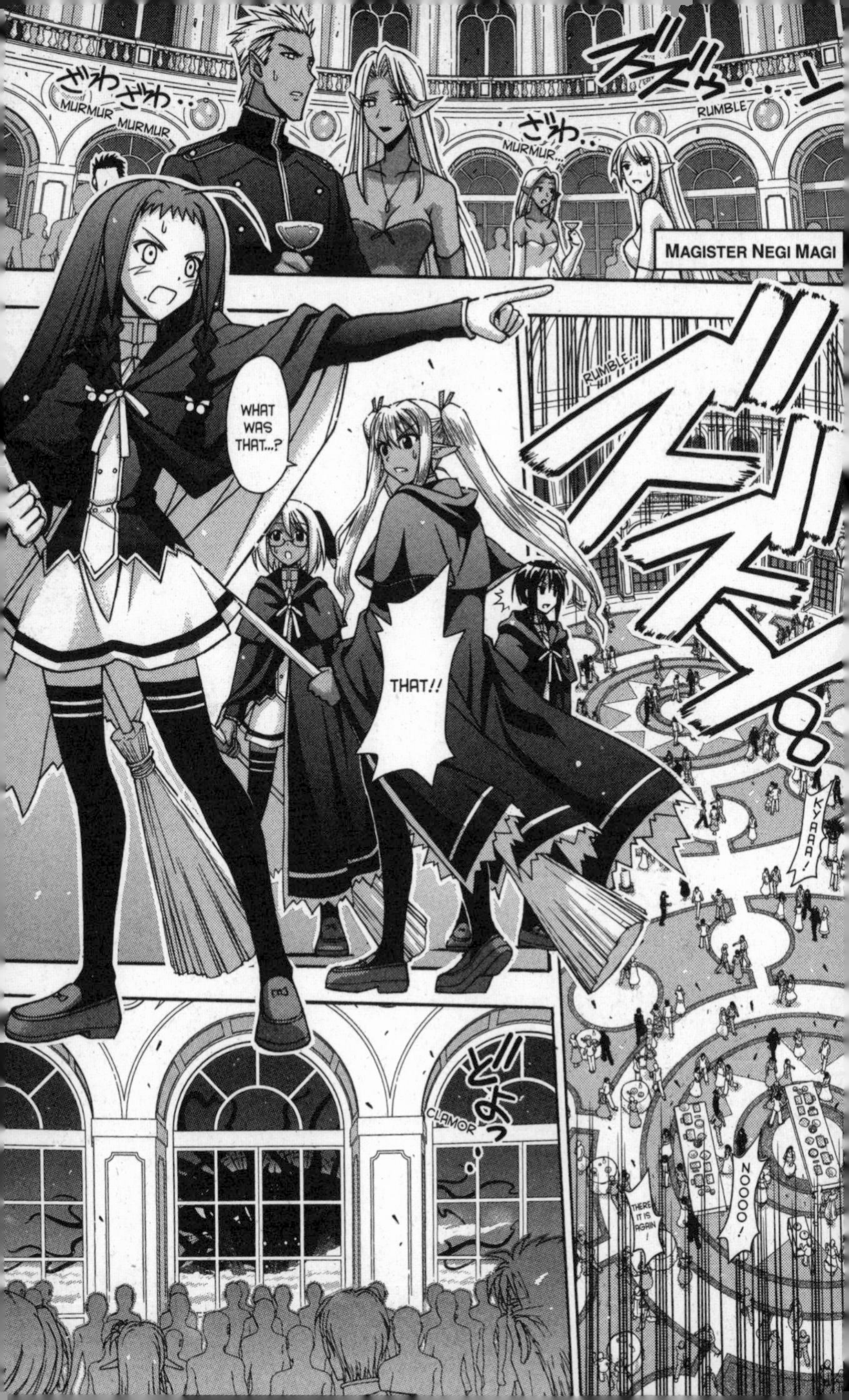

ずずぅ…ン
RUMBLE
ざわ…
MURMUR…
ざわざわ…
MURMUR MURMUR
RUMBLE…
KYAAA!
NOOOO!
THERE IT IS AGAIN!
WHAT WAS THAT…?
THAT!!
どよっ
CLAMOR

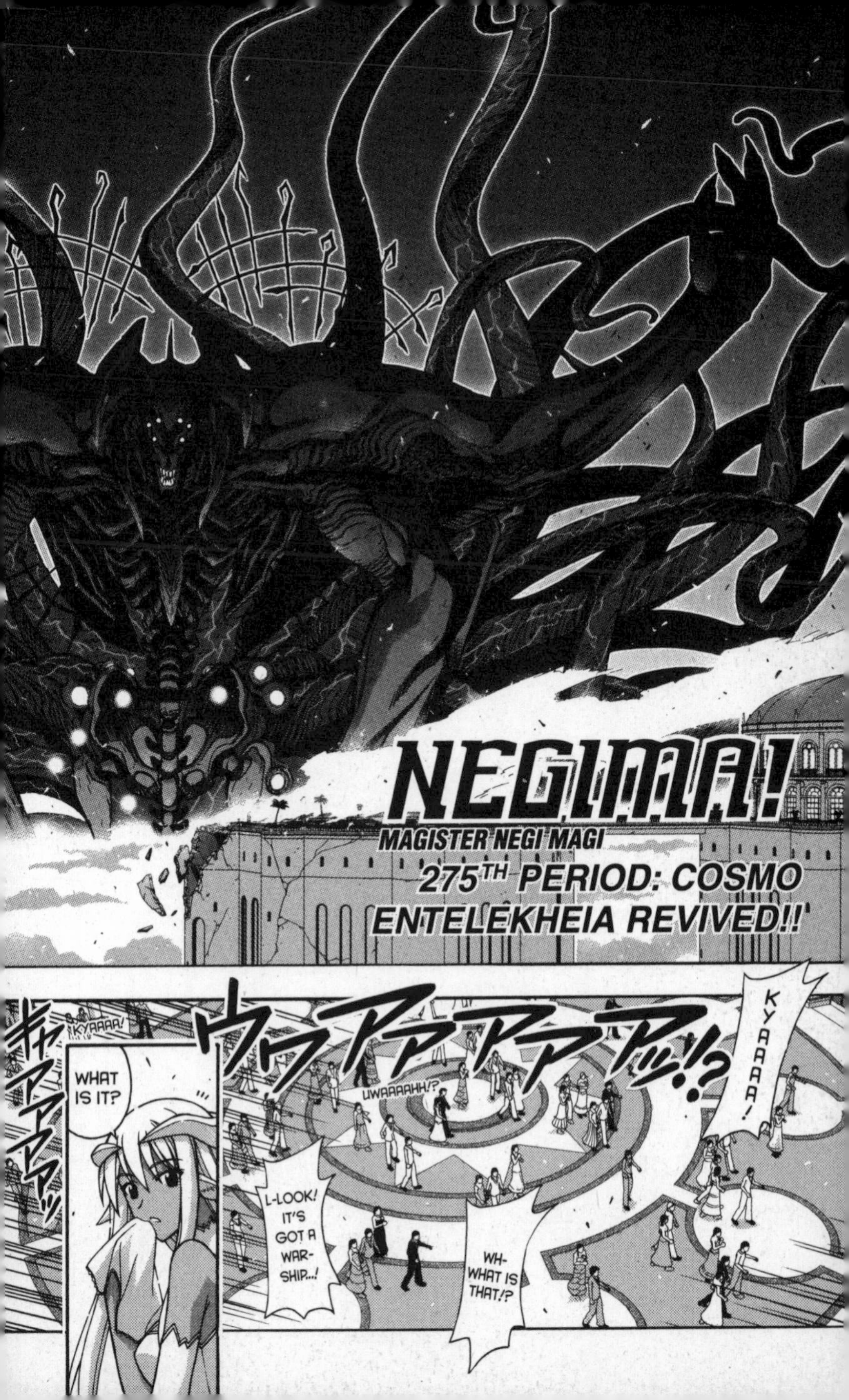
NEGIMA!
MAGISTER NEGI MAGI
275TH PERIOD: COSMO ENTELEKHEIA REVIVED!!
KYAAAAA!
ウワアアアアッ!?
UWAAAAAHH!?
KYAAAAA!
キャアアアアッ
WH-WHAT IS THAT!?
L-LOOK! IT'S GOT A WAR-SHIP...!
WHAT IS IT?

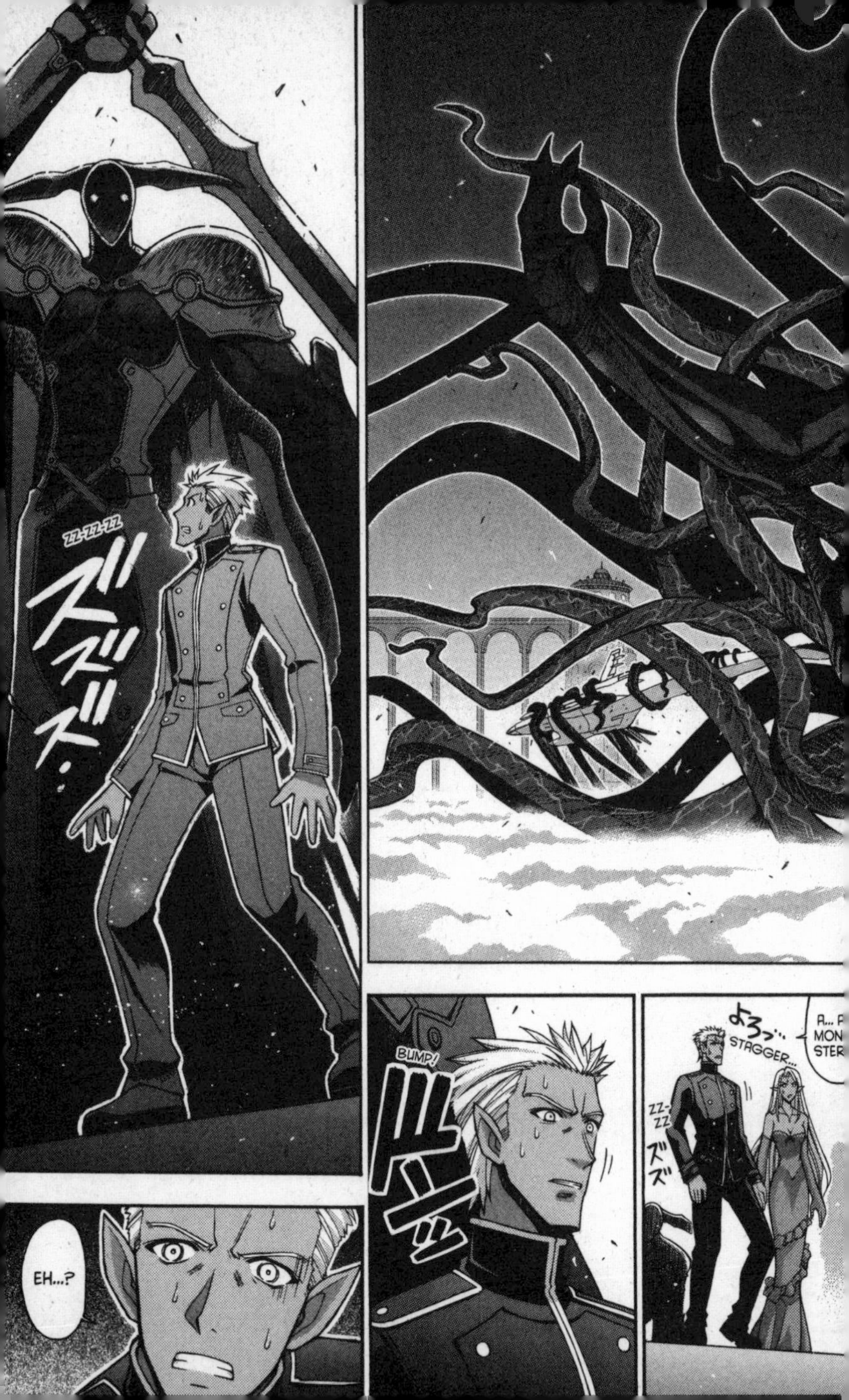
ZZ-ZZ-ZZ
ズズズ…
よろっ… STAGGER...
A... A MONSTER
ZZ-ZZ ズズ
BUMP!
EH...?

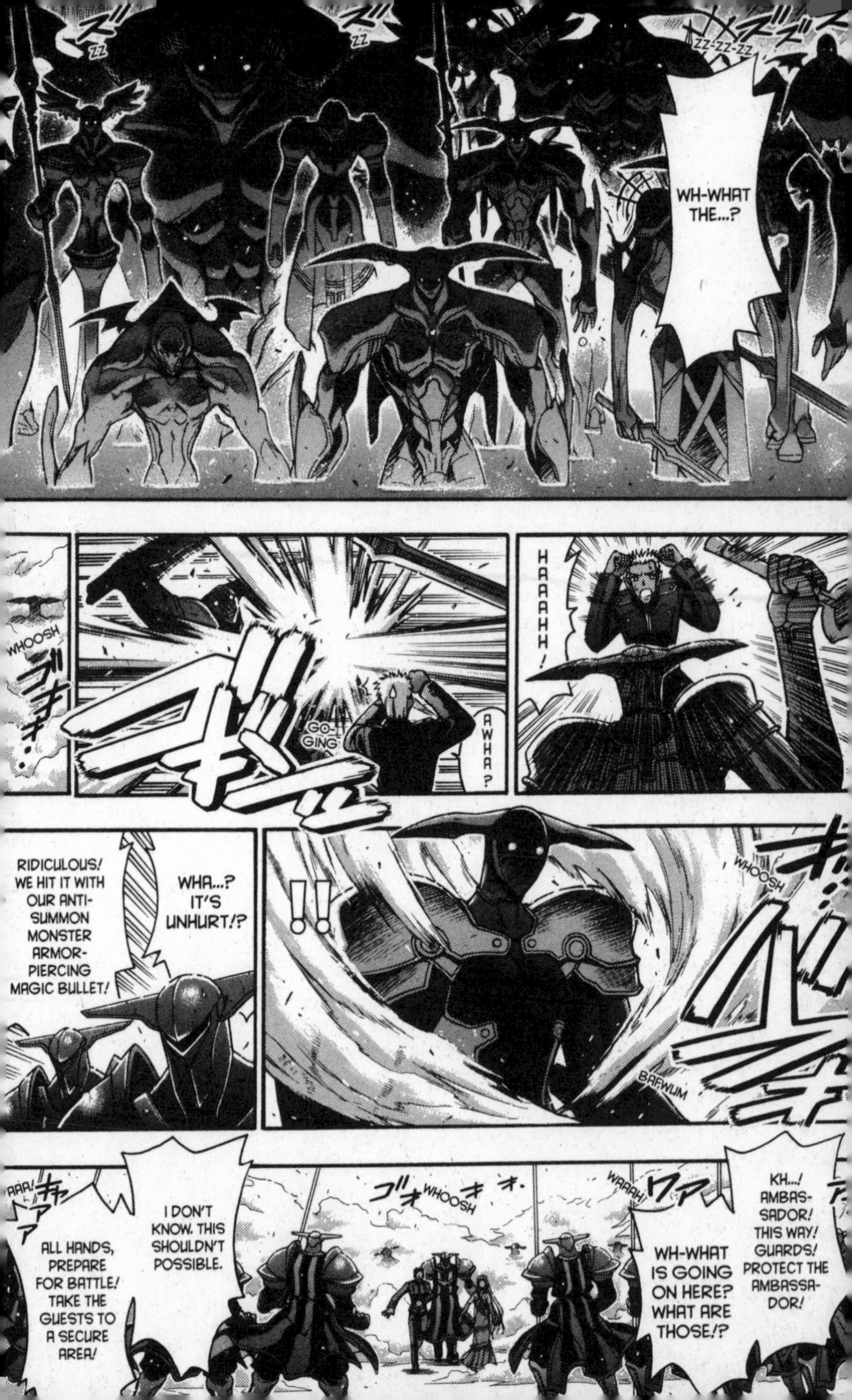
ZZ-ZZ-ZZ
WH-WHAT THE...?
ZZ
ZZ
HAAAAHH!
AWHA?
GO-GING
WHOOSH
WHOOSH
BAFWUM
WHA...? IT'S UNHURT!?
RIDICULOUS! WE HIT IT WITH OUR ANTI-SUMMON MONSTER ARMOR-PIERCING MAGIC BULLET!
KH...! AMBAS-SADOR! THIS WAY! GUARDS! PROTECT THE AMBASSA-DOR!
WH-WHAT IS GOING ON HERE? WHAT ARE THOSE!?
WAAAH!
WHOOSH
I DON'T KNOW. THIS SHOULDN'T POSSIBLE.
ALL HANDS, PREPARE FOR BATTLE! TAKE THE GUESTS TO A SECURE AREA!
AAA!

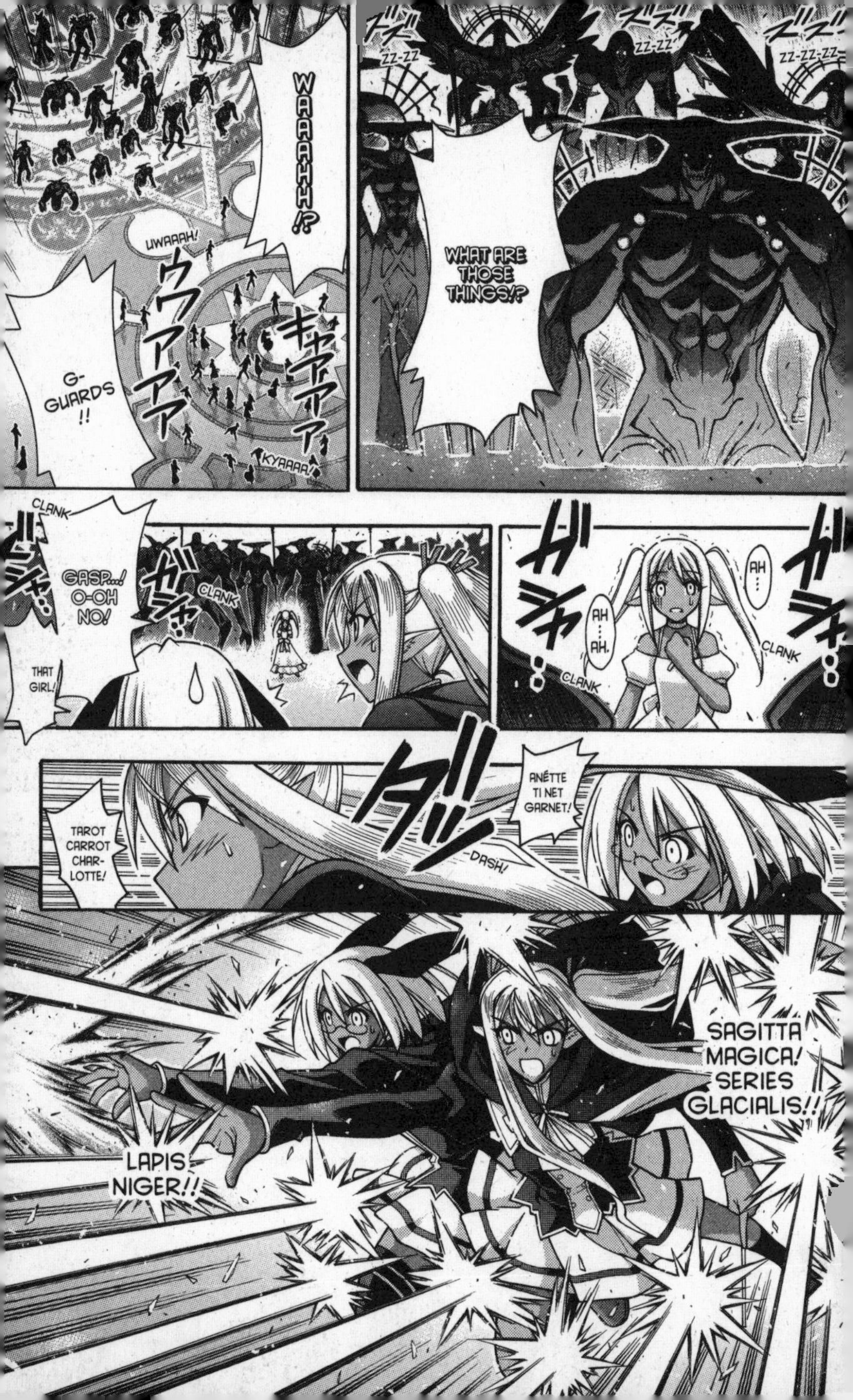
ZZ-ZZ
ZZ-ZZ!
ZZ-ZZ-ZZ
WHAT ARE THOSE THINGS!?
WAAAAHHH!?
UWAAAH!
KYAAAA!
G-GUARDS!!
AH...
AH... AH.
CLANK
CLANK
CLANK
GASP...! O-OH NO!
CLANK
THAT GIRL!
ANÉTTE TI NET GARNET!
DASH!
TAROT CARROT CHAR-LOTTE!
SAGITTA MAGICA! SERIES GLACIALIS!!
LAPIS NIGER!!

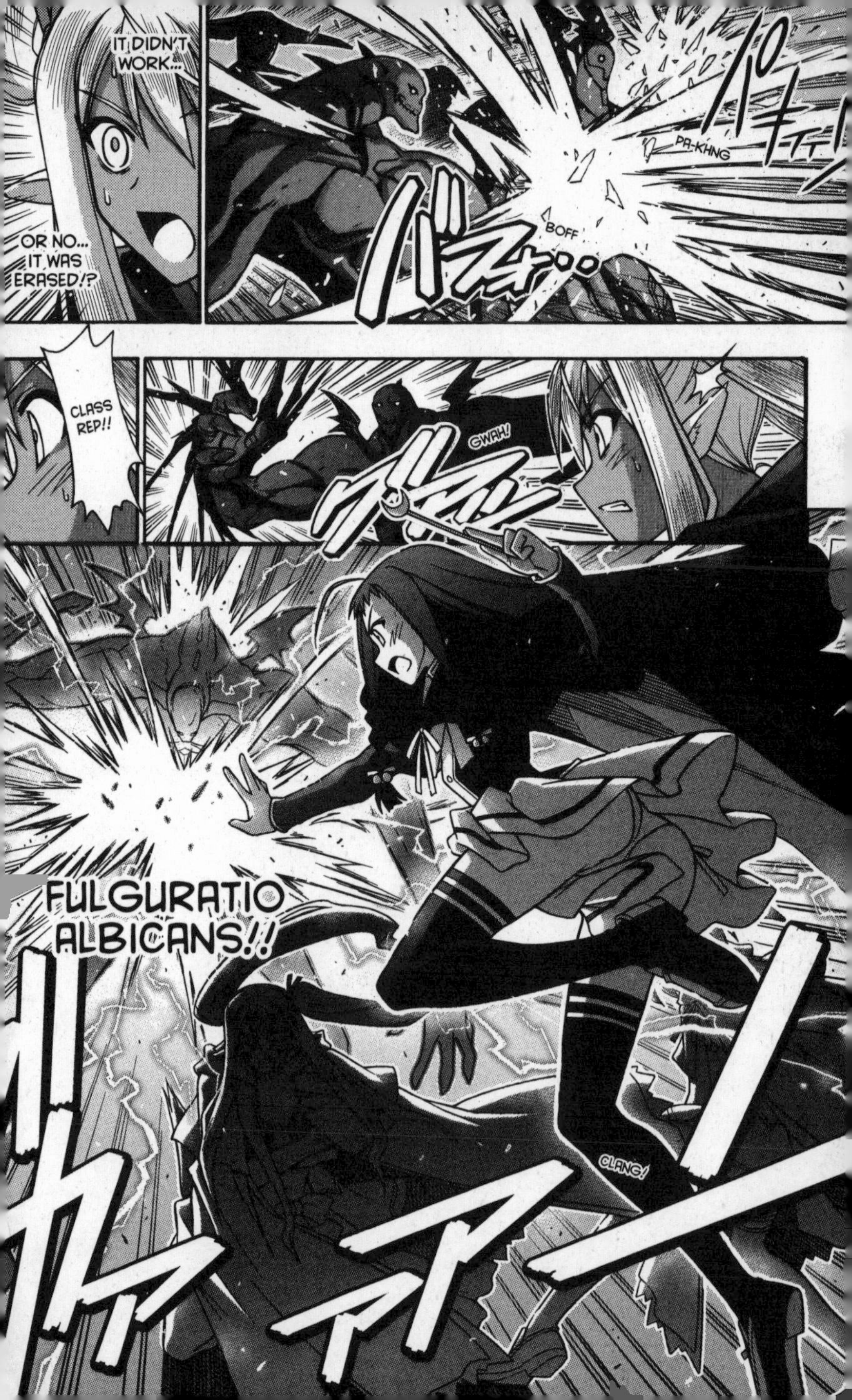
PA-KHNG
BOFF
IT DIDN'T WORK...
OR NO... IT WAS ERASED!?
GWAH!
CLASS REP!!
FULGURATIO ALBICANS!!
CLANG!

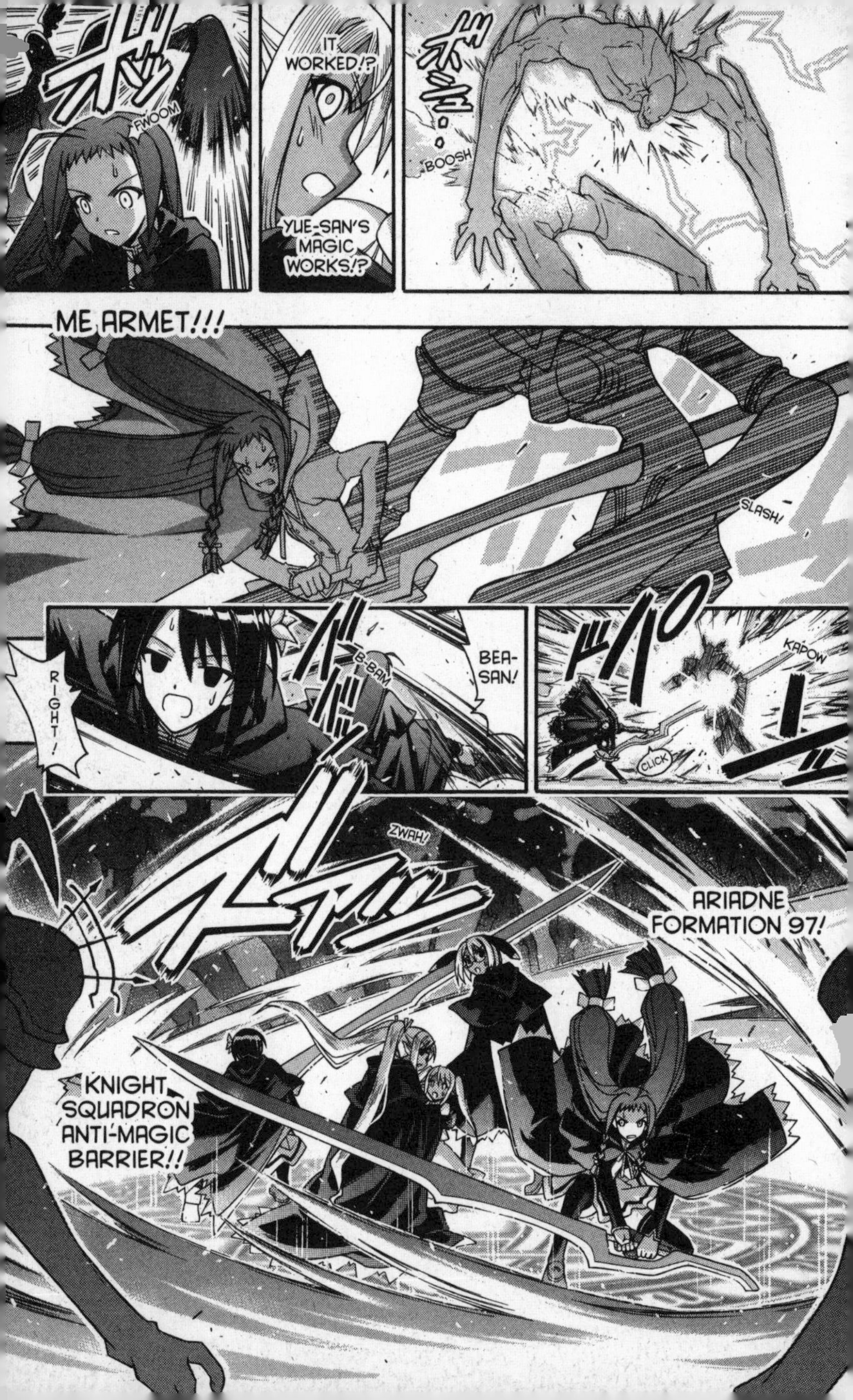
BOOSH
IT WORKED!?
YUE-SAN'S MAGIC WORKS!?
FWOOM
ME ARMET!!!
SLASH!
KAPOW
CLICK
BEA-SAN!
B-BAM
RIGHT!
ARIADNE FORMATION 97!
ZWAH!
KNIGHT SQUADRON ANTI-MAGIC BARRIER!!

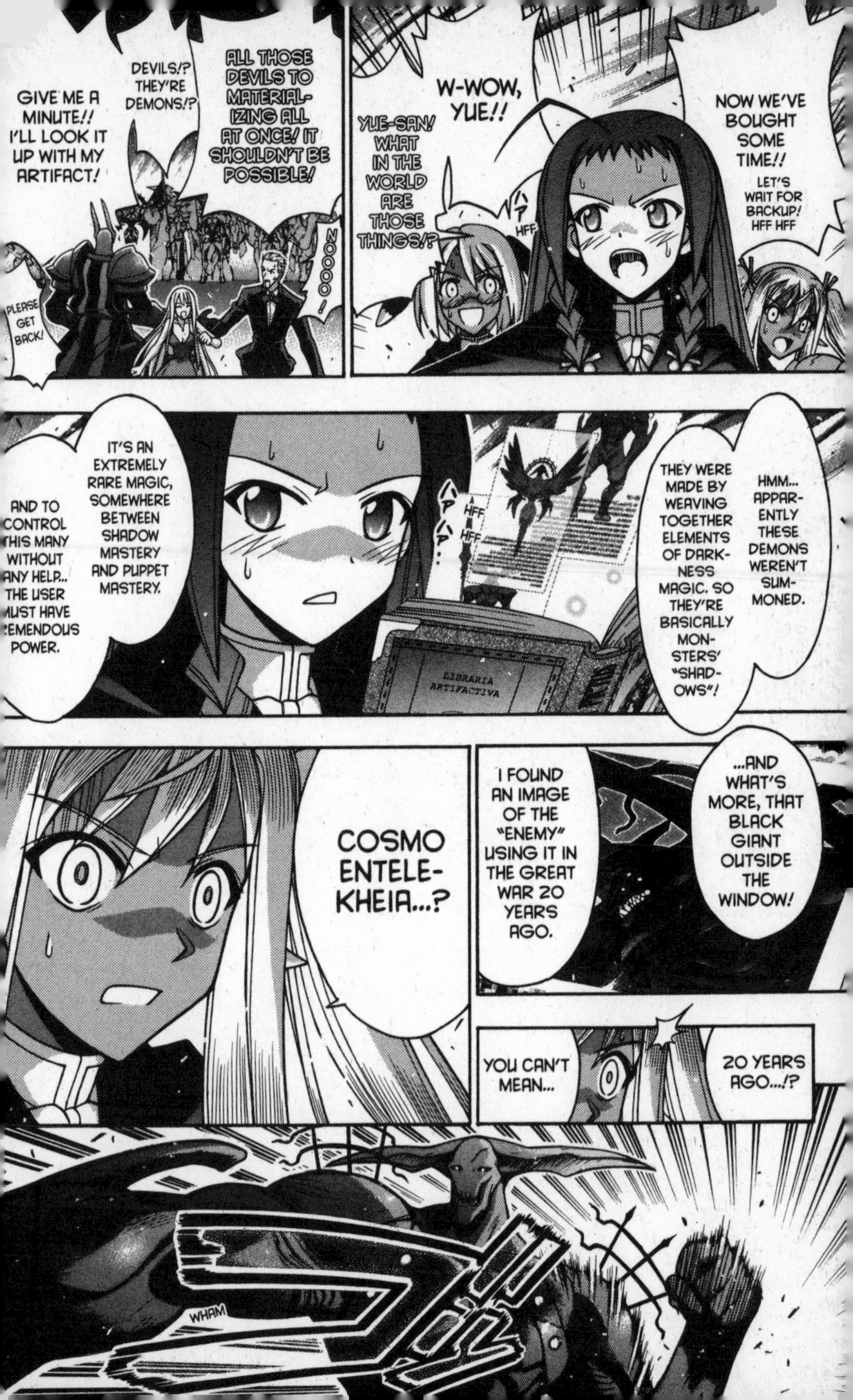
NOW WE'VE BOUGHT SOME TIME!!
LET'S WAIT FOR BACKUP! HFF HFF
W-WOW, YUE!!
YUE-SAN! WHAT IN THE WORLD ARE THOSE THINGS!?
HFF
ALL THOSE DEVILS TO MATERIALIZING ALL AT ONCE! IT SHOULDN'T BE POSSIBLE!
DEVILS!? THEY'RE DEMONS!?
GIVE ME A MINUTE!! I'LL LOOK IT UP WITH MY ARTIFACT!
NOOOO!
PLEASE GET BACK!
HMM... APPARENTLY THESE DEMONS WEREN'T SUMMONED.
THEY WERE MADE BY WEAVING TOGETHER ELEMENTS OF DARKNESS MAGIC. SO THEY'RE BASICALLY MONSTERS' "SHADOWS"!
HFF HFF
LIBRARIA ARTIFACTIVA
IT'S AN EXTREMELY RARE MAGIC, SOMEWHERE BETWEEN SHADOW MASTERY AND PUPPET MASTERY.
AND TO CONTROL THIS MANY WITHOUT ANY HELP... THE USER MUST HAVE TREMENDOUS POWER.
...AND WHAT'S MORE, THAT BLACK GIANT OUTSIDE THE WINDOW!
I FOUND AN IMAGE OF THE "ENEMY" USING IT IN THE GREAT WAR 20 YEARS AGO.
20 YEARS AGO...!?
YOU CAN'T MEAN...
COSMO ENTELEKHEIA...?
WHAM

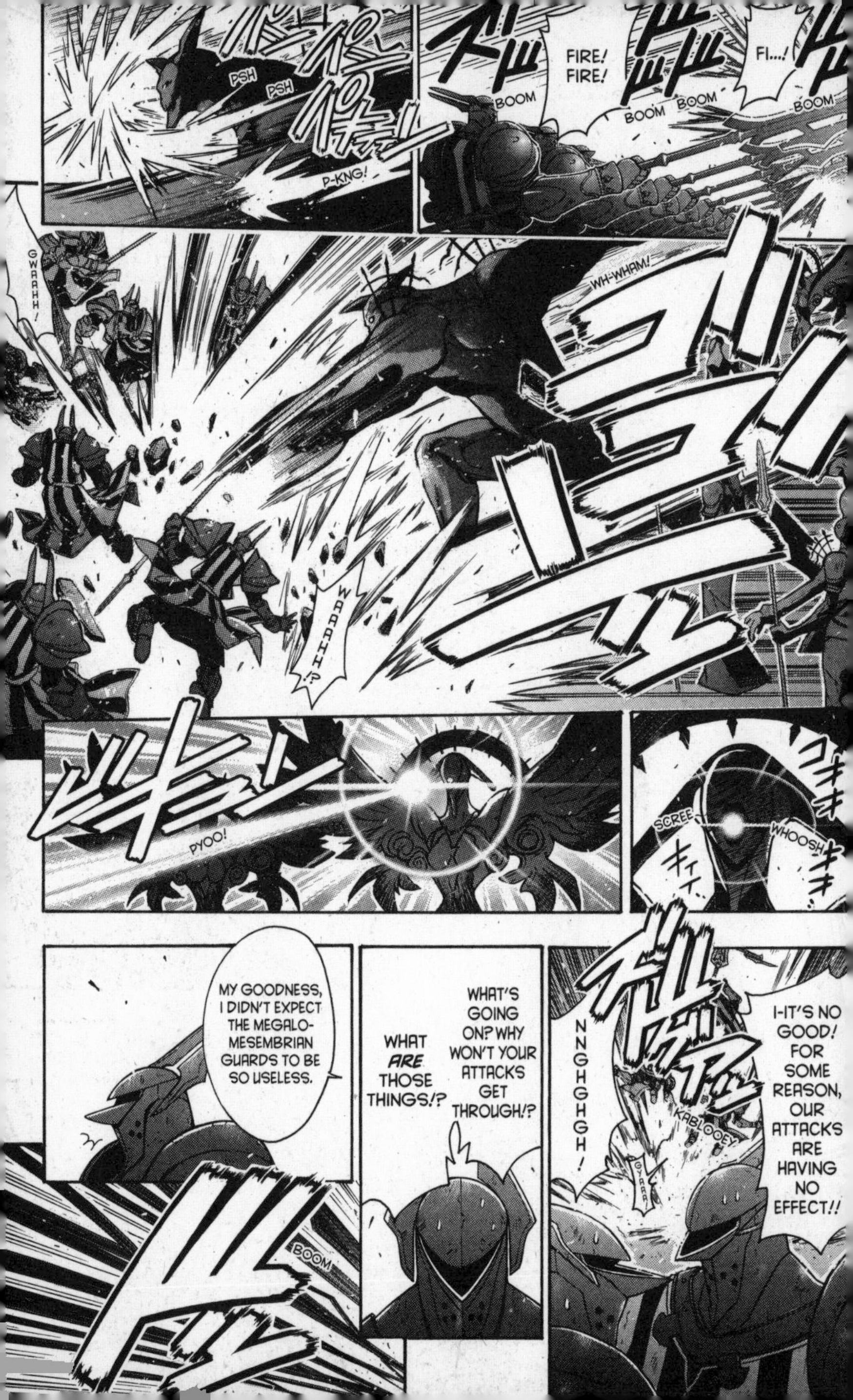
FIRE! FIRE!
BOOM
BOOM
BOOM
FI...!
BOOM
PSH
PSH
P-KNG!
WH-WHAM!
GWAAHH!
WAAAHH!?
SCREE
WHOOSH
PYOO!
I-IT'S NO GOOD! FOR SOME REASON, OUR ATTACKS ARE HAVING NO EFFECT!!
NNGHGHGH!
KABLOOEY
GYRRR
WHAT'S GOING ON? WHY WON'T YOUR ATTACKS GET THROUGH!?
WHAT *ARE* THOSE THINGS!?
MY GOODNESS, I DIDN'T EXPECT THE MEGALO-MESEMBRIAN GUARDS TO BE SO USELESS.
BOOM

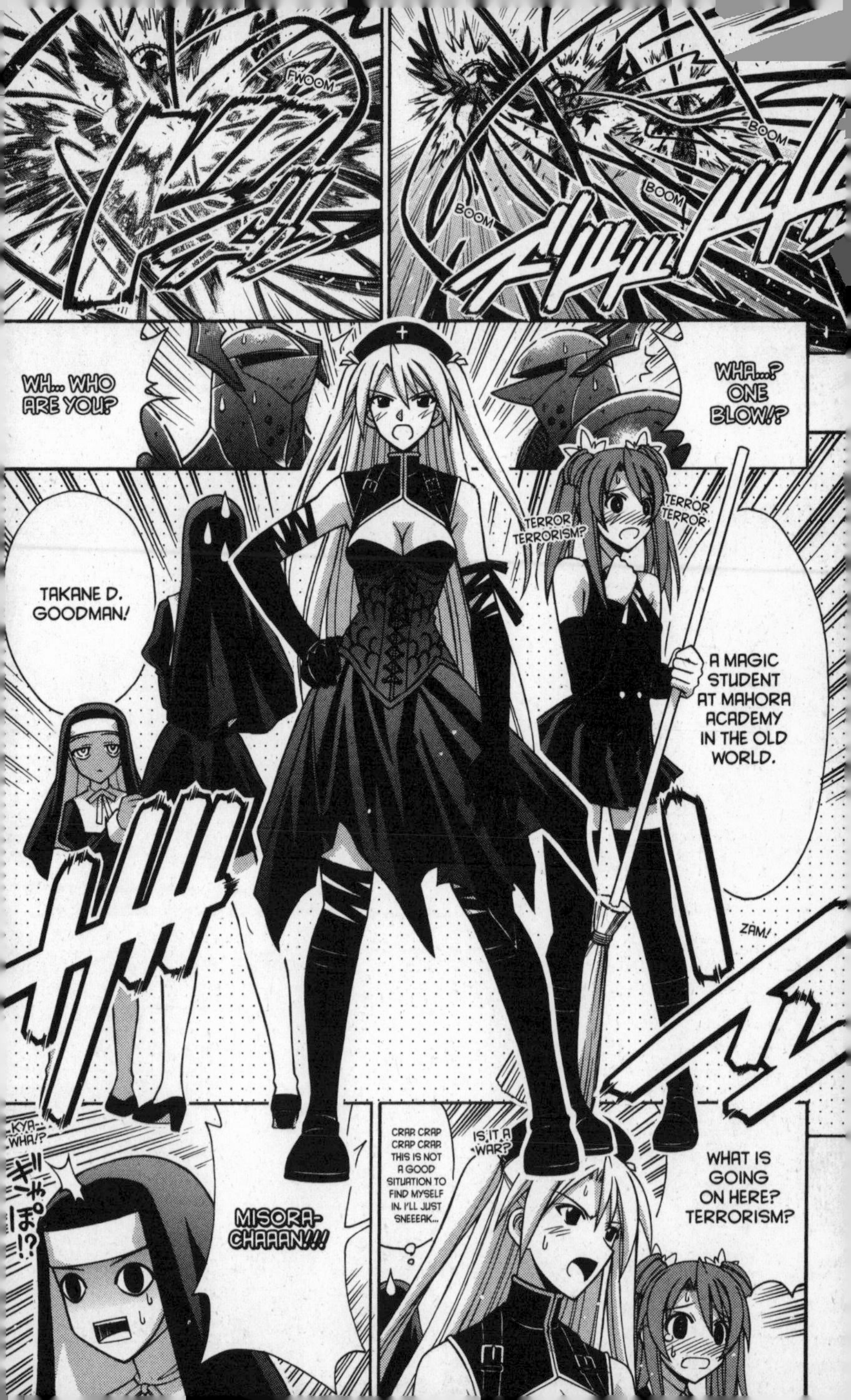
BOOM
BOOM
BOOM
FWOOM
WHA...? ONE BLOW!?
WH... WHO ARE YOU!?
TERROR TERROR
TERRORISM?
TAKANE D. GOODMAN!
A MAGIC STUDENT AT MAHORA ACADEMY IN THE OLD WORLD.
ZAM!
WHAT IS GOING ON HERE? TERRORISM?
IS IT A WAR?
CRAP CRAP CRAP CRAP THIS IS NOT A GOOD SITUATION TO FIND MYSELF IN. I'LL JUST SNEEEAK...
MISORA-CHAAAN!!!
KYA-WHA!?
ギャぽ!?

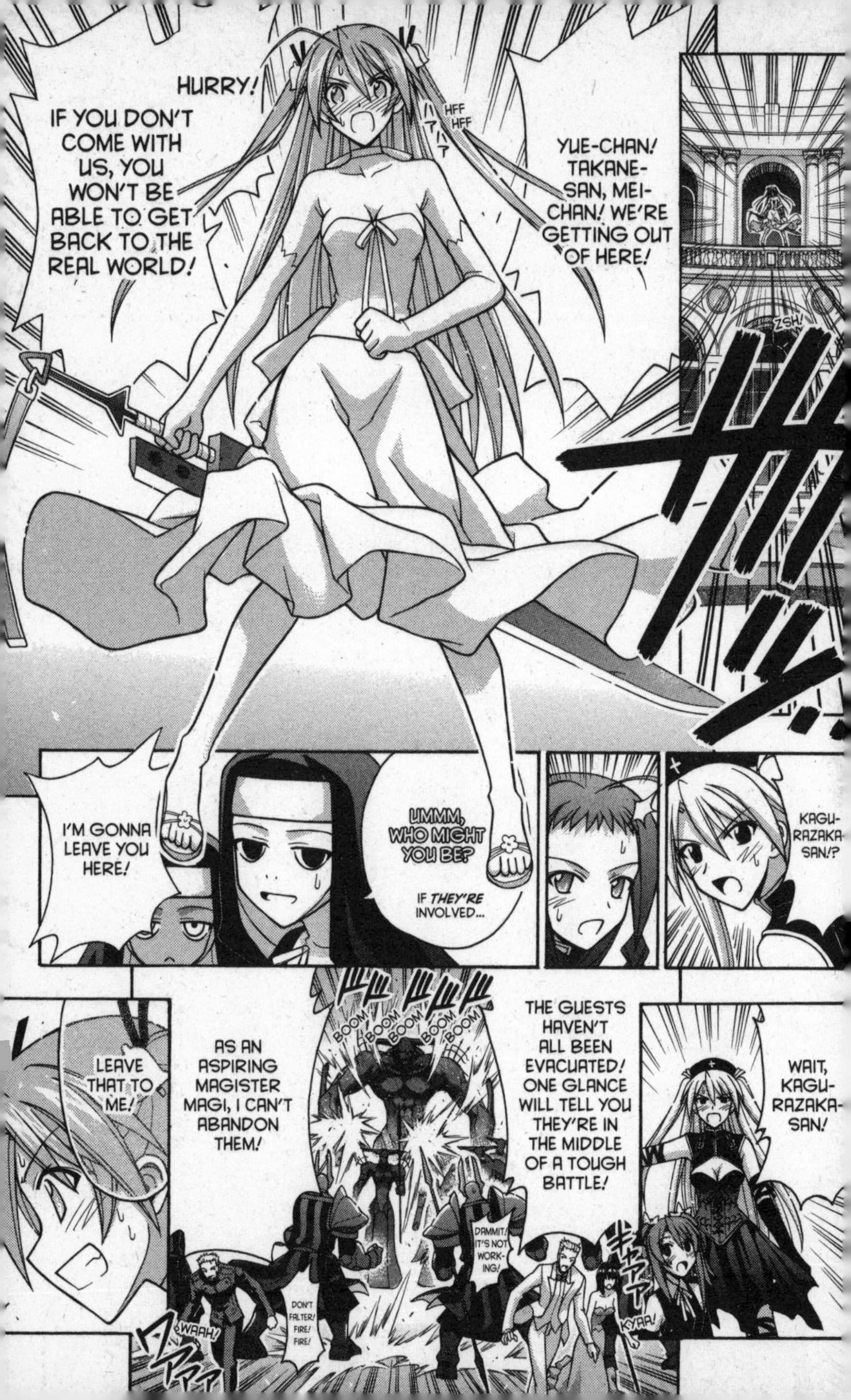
ZSH!
YUE-CHAN! TAKANE-SAN, MEI-CHAN! WE'RE GETTING OUT OF HERE!
HFF HFF
HURRY!
IF YOU DON'T COME WITH US, YOU WON'T BE ABLE TO GET BACK TO THE REAL WORLD!
KAGU-RAZAKA-SAN!?
UMMM, WHO MIGHT YOU BE?
IF *THEY'RE* INVOLVED...
I'M GONNA LEAVE YOU HERE!
WAIT, KAGU-RAZAKA-SAN!
KYAA!
THE GUESTS HAVEN'T ALL BEEN EVACUATED! ONE GLANCE WILL TELL YOU THEY'RE IN THE MIDDLE OF A TOUGH BATTLE!
DAMMIT! IT'S NOT WORKING!
BOOM BOOM BOOM BOOM BOOM
AS AN ASPIRING MAGISTER MAGI, I CAN'T ABANDON THEM!
DON'T FALTER! FIRE! FIRE!
WAAH!
LEAVE THAT TO ME!

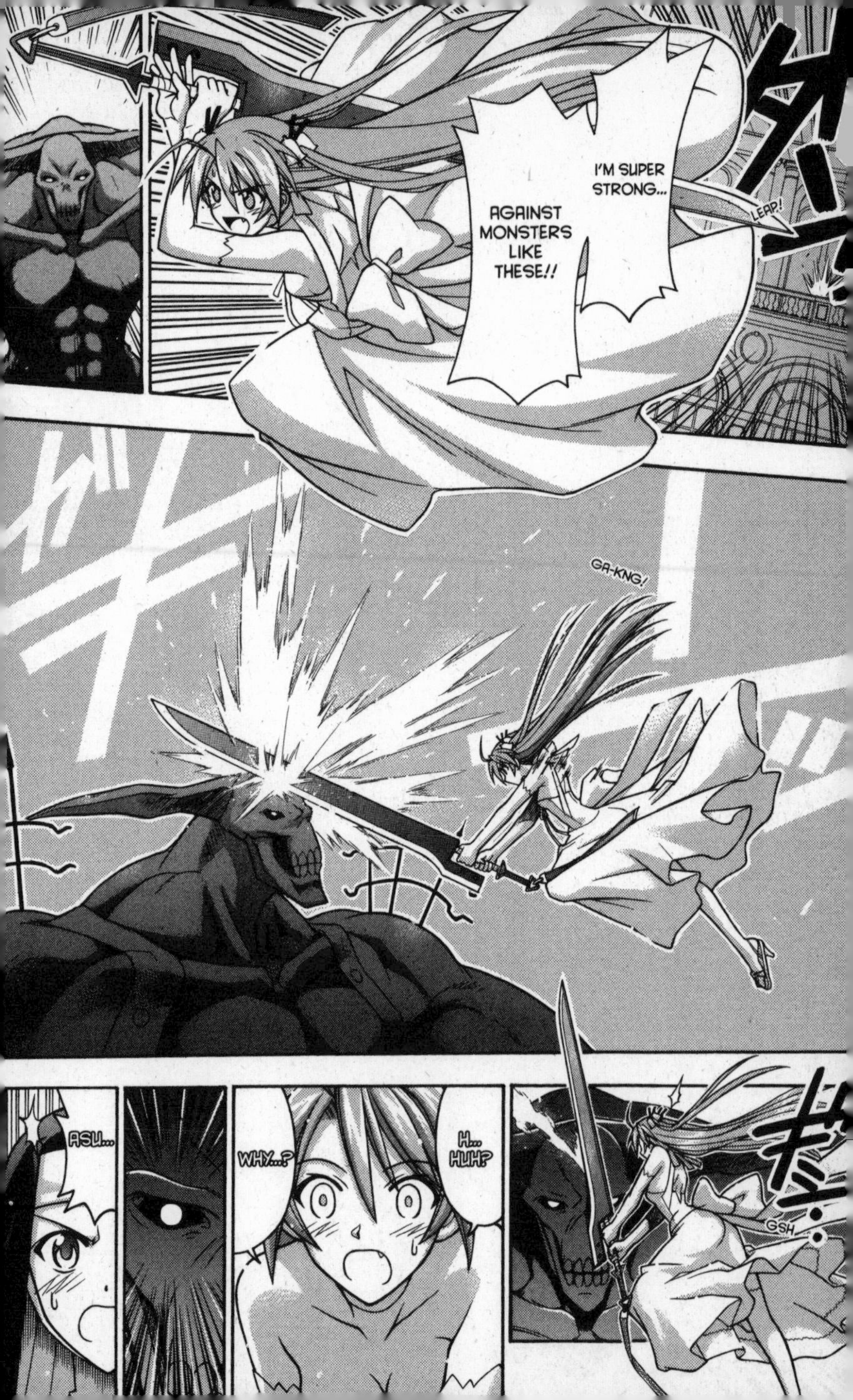
I'M SUPER STRONG...
AGAINST MONSTERS LIKE THESE!!
LEAP!
GA-KNG!
GSH
H... HUH?
WHY...?
ASU...

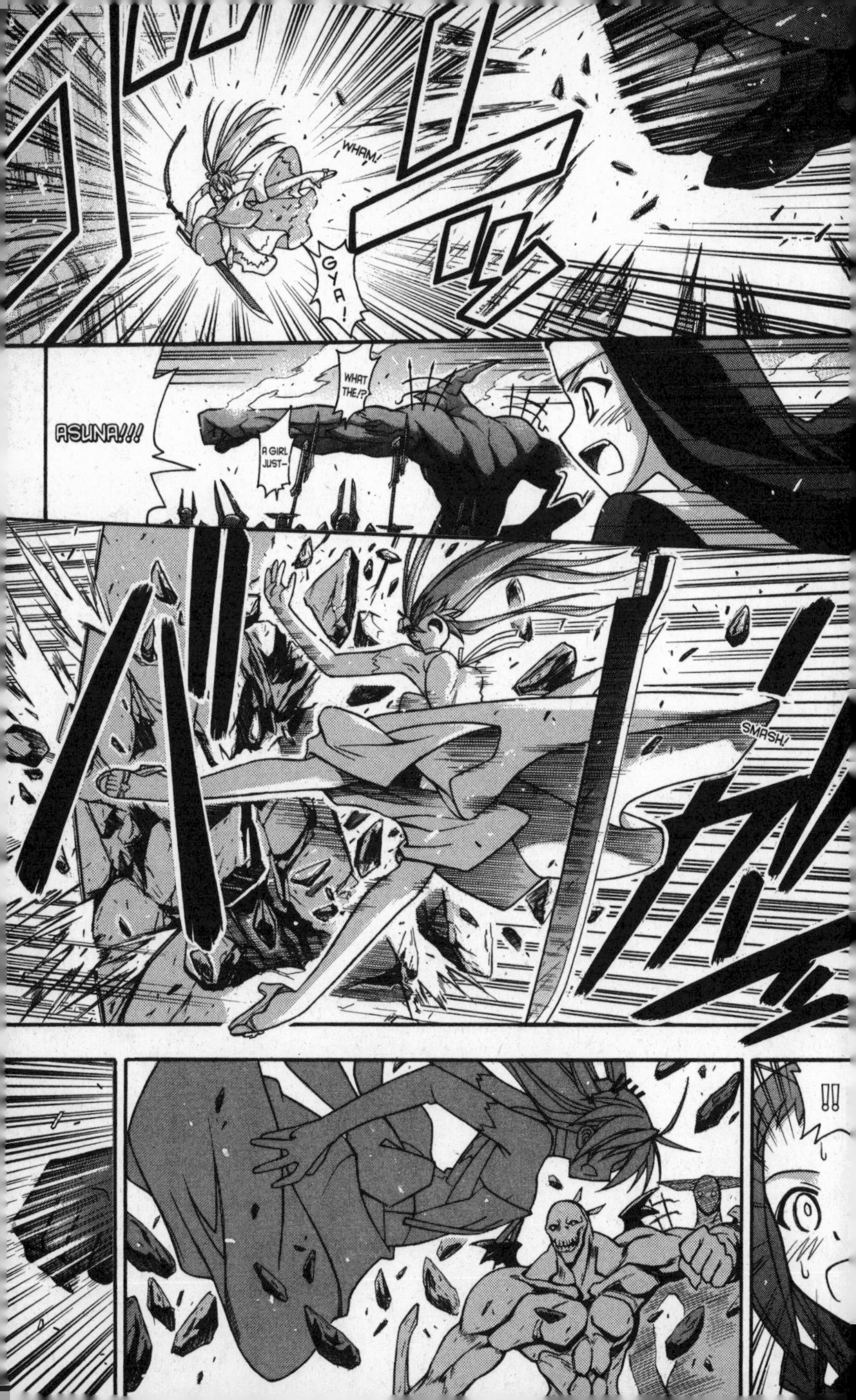
WHAM!
GYA!
WHAT THE!?
A GIRL JUST-
ASUNA!!!
SMASH!
!!

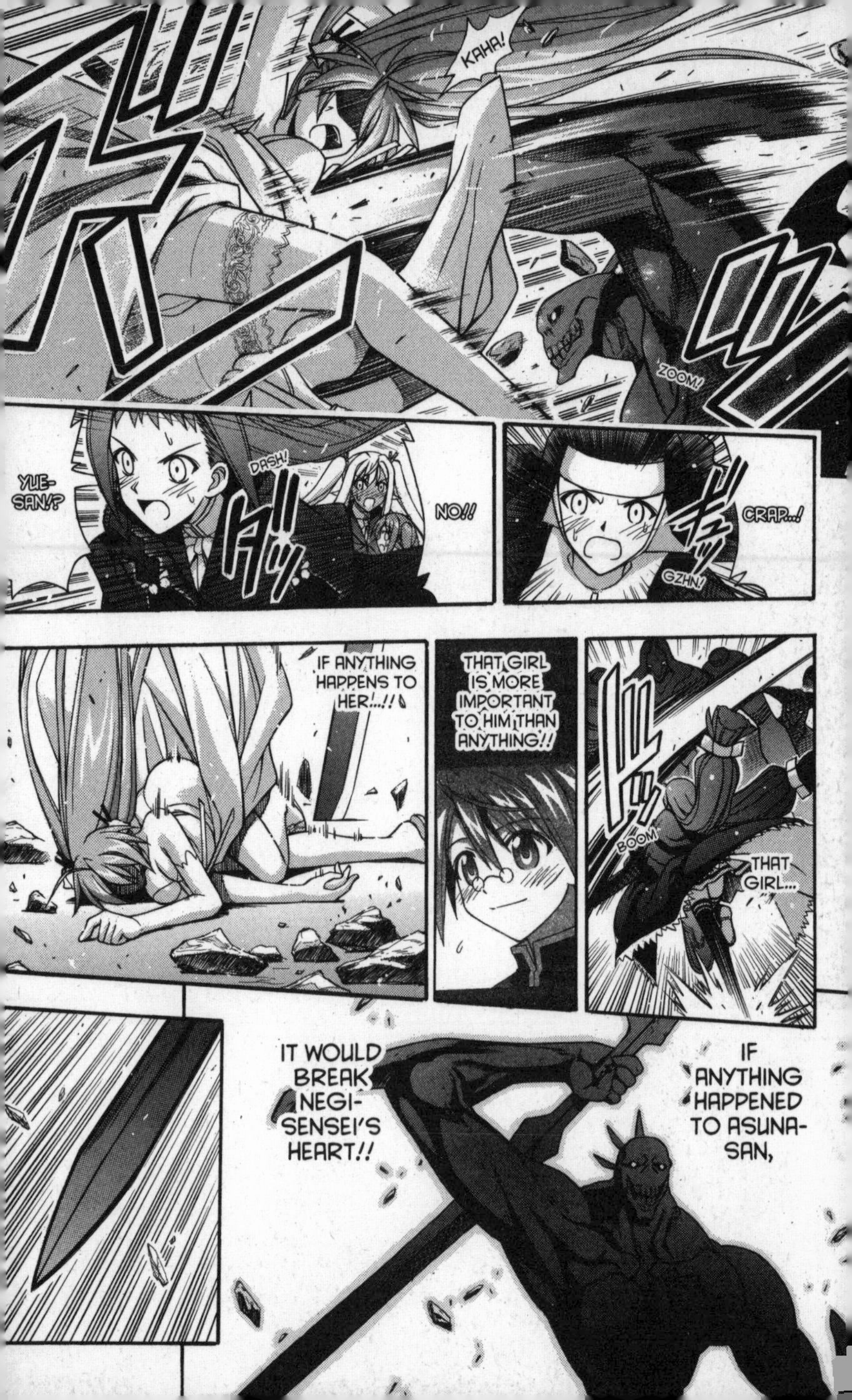
KAHA!
ZOOM!
CRAP...!
GZHN!
NO!!
DASH!
YUE-SAN!?
THAT GIRL...
BOOM!
THAT GIRL IS MORE IMPORTANT TO HIM THAN ANYTHING!!
IF ANYTHING HAPPENS TO HER...!!
IF ANYTHING HAPPENED TO ASUNA-SAN,
IT WOULD BREAK NEGI-SENSEI'S HEART!!

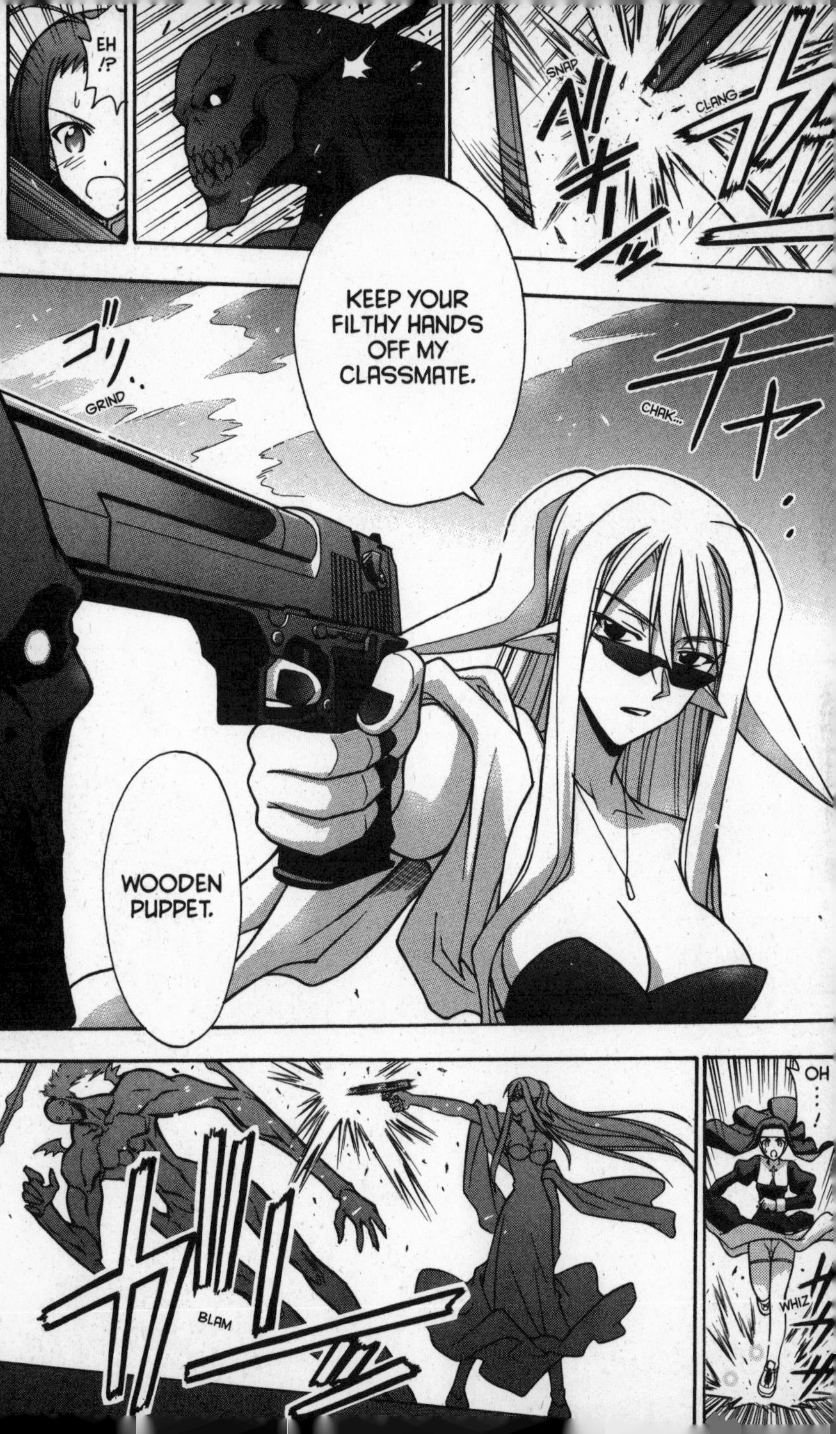
SNAP
CLANG
EH !?
CHAK...
KEEP YOUR FILTHY HANDS OFF MY CLASSMATE.
GRIND
WOODEN PUPPET.
OH...!
WHIZ
BLAM

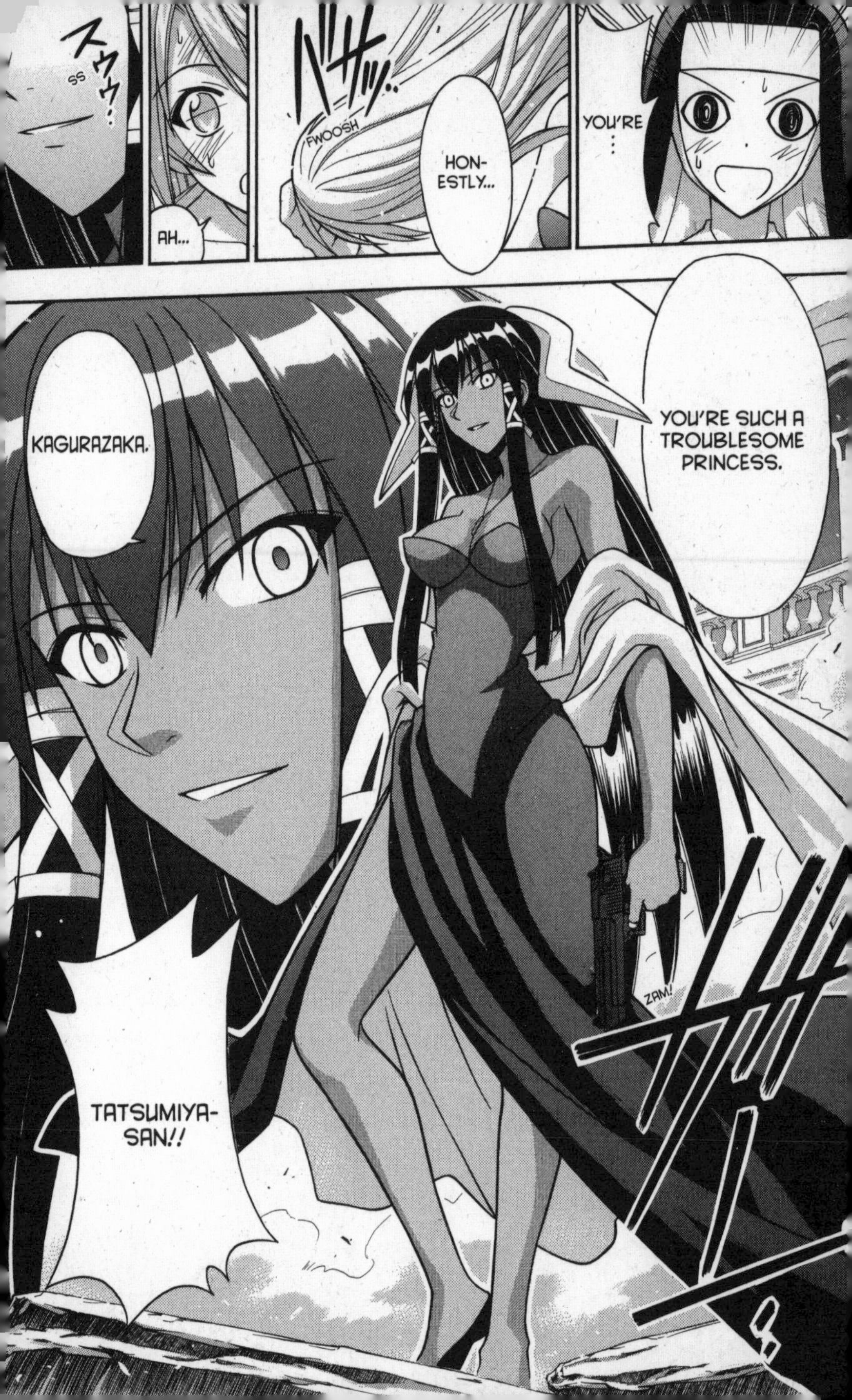
YOU'RE
...
FWOOSH
HON-ESTLY...
AH...
SS
YOU'RE SUCH A TROUBLESOME PRINCESS.
KAGURAZAKA.
ZAM!
TATSUMIYA-SAN!!

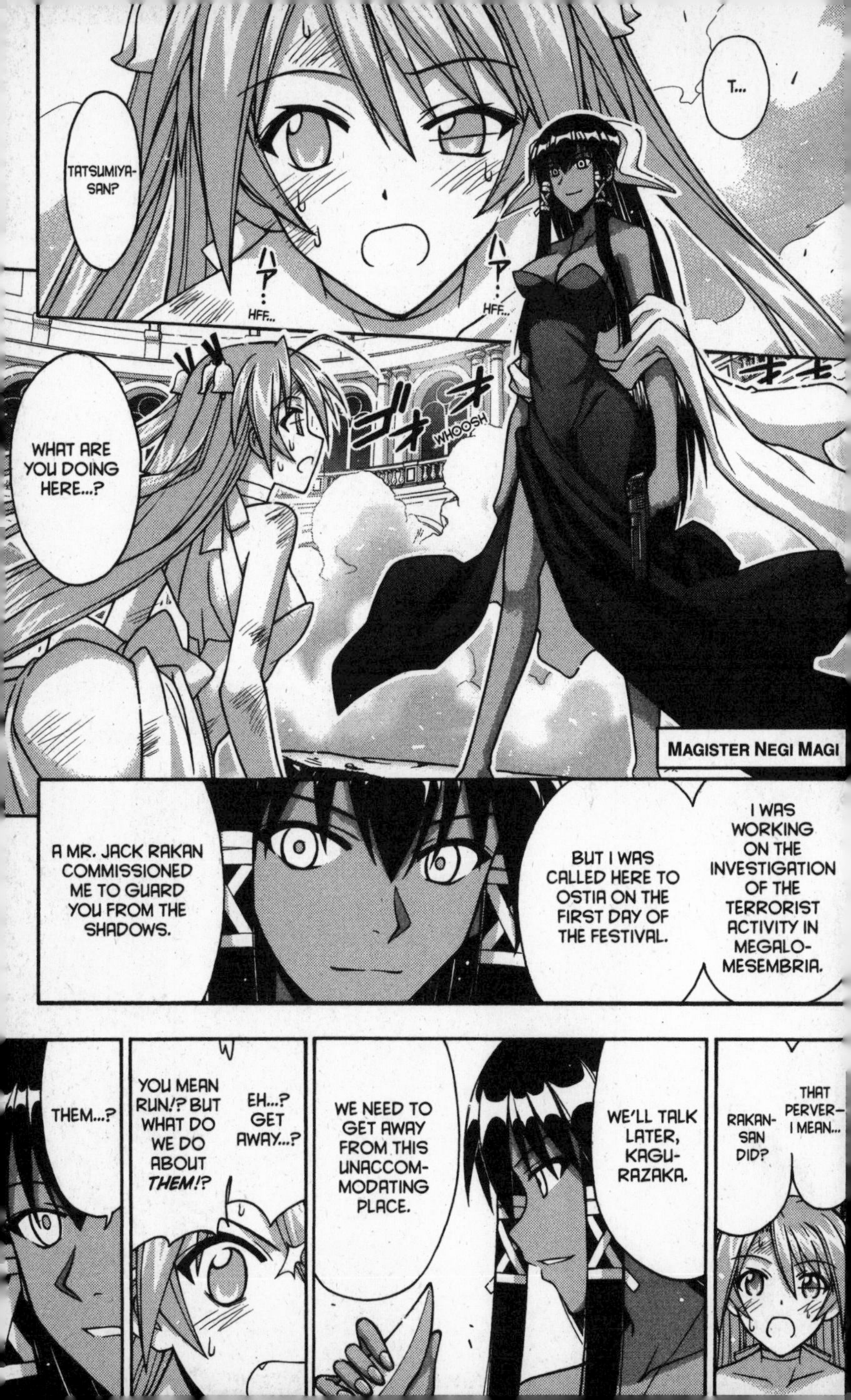
T...
TATSUMIYA-SAN?
ハァ
HFF...
ハァ
HFF...
WHAT ARE YOU DOING HERE...?
ゴオォ
WHOOSH
MAGISTER NEGI MAGI
I WAS WORKING ON THE INVESTIGATION OF THE TERRORIST ACTIVITY IN MEGALO-MESEMBRIA.
BUT I WAS CALLED HERE TO OSTIA ON THE FIRST DAY OF THE FESTIVAL.
A MR. JACK RAKAN COMMISSIONED ME TO GUARD YOU FROM THE SHADOWS.
THAT PERVER- I MEAN...
RAKAN-SAN DID?
WE'LL TALK LATER, KAGU-RAZAKA.
WE NEED TO GET AWAY FROM THIS UNACCOM-MODATING PLACE.
EH...? GET AWAY...?
YOU MEAN RUN!? BUT WHAT DO WE DO ABOUT *THEM!?*
THEM...?

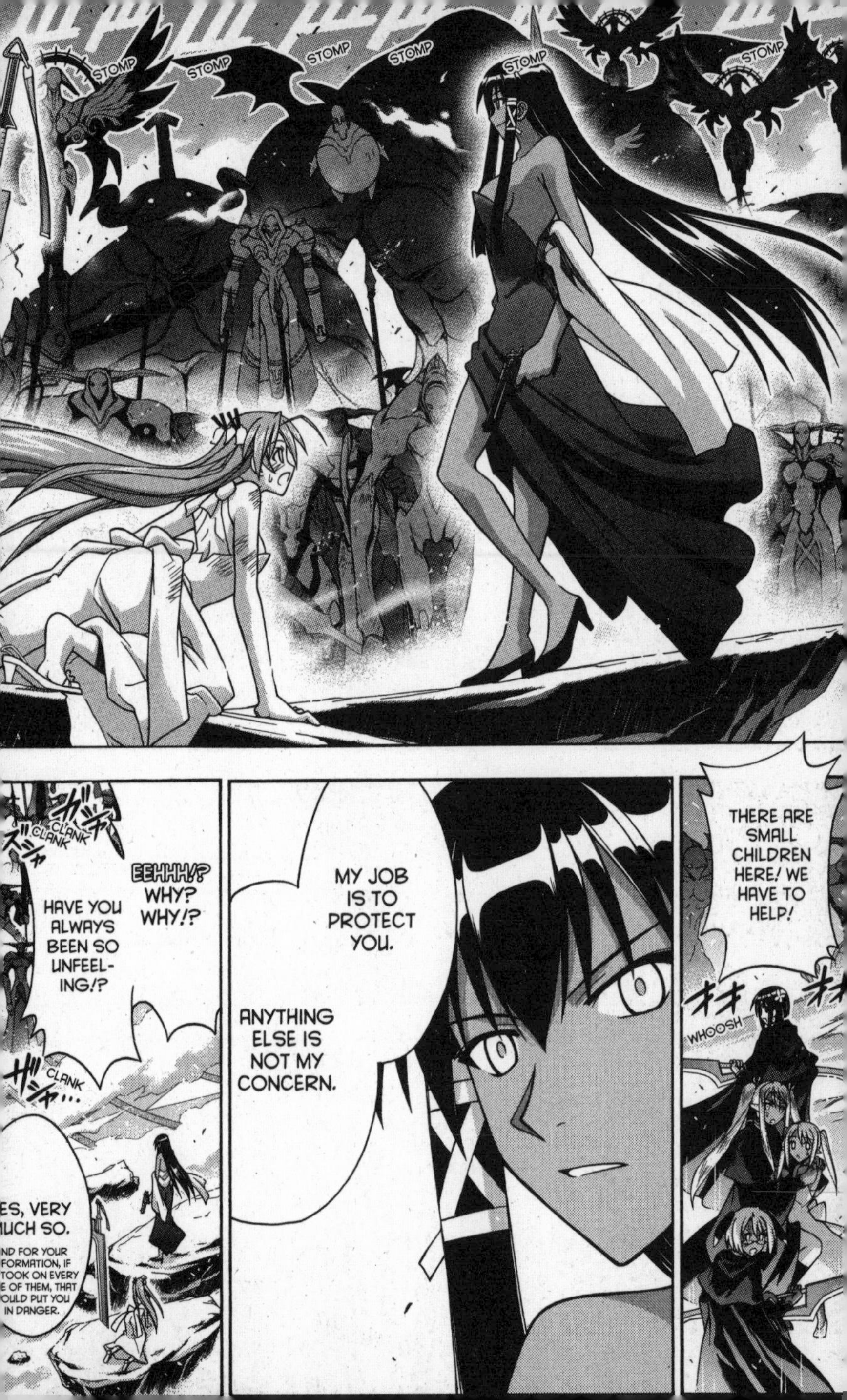
STOMP
STOMP
STOMP
STOMP
STOMP
STOMP
THERE ARE SMALL CHILDREN HERE! WE HAVE TO HELP!
WHOOSH
MY JOB IS TO PROTECT YOU.
ANYTHING ELSE IS NOT MY CONCERN.
CLANK CLANK
EEHHH!? WHY? WHY!?
HAVE YOU ALWAYS BEEN SO UNFEEL-ING!?
CLANK...
ES, VERY MUCH SO.
ND FOR YOUR FORMATION, IF TOOK ON EVERY E OF THEM, THAT OULD PUT YOU IN DANGER.

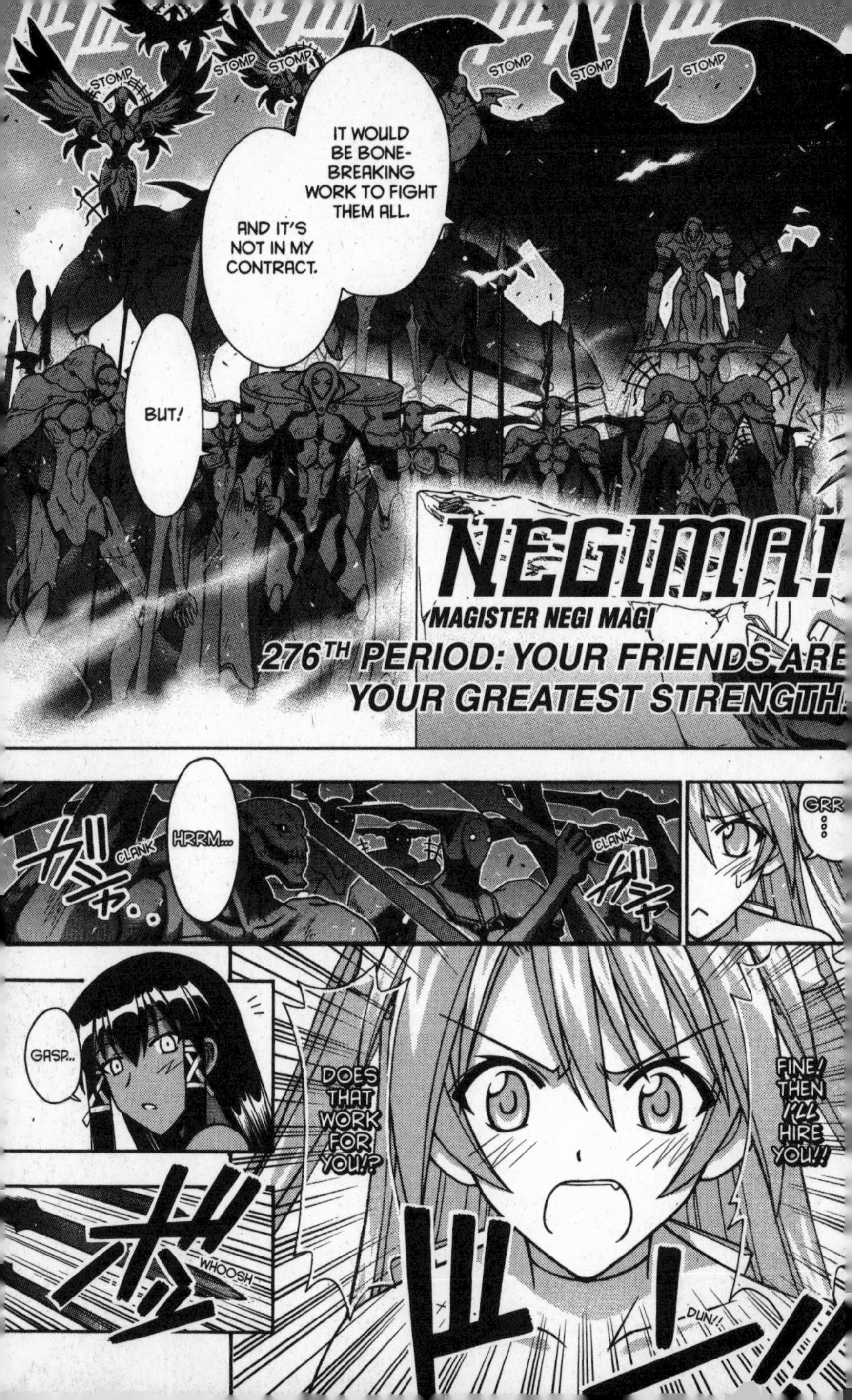
STOMP
STOMP
STOMP
STOMP
STOMP
STOMP
IT WOULD BE BONE-BREAKING WORK TO FIGHT THEM ALL.
AND IT'S NOT IN MY CONTRACT.
BUT!
NEGIMA!
MAGISTER NEGI MAGI
276TH PERIOD: YOUR FRIENDS ARE YOUR GREATEST STRENGTH!
GRR...
CLANK
HRRM...
CLANK
FINE! THEN I'LL HIRE YOU!!
DOES THAT WORK FOR YOU!?
DUN!!
GASP...
WHOOSH

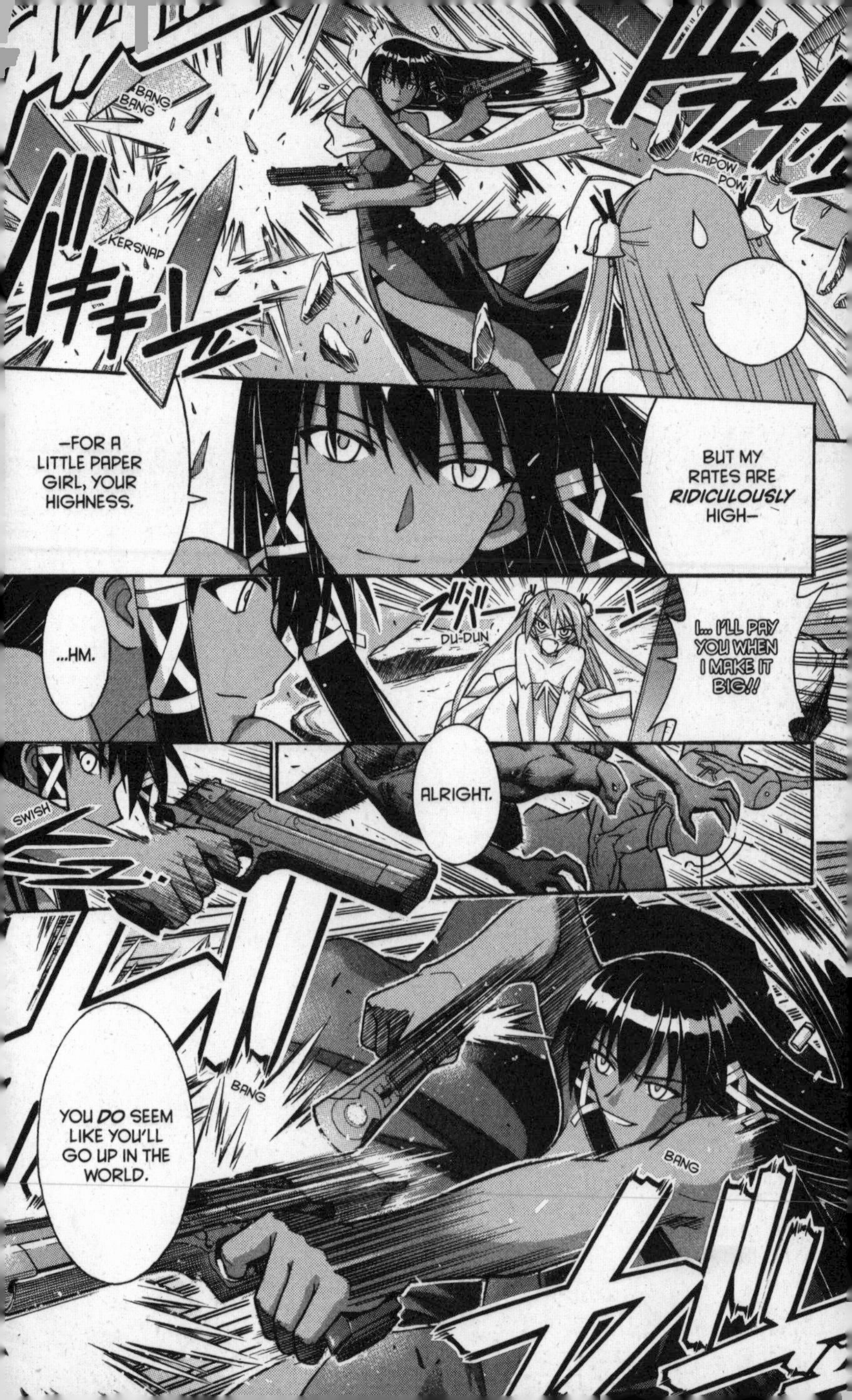
KAPOW
POW
BANG
BANG
KERSNAP
BUT MY RATES ARE *RIDICULOUSLY* HIGH—
—FOR A LITTLE PAPER GIRL, YOUR HIGHNESS.
I... I'LL PAY YOU WHEN I MAKE IT BIG!!
DU-DUN
...HM.
ALRIGHT.
SWISH
BANG
BANG
YOU *DO* SEEM LIKE YOU'LL GO UP IN THE WORLD.

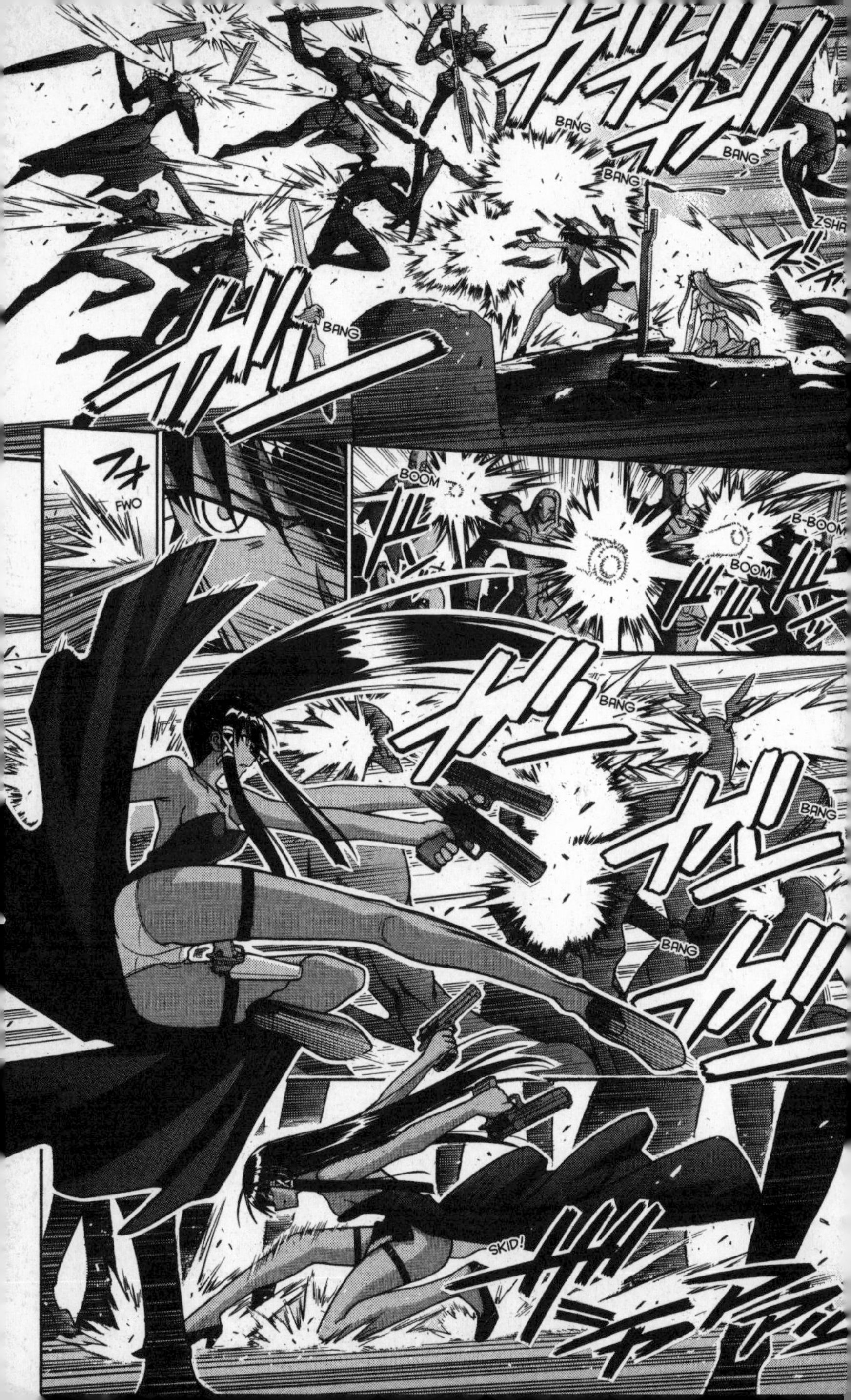
BANG
BANG
BANG
ZSHA
BANG
B-BOOM
BOOM
BOOM
FWO
BANG
BANG
BANG
SKID!

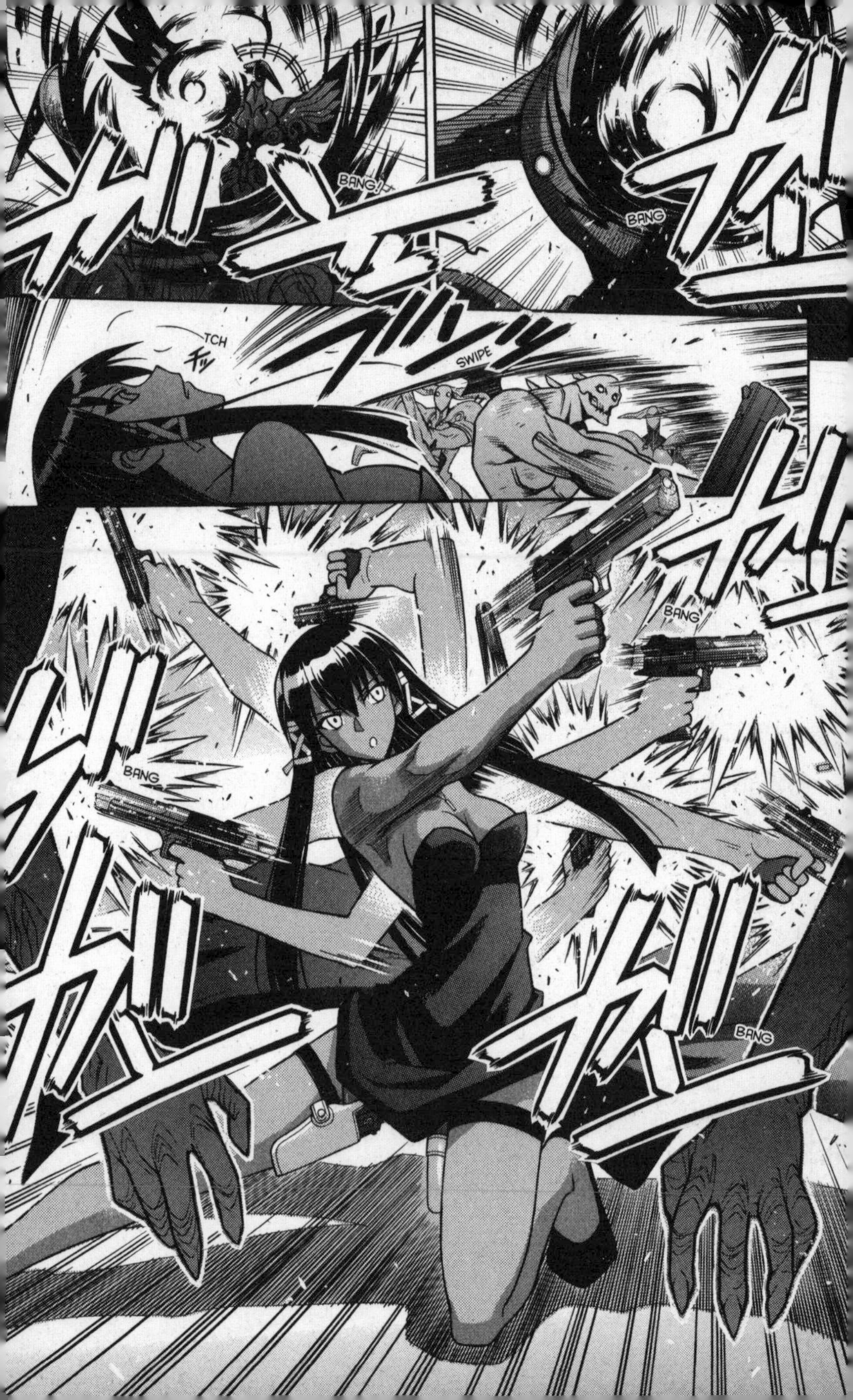
BANG
BANG!
SWIPE
TCH
チッ
BANG
BANG
BANG

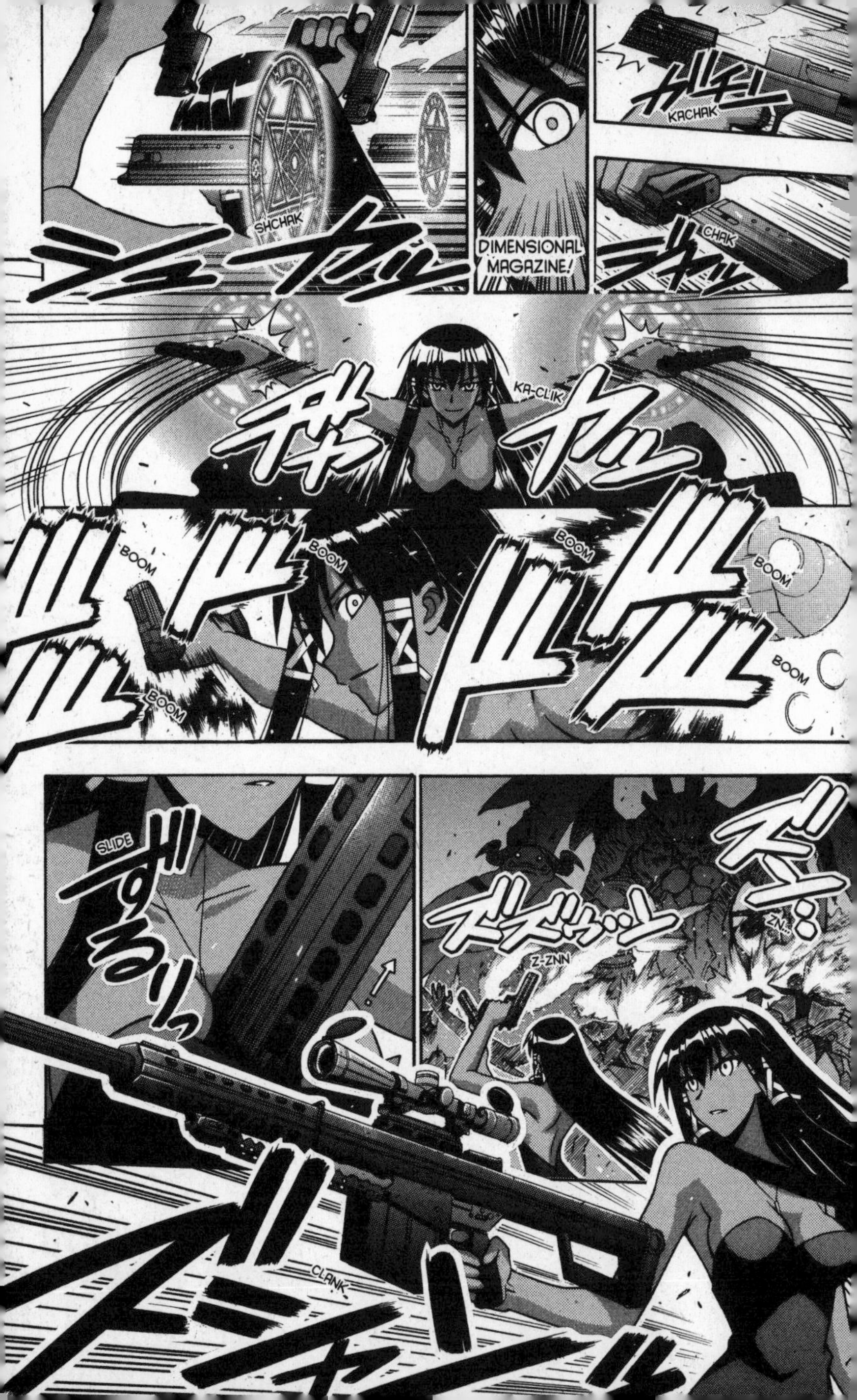

KACHAK
CHAK
DIMENSIONAL MAGAZINE!
SHCHAK
KA-CLIK
BOOM
BOOM
BOOM
BOOM
BOOM
BOOM
ZN...
Z-ZNN
SLIDE
CLANK

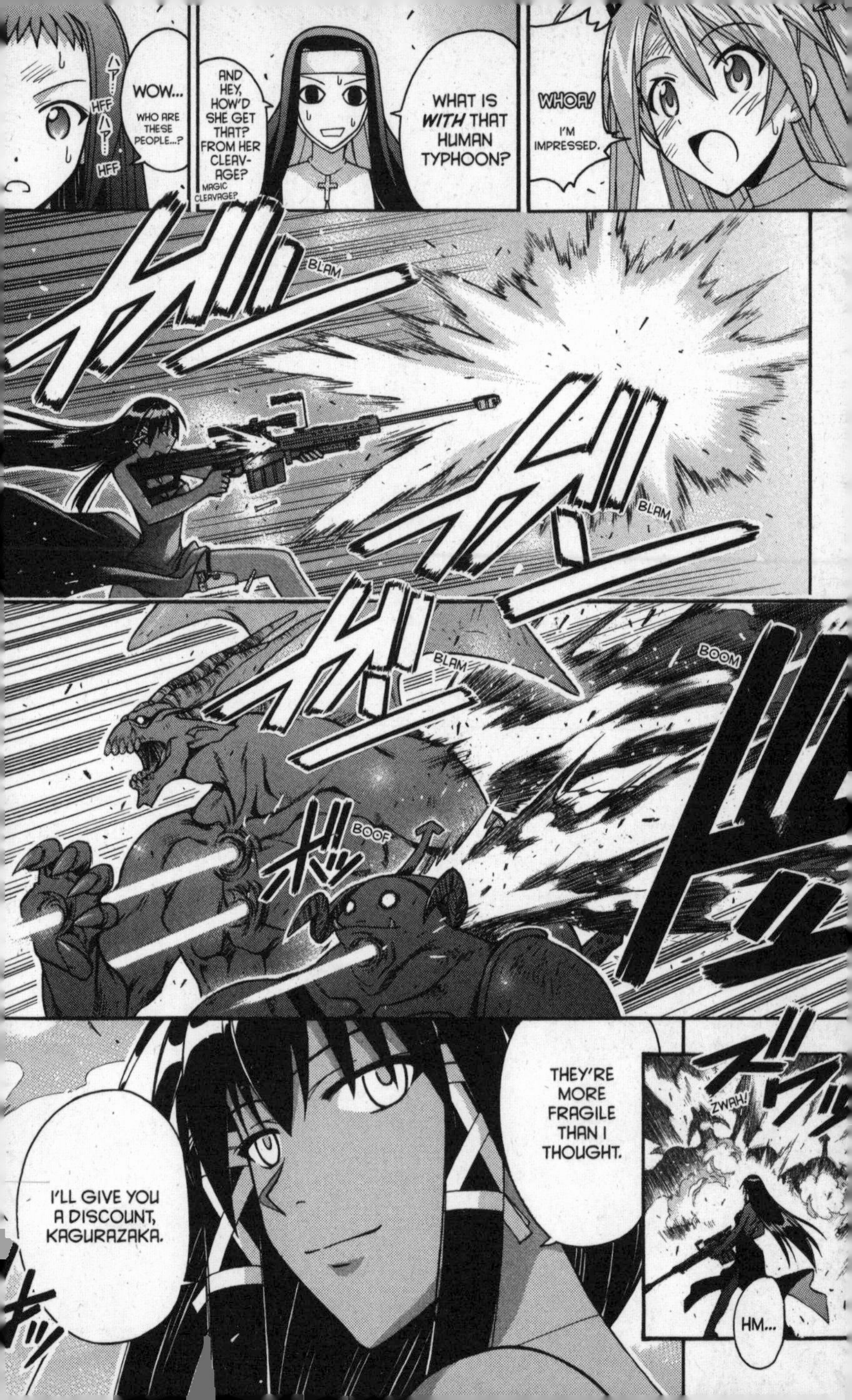
WHOA!
I'M IMPRESSED.
WHAT IS *WITH* THAT HUMAN TYPHOON?
AND HEY, HOW'D SHE GET THAT? FROM HER CLEAVAGE?
MAGIC CLEAVAGE?
WOW... WHO ARE THESE PEOPLE...?
HFF
HFF
BLAM
BLAM
BOOM
BLAM
BOOF
ZWAH!
HM...
THEY'RE MORE FRAGILE THAN I THOUGHT.
I'LL GIVE YOU A DISCOUNT, KAGURAZAKA.

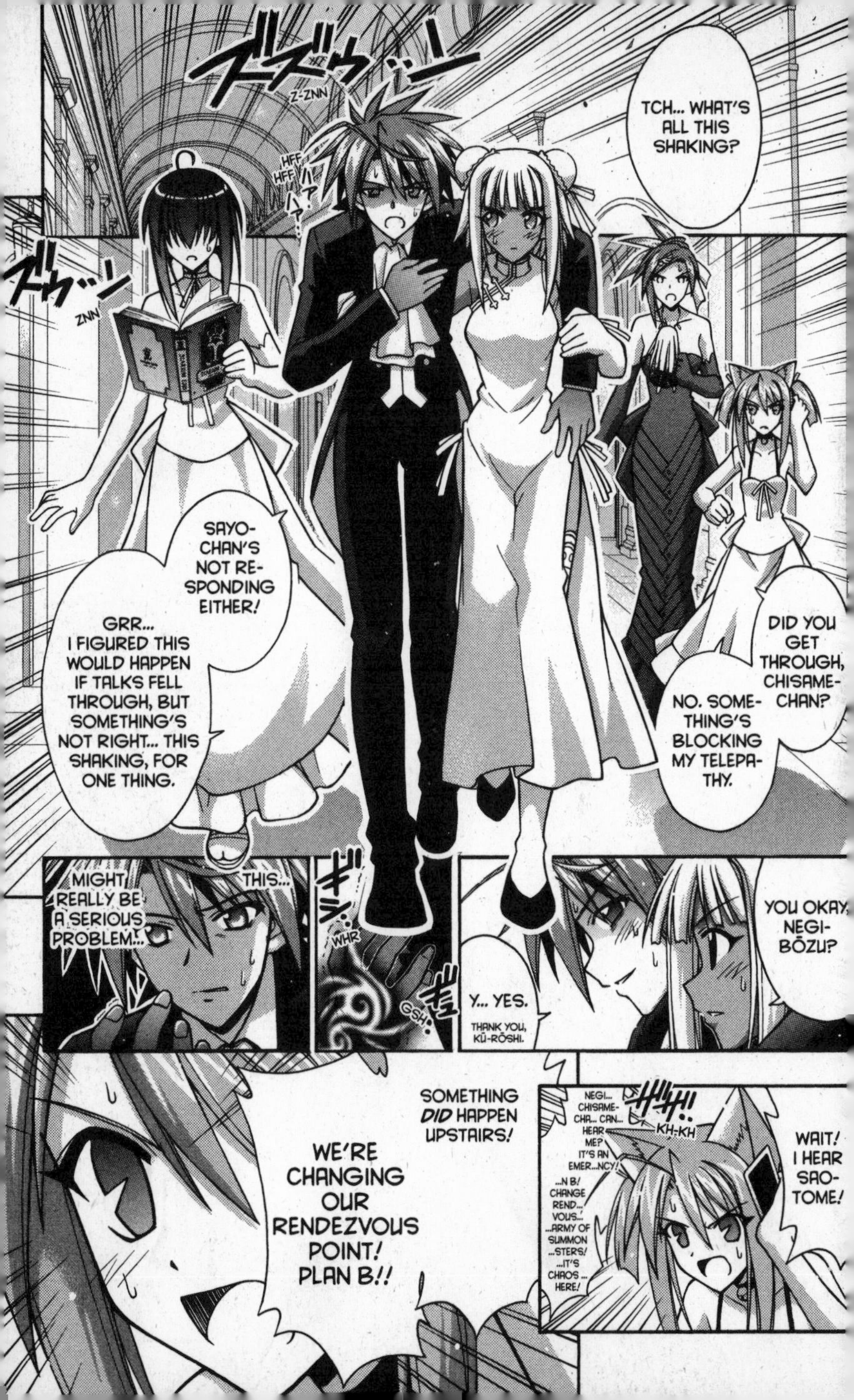
TCH... WHAT'S ALL THIS SHAKING?
Z-ZNN
HFF HFF
ZNN
DID YOU GET THROUGH, CHISAME-CHAN?
NO. SOMETHING'S BLOCKING MY TELEPATHY.
SAYO-CHAN'S NOT RESPONDING EITHER!
GRR... I FIGURED THIS WOULD HAPPEN IF TALKS FELL THROUGH, BUT SOMETHING'S NOT RIGHT... THIS SHAKING, FOR ONE THING.
YOU OKAY, NEGI-BŌZU?
Y... YES.
THANK YOU, KŪ-RŌSHI.
WHR
GSH
THIS...
MIGHT REALLY BE A SERIOUS PROBLEM...
WAIT! I HEAR SAOTOME!
KH-KH
NEGI... CHISAME-CHA... CAN... HEAR ME? IT'S AN EMER...NCY! ...N B! CHANGE REND... VOUS... ...ARMY OF SUMMON ...STERS! ...IT'S CHAOS ... HERE!
SOMETHING *DID* HAPPEN UPSTAIRS!
WE'RE CHANGING OUR RENDEZVOUS POINT! PLAN B!!

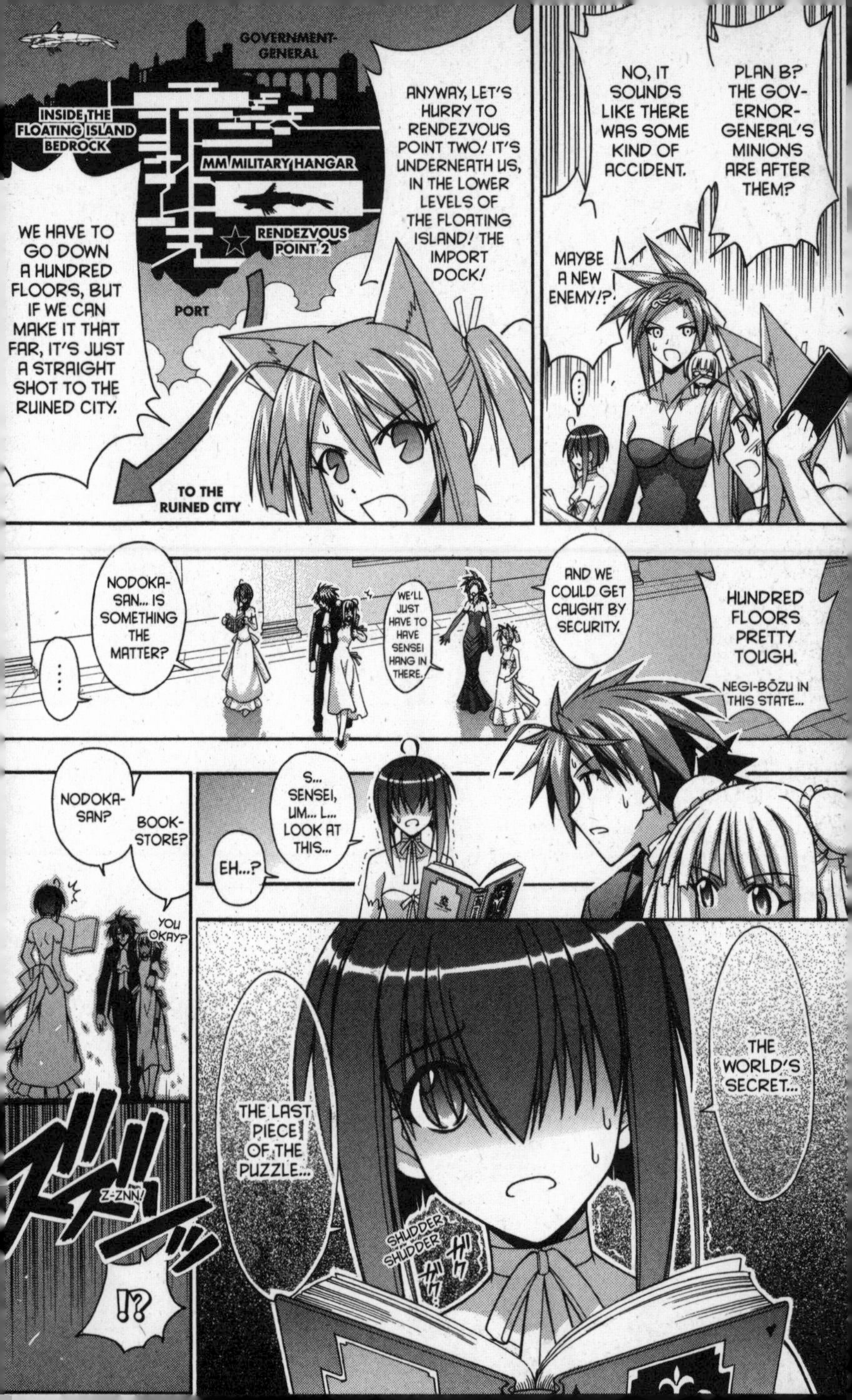
PLAN B? THE GOV-ERNOR-GENERAL'S MINIONS ARE AFTER THEM?
NO, IT SOUNDS LIKE THERE WAS SOME KIND OF ACCIDENT.
MAYBE A NEW ENEMY!?
...
ANYWAY, LET'S HURRY TO RENDEZVOUS POINT TWO! IT'S UNDERNEATH US, IN THE LOWER LEVELS OF THE FLOATING ISLAND! THE IMPORT DOCK!
GOVERNMENT-GENERAL
INSIDE THE FLOATING ISLAND BEDROCK
MM MILITARY HANGAR
RENDEZVOUS POINT 2
WE HAVE TO GO DOWN A HUNDRED FLOORS, BUT IF WE CAN MAKE IT THAT FAR, IT'S JUST A STRAIGHT SHOT TO THE RUINED CITY.
PORT
TO THE RUINED CITY
HUNDRED FLOORS PRETTY TOUGH.
NEGI-BŌZU IN THIS STATE...
AND WE COULD GET CAUGHT BY SECURITY.
WE'LL JUST HAVE TO HAVE SENSEI HANG IN THERE.
NODOKA-SAN... IS SOMETHING THE MATTER?
...
S... SENSEI, UM... L... LOOK AT THIS...
EH...?
BOOK-STORE?
NODOKA-SAN?
THE WORLD'S SECRET...
THE LAST PIECE OF THE PUZZLE...
SHUDDER SHUDDER
YOU OKAY?
Z-ZNN!
!?

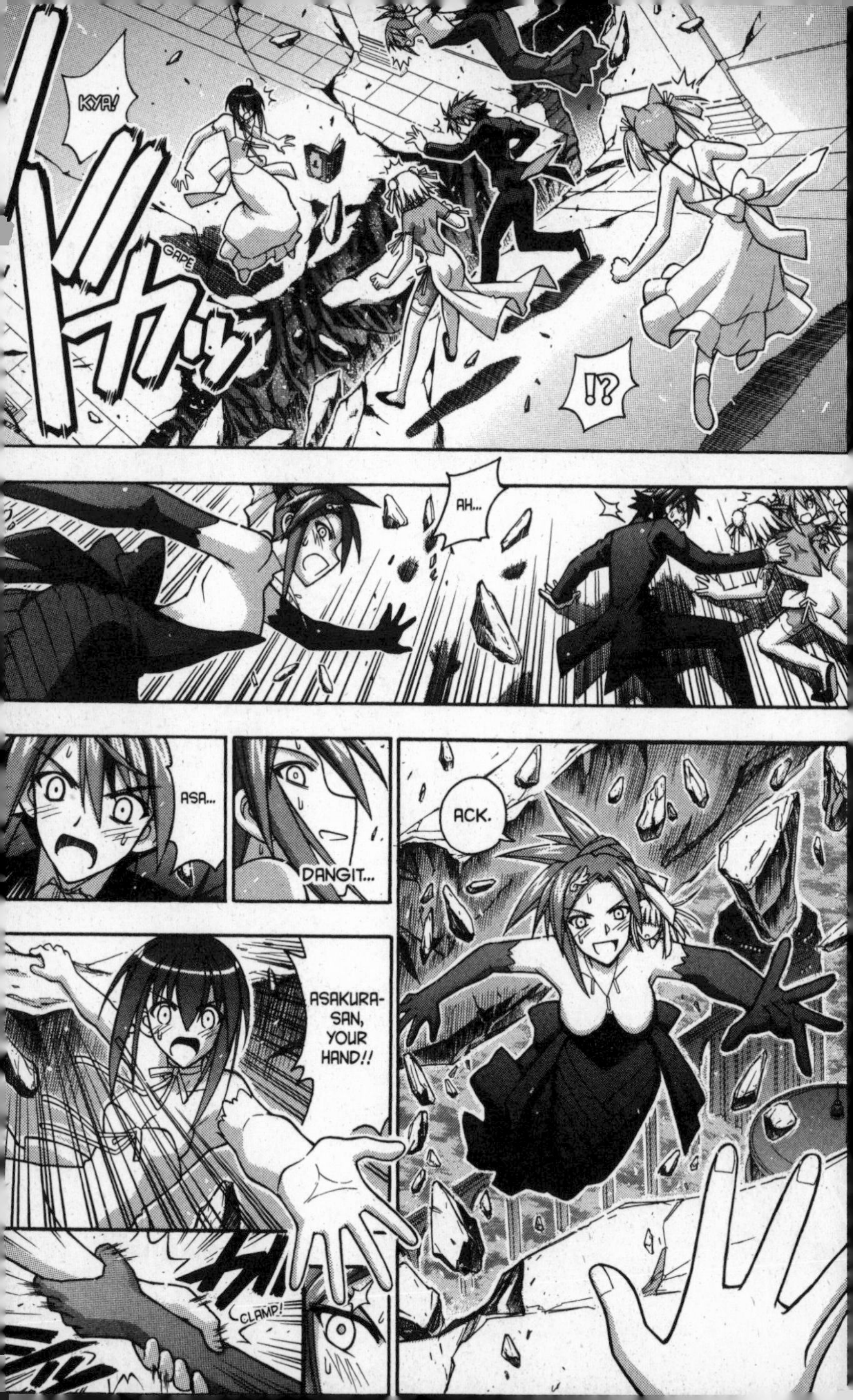
!?
KYA!
GAPE
AH...
ACK.
DANGIT...
ASA...
ASAKURA-SAN, YOUR HAND!!
CLAMP!

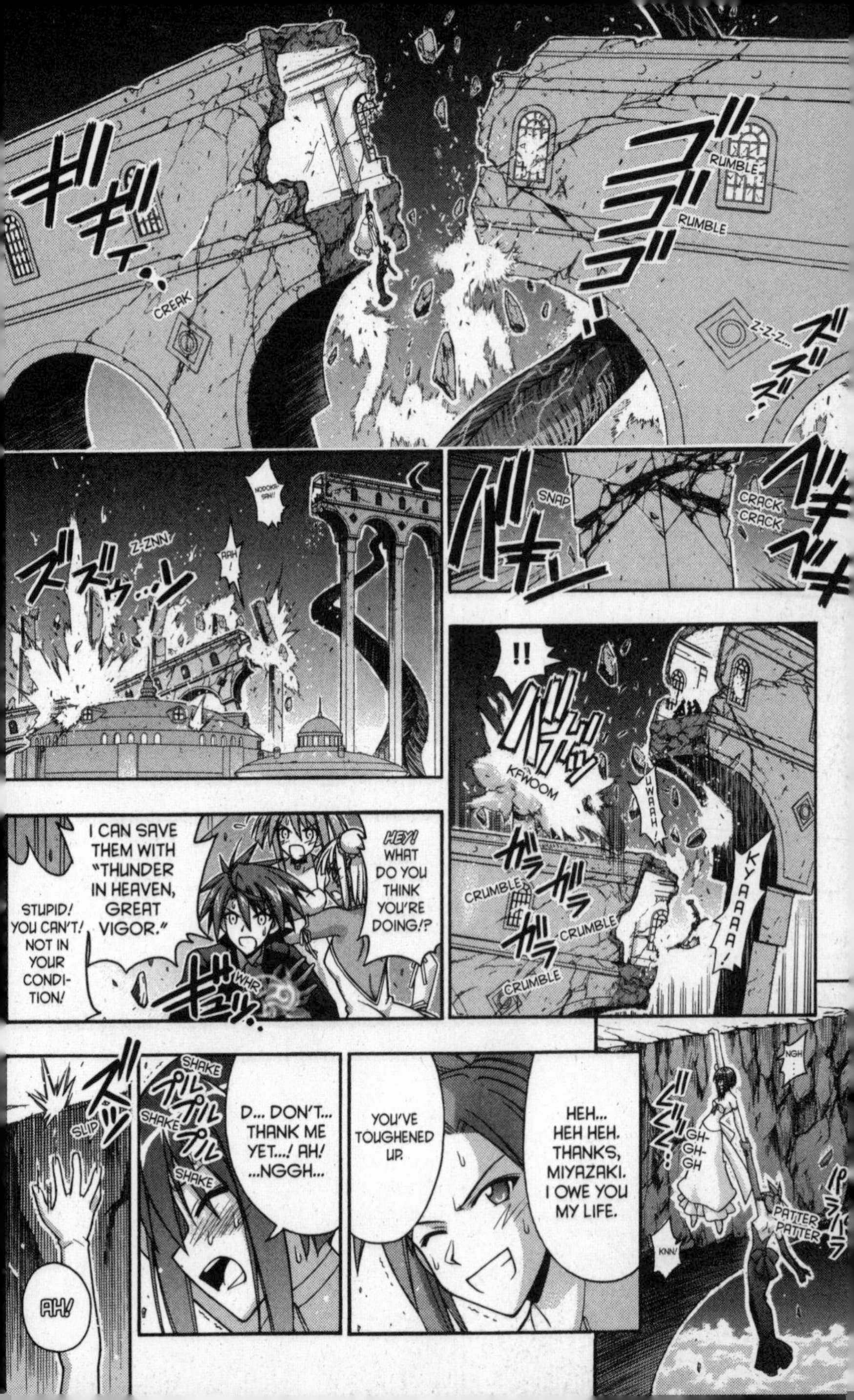
RUMBLE
RUMBLE
Z-Z-Z...
CREAK
CRACK
CRACK
SNAP
NODOKA-SAN!
AAH!
Z-ZNN
!!
KFWOOM
UWAAH!
KYAAAAA!
CRUMBLE
CRUMBLE
CRUMBLE
HEY! WHAT DO YOU THINK YOU'RE DOING!?
I CAN SAVE THEM WITH "THUNDER IN HEAVEN, GREAT VIGOR."
STUPID! YOU CAN'T! NOT IN YOUR CONDITION!
WHR
NGH
GH-GH-GH
PATTER PATTER
KNN!
HEH... HEH HEH. THANKS, MIYAZAKI. I OWE YOU MY LIFE.
YOU'VE TOUGHENED UP.
D... DON'T... THANK ME YET...! AH! ...NGGH...
SHAKE
SHAKE
SHAKE
SLIP
AH!

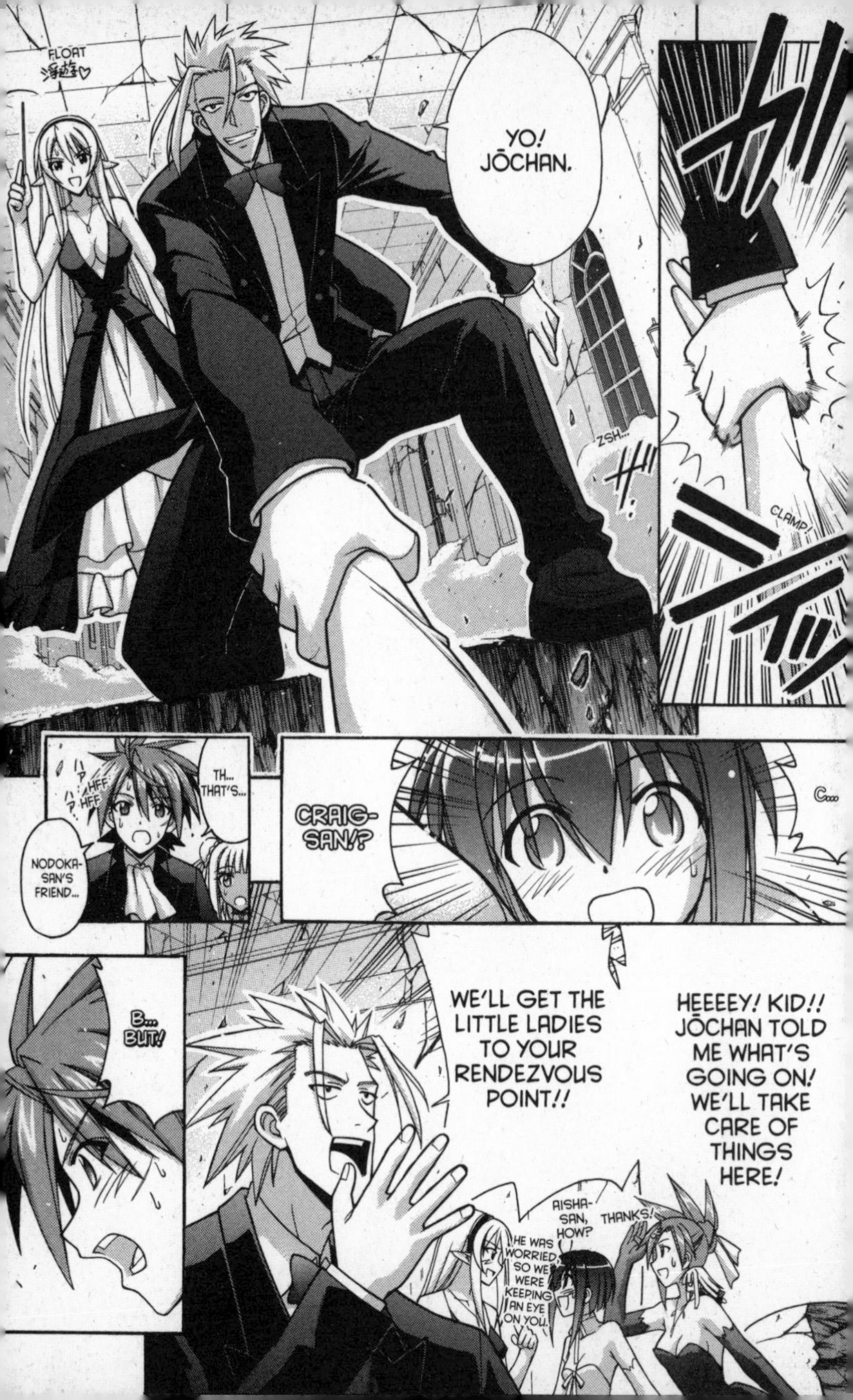
CLAMP!
YO! JŌCHAN.
FLOAT
ZSH...
C...
CRAIG-SAN!?
TH... THAT'S...
HFF HFF
NODOKA-SAN'S FRIEND...
HEEEEY! KID!! JŌCHAN TOLD ME WHAT'S GOING ON! WE'LL TAKE CARE OF THINGS HERE!
WE'LL GET THE LITTLE LADIES TO YOUR RENDEZVOUS POINT!!
THANKS!
AISHA-SAN, HOW?
HE WAS WORRIED, SO WE WERE KEEPING AN EYE ON YOU.
B... BUT!

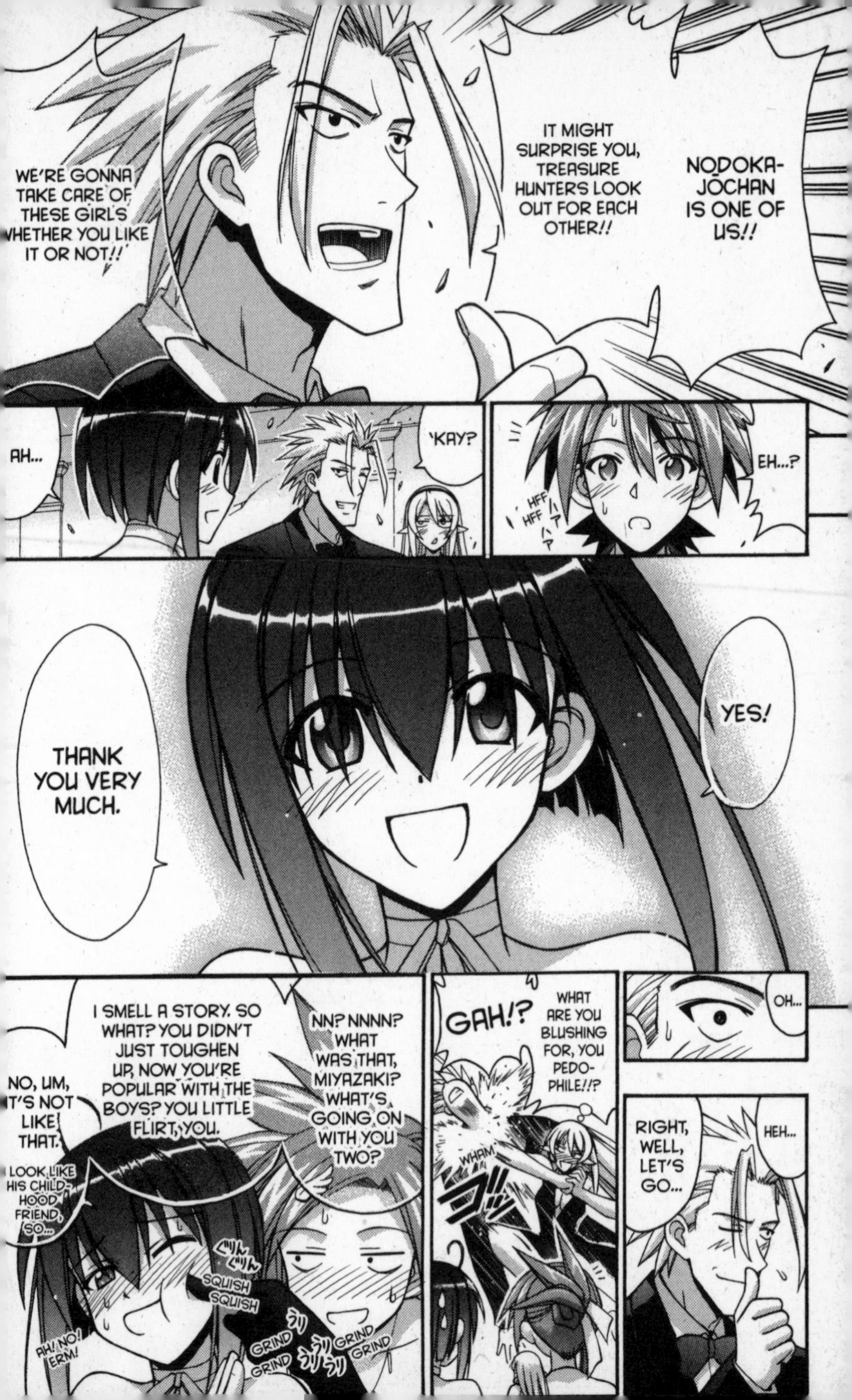
NODOKA-JŌCHAN IS ONE OF US!!
IT MIGHT SURPRISE YOU, TREASURE HUNTERS LOOK OUT FOR EACH OTHER!!
WE'RE GONNA TAKE CARE OF THESE GIRLS WHETHER YOU LIKE IT OR NOT!!
EH...?
HFF HFF
'KAY?
AH...
YES!
THANK YOU VERY MUCH.
OH...
HEH...
RIGHT, WELL, LET'S GO...
WHAT ARE YOU BLUSHING FOR, YOU PEDO-PHILE!!?
GAH!?
WHAM
NN? NNNN? WHAT WAS THAT, MIYAZAKI? WHAT'S GOING ON WITH YOU TWO?
I SMELL A STORY. SO WHAT? YOU DIDN'T JUST TOUGHEN UP, NOW YOU'RE POPULAR WITH THE BOYS? YOU LITTLE FLIRT, YOU.
NO, UM, IT'S NOT LIKE THAT.
I LOOK LIKE HIS CHILD-HOOD FRIEND, SO...
SQUISH SQUISH
GRIND GRIND GRIND GRIND
AH! NO! ERM!

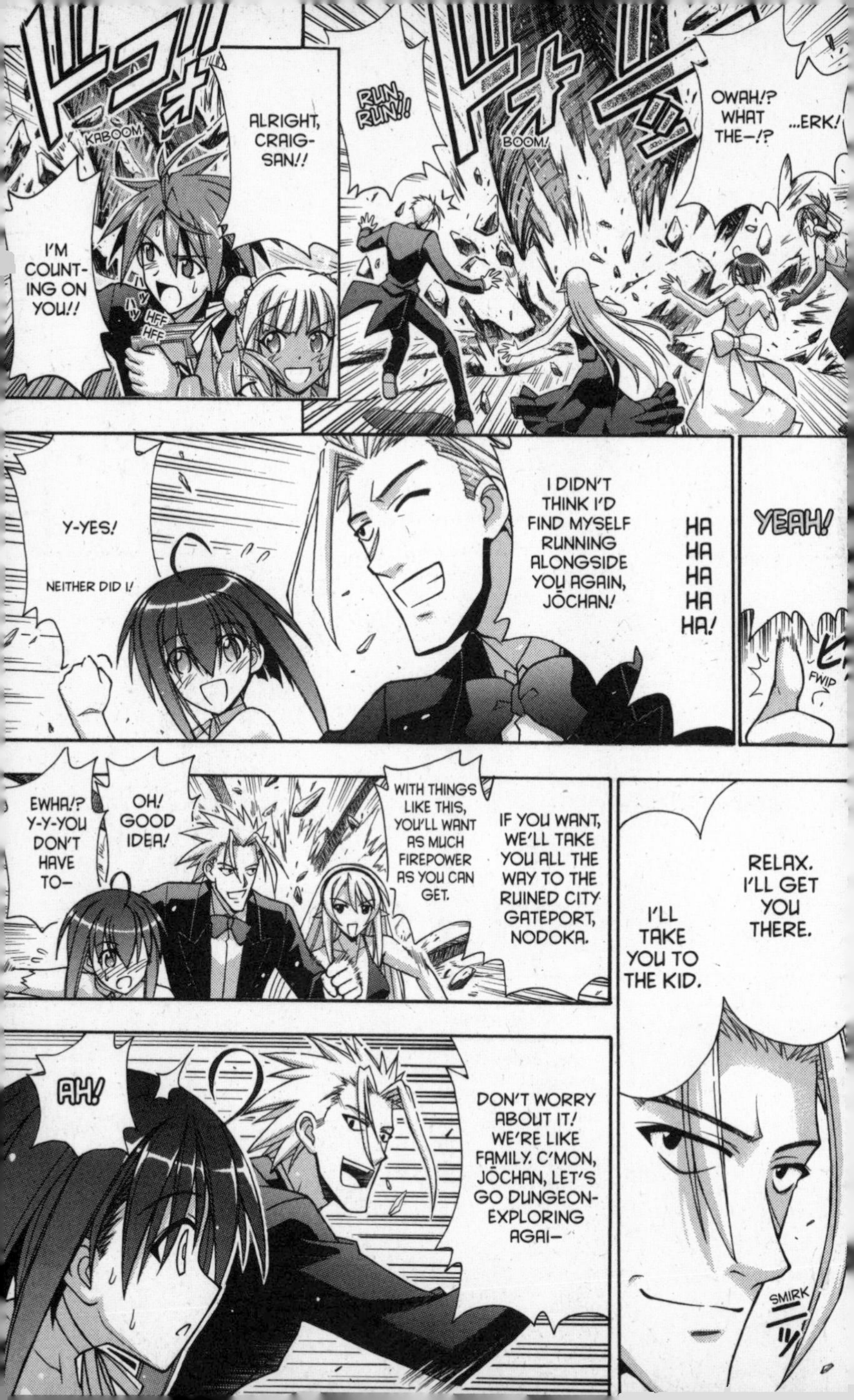
...ERK!
OWAH!? WHAT THE—!?
BOOM!
RUN, RUN!!
KABOOM
ALRIGHT, CRAIG-SAN!!
I'M COUNTING ON YOU!!
HFF HFF
YEAH!
FWIP
HA HA HA HA HA!
I DIDN'T THINK I'D FIND MYSELF RUNNING ALONGSIDE YOU AGAIN, JŌCHAN!
Y-YES!
NEITHER DID I!
RELAX. I'LL GET YOU THERE.
I'LL TAKE YOU TO THE KID.
SMIRK
IF YOU WANT, WE'LL TAKE YOU ALL THE WAY TO THE RUINED CITY GATEPORT, NODOKA.
WITH THINGS LIKE THIS, YOU'LL WANT AS MUCH FIREPOWER AS YOU CAN GET.
OH! GOOD IDEA!
EWHA!? Y-Y-YOU DON'T HAVE TO—
DON'T WORRY ABOUT IT! WE'RE LIKE FAMILY. C'MON, JŌCHAN, LET'S GO DUNGEON-EXPLORING AGAI—
AH!

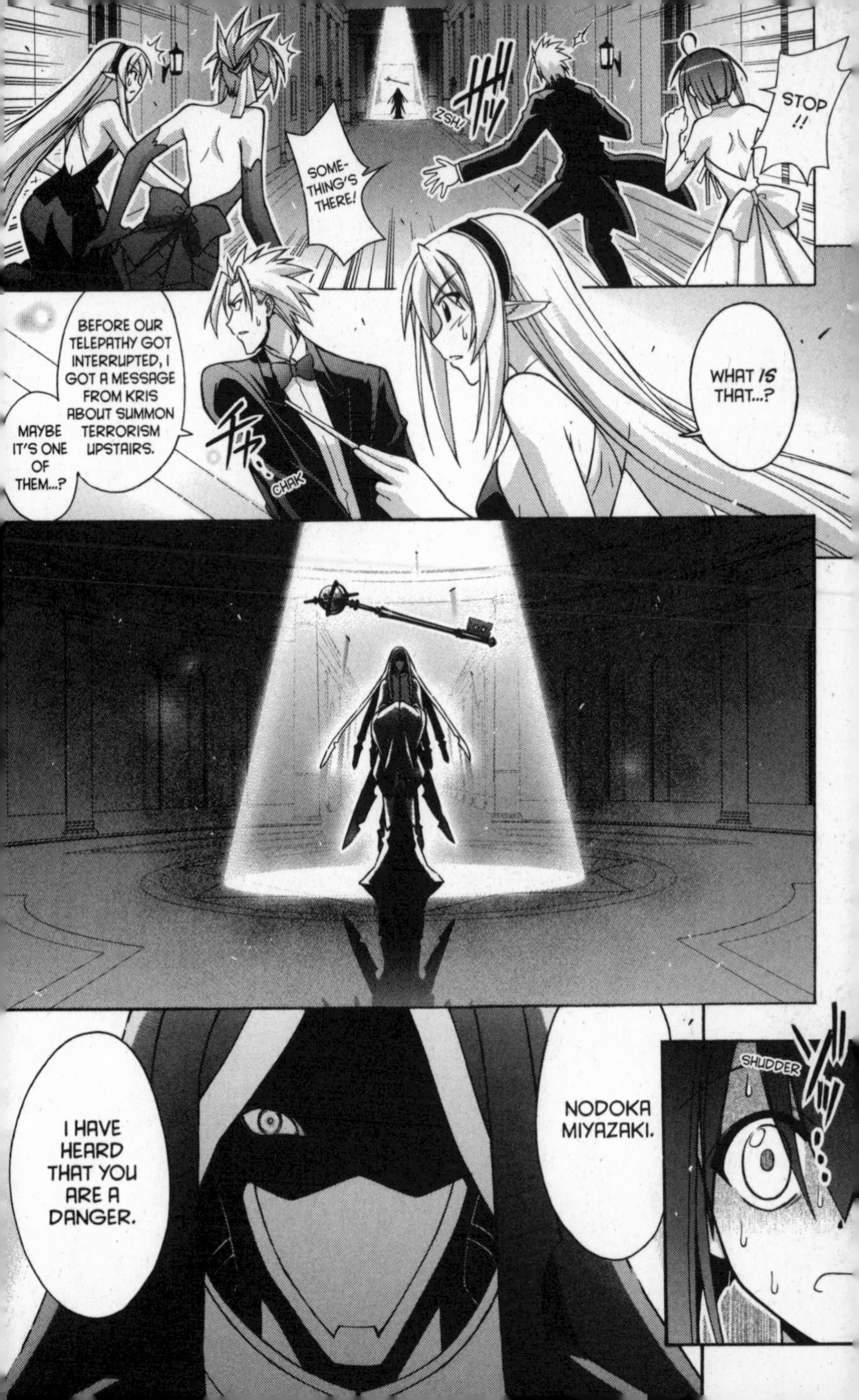
STOP !!
ZSH!
SOME-THING'S THERE!
WHAT *IS* THAT...?
BEFORE OUR TELEPATHY GOT INTERRUPTED, I GOT A MESSAGE FROM KRIS ABOUT SUMMON TERRORISM UPSTAIRS.
CHAK
MAYBE IT'S ONE OF THEM...?
SHUDDER
NODOKA MIYAZAKI.
I HAVE HEARD THAT YOU ARE A DANGER.

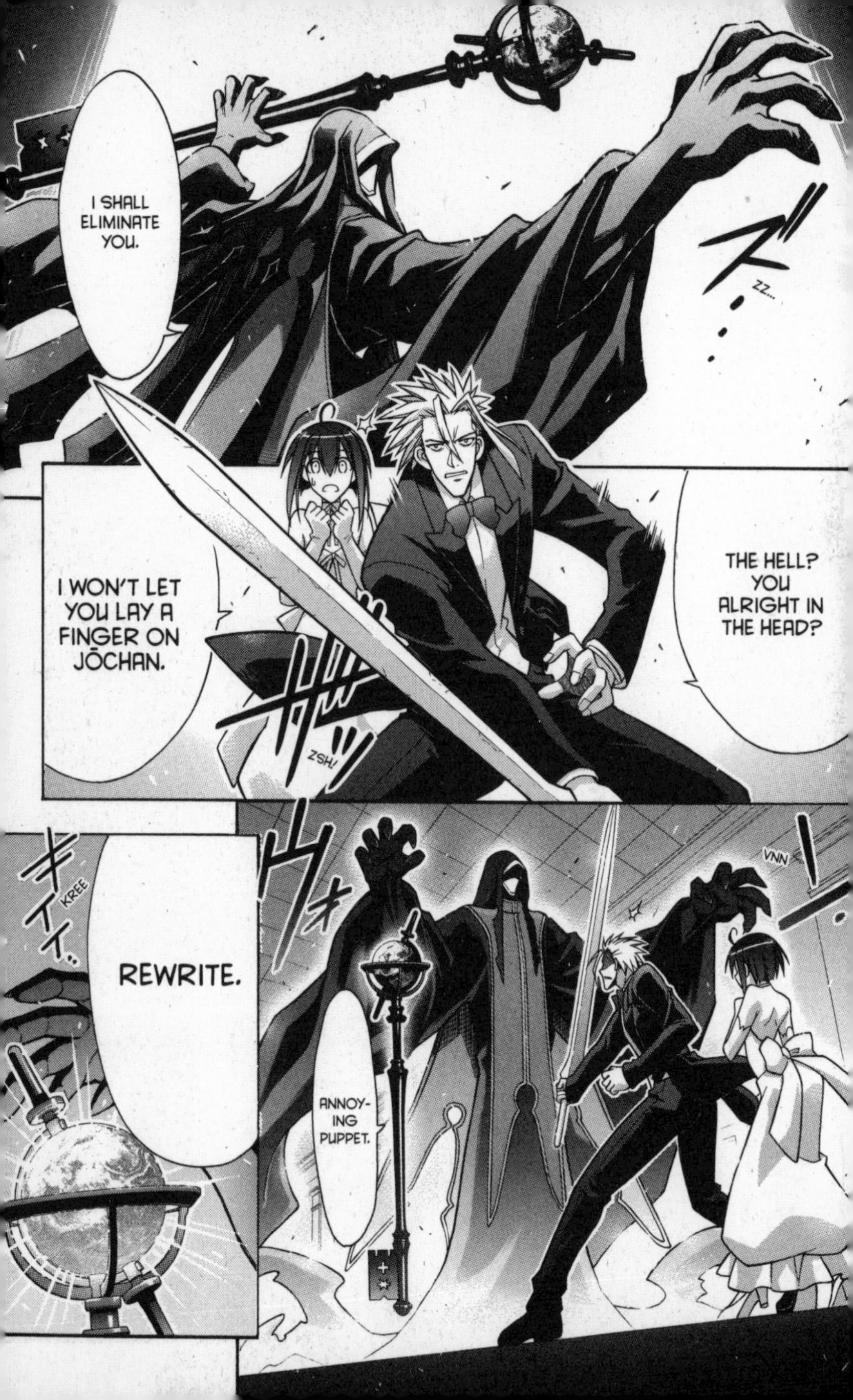
ZZ...
I SHALL ELIMINATE YOU.
THE HELL? YOU ALRIGHT IN THE HEAD?
I WON'T LET YOU LAY A FINGER ON JŌCHAN.
ZSH!
VNN
ANNOY-ING PUPPET.
KREE
REWRITE.

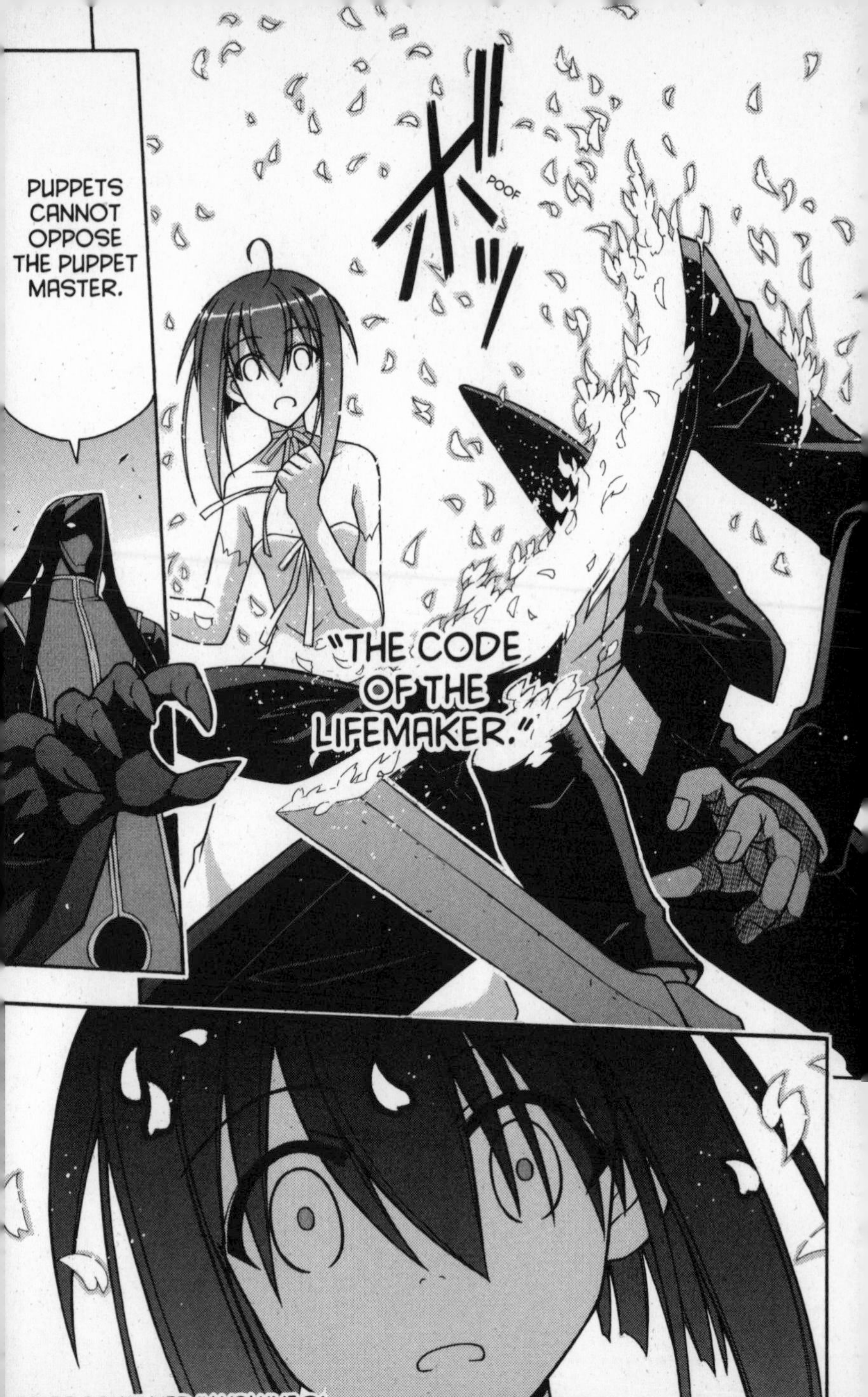
POOF
PUPPETS CANNOT OPPOSE THE PUPPET MASTER.
"THE CODE OF THE LIFEMAKER."

TO BE CONTINUED IN VOLUME 31

-STAFF-

Ken   Akamatsu

Takashi   Takemoto

Kenichi   Nakamura

Keiichi   Yamashita

Tohru   Mitsuhashi

Yuichi   Yoshida

Susumu   Kuwabara

Thanks   to

Ran   Ayanaga

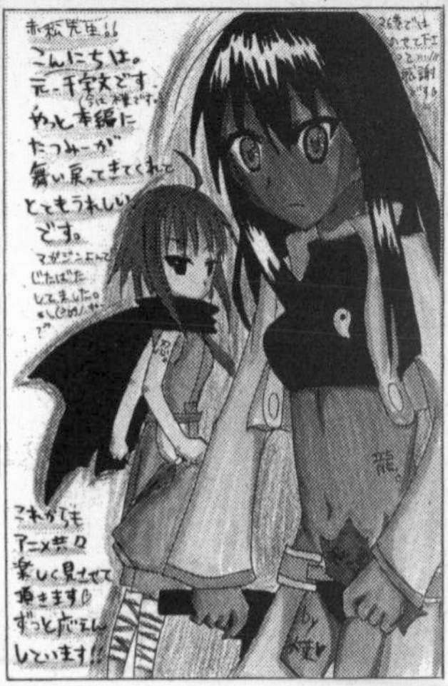
赤松先生!!
こんにちは。

THOSE ARE CUTE PROPORTIONS ON TATSUMIYA.

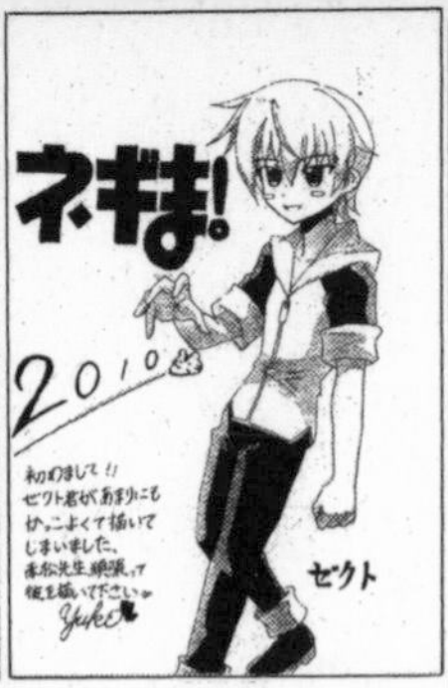
ネギま!
2010
ゼクト

▲THIS IS A GREAT ZECHT!

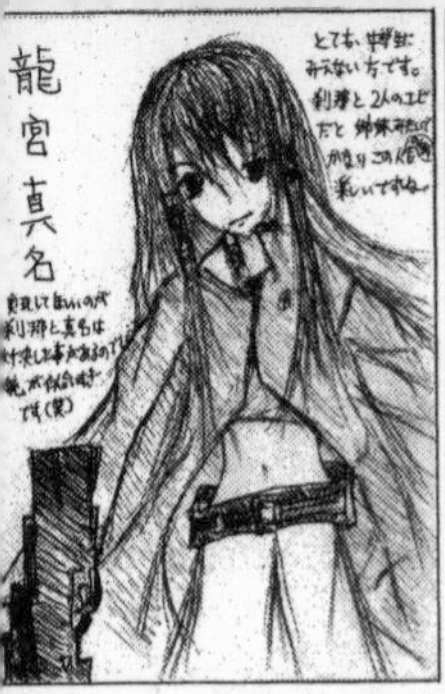
龍宮真名

▲GOOD ROUGH TOUCHES♪

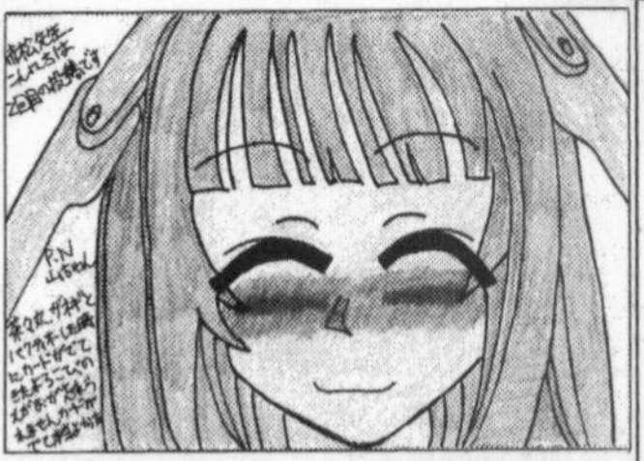

▼SHE'S SMILING EAR-TO-EAR.

NEGIMA! FAN ART CORNER

THIS VOLUME'S MOST DRAWN CHARACTER IS NATSUMI♪ SHE HAS BEEN REALLY ACTIVE IN THE STORY LATELY. WHAT WILL HAPPEN WITH HER AND KOTA-KUN? (LAUGH) OH, AND WE'RE GETTING MORE COMMANDER TATSUMIYA, TOO. (LAUGH) WE'RE WAITING FOR DRAWINGS OF ALL THE CHARACTERS♪ PLEASE SEND THEM TO THE KODANSHA EDITORIAL DEPARTMENT ADDRESS AT THE END OF THE BOOK★

TEXT BY MAX

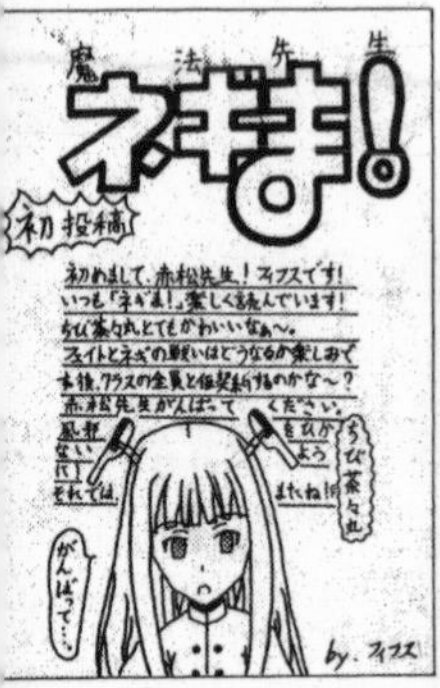
魔法先生
ネギま!
初投稿

▲A HUMBLE CHIBI-CHACHA

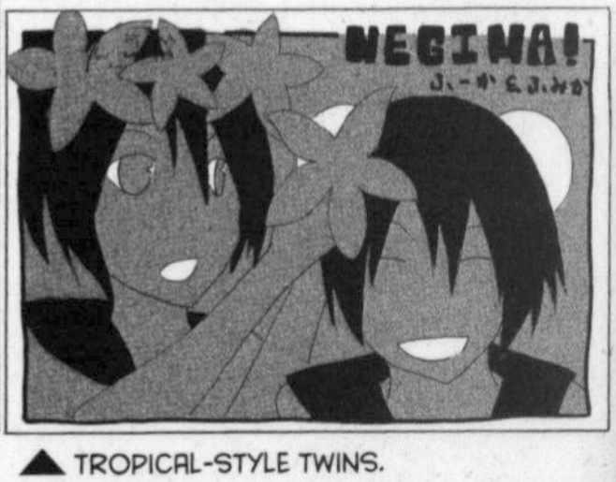
NEGIMA!

▲TROPICAL-STYLE TWINS.

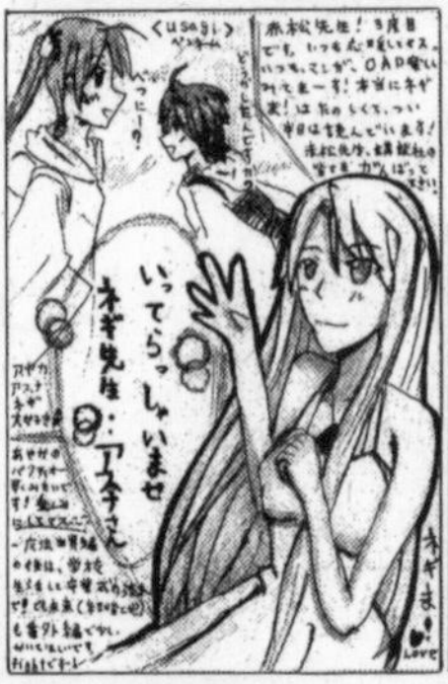
いってらっしゃいませ
ネギ先生

▲I WANT TO SEE THIS CLASS REP, TOO.

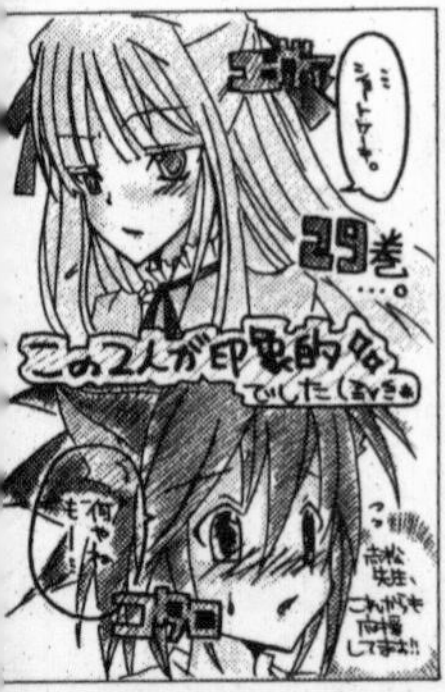
29巻…。

▲YOU'VE TONED DOWN THE MOÉ, I SEE.

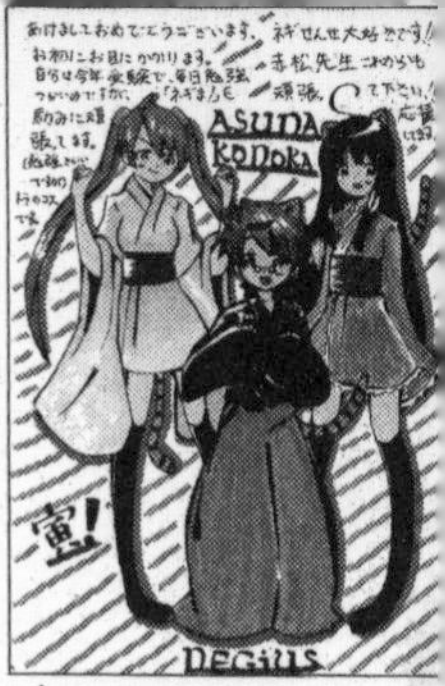
ASUNA
KONOKA
寅!

▲ I LIKE THE TIGER COSTUMES.

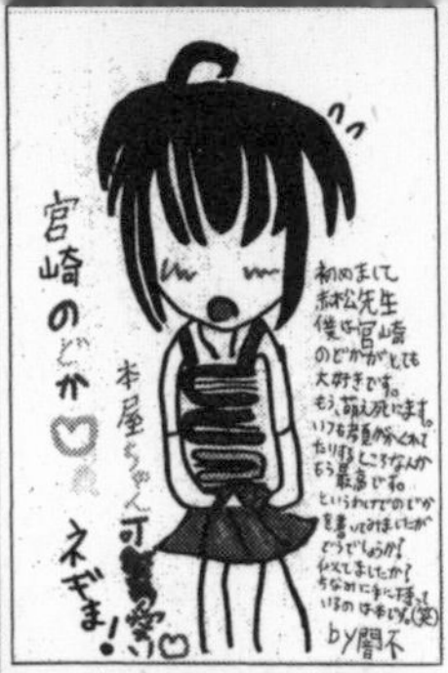
宮崎のどか♡
ネギま!

▲ NODOKA'S CUTE HIDING HER FACE, TOO.

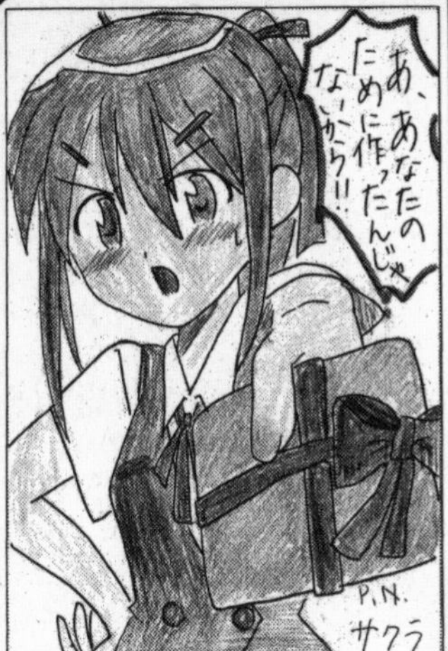
あ、あなたのために作ったんじゃないから!!
P.N. サクラ

▲ THIS IS WHAT THEY CALL "TSUNDERE."

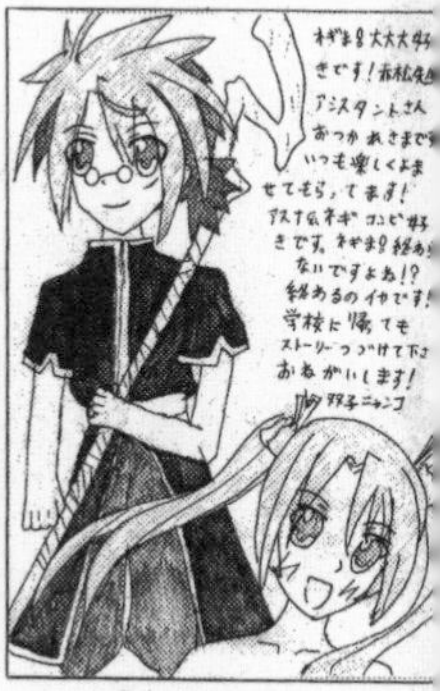

▲ THEY'RE A GOOD TEAM.

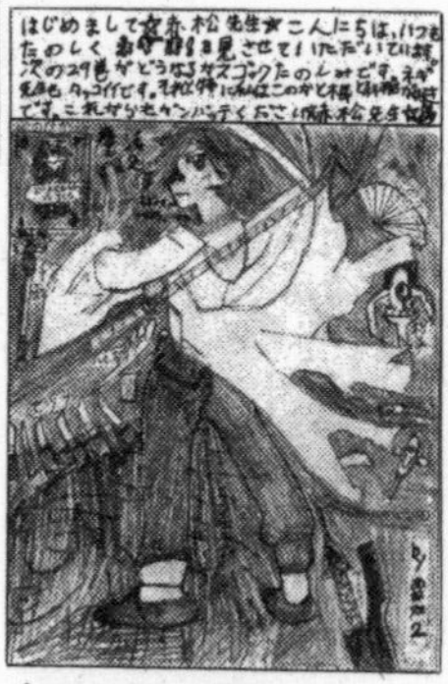

▲ NEGI-KUN GETS STRONGER AND STRONGER.

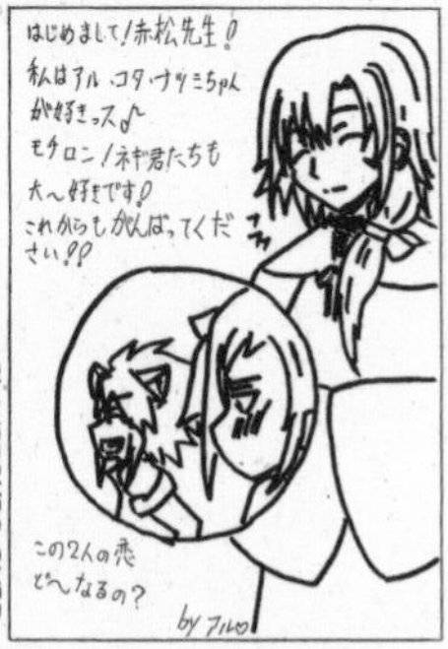
はじめまして!赤松先生!
私はアル、コタ、ナツミちゃんが好きっス♪
モチロン!ネギ君たちも大〜好きです!!
これからもがんばってください!!
この2人の恋どーなるの?

▲ AL WATCHES OVER THEM WITH A SMILE.

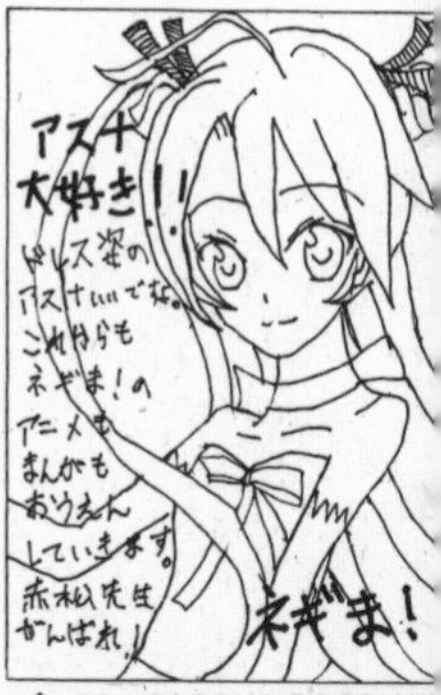
アスナ大好き!!
ドレス姿のアスナいいですね。これからもネギま!のアニメもまんがもおうえんしていきます。赤松先生がんばれ!
ネギま!

▲ ASUNA LOOKS GOOD IN HER GOWN.

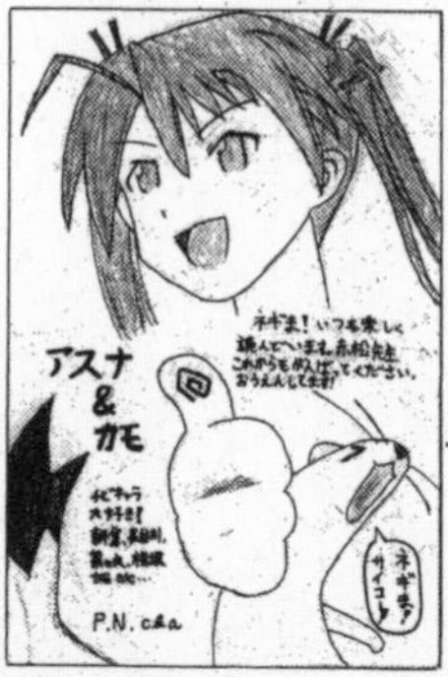
アスナ & カモ
P.N. c&a

▲ HIGH-ENERGY CHAMO-KUN.

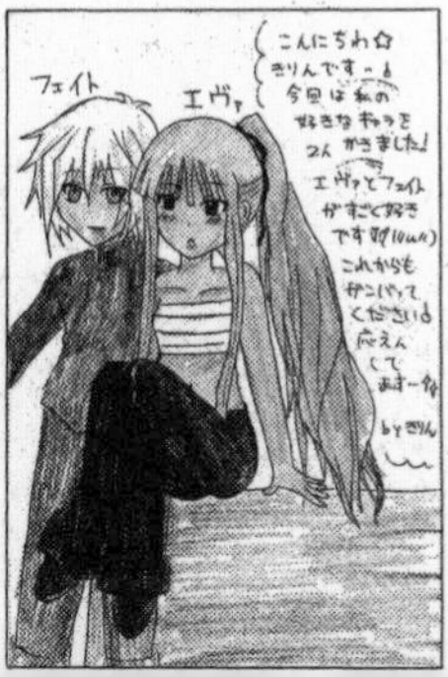
フェイト
エヴァ
by きりん

▲ EVA WEARING SARASHI COTTON WRAPPINGS. IT KINDA SUITS HER★

NEGI

MAHORA

MA!

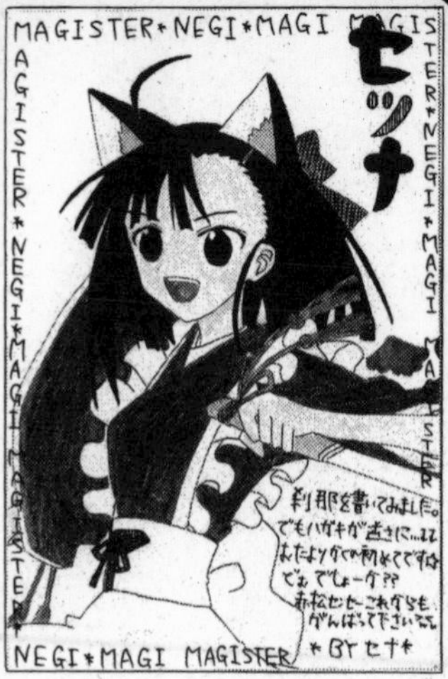
MAGISTER*NEGI*MAGI MAGISTER*NEGI*MAGI MAGISTER
セツナ
刹那を書いてみました。
赤松先生これからもがんばって下さい
NEGI*MAGI MAGISTER
▲ AN ENERGETIC SETSUNA.

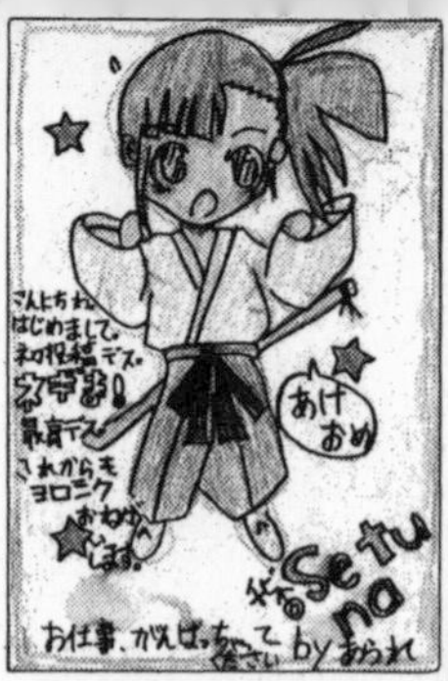
あけおめ
Setsuna
お仕事、がんばって下さい byあられ
▲ I WANT TO SEE LI'L SETSUNA AGAIN.

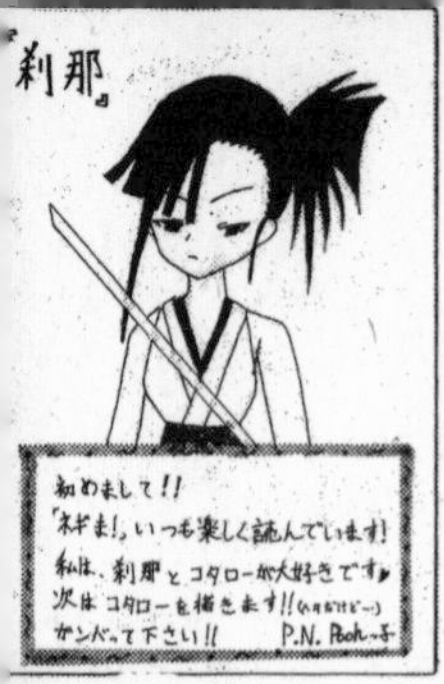
「刹那」
初めまして!!
「ネギま!」いつも楽しく読んでいます!
私は、刹那とコタローが大好きです。
次はコタローを描きます!!
ガンバって下さい!!
▲ SETSUNA GIVES A SHARP GAZE.

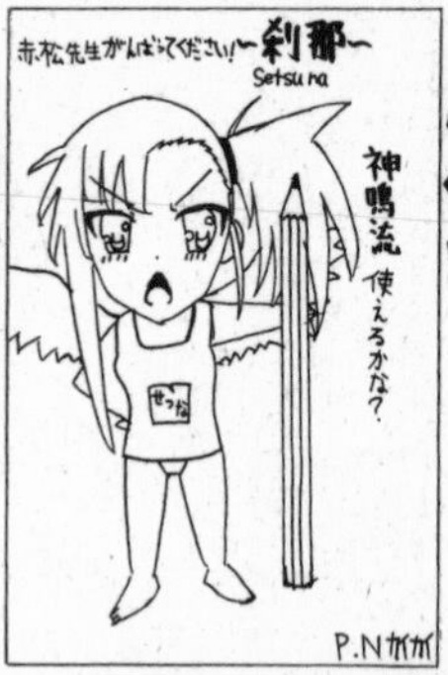
赤松先生がんばってください!~刹那~
Setsuna
神鳴流 使えるかな?
せつな
▲ SHE'S CUTE HOLDING THAT PENCIL.

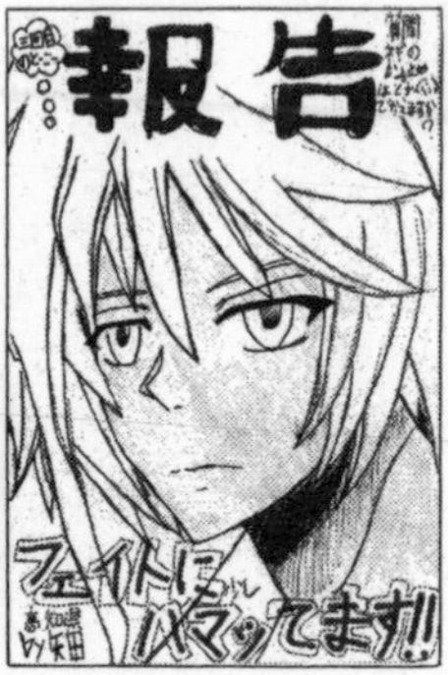
報告
フェイトにハマってます!!
▲ ADULT FATE.

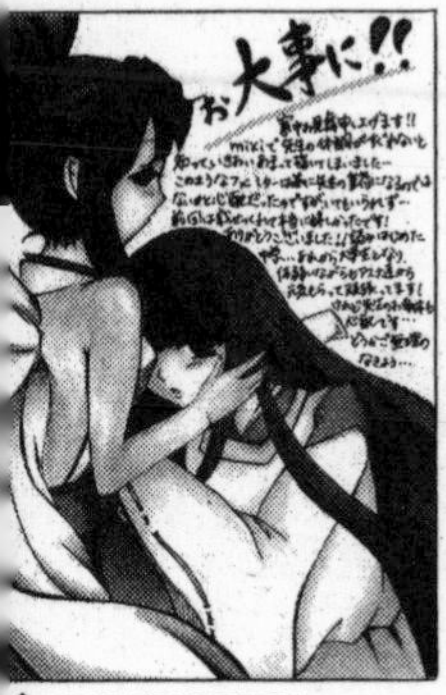
お大事に!!
▲ IT'S KONOSETSU.

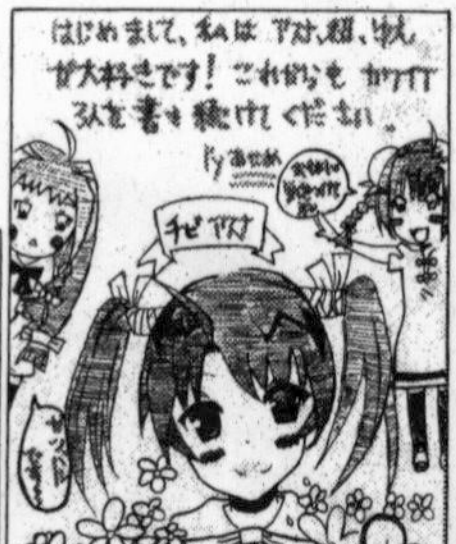
はじめまして、私は アスナ、刹那、ゆえ が大好きです! これからも カワイイ 3人を書き続けてください。
チビアスナ
▲ A LOVELY LI'L ASUNA.

THEY LOOK JUST LIKE DOLLS.
▼

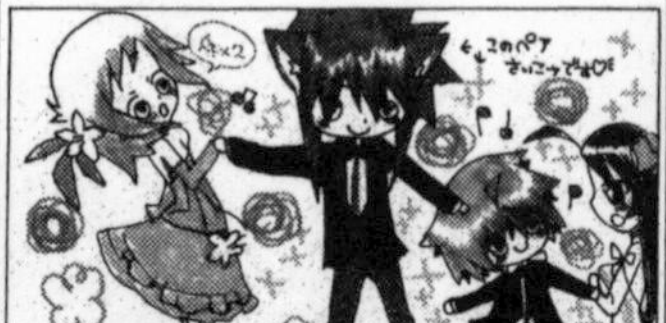
のせて下さい!
これからもがんばって下さい!

▼ THE TWO RIVALS.

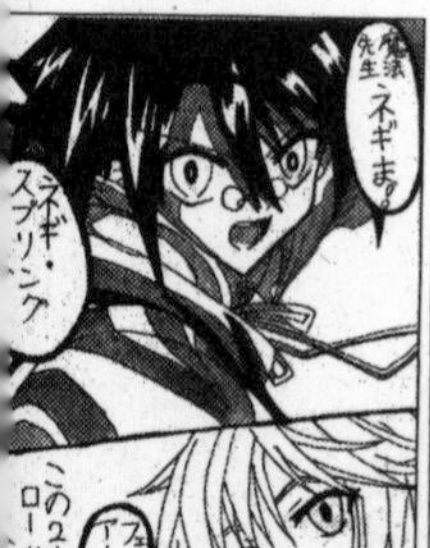
魔法先生ネギま!
ネギ・スプリングフィールド
フェイト・アーウェルンクス

THIS VOLUME'S MOST DRAWN CHARACTER!

NATSUMI MURAKAMI RANKING

1ST PLACE

夏美♡

コンニチは赤松先生
二回目の投こうデス

ところで、私は29巻
以来、夏美が大好きに
なりました♪

以後、夏美の活
役を期待しつつ、
赤松先生、スタッフの皆サン
を応援します。

皆さんガンバッて下さい♡

P.N
MIYU

2ND PLACE

ネギま！

初ピーシー
アル♪

あられ
GET☆

はじめまして☆ネギま大好きな女子大生、蘭634(あらむさし)
と申します(^^) 29巻のなっちゃんはホンマ可愛いかったです！や
っぱりフリーの女の子っていいですね～。ドラマCDもすごく楽寿でし
た♪ 毎回限定版出すのが楽しみで仕方ありません。
上のイラストは少し季節外れかもしれませんが、コク裏ひな祭り
ver.ですw P.S.スウェーデンに旅行に行ったら本屋にネギまがありました！

NATSUMI IS VERY POPULAR LATELY♥
SHE JUST CAN'T BE HONEST ABOUT
HER FEELINGS FOR KOTARO,
BUT SHE IS AN OLDER WOMAN,
SO SHE CAN'T HELP IT.

EHH?! YOU SAW THE SERIES IN
SWEDEN?! I WONDER WHO'S POPULAR
OVER THERE! THE KŪ-CHAN IN THE
TOP CORNER IS CUTE, TOO. (^^)

28番村上
夏美

こんにちは♪

いつも楽しくねま割ん読んでいます。
29巻マス夏美 コタロハこんパーティーの
ときには冥土にごいっぱいでした。
夏美がマスネルアーティファクトが見（は）
たいんです。

どうして夏美はこんな
かわいいんですか？！
こんなかわいいのは
そうそういません。

赤松センセー
がんばって♡

3RD PLACE

I SUPPOSE GIRLS DO GET
PRETTIER WHEN THEY'RE IN
LOVE. PLEASE BE PATIENT, AND
YOU'LL SEE HER ARTIFACT.

(AKAMATSU)

NON-CLASSMATE EDITION

THE WHAT AND WHY OF NEGIMA!

NAGI PARTY

Nagi Party

■ Nagi has a probationary contract with Albireo and Rakan. Does he have a probationary contract with Gateau and Zecht, too?

★ **He does not have one with Gateau. And Zecht is Nagi's master, so he doesn't have a contract with him, either.**

■ IAbout Albireo Imma's hair. In the present day, it's colored with tone, but in the past, it was painted black with ink. Was that intentional?

★ **I'm glad you noticed! Of course that was intentional.**

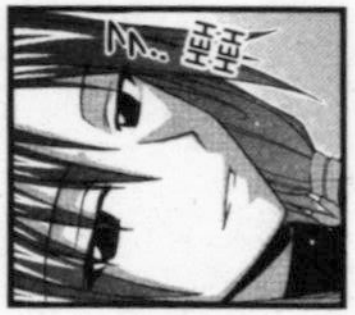
M...
HEH HEH

■ Rakan used dark magic. Did he learn it from someone, or did he just do it on his own?

★ **Rakan is a genius, so he can learn dark magic and Shinmei School techniques just by watching them.**

■ Zecht has the body of a child, but how old is he really?

★ **I'm told he is hundreds of years old, like Eva.**

■ If the present Kurt and Takamichi were to fight each other, who would win?

★ **Kurt is a very busy politician, so when it comes to battle, his skills might have fallen behind Takamichi's.**

■ I think that Eishun-san has aged too much, especially compared to Rakan-san...

★ **Eishun has always looked old. Rakan comes from a race with long lives, so he doesn't age much.**

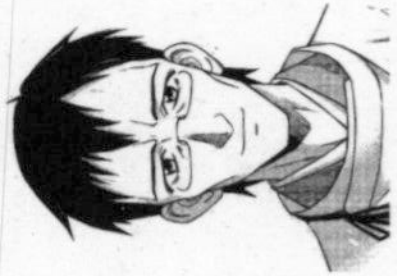

Fate Party

■ Is Tsukuyomi human? Or is she a half-breed?

★ **Tsukuyomi is human. But when she is under the control of the dark side of the Shinmei School, her eyes look like a demon's.**

■ Was Homura born with the ability to produce fire from her left eye?

★ **That is technically her artifact's ability, but she was born with an aptitude for it. Please think of it as an enhanced power.**

■ **Why doesn't Tamaki wear panties?**

★ **She can't wear panties because she has a thick tail. No one from her race wears underwear.**

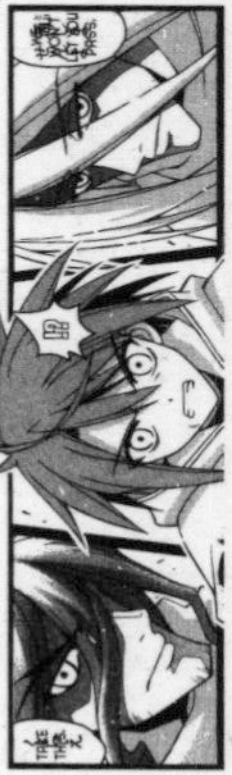
WE WON'T LET YOU PASS.
!?
TAKE THIS

■ **What happened to the big, burly fire and water mages in the final battle between Nagi's Party and Fate's Party?**

★ **They were each defeated by Rakan and Zecht, respectively. The only survivor from Fate's side was the mage in black.**

■ **Did Koyomi get her artifact from Fate?**

★ **That's right. He also gave her her name, or rather, her code name. They each have names that have something to do with their abilities. Those aren't their real names.**

The Magic Teachers

■ **In the 106th Period, Takamichi is chewing on something. Is that some kind of item to help them escape?**

★ **That's exactly right. Due to the way the story flowed, I couldn't draw the moment that they made their escape. It was a story composition mistake that I still regret.**

Nagi Party

■ Nagi has a probationary contract with Albireo and Rakan. Does he have a probationary contract with Gateau and Zecht, too?

★ **He does not have one with Gateau. And Zecht is Nagi's master, so he doesn't have a contract with him, either.**

■ How strong is Professor Akashi as a wizard?

★ **He's more of an investigation and analysis guy, so compared to the fighting teachers, he's not very strong.**

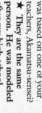

■ What does Shadebeard-sensei, also known as Kataragi-san, use to activate his magic? He's not holding anything, and it doesn't look like he's wearing a ring. Don't tell me he uses the shades!?

★ **That's a distinct possibility (laugh). Because there has never been and never will be a scene where he uses magic without them.**

■ Is Donet the partner of the Headmaster of Merdiana Magic Academy?

★ **Yes, she is. We first saw her in chapter fifteen. She may not look it, but she's around forty.**

■ Is there any relation between the "Magia Erebea" marks on Negi's body and the spell patterns on Chao's body?

★ **They are indeed related. And both of them lead to destruction if used too much.**

■ Who is stronger: Konoemon Konoe or the headmaster of Merdiana Magic Academy?

★ **I think they're almost equally matched.**

Mahora Academy and the People of the Real World

■ Is Nitta-sensei the same Nitta-sensei that was in AI Love You? And is it true that he was based on one of your teachers, Akamatsu-sensei?

★ **They are the same person. He was modeled after my high school homeroom teacher, and he even appears in my debut work from when I won the newcomer award for Shonen Magazine.**

■ What club is Kaoru G tokuji in?

★ **The yell squad.**

■ How does Chachazero move?

★ **She runs on Eva's magic. Because of that, she can't move very well in Mahora Academy, where's Eva's magic power is limited.**

■ What happened to the high school students Eiko-san and Naoya-san?

★ **Eiko still hasn't figured out how Naoya feels. She won't for a while.**

■ Are things going well with Yuki-chan and Haruki-kun?

★ **Yuki is more assertive, so I think things are going well for them.**

■ Megumi Natsume was managing the school computers with Professor Akashi. Is she as smart as Hakase?

★ **She's not as smart as Hakase, but she does excel as an operator. She's also skilled in attack magic, so she might be a pretty handy person to have around.**

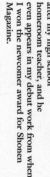

NON-CLASSMATE EDITION

■ Is it alright for Kotar not to hide his dog ears and tail?
★ **At that school, they'd probably just think it's a costume. They don't even care when there's a robot going to school.**

■ What exactly is Kei'ichi Yamashita's 3D jujitsu...?
★ **Apparently, it's a jujitsu technique that can attack from all angles. Also, it can repeat the same move several times over.**

■ Is Takane so easy to strip because she has low defensive power?
★ **Takane's defensive power is top class, even among magic students. She just keeps going up against the wrong opponents....**

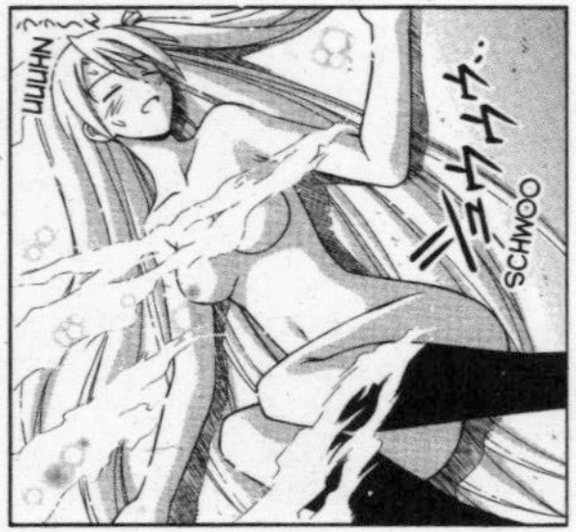
UUUHHN
SCHWOO

■ Mei Sakura has an artifact, but does she have a master?
★ **Her master is Takane. Takane is Nutmeg's master, too. She may not look it, but On -sama is pretty popular.**

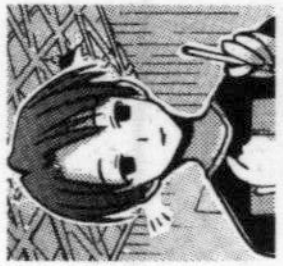

■ What club was Ninomiya-sensei in when she was a student?
★ **Rhythmic gymnastics, naturally. She has rather good proportions, too.**

■ Are Nekane and Negi genuine, bona fide brother and sister? If so, does Nekane have enormous magic power, too?
★ **They are not really siblings. And Nekane's magic power is nothing very special.**

People from the Magical World
■ How does Ricardo get his hair like that?
★ **He doesn't do anything to it; it's like that naturally.**

■ Is Beatrix Emily's minister magi?
★ **They don't have a probationary contract, so they aren't officially partners. It's more like Emily is from a family of nobles, and Beatrix is her servant.**

■ How strong is Craig in battle?
★ **He's the main fighter of their party, so he's pretty strong. He probably has an attack power of about 300.**

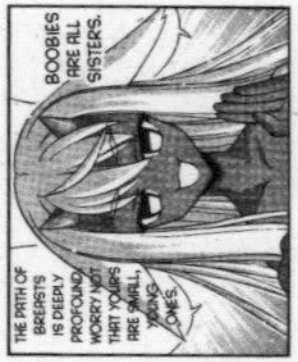
BOOBIES ARE ALL SISTERS.
THE PATH OF BREASTS IS DEEPLY PROFOUND. WORRY NOT THAT YOURS ARE SMALL, YOUNG ONES.

■ In 268th Period, was it Paio Zi that Nagi saved?
★ **That's right. It's still a mystery why she grew into such a pervert.**

■ Morborgran from Canis Niger is a demon. Can demons go freely between the Magical World and the demon world, or was he summoned?
★ **It's extremely rare, but it would seem that it is possible for them to go freely between worlds. The presence of several other demons has been confirmed, as well.**

■ What does Chiko[STAR] Tan look like after he transforms?
★ **There are many theories--like he turns into a giant monkey, he starts using polite language, etc. But I think it's probably not anything special.**

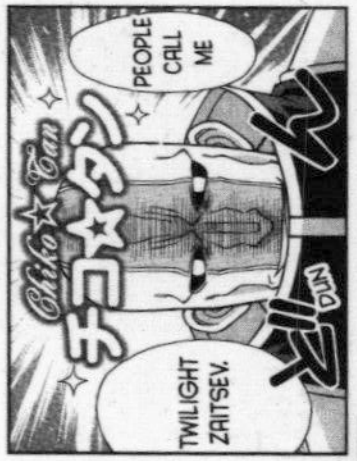
PEOPLE CALL ME
Chiko☆Tan
チコ☆タン
TWILIGHT ZAITSEV.
DUN

■ Does Theo-sama like Rakan?
★ **She probably does. She probably wants him to propose, but Rakan treats her like a kid, so that's not likely to happen for a while.**

NEGIMA! HÀNZÌ CONVERSION

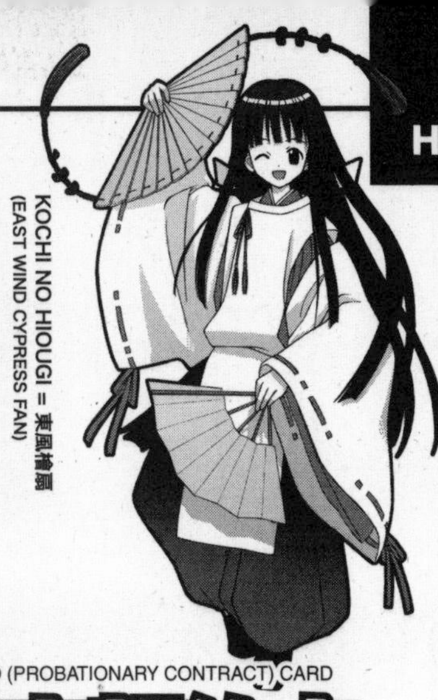

ON THIS PAGE, WE WOULD LIKE TO CONTINUE OUR INTRODUCTION OF THE TAIWANESE VERSION OF *NEGIMA!* FROM VOLUME 23; WE CALL IT THE *NEGIMA!-ESE HÀNZÌ* CONVERSION PAGE.

THERE ARE SOME WITH MORE INFORMATION IN THEIR NAMES THAN THE ORIGINAL, LIKE "GATEPORT=伝送門港 (TRANSMISSION GATEPORT)" AND "TAKAMICHI (WRITTEN IN KATAKANA WITH NO SPECIFIC MEANING GIVEN)=隆道 (NOBLE ROAD)." THERE ARE SOME THAT ARE MAKE SENSE, LIKE "CELL PHONE=手電話 (HAND PHONE)," "BADGE=胸章 (CHEST BADGE)," AND "AEGIS CRUISER=神盾艦 (DIVINE SHIELD WARSHIP)." THERE ARE SOME THAT MAKE YOU LAUGH IN SPITE OF YOURSELF, LIKE "TOSAKA-SAN=雞冠頭先生 (MR. CHICKEN CROWN HEAD)" AND "MAID=女僕 (WOMAN SERVANT, BUT LOOKS LIKE WOMAN ME, OR WOMAN BOY)." THERE SOME THAT ARE LEFT AS-IS, LIKE "KAGETARŌ (影太朗)" AND FATE'S SERVANTS, AS WELL AS AN UNTRANSLATED "暴走中の茶々丸 (ROGUE CHACHAMARU)." ...AND NOW WE WOULD LIKE TO 上載 (UPLOAD) PLENTY MORE TRIVIA FOR YOU. FIRST, LET'S START WITH THE CARDS.

KOCHI NO HIOUGI = 東風檜扇 (EAST WIND CYPRESS FAN)
HAE NO SUEHIRO = 西風末廣 (WEST WIND FOLDING FAN)
HAMA NO TSURUGI = 破魔之劍 (SWORD OF DEMON DISPELLING)

WHEN KONOKA SLURS THE NAME TO MAKE IT EASIER TO SAY, IT'S TRANSLATED AS "契約卡(CONTRACT CARD)," AND WHEN IT'S PRONOUNCED CORRECTLY, IT'S TRANSLATED AS "暫定契約卡 (TEMPORARY CONTRACT CARD)." THE TRANSLATION IS SO DETAILED.

PACTIO (PROBATIONARY CONTRACT) CARD

暫定契約卡

盾牌少女 (SHIELD PLACARD GIRL)
... SHIELD MAIDEN)
裝甲卡 (ARMOR CARD)
... ARMOR CARD
服裝卡 (COSTUME CARD)
... COSPLAY CARD
爛卡 (ROTTEN CARD)
... BOTCHED CARD

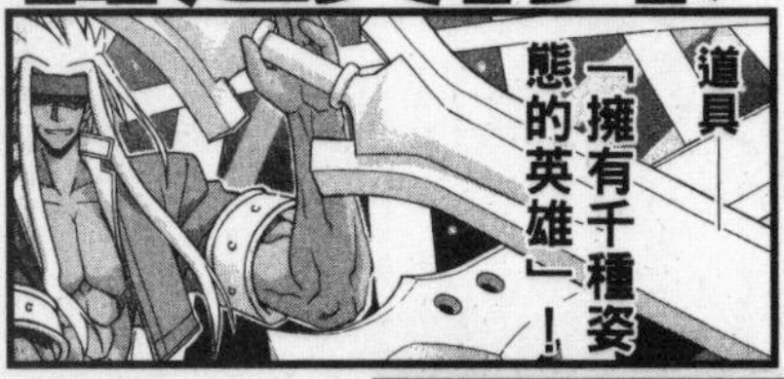
道具「擁有千種姿態的英雄」!

ARTIFACT: HERO WITH A THOUSAND FACES

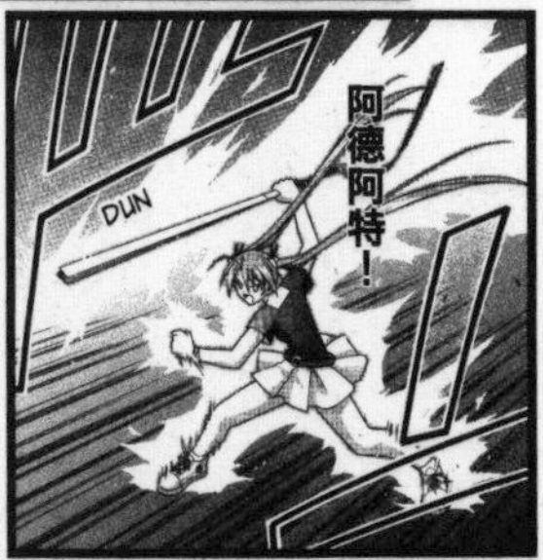
阿德阿特!
DUN

ADEAT!

塗鴉帝國 (PAINT CROW" EMPIRE)
... IMPERIUM GRAPHICES
"THE CHARACTERS "PAINT CROW" FORM THE CHINESE WORD FOR "SCRIBBLE."
本我繪圖日記 (BOOK SELF PICTURE DRAWING DIARY)
... DIARIUM EJUS
世界圖繪 (WORLD DRAWING PICTURE)
... ORBIS SENSUALIUM PICTUS

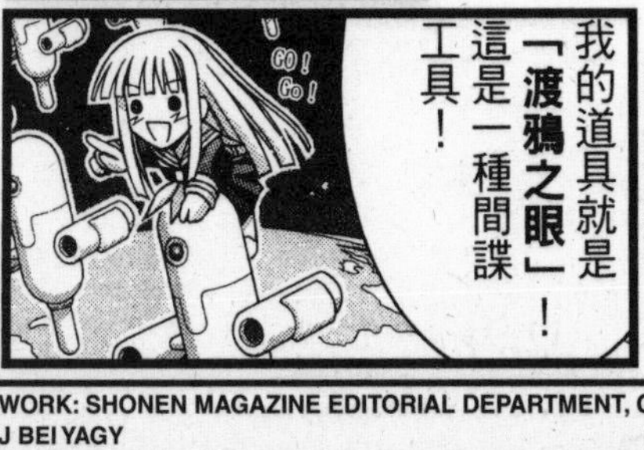
我的道具就是「渡鴉之眼」!這是一種間諜工具!
GO! GO!

MY ARTIFACT IS "OCULUS CORVINUS," THE "RAVEN'S EYE"!! AS THE NAME SUGGESTS, IT'S A SPY ITEM!

魔法老師! MAGISTER NEGI MAGI

WORK: SHONEN MAGAZINE EDITORIAL DEPARTMENT, COOPERATION: J BEI YAGY

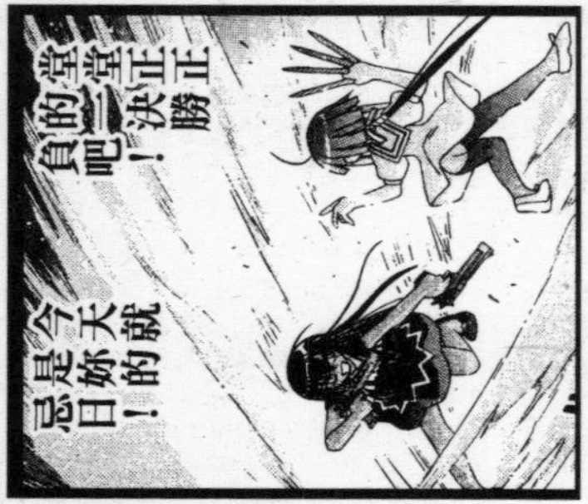
堂堂正正的一決勝負吧！
TO A FAIR FIGHT!
今天就是妳的忌日！
THIS DAY WILL BE YOUR LAST!

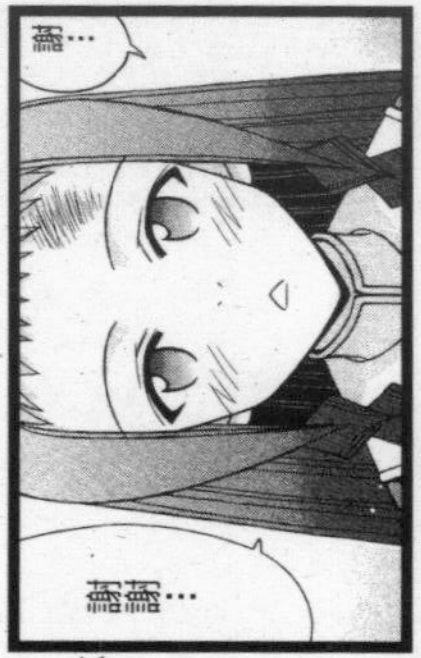
謝…
TH...
謝謝…
THANK YOU...

帝國船 帝國 IS A MORE COMPLEX VERSION OF THE JAPANESE 帝国 (EMPIRE). 船 MEANS WARSHIP, SO... ➡ IMPERIAL SHIP

偉大春春女王號 號 IS THE CHINESE VERSION OF 号, A JAPANESE SUFFIX THAT IN THIS CASE MEANS THAT THIS IS THE NAME OF A SHIP. 春奈 IS HARUNA, WHICH REFERS TO PARU. ➡ THE GREAT PARU-SAMA

無聲脫衣術 NO SOUND REMOVE CLOTHING TECHNIQUE. ➡ SILENT STRIP TECHNIQUE

超級河童小弟 SUPER... KAPPA... AND LITTLE BROTHER, THE CHINESE VERSION OF -KUN. ➡ SUPER KAPA-KUN

起源魔法師 起源 MEANS BEGINNING, 師 MEANS SOMEONE WHO PRACTICES (IN THIS CASE) 魔法, OR MAGIC. ➡ THE MAGE OF THE BEGINNING

我問汝的真正名字 I ASK YOUR REAL NAME ➡ WHAT IS YOUR NAME?

涅吉少組 THE FIRST KANJI COMBINATION SAYS "NEGI." THE SECOND COMBINATION MEANS "SMALL GROUP." FOR FATE'S ____, IT WOULD BE 菲特少組. ➡ NEGI PARTY

夢幻世界 幻想的世界 DREAM WORLD, ILLUSION WORLD. USUALLY SAID BY CHISAME ➡ FANTASY (WORLD)

千羽大人 REFERS TO CHISAME. 大人 IS A CHINESE HONORIFIC MEANING "GREAT PERSON." WHY WOULD IT BE 羽 (YŪ, WING) INSTEAD OF 雨, THE NORMAL SECOND KANJI IN CHISAME'S NAME? ➡ CHIU-SAMA, CHIU-TAMA

色色的危機 A COLORFUL CRISIS. IN THIS CASE, "COLOR" ALSO REFERS TO SENSUALITY. WHEN CHISAME'S CLOTHES ARE MELTED BY THE OCTOPUS BEAST... ➡ EROTIC DILEMMA

不顯眼的幽靈 不顯眼的 LOOSELY MEANS "NOT EYE-CATCHING." 幽靈 IS THE MORE COMPLEX CHINESE VERSION OF 幽霊 (GHOST). IT REFERS TO SAYO. ➡ BORING GHOST

魔法世界的女僕 TRANSLATED LITERALLY, IT MEANS "MAGIC WORLD MAID-SAN" ➡ MAID IN THE MAGICAL WORLD (194TH PERIOD'S TITLE)

帝國船 帝國 IS A MORE COMPLEX VERSION OF THE JAPANESE 帝国 (EMPIRE). 船 MEANS WARSHIP, SO...

NEGI-KUN'S NICKNAMES: BŌYA (EVA) IS 小鬼 (LITTLE DEMON, LITTLE BRAT), KID (RAKAN) IS 小弟 (LITTLE BROTHER, LITTLE DISCIPLE), MASTER (CHACHAMARU) IS 主人 (MASTER).

REVERSE DICTIONARY (INCLUDING WORDS NOT SPECIFIC TO NEGIMA!)

Cell phone ▸ 手機 (hand machine), 行動電話 (mobile phone)

Laptop ▸ 筆記過型電腦 (note-taking type electric brain)

Keyboard ▸ 鍵盤 (board for keys)

Mouse ▸ 滑鼠 (sliding mouse)

Hard disk ▸ 硬碟 (hard plate)

Magneto-optical disk ▸ 光碟片 (light plate sheet)

Save ▸ 儲存 (earnings keeping)

Load ▸ 讀取 (読取) (read)

Net ▸ 網路 (net road)

Access ▸ 連線 (connect line)

Password ▸ 密碼 (secret symbol)

Account ▸ 帳號 (號=号) (account name/number)

Copy & Paste ▸ 複製&貼上 (copy & paste)

Format ▸ 格式化 (format)

Download ▸ 下載, 下傳 (put down, transmit down)

Upload ▸ 上載, 上傳 (put up, transmit up) (傳=伝, transmit)

Backup ▸ 備份 (equipped portion)

Program ▸ 程式 (formula system)

Rogue ▸ 失控 (lost inhibitions) (sometimes refers to Chachamaru)

WE'VE GOT A HACKER IN THE ACADEMY SECURITY'S CENTRAL COMPUTER!

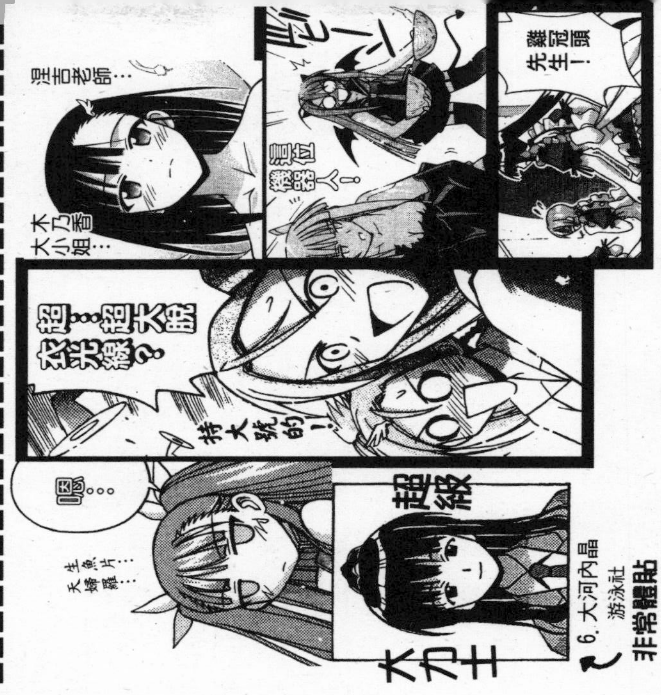

涅吉老師…
木乃香大小姐…
這位機器人！
ビーッ
雞冠頭先生！
超…超大脱衣光線？
持大號的！
嗯…
生魚片…天婦羅…
超級大力士
6. 大河內晶
游泳社
非常體貼

NEGI-SENSEI

KONOKA-OJŌSAMA

YOU! ROBOT!

TOSAKA-SAN!

S... SUPER BIG STRIPPER BEAM?

HELLA BIG!!

ERK...

SASHIMI AND TEMPURA...

SUPER

STRONG

AKIRA ŌKŌCHI SWIM TEAM VERY KIND

老子 (LĂOSHI) IS "SENSEI" IN JAPANESE. 先生(XIĀNSHENG IN CHINESE, SENSEI IN JAPANESE) IS THE CHINESE EQUIVALENT OF THE JAPANESE -SAN.
FATE: 再見 (ZÀIJIÀN) SEE YOU AGAIN.

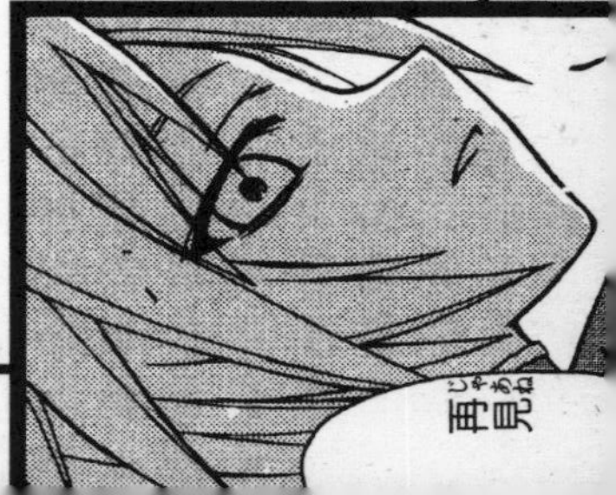

再見

AFTER HER TEARS,
TREASURE HUNTER NODOKA MIYAZAKI.
HFF
31
NEGIMA
MAGISTÉR NEGI MAGI

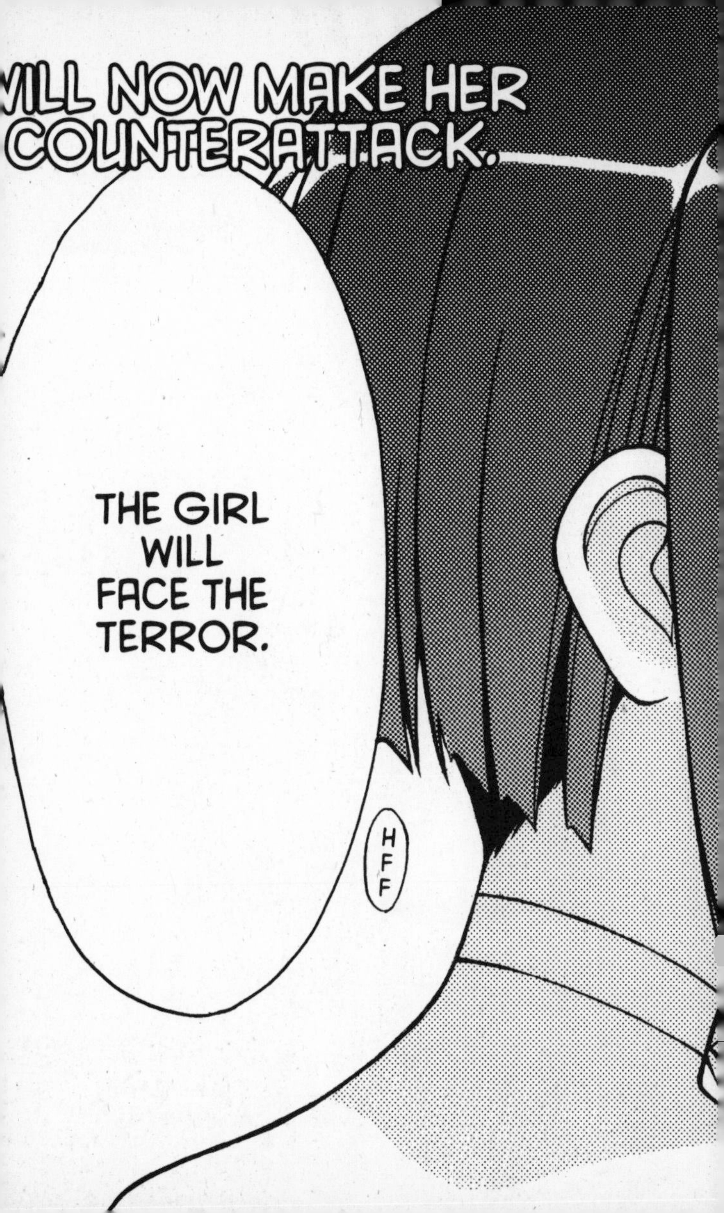
ILL NOW MAKE HER COUNTERATTACK.
THE GIRL WILL FACE THE TERROR.
HFF

NEGIMA!
MAGISTER NEGI MAGI

Ken Akamatsu

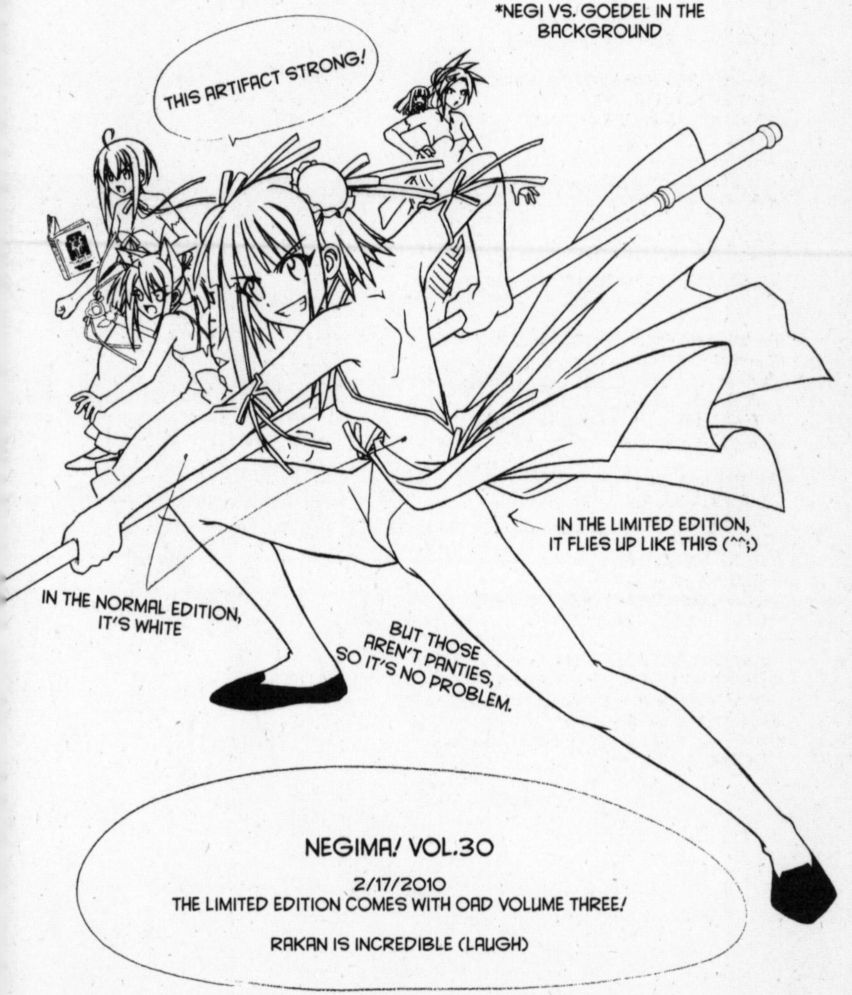
*NEGI VS. GOEDEL IN THE BACKGROUND
THIS ARTIFACT STRONG!
IN THE LIMITED EDITION, IT FLIES UP LIKE THIS (^^;)
IN THE NORMAL EDITION, IT'S WHITE
BUT THOSE AREN'T PANTIES, SO IT'S NO PROBLEM.
NEGIMA! VOL.30
2/17/2010
THE LIMITED EDITION COMES WITH OAD VOLUME THREE!
RAKAN IS INCREDIBLE (LAUGH)

(26) EVANGELINE A.K. MCDOWELL

NEGI'S FIRST AND MOST VILLAINOUS
MASTER (LAUGH). SHE'S A VERY
POPULAR CHARACTER, SO I PUT HER IN
THE MAGICAL WORLD ARC AS THE SPIRIT
IN THE SCROLL. (AND LOGICALLY, IT'S
BETTER FOR EVA TO TEACH HIM DARK
MAGIC THAN RAKAN.)

SHE'S HEAD OVER HEELS IN LOVE WITH
NAGI, BUT SHE DOESN'T HATE NEGI,
EITHER, SO SHE HELPS HIM OUT A LOT.
(^^;)

AS YOU MAY HAVE FIGURED OUT FROM
THE "ASK HER ADVICE IF YOU'RE IN
TROUBLE" NOTE IN THE CLASS ROSTER,
I CREATED HER WITH THE INTENT OF
HAVING HER TRAIN NEGI AS HIS MASTER,
AND I'M VERY ATTACHED TO HER.

IN THE ANIME, SHE'S VOICED BY
YUKI MATSUOKA-
SAN. SHE IS THE
ONLY ONE WHO
CAN RECREATE EVA'S
CACKLE!! EVERYONE IN THE
RECORDING STUDIO RELIES ON HER,
TOO.

IN THE LIVE-ACTION DRAMA, SHE IS
PLAY BY SAKINA KUWAE. LIKE EVA,
SHE'S SMALL BUT HAS A BIG PRESENCE.
AND ON TOP OF THAT, SHE'S A
SINGING, DANCING SUPER IDOL. SHE'S
ADORABLE♡

OY.

SUCH A
TSUNDERE.

AKAMATSU

About the Creator

Negima! is only Ken Akamatsu's third manga, although he started working in the field in 1994 with *AI Ga Tomaranai* (released in the United States with the title *A.I. Love You*). Like all of Akamatsu's work to date, it was published in Kodansha's *Shonen Magazine*. *AI Ga Tomaranai* ran for five years before concluding in 1999. In 1998, however, Akamatsu began the work that would make him one of the most popular manga artists in Japan: *Love Hina*. *Love Hina* ran for four years, and before its conclusion in 2002, it would cause Akamatsu to be granted the prestigious Manga of the Year Award from Kodansha, as well as going on to become one of the best-selling manga in the United States.

Translation Notes

Japanese is a tricky language for most Westerners, and translation is often more art than science. For your edification and reading pleasure, here are notes on some of the places where we could have gone in a different direction with our translation of the work, or where a Japanese cultural reference is used.

He tried to turn them, but they turned him instead, page 53

The Japanese phrase Haruna uses here is, "he went to get a mummy and became one himself." One theory is that the saying comes from the practice in the Middle Ages of grinding mummies into powder to make into medicine. But finding a mummy was not always easy, and those who went in search of them would die themselves. These days, the phrase is used to refer to going to find someone and becoming lost yourself or, as in Kurt's case, going to convince someone of the error of their ways and instead being turned to the other side.

Rúyì Jīngū Bàng, page 104

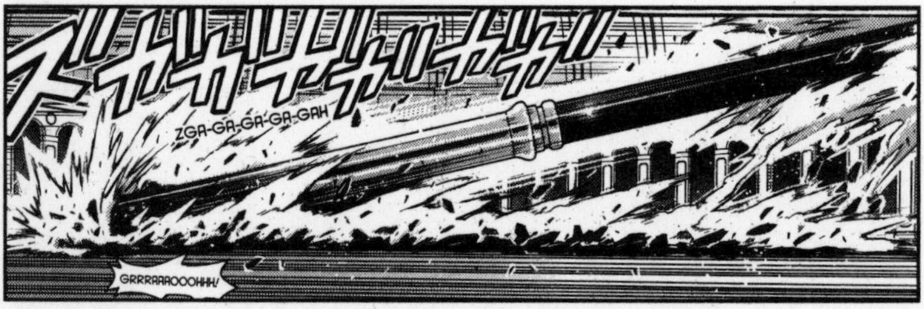
ZGA-GA-GA-GA-GAH
GRRRAAAOOOHHH!

According to legend, the great monkey king Sun Wukong, known in Japan as Son Gokū, had a magical staff that could change in size, extending and contracting in accordance with its master's wishes. Because it is so compliant, its name means roughly "as-you-wish gold-bound staff."

Tengu no Kakuremino, page 114

This is the name of Kaede's artifact. A tengu is a Japanese mythological that is usually depicted as a sort of bird-like human. According to legend, tengu have special cloaks of invisibility, or kakuremino (hiding rain-coat).

Takemikazuchi, page 117

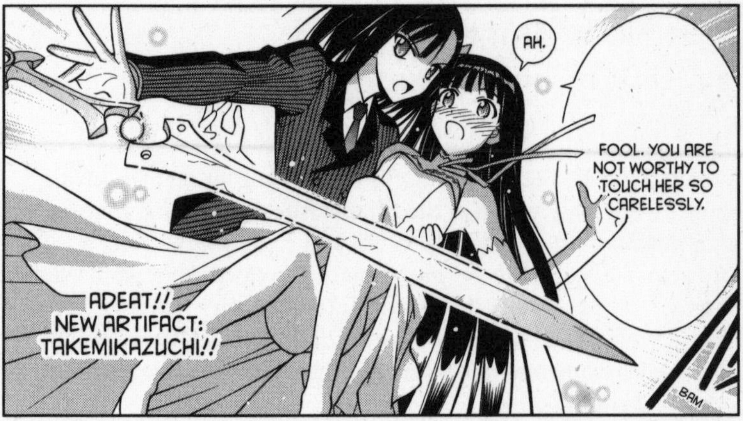
AH.
FOOL. YOU ARE NOT WORTHY TO TOUCH HER SO CARELESSLY.
ADEAT!! NEW ARTIFACT: TAKEMIKAZUCHI!!
BAM

Setsuna's new artifact, based on her contract with Konoka. The artifact gets its name from Takemikazuchi-no-mikoto, a Japanese lightning and sword deity.

Yell squad, page 167

A Japanese ōendan, or yell squad, is like a cheer squad, but instead of girls in short skirts, it consists of boys in gakuran, the high-collared male school uniforms. They make a lot of noise with drums, megaphones, etc., leading their schools in cheering for their teams as well as taunting their opponents. Anyone who remembers Gōtokuji from the Mahora Budōkai will remember his distinctive hairstyle—a stereotypical hairstyle of yell squad members.

Preview of *Negima!* Volume 31

We're pleased to present you a preview from volume 31. Please check our website, www.delreymanga.com, to see when this volume will be available in English. For now you'll have to make do with Japanese!

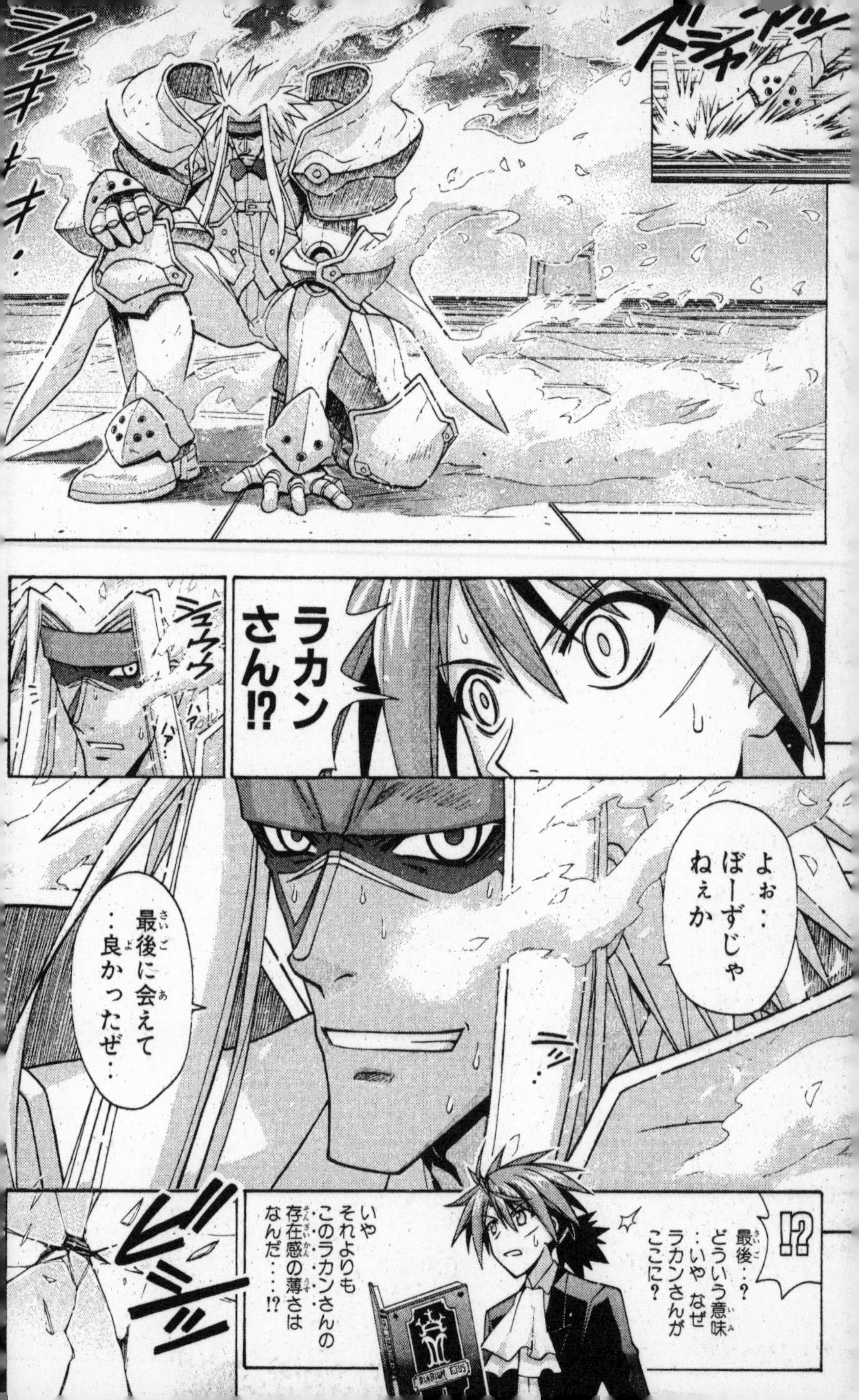
ズジャッ
シュキキキ…
ラカンさん!?
シュウウ
ハァ ハァ…
よぉ…ぼーずじゃねぇか
最後に会えて…良かったぜ…
!?
最後…? どういう意味…いや なぜラカンさんがここに?
いやそれよりもこのラカンさんの存在感の薄さはなんだ…!?

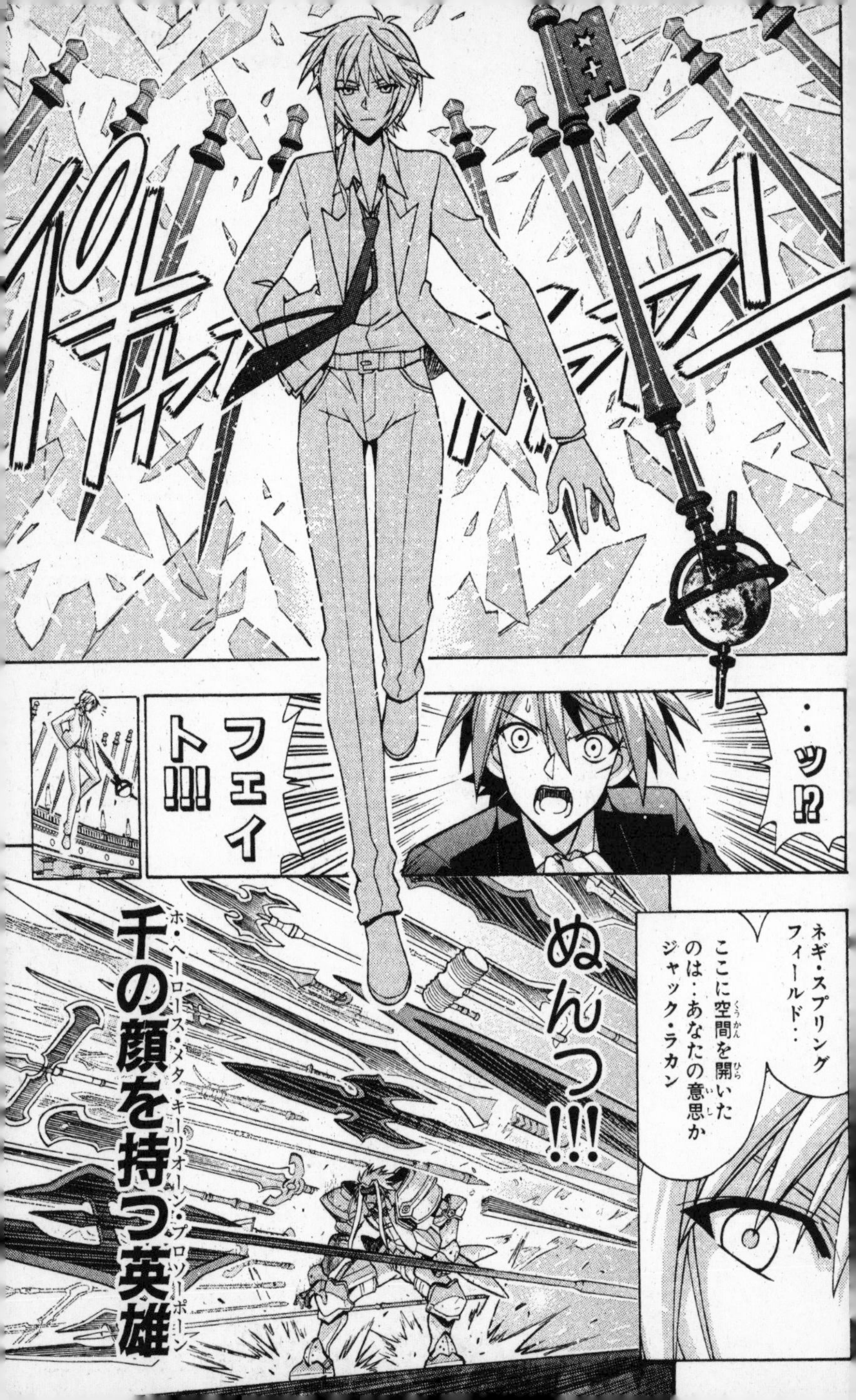
・・ッ!?
フェイト!!!
ネギ・スプリングフィールド・・
ここに空間を開いたのは・・あなたの意思か
ジャック・ラカン
ぬんっ!!!
千の顔を持つ英雄(ホ・ヘーロース・メタ・キーリオーン・プロソーポーン)

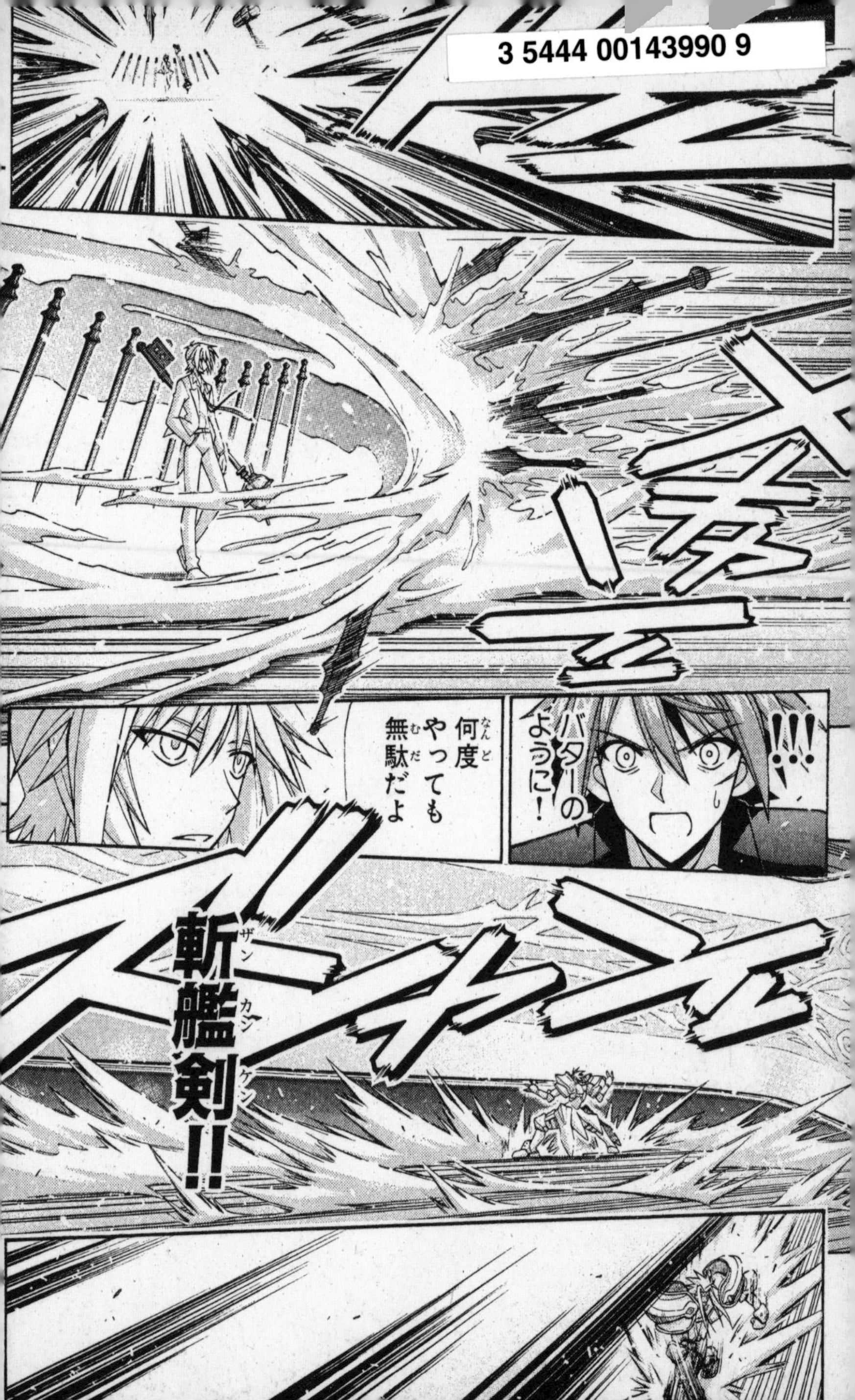
!!!
バターのように!
何度やっても無駄だよ
斬艦剣!!

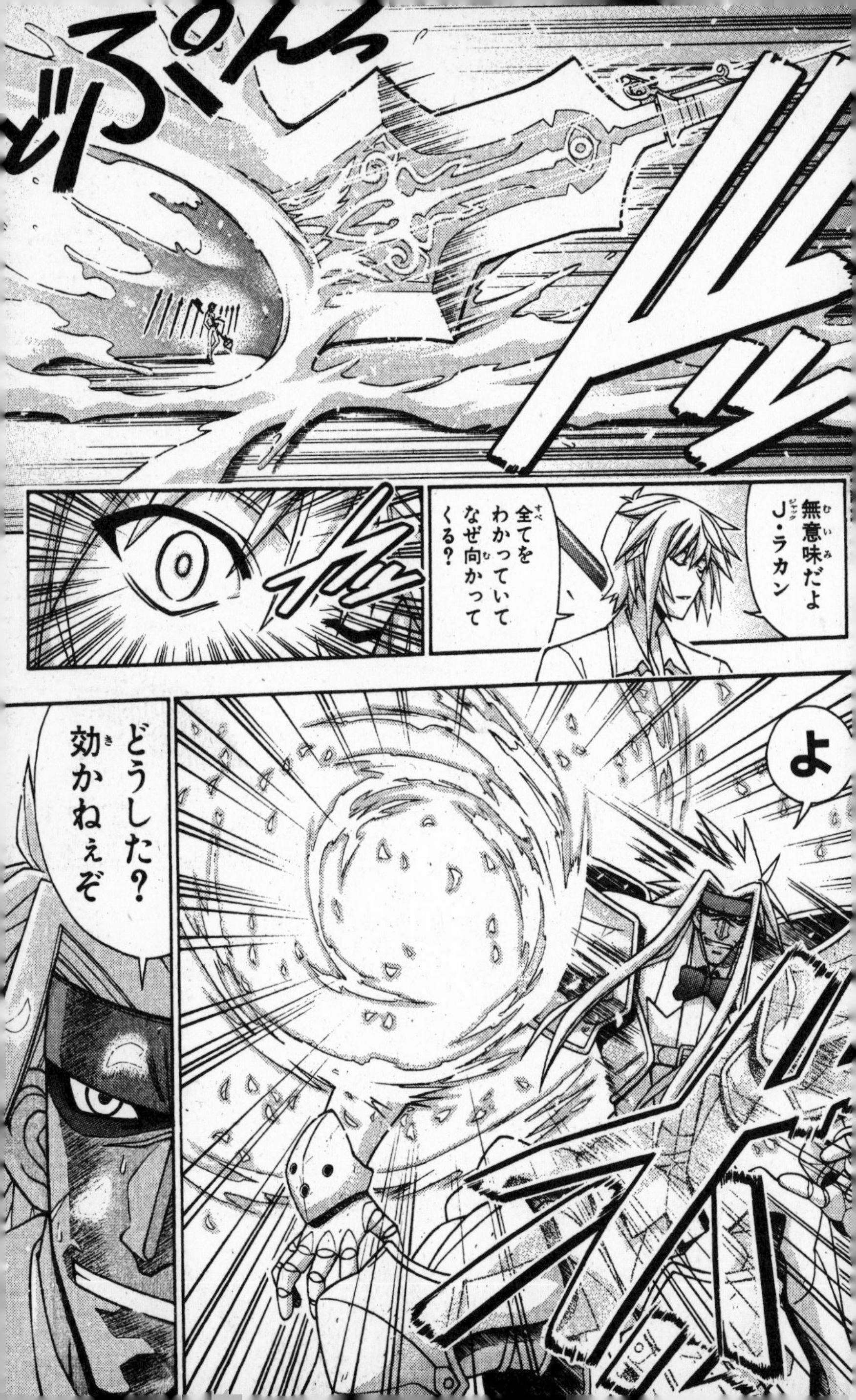
ズッ
どぷん
無意味だよ J・ラカン
全てを わかっていて なぜ向かって くる?
よ
どうした? 効かねぇぞ

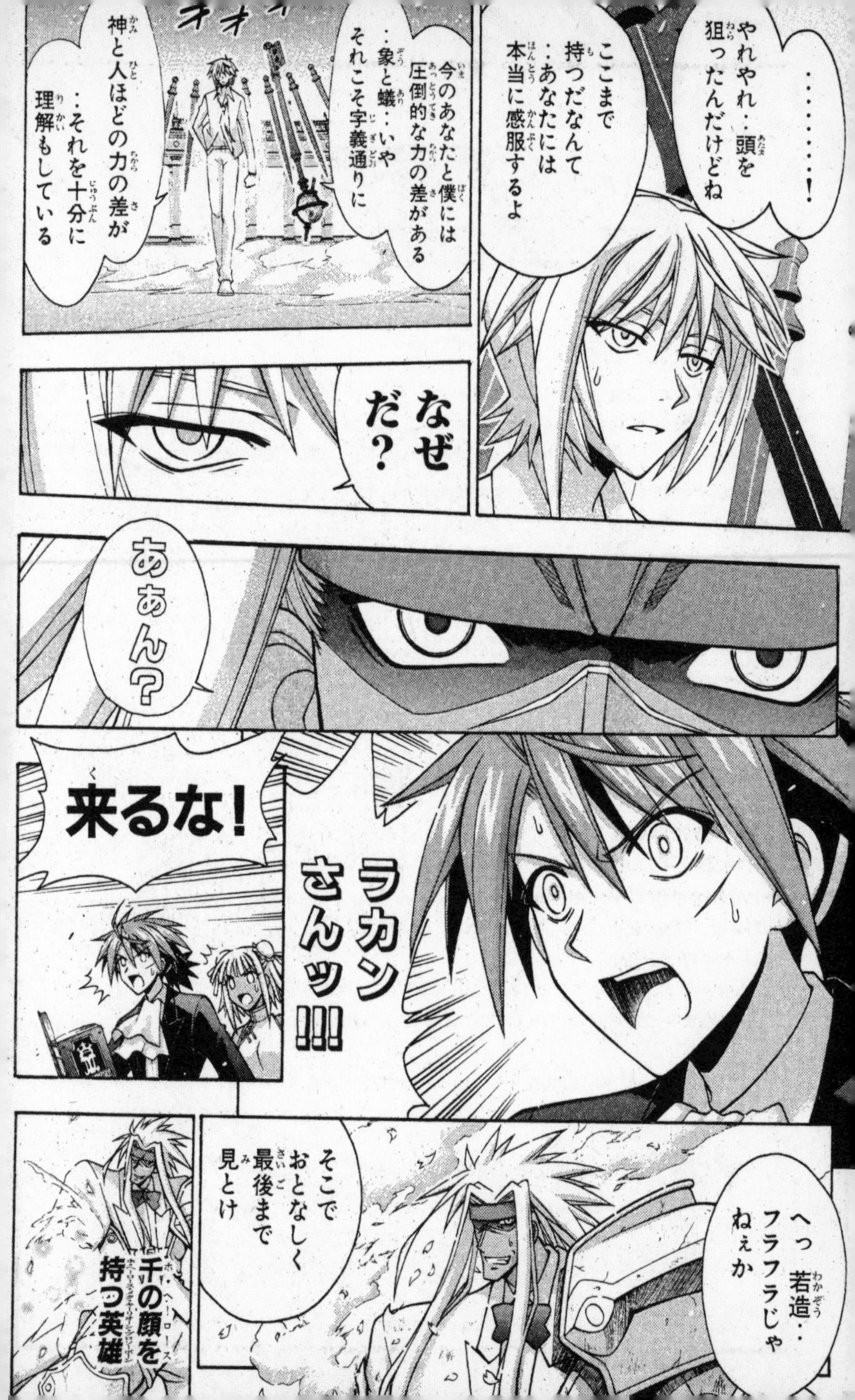
……！
やれやれ…頭を狙ったんだけどね
ここまで持つだなんて…あなたには本当に感服するよ
オオ
今のあなたと僕には圧倒的な力の差がある
…象と蟻…いや それこそ字義通りに
神と人ほどの力の差が
…それを十分に理解もしている
なぜだ？
あぁん？
ラカンさんッ!!!
来るな！
へっ 若造…フラフラじゃねぇか
そこでおとなしく最後まで見とけ
千の顔を持つ英雄

BY OH!GREAT

Itsuki Minami needs no introduction—everybody's heard of the "Babyface" of the Eastside. He's the strongest kid at Higashi Junior High School, easy on the eyes but dangerously tough when he needs to be. Plus, Itsuki lives with the mysterious and sexy Noyamano sisters. Life's never dull, but it becomes downright dangerous when Itsuki leads his school to victory over vindictive Westside punks with gangster connections. Now he stands to lose his school, his friends, and everything he cares about. But in his darkest hour, the Noyamano girls give him an amazing gift, one that just might help him save his school: a pair of Air Trecks. These high-tech skates are more than just supercool. They'll enable Itsuki to execute the wildest, most aggressive moves ever seen—and introduce him to a thrilling and terrifying new world.

Ages: 16 +

Special extras in each volume! Read them all!

TOMARE!

[STOP!]

You're going the wrong way!

Manga is a completely different type of reading experience.

To start at the *beginning*, go to the *end*!

That's right! Authentic manga is read the traditional Japanese way—from right to left, exactly the *opposite* of how American books are read. It's easy to follow: Just go to the other end of the book, and read each page—and each panel—from right side to left side, starting at the top right. Now you're experiencing manga as it was meant to be.